MW01153832

Stormy Passage

Stormy Passage

Mexico from Colony to Republic, 1750–1850

Eric Van Young

ROWMAN & LITTLEFIELD
Lanham • Boulder • New York • London

Published by Rowman & Littlefield

An imprint of The Rowman & Littlefield Publishing Group, Inc.
4501 Forbes Boulevard, Suite 200, Lanham, Maryland 20706
www.rowman.com

86-90 Paul Street, London EC2A 4NE

British Library Cataloguing in Publication Information Available

Library of Congress Cataloging-in-Publication Data

Names: Van Young, Eric, author.
Title: Stormy passage : Mexico from colony to republic, 1750-1850 / Eric
    Van Young.
 Other titles: Mexico from colony to republic, 1750-1850
Description: Lanham : Rowman & Littlefield, [2022] | Includes
    bibliographical references and index.
Identifiers: LCCN 2021053338 (print) | LCCN 2021053339 (ebook) | ISBN
    9781442209015 (cloth) | ISBN 9781442209039 (epub)
Subjects: LCSH: Mexico--History--Spanish colony, 1540-1810. |
    Mexico--History--Wars of Independence, 1810-1821. |
    Mexico--History--1821-1861.
Classification: LCC F1231 .V368 2022 (print) | LCC F1231 (ebook) | DDC
    972/.02–dc23/eng/20211214
LC record available at https://lccn.loc.gov/2021053338
LC ebook record available at https://lccn.loc.gov/2021053339

For Maggie; my children, Marin and Adrian;
their children, Arden, Sebastian, Dashiell, and August;
and for the Mexican friends and other scholars
from whom I have learned so much
over the past fifty years or so

Contents

Acknowledgments

Meant for an interested general audience and perhaps for undergraduate readers, this book was originally intended as a sort of overview and introduction, perhaps in long article format, to my recently published biography (Yale University Press, 2021) of one of the era's central political players, Lucas Alamán, who shows up repeatedly in these pages. It was to be a therapeutic head clearing, but one thread led to another and one moderate-sized issue after another morphed into a larger one. The seemingly endless research and writing on that book, the pressure of other professional commitments, and the unanticipated twists of personal life have turned the essay into a book.

A small group of friends and colleagues have helped me along the way by offering counsel in written or conversational form, supplying information, helping with technical aspects of the book, lending me pieces of their own work, reading passages or chapters of the manuscript at various points, or simply being patient and encouraging. Susan McEachern, my editor at Rowman & Littlefield, was infinitely forbearing with me over the decade or so it took to complete this project while I gave the Alamán biography precedence at every turn. She tactfully suggested that an early approach to a first draft was a bit too dry and prissy; she was right. Katelyn Turner at Rowman & Littlefield took over the project with grace and competence upon Susan's retirement and has helped me bring it to conclusion. The friends who helped me include María Bárbara Zepeda Cortés, Roberto Breña, Will Fowler, Peter Gourevitch, and Tom Passananti. Cynthia Radding did a painstaking reading of the manuscript and gave me a mountain of queries, suggestions, and corrections. I have by no means attended to all of these, nor to the astute comments offered by the other two anonymous readers for Rowman & Littlefield, but as a whole they were extremely helpful and I have followed their advice in many instances. The two likewise "anonymous" readers of the initial book proposal, Margaret Chowning and Gilbert Joseph, made helpful and charitable suggestions. I find it difficult to respect his wish to remain anonymous, but another friend lent me his computer and editing skills, as he has done twice before, to put my manuscript into shape for the publisher. Jenny Jaramillo applied her great ingenuity and internet expertise in locating the images and getting permission to use them.

PART I

Colonial Twilight

Chapter 1

Introduction

MEXICO AND ITS MODERNIZATIONS

At 758,449 square miles in area, Mexico is slightly larger than France, Spain, Italy, Germany, and the United Kingdom put together. The country's population is about 130,000,000 people, the combined total of the United Kingdom and France. The tropical lowlands bordering the Gulf of Mexico rise to a central plateau at about 8,000 feet at Mexico City in the temperate-to-cold uplands, while the Mexican north embraces hundreds of thousands of square miles of desert and semidesertic terrain. Blessed with few navigable rivers, the country therefore lacks the possibility of constructing the canals that proved so important to national integration and economic development in Britain and the United States before railroads. The longest of these waterways in Mexico are the Colorado River and the Rio Grande (aka Rio Bravo), both of which originate in the United States, while with few exceptions the others are either quite short or in out-of-the-way regions. Mountain ranges extend up the east and west sides, and a volcanic axis traverses Mexico from the Gulf to the Pacific. The peaks of the two highest volcanic mountains, to the east of the capital, rise to some 18,000 feet; a new volcano, Paricutín, was born in the western part of the country as recently as 1943. Mexico hosts one of the most biologically diverse ecosystems in the world, while the horizontal and vertical dimensions of the country posed significant challenges to European domination. In the prerailroad age, before electronic means of communication appeared on the scene, it was not an easy corner of the world to unify politically or economically. Only as late as 1940 did mass communication media (radio, films), the wide use of the automobile, and the definitive extension of state authority finally knit together this large and geographically complex country.[1]

3

When did Mexico begin modernization, achieve it, or even count itself well advanced along the path to it? If the modernization process was impeded or slowed when it might have developed, why and how did this happen? How essential was national integration to modernization in Mexico? Some historians have put the flowering of the extended process of modernization, and with it the maturing of nationhood, only as late as 1940. At least one distinguished observer of the country, the late Mexican journalist Carlos Monsiváis, suggested playfully that the transition into modernization essentially was skipped, quipping that Mexico had passed from a state of premodernity to one of postmodernity without ever experiencing modernity. Lucas Alamán (1792–1853), the great statesman-historian of the early republican period who will serve here as a sort of Virgil to our Dante, anticipated Monsiváis along roughly the same lines by more than a century. He wrote in 1849 that Mexico had "arrived from infancy to decrepitude without enjoying more than a glimmer of the happiness of youth."[2] Other scholars have written that Mexico was born under the sign of modernity at its conquest by Fernando Cortés in 1521. The principal argument in support of this view is that the society was never feudal, the phase of historical development that preceded modernization in most of the European world, but embryonically capitalist from its inception and therefore edging its way into modernity through the door of European domination even while Europe itself was beginning to modernize. In this scenario, Mexico was a child of the first great globalization that began with Christopher Columbus and drew much of the world, including the Americas, into the orbit of Europe, from where modernization eventually spread to embrace most of mankind. This interpretation suggests that colonial empires were not antithetical to modernization but essential to it. Colonization was completely to restructure the economic, social, political, and cultural arrangements of colonized societies through the development of capitalism. The advent of capitalism was fueled by the trade in the tropical products and mineral wealth of the New World and by the trans-Atlantic trade in African slaves, along with the expropriation of the land, labor, and bodies of other peoples of color, who fell violently under the hegemony of the Europeans, thus tragically bearing the costs of empire.

There are other candidates for the beginning of this momentous transition in Mexico, or for significant milestones along the way. One of these is the so-called Bourbon Reforms (named for the eponymous reigning dynasty of the Spanish Empire after 1715, whose heirs still occupy the Spanish throne), most of them carried out in the latter half of the eighteenth century. Under the auspices of the enlightened despotism common to European monarchies of the time, the reforms aimed at overhauling the creaky Spanish Empire through a form of state-directed modernization—change from the top down. A more conventional periodization of Mexican history locates the inflection from "traditional" society to forms of modernization introduced after independence from the Spanish Empire in 1821, a view for which there is much to be said. The question of decolonization is obviously a corollary to the independence = modernization equation, and in fact the processes of decolonization and modernization wind like a double helix through much of this book. One can also make the onset-of-modernization case for the Porfirian era (1876–1911), dominated by the figure of perennial president-dictator Porfirio Díaz (1830–1915). The extension of a robust railway network throughout the country, moderate but significant population growth, the in-pouring of foreign investment and introduction of a banking system, the relatively rapid advance of industrialization, and the invention of a nationalist mythology to legitimize state and nation were the instruments of the Porfirian regime's self-conscious modernization project.

The Mexican Revolution of 1910–1921 that overthrew Díaz—the revolution of Pancho Villa and Emiliano Zapata—is sometimes seen as a definitive transition point along the path to modernization. The reach of the postrevolutionary state after the early 1920s increased thanks to political stability based upon the later construction of a hegemonic party, the Partido Revolucionario Institucional (Institutional Revolutionary Party, or PRI). It penetrated deep into the organs of governance and Mexican society and remained dominant for seventy years draped in the fig leaf of a nominally democratic regime. With the "Mexican Miracle" of the post–World War II era the country underwent rapid industrialization, population growth, urbanization, rising living standards, improvements in educational levels and public health, etc., but at the cost of the imposition of a *dictablanda* undermining an ostensible commitment to political democracy, liberal citizenship, and opportunity for all.[3] It will have occurred to readers that these points of inflection were more like halting but discernible steps along a modernizing path rather than sharp breaks or disjunctive forward plunges.

Cumulative alterations in the economic, political, and social spheres have brought the country to a leading position in Latin America and today's world. By some indicators Mexico enjoys a notable level of development masked by the acuteness of its many challenges. The country is a member of the G20 group, composed of the world's twenty largest advanced and emerging economies. By most estimates its gross domestic product places it in about tenth or twelfth position among the world's nations. Its economy is dwarfed by those of China, the European Union, and the United States at about twenty times its size, but its gross domestic product (GDP) is nearly twice that of Argentina or Sweden, for example, even though GDP is an admittedly crude measure of economic advancement. Mexico does not begin to have the social safety net, healthcare systems, or even the elevated living standards of some much smaller nations, such as the Scandinavian countries, which also have a more equitable distribution of wealth and functioning democracies.

Going back in time to the first half of the nineteenth century, however, to the birth of the independent nation, we can say that during the early republican period (1821–ca. 1860) Mexico suffered a serious economic reverse—not just a period of stagnation but an actual decline in the national economy as represented by national income estimates. Some comparisons with other Atlantic economies to which Mexico looked as models for economic and political modernization illuminate this point. In contrast to Great Britain, for example, per capita income in Mexico declined from about a third of Great Britain's in 1800 to around a sixth in 1845 and persisted at even slightly lower levels until 1910.[4] Compared with its northern neighbor, the young American republic, in 1800 both the national income and per capita income of Mexico were around 50 percent those of the United States but had fallen by 1845 to about 20 percent and 8 percent, respectively. By 1860 the disparity had become still more pronounced: the national income calculation for the United States had grown by about 1,300 percent, while Mexico's had continued to decline.

In Mexico's case both national and per capita incomes were determined in large part by silver exports. Because this produced an extremely concentrated distribution of wealth, per capita income calculations are not representative of the welfare of the general population. Furthermore, there is evidence that Mexico's silver economy had begun to falter before 1800 and collapsed almost entirely during the insurgency of 1810–1821; there are other indicators of an economic softening in the late colonial economy. If we take 1800 as an overall baseline, it is clear that the decade of the independence struggle, followed by the political turmoil of the 1821–1855 period, did great damage to the economy and the society as a whole. The loss of half the national territory to the United States after 1848 and the civil wars at mid-century associated with the Liberal Reform had enormous costs for the country in terms of economic development. A sharp drop in per capita GDP occurred between 1800 and 1820; then between 1820 and 1845 the decline in GDP per capita amounted to about 25 percent in total—that is, a shrinkage in the Mexican economy of about a quarter. The first half of the nineteenth century therefore saw a prolonged crisis in the country's development. Had these disruptions not occurred, Mexico might have reached its twentieth-century levels of development and well-being decades earlier.

This bird's-eye view of Mexican economic history directs our attention to the late eighteenth and early nineteenth centuries for insight into the country's stuttering development. Should the period be broken in two at the independence struggle (ca. 1808–1821) in the more traditional manner, with colonial New Spain on one side and independent Mexico on the other, or should it be seen in many ways as a single unit? Viewed from the long perspective of a hundred years, the era is rife with contradictions. The project of the Bourbon Reforms (ca. 1760–1810) as it applied to New Spain, for example, meant the "recolonization" of Mexico as one element in an overhaul of the faltering Spanish Empire for the benefit of the metropolis. Local elites in New Spain were in some ways disenfranchised from the political position they had come to occupy by default during the period from 1650 to 1750, when the imperial center in Old Spain went into a long slide and power devolved upon the wealthy and powerful of the colony. The Bourbon modernization program therefore sowed the seeds of its own destruction by generating discontent among the upper reaches of the population. Furthermore, in the republican era the Indigenous majority of the country nominally transited from "subjects" to "citizens," but against a backdrop of poverty, racial prejudice, and social subjugation as an ethnically marked underclass. Effective citizenship was thus highly circumscribed, and the status of Indians in most respects—economically, socially—seems actually to have worsened with independence.[5] The thing about contradictions, of course, is that if the terms are disaggregated they cannot be visualized or understood in relation to each other, so they become difficult or impossible to describe, let alone explain. Viewing the century from 1750 to 1850 as a single unit thus allows us to see both continuity and change more clearly, and the ways in which the two illuminate each other.

MODERNIZATION[6]

The turbulent interaction of modernization and decolonization is represented in the stormy passage of my title. The genealogy of modernity is not unproblematic, of course, and has long been argued about. The liberal statesmen, writers, and entrepreneurs of the early Mexican republic, but also many conservatives, were very much self-conscious modernizers in their vision of the nation's future. For the Bourbon reformers of the late eighteenth century, the captive colony was like a lover—too much reform and liberalization and it would get away; not enough and it would be smothered. Modernization to political men of the nineteenth century meant substantive change in the society; the question was how much of it was good for the country as a whole and who should enjoy its benefits? The modernizing vision required optimism about national possibilities sharing much with contemporaries elsewhere in Latin America and even with public figures and thinkers such as Alexander Hamilton in the fledgling United States some decades earlier. The Mexicans of this generation spoke and wrote of national economic development, an ordered political life, and a strong state as characteristics of the great Euro-Atlantic societies they wished to emulate. They paid much less attention to social and cultural change, although these were implicitly presumed to follow in the wake of economic development and viable political institutions. Mexico's capacity to "become modern" was linked by virtually all thinkers and statesmen of the early republican period to the emergence of the autonomous nation and the consolidation of the state—to decolonization toward viable nationhood. Obsessed as we are with the history of those great invented clans called nations, the issue remains at the center of Western social science and public conversation in an era of globalization.

Modernity, the product of modernization (the first being a condition, the second a process), can be defined in many ways. Among its chief manifestations are the condition of constant, rapid, and discrepant change in the economic, social, political, and cultural realms; the disenchantment of the world from a religious point of view and its reenchantment from a scientific one; and the rise of the centralized and hegemonic state with its "iron cage" of bureaucratic rationality. There are a number of other diagnostic elements, among them rapid rates of urbanization, industrialization, increasing literacy, and rising living standards and life expectancy. On the part of Mexican public men of the early nineteenth century there was apparently no coherent, explicit project to achieve any such thing as modernization and no elaborated program about what decolonization might mean much beyond political independence from Spain. The impulse toward modernity was primarily mimetic, seeking models to follow—for some the United States, for others Britain and/or France. From the late eighteenth century, the inspiration of the British model—not only what Enlightenment figures like Adam Smith were writing but also what was happening in the British economy and political sphere—was clearly at work in the thinking of reformers all over the Spanish world. In political terms, what was initially at issue for public actors during the Mexican independence struggle of 1810–1821 was autonomy and some form of "home rule" within a revived Spanish worldwide monarchy rather than independence as such. As the intransigence of Spain stiffened in the face of unfolding events in the Americas, however, and as political fragmentation emerged within insurgent groups, independence seemed the only viable option.

Hovering over all the processes of independence in Ibero-America was the long shadow of the French Revolution. One outward rippling shock wave generated by this seismic event was the bloody slave uprising and revolution on the French sugar island of St. Domingue in 1791. The Haitian Revolution frightened autonomy-minded elites in Spanish America (as well as those of Brazil and the southern United States) with the specter of mass social violence by people of color. Those elites therefore withheld support after 1808 from a number of popular movements in the colonies, including in New Spain (as Mexico was then known), that might otherwise have attracted their alliance against the colonial regime. The Haitian episode, in fact, points to one of the chief questions of the decolonization era regarding the development of national sensibilities: the intersection of race, citizenship, and class and beyond that how inclusive the idea of the "nation" might be.

DECOLONIZATION

The processes of decolonization have, like modernization, generated an entire scholarly discipline lying at the intersection of the humanities and social sciences, that of postcolonial studies. It was possible to put into practice elements of a modernization program during colonial times, and it was limited forms of these that the Bourbon Reforms aspired to introduce. But many statesmen of the early republican period rejected this statist (that is, top-down) form of modernization as just another form of metropolitan oppression, which in many ways it was. In terms of the political sphere of life, decolonization can be viewed at the most elemental level as the outcome of the movement(s) in New Spain to throw off the rule of Old Spain. However, decolonization amounted to much more than severing the bonds with the Spanish monarchy, telling people they were now citizens rather than subjects, and inventing the device on a flag. It moved on several different tracks at different speeds—political, social, economic, and cultural—producing changes that moved Mexico incrementally toward modernization. In the political sphere it was a relatively easy matter to enact the category of "citizen" to replace that of "subject" by constitutional charter or law. But it was harder to perform it because it was not clear at first what being a citizen of Mexico meant, let alone who citizens were or what rights and responsibilities might pertain to them. Social decolonization stretched well beyond independence and had to do with changes in social structure, the emergence of new ruling elites, ideas about race and class, and so forth. One very concrete aspect of this prolonged process in Mexico, for example, was the abolition of the titled aristocracy (1826–1827) and its replacement with a class of *hombres de bien* (the closest English translation here would be "gentlemen"), a natural aristocracy of talent, education, and material comfort much discussed in the nineteenth-century Atlantic world. Operationalizing this often boiled down to imposing property qualifications for the vote, the idea that economic worth translated directly into stake holding in the society and therefore into political seriousness. Another event along the way was the abolition in 1829 of African slavery, an institution already moribund but still symbolically important. Independence opened Mexican society up to some degree to people of color, clearly, but there were (*are still*) long-lingering traces of the ethnically graded social hierarchy, the *sistema de castas* (discussed in chapter 2).

Economic decolonization took longer still. New polities like Mexico needed to reenter the hemispheric and global economies within frameworks different from the extractive and monopolistic ones typical of the colonial relationships. The terms of such a reintegration would still be highly asymmetrical but were defined by market and other economic forces rather than by formal political mechanisms of extraction such as tribute payments by people of color, taxation, and closed trading arrangements and exclusions that favored metropolitan mercantile interests. Often referred to as "neocolonialism," this was a state of uneven terms of trade and national welfare that dependency theory, developed in the twentieth century, was invented to explain. Finally, cultural decolonization took the longest of any of these processes and has been explored by the development of postcolonial studies. Decolonization in the political sense is a process with a beginning and an end, while postcoloniality inhabits the cultural sphere as a long-lived condition. One famous example is the centrality of the Virgin of Guadalupe to Mexican cultural and political life and to national identity. Officially declared patroness of New Spain in 1754, her devotion has a long history stretching from mid-colonial times to the present. The original apparition of the Virgin in this advocation dates to 1531, a decade after the conquest, when she appeared to the humble Indigenous man Juan Diego, canonized by Pope John Paul II in 2002. Her history is emblematic of the sort of rebranding of heavily freighted cultural icons that can go on from colonial to postcolonial situations but whose objects never entirely shed their resonances with earlier traditions.

THE BOOK'S APPROACH

Sociological considerations and aggregate numbers by no means tell the entire story of this turbulent century, however. Mexican conservatives and liberals struggled after 1821 to assert their competing but in many cases overlapping visions for the country's future. Social change in any direction, whether backward or forward, was actually *lived* for the most part by the mass of the Mexican population outside a few thousand men (and they were exclusively men) who made up what I have called the "political nation." This was composed of those political generals, civilian politicians, educated professionals, and officials at all levels of government who among them controlled the nation's fate in the national capital. They manned the state legislatures and governors' mansions, the upper reaches of the army and Church, and informal social networks defined by common geographical origins, education, wealth, mutual interest, and kinship. Although poor, with no prospect of upward social mobility and largely voiceless politically, ordinary people could still enjoy public celebratory life, the consolations of religion, the intimacy of the domestic sphere, and the other human pleasures—emotional, aesthetic, sensual, and interpersonal—available to even the most abject people in human history. The problem for the historian interested in the common people whose lives flow on under the great events of war, politics, and epochal change is that their voices are difficult to recover. In our own information-saturated environment, we may forget that ordinary people in a society such as Mexico 150 or 200 years ago tended to leave documentary traces only when they bumped up against the state in some way. Such moments of contact typically consisted of legal scrapes or when disposing of property through inheritance or market transactions. The latter was much less likely to leave evidence among vast numbers of poor people because they had little disposable property in the first place. But where I can show what ordinary Mexicans were thinking, feeling, and doing during this century, I will try to do so.

Finally, a word about what I have emphasized in this book and left out of it. Important aspects of the period's history have been glossed over quickly or simply left aside entirely in keeping with the modest dimensions of the work and the intellectual idiosyncrasies of its author. I have felt that it was preferable to deal with some central themes more deeply than try to achieve an encyclopedic account of this century of Mexican history, a strategy that therefore locates the book more in the category of an extended interpretive/ synthetic essay than a survey. There is little on the structures of rule under the colonial regime except as they came to be the objects of reform efforts during its last three generations or so. Interpersonal relationships, marriage, illicit unions, family, and the raising of children are scarcely alluded to. A major related theme touched upon only in passing is the role of women in Mexican society and changes in gender expectations and practices. Steps toward modernization occurred here, too, as in the elevation of republican motherhood as a gender ideal for women (a similar trend took hold in the United States) and the complementary retraction of the nun as feminine role model, but there were other major changes as well.

Stretching from the Gulf of Mexico to the Pacific and from Zacatecas up to the Pacific Northwest, the Mexican North stood in a peripheral relationship both geographically and politically to the rest of the country for most of our period, and after Texas won its independence in 1836 the vast region became as much a problem as a potential resource (see map 1.1). Historian Peter Guardino has put this well: "Before Texas became independent [1836], the northern territories that [President] Polk coveted had been quite marginal to Mexican political debates, and probably also to Mexican ideas about what Mexico was. The loss of Texas made Texas and the looming danger the United States posed to other northern territories symbols of national sovereignty and self-respect."[7]

The Viceroyalty
of New Spain
ca. 1800

Disputed
Territory

Government of
New California

Louisiana

Government of
New Mexico

Arizpe

Province of
Texas

Florida

Monterrey

Durango

5 6

Zacatecas

San Luis Potosi

4

2

7

Guadalajara

Guanajuato

8

Yucatán

Valladolid

Mérida

3

Mexico

Veracruz

Puebla

1

9

10

7

Oaxaca

Chinpas

Comayagun

Guatemala

San Salvador

León

Costa Rica

Principal Intendencies of Central New Spain

1. Intendency of Mexico
2. Intendency of Guanajuato
3. Intendency of Valladolid
4. Intendency of Guadalajara
5. Intendency of Zacatecas
6. Intendency of San Luis Potosi
7. Intendency of Vera Cruz
8. Government of Tiaxcala
9. Intendency of Puebla
10. Intendency of Oaxaca

Viceregal Audiencia of Mexico

Captaincy-General of Guatemala

Captaincy-General of Cuba

Adapted from Lombardi and Lombardi, 1983

Map 1.1. Late colonial New Spain. Cathryn L. Lombardi, John V. Lombardi, with K. Lynn Stoner, *Latin American History in Maps: A Teaching Atlas* (Madison: University of Wisconsin Press, 1983), 31.

In many ways the North had a quite different culture—ecologically, ethnically, economically—from the more central parts of the country; doing it justice would require much more space than is available here. So while the Mexican North is frequently alluded to in these pages, it has largely been left aside in my treatment in favor of the more densely settled central areas of the country. Similarly, although chapters 5 through 7 deal at length with the Mexican independence movement, on which I have been writing for a number of years, it concentrates on the social and political aspects of the extended rebellious decade from 1808 to 1821 and less on battles, other events, and distinct individuals. The same general approach holds for the sections of the book devoted to early republican history, where I have opted for a synoptic/interpretive treatment rather than a detailed narrative account.

There is throughout a great deal of explicit emphasis on the economy and economic change. But political modernization was also occurring, manifested in debates over the separation of church and state, how inclusive democratic practices were to be, and the formal structure of the state and its ruling institutions. Some attention is devoted to politics in the broadest sense, meaning the way people distributed power and struggled over it in formal and often informal settings; with some exceptions, these processes are woven into the book's narrative flow rather than singled out analytically. I have also devoted attention throughout to questions such as race, racial classification systems, social mobility, and life in the countryside. These broad themes, and a few others, begin to account for how people identified themselves and were identified by other people, how they earned their living and how wealth was distributed in Mexican society, and whose authority they obeyed, or did not, through the action of formal institutions and sometimes violent resistance.

NOTES

1. For an interesting treatment of how geography to some extent influenced the consolidation of the postrevolutionary Mexican state, see Paul Gillingham, *Unrevolutionary Mexico: The Birth of a Strange Dictatorship* (New Haven, CT: Yale University Press, 2021).

2. Lucas Alamán, *Historia de Méjico desde los primeros movimientos que prepararon su independencia en el año de 1808, hasta la época presente*, second edition, 5 vols. (Mexico City: Editorial Jus, 1968).

3. *Dictablanda* is a virtually untranslatable Spanish neologism playing on the word *dictadura*, "dictatorship," and *blanda*, meaning "soft" in Spanish. So we have in *dictablanda* a "soft dictatorship," more or less; see Paul Gillingham and Benjamin T. Smith, eds., *Dictablanda: Politics, Work, and Culture in Mexico, 1938–1968* (Durham: Duke University Press, 2014).

4. John H. Coatsworth, *Los orígenes del atraso: Nueve ensayos de historia económica de México en los siglos XVIII y XIX*, trans. Juan José Trujilla (Mexico City: Alianza Editorial, 1990), 80–84.

5. The terms "Indian" and "Indigenous" are used here interchangeably to avoid repetitiveness.

6. The discussion of modernization and decolonization here appears in a somewhat more developed form in Eric Van Young, *A Life Together: Lucas Alamán and Mexico, 1792–1853* (New Haven, CT: Yale University Press, 2021), 707–15.

7. Peter Guardino, *The Dead March: A History of the Mexican-American War* (Cambridge, MA: Harvard University Press, 2020), 74.

Chapter 2

Society in New Spain

COLONIAL TWILIGHT TO INDEPENDENCE, 1750–1810

A humble Indigenous farmer born in 1700 would have seen little change in his daily life by 1750, nor very much even over the next century.[1] Had he miraculously lived until 1900, however, Mexico would have been very different. By the beginning of the twentieth century he could walk from his village to a nearby town and might travel by train to a distant city. He might migrate to Mexico City, Veracruz, Monterrey, or Guadalajara to join the growing sector of urban workers laboring in textile factories, breweries, or other industrial settings. Leaving the men in her family behind to work the fields, his daughter might find a position as a domestic in one of the more affluent homes in the Mexico City downtown area or the growing western suburbs of the city, by 1900 a humming capital of about 500,000 (quadrupling its 1800 population). If in 1900 he committed a crime of more than ordinary violence and fled the scene, his movements could be traced by authorities through the telegraph. Or if a bandit, he might be pursued by President Diaz's famous mounted constabulary, the Rurales. Assuming he had the wherewithal, he might occasionally go to a cantina in the nearby town to drink a bottled beer. His wife, however, was still making the family's clothing by hand in 1850 out of homespun or inexpensive cotton purchased in the town or perhaps from a traveling peddler. Most likely even by 1900 she did not have one of the recently introduced Singer sewing machines, a treadle affair that in the absence of electricity worked on female leg power. Her burdens she probably carried in an *ayate*, a sort of multipurpose sling woven of agave fiber harvested from the leaves of the same cactus from whose fibrous heart the intoxicant *pulque* was fermented. She would have spent much of her day preparing maize in a *metate*, a grinding stone of age-old design, and another large chunk of her waking hours making tortillas, the staple of the family diet, prepared

15

over a simple charcoal-fired hearth on a round clay griddle, the *comal*. Her husband would have carried a stack of cold tortillas with him to his work in the fields, along with some mild chiles and a pinch of salt as condiments and perhaps some cold *quelites*, a generic name for different sorts of edible wild plants prepared by boiling, some tasting like spinach. The couple's children might split their days between farm or household labor and a few hours in a village school learning their first letters and numbers from an underpaid school master. Overall literacy rates remained quite low outside the cities (today they reach about 95 percent of adults nationwide), and virtually no peasant child progressed further than the earliest grades of school.

RACE AND THE SOCIAL HIERARCHY

In most respects, then, the lives of ordinary people in the Mexican countryside or even in the cities did not change much between 1750 and 1850 in relation to material goods, the work they did, their family life, and the religious and celebratory calendar. One alteration in the human environment that our villager might have noticed was in the complexion of the people around him, especially in the larger villages or smaller towns to which he might occasionally travel. Of the country's approximately 4.5 million inhabitants in 1750, the vast majority were Indigenous peasants.[2] Table 2.1 shows the approximate racial groupings a half century or so later, on the eve of the independence struggle.

Despite some debate among scholars as to the total population of New Spain at the outbreak of the 1810 insurgency, the percentages presented in table 2.1 are widely accepted. The tiny proportion of European-born Spaniards (known as *españoles europeos*, *peninsulares*, or by derogatory terms such as *gachupines*) remained fairly steady at 15,000 during the last half century of colonial rule; "Creoles" were those Mexican-born people who claimed "pure" European (Spanish) descent. The share of the population consisting of

Table 2.1. Racial groups in New Spain in about 1810.

Source: Eric Van Young, *The Other Rebellion: Popular Violence, Ideology, and the Mexican Struggle for Independence, 1810–1821* (Stanford: Stanford University Press, 2001), 46. *Note*: The figures offered in the table are only approximations, based primarily on estimates by late colonial observers. The percentage of European Spaniards in the total, at 0.002, is statistically almost insignificant despite their qualitative importance in the population of New Spain. Their number, about 15,000, has been included in the figure for Creoles for purposes of the table, and that number rounded up just slightly so that the percentages add up to 100.

Group	Number	Percentage
Spaniards	1,108,000	18.0
Europeans	*15,000*	*0.002*

Creoles	*1,093,000*	*18.0*
Indians	3,676,000	60.0
Mixed Castes	1,338,000	22.0
Mestizos/Castizos	—	—
Blacks	—	—
Total	6,122,000	100

a mixture of Indigenous people and those of European stock, known as *mestizos*, grew rapidly from the end of the sixteenth century and has continued to do so. This makes Mexico substantially a mestizo nation, although there has often been a strong case made for the country's Indian essence, at least cultural if not biological.[3]

The percentage of Indigenous Mexicans has steadily declined until our own day, when they make up 10 to 14 percent of the national population of about 130,000,000. Some native languages have disappeared but many still survive, chief among them Náhuatl, even now the most widely spoken Indigenous tongue. But there are still hundreds of thousands of Yucatec Maya, Mixtec, Zapotec, Otomí, and Purépecha speakers, as well as speakers of about sixty or so other languages. Efforts by the colonial regime to suppress native languages in favor of Spanish were unsuccessful. Where rural schools existed it was much more likely that the Indigenous students would acquire some rudiments of the conquerors' tongue than lose their own. By 1750 most Indians spoke their own languages exclusively, with perhaps a smattering of Spanish; others were effectively bilingual; while a still smaller group had lost the use of their native non-Spanish tongue completely.[4]

Changes in racial structure were most significant in a social sense. In the mid-eighteenth century, Mexicans of mixed race, most particularly those with an admixture of African blood, still suffered the negative stereotyping of being "mongrels," feared as tempestuous, violent social misfits by the Indian peasant population and disdained for the same reasons by the small minority of "white" Mexicans. Some of these people blended into the Indigenous population through intermarriage or illegitimate unions, while some joined the rural work force as day laborers and faded into the general population. Others headed for the cities and towns of the viceroyalty, assuming menial jobs or joining the multitude of urban homeless people, petty criminals, or outright beggars. Many of these made up the *léperos* (literally lepers, but figuratively the socially marginal poor) whose ubiquitous presence in Mexico City drew the comment of visitors to the capital at least until the later nineteenth century. Ethnically and often phenotypically intermediate between those of European and those of native descent, mestizos were also structurally intermediate, filling the niches that kept colonial society humming along. Among these were the occupations of mule drivers, artisans, petty tradesmen, and lower-level management personnel in the countryside. But this indeterminacy and even marginality also allowed for upward mobility within the middle reaches of society. Through integration into commercial circuits, accumulation of capital, and judicious borrowing a mestizo mule driver, for example, might become a small-scale merchant in a town. Or a mestizo woman could marry a Spanish man of modest standing, thus moving up a rung in a very color-and ethnic-conscious society with nonetheless somewhat porous social boundaries.

The socioethnic structure of late colonial New Spain was even more complicated than that, however. It was embodied in the *sistema de castas* arrangement of racial distinctions prevailing in the Spanish New World realms. This was not the rigidly determinative, religiously sanctified, birth-based caste system hierarchy familiar from India, Brahmins at the top and "untouchables" at the bottom and in between hundreds of distinctions corresponding to an occupational pyramid. Rather, the classifications in Mexico were based upon a variety of factors, chiefly including phenotype, lifestyle (including dress, diet, and so forth), language, social context, parents and place of birth, and self-ascription, among others. Categorization in one group or another was thus somewhat arbitrary; the "system" included a good deal of "passing" and overlap, and assignment could inevitably be highly subjective. For example, around 1811, just after the outbreak of the independence rebellion, a group of captured men alleged to be rebels were herded into an old Inquisition prison in Mexico City. When asked the standard question about his *calidad* (race) by an official taking the initial statements, one man interrogated identified himself as an Indian. The examining official noted, "He says he is Indian, but appears to be of quite mixed race (*de calidad bastante revuelta*)." The prisoner may have self-identified as Indian in the hope of drawing a lighter punishment for rebellion against the Spanish crown because Indians were considered to have less developed mental faculties and were therefore less responsible for their own actions. But the reverse self-ascription might also occur, as when Indians described themselves as belonging to other groups to avoid the tribute tax imposed on Indigenous people by right of the Spanish conquest. On the other hand, the interrogating official might simply have been wrong, and the prisoner was of the racial ascription he asserted; one can see the problem here.

In colonial Mexico the basic elements of the ethnic hierarchy were European whites, almost exclusively Spaniards; Indigenous peoples; and Black Africans. Virtually all male and predominantly from the Castilian and Basque regions, European Spaniards continued to migrate to colonial Mexico during the eighteenth century. They came as government officials and churchmen, military officers and soldiers, merchants and clerks, skilled professionals, and to enter the silver mining industry. During their own lives either through ill luck, bad economic choices, or profligacy, or over a couple of succeeding generations, there was a constant recruitment at the top of the group to compensate for a continual downward social drainage. An old proverb of the Spanish world in one of its Mexican versions ran "Abuelo minero, hijo caballero, nieto pordiosero"—"Father miner, son gentleman, grandson beggar." This suggests that fortunes made in the first generation by an entrepreneur in silver mining, possibly a Spanish immigrant, might be dissipated by the third generation. A classic pattern among immigrants was to arrive relatively young, establish themselves economically in a business owned by a senior male relative, and marry a Creole woman, perhaps the boss's daughter or even his widow. An illustrative example of this pattern was the family history of Lucas Alamán (1792–1853), viewed by many historians as one of the early republic's greatest statesmen and certainly the nineteenth century's greatest writer of history (see figure 2.1). His father came to the great silver mining city of Guanajuato from a small town in northern Spain around 1770, married a wealthy widow, established himself in commerce and the mining industry, and made his own modest fortune. His wife's great-grandfather, a silver miner, had some generations earlier acquired a large fortune and a Spanish noble title. By the end of the eighteenth century, however, the volatile nature of the industry, the reproductive vigor of the intervening generations and established inheritance patterns, and the profligacy of some descendants had dissipated the family fortune considerably. And while Alamán himself was never less than well off, he never had the fortune to which he aspired and that the history of the family might have prepared him to expect.

Mexico's Indigenous peoples had counted in the tens of millions at the arrival of the Spanish around 1520, but by 1650 or so their numbers had declined by 90 to 95 percent. This demographic apocalypse was due primarily to the introduction of Old World diseases to which they had no immunity because of the long geographic isolation of the New World from the Old. From its nadir around 1650 the Indian population began to rebound, so that by 1810 it comprised over half the country's inhabitants, but never again would it reach its pre-Columbian numbers of perhaps 20 to 30 million souls. By the time of the Conquest the Aztec Empire embraced much of the most densely populated parts of an extended Valley of Mexico, although other kingdoms and chieftainships existed on all sides, some tributary to the Aztecs, others uneasily independent. The most important of these smaller polities was the Tarascan kingdom to the west, in what is now the state of Michoacán, which managed to maintain its political autonomy by virtue of intermittent warfare and political negotiation with the Aztecs. Another was the small but hardy kingdom of Tlaxcala directly to the east of the Aztec realms, also of Náhuatl speech, which maintained its independence by engaging in diplomacy and highly regulated ritual warfare with its larger, more powerful Aztec neighbor.

Figure 2.1. Lucas Alamán (1792–1853), statesman, historian, and entrepreneur. Pelegrín Clavé y Roqué, 1853. Eduardo Galindo Vargas, courtesy Museo Nacional de San Carlos, INBAL.

The Maya societies to the southeast, in the region of the Yucatán Peninsula and Central America, inhabited another densely populated area, but for causes still debated their complex social forms had long since passed from the scene by the arrival of the Spanish. By 1750 population loss, Spanish labor and land policies applied to the subject peoples, Christian evangelization by various regular religious orders over two centuries, colonial administrative law, and a variety of other factors had swept away nearly every vestige of the upper and intermediate levels of these state-level societies, reducing the preconquest sociopolitical complexity to a vast village-dwelling peasantry. Most of the white colonial elite saw the Indians as a homogeneous mass of lazy, libidinous, drunken, improvident, benighted, credulously pious human worker bees dominated by their village priests. But local Indian society in reality maintained a surprising degree of cultural integrity. In the eighteenth century there is evidence of a reemergence of Aztec cultural and even political consciousness, particularly at the upper levels of Indigenous society, as demonstrated, for example, in Indigenous naming practices. Indigenous languages were still spoken and could not be stamped out despite efforts by the Spanish crown to do so, and village governing structures preserved many pre-Conquest elements. The rituals, beliefs, and celebratory life of Christianity as practiced by Indigenous people reflected a blend of European and ancient Indian elements, with native religious practices flowing strongly beneath the surface of society in certain areas. The conquerors did not realize that despite the arrangements they imposed there persisted much native habit in the spatial distribution of village political power, rotation in office, and governing practices, especially where religious observance was concerned. As late as 1820, for example, after three centuries of more or less intense efforts on the part of the Catholic Church to make Indians into good Christians, a priest in the area of Toluca, just to the west of Mexico City, stumbled upon a cave in the countryside much in use by local Indigenous villagers for religious rites that had escaped the padre's oversight. In it he discovered an altar with strange sorts of food obviously intended as propitiatory offerings to a mixture of both ancient native gods and Christian saints, as well as what he described as *muñecos* (dolls or figurines) completely unfamiliar to him, which he interpreted as representations of native deities or even satanic entities.

The third human element in the racial makeup of New Spain consisted of some 200,000 Black Africans imported as slaves, chiefly during the colony's first century; after that time those people identified as *negros* or in some derived category were mainly born in the country. Africans arriving in New Spain in bondage made up a tiny fraction of the twelve million or so shipped to the Americas over nearly four centuries but did leave a significant imprint. There are trace amounts of African DNA in most phenotypically non-African Mexicans today, and African culture—in material life, in music, in foodways—is quite visible in contemporary Mexico, especially in pockets along the Gulf and Pacific coasts. The decline in the Indigenous population of Mexico under the impact of European diseases during the sixteenth and seventeenth centuries made the labor issue critical for the colonizers, loath to labor themselves, and Black African slavery offered a partial solution. These people worked on sugar plantations in the tropical lowland areas of the country but also in other rural settings and in the cities of New Spain, where they might attain a fair degree of autonomy working for their masters as domestics, rented out as waged laborers, or in urban craft and service occupations. By 1750 there were perhaps 20,000 Black slaves in New Spain. A large group of Africans had gained their freedom through self-purchase or manumission by their owners. Even those Africans who gained their freedom, however, found themselves at a distinct social disadvantage owing to official color bars and implicit anti-Black prejudices. By the late colonial period, however, there were Afro-Mexican military regiments made up of free urban Blacks as well as entire villages with a distinctly African complexion, especially on the eastern side of the country. As the Indian population rebounded after 1650 or so, it became too expensive to import slaves while free labor was much cheaper. By the late colonial period slavery had drastically declined in New Spain and shortly after independence was finally abolished in 1829.

By 1800 the notional racial hierarchy in New Spain had become quite explicit, complex, and formalized, the rigidity increasing in direct proportion to elite anxieties about racial mixing among common people. What was at stake was social and economic dominance based on the degree of whiteness, a form of leverage that the white population was little short of desperate to retain. This preoccupation was exemplified in the famous *casta* paintings done by various Mexican artists, chiefly in the latter part of the century. Here the three primary racial categories and their various crossings were represented pictorially, depicted in stereotypical domestic scenes, usually showing a male-female couple and a young child, with racial labels inscribed at the foot of each image (see figure 2.2). The famous form of representation was a canvas divided into sixteen cells, each displaying a racial pairing, read from the top left to the bottom right. The child exemplified the racial category produced by the adult pair. A Spanish man (whether of European birth or a Creole) and woman produced a Spanish child, a mestizo couple a mestizo, an Indian couple an Indian, a mulatto couple a mulatto, and a Black couple a Black child. After that, things became increasingly complicated and the racial terms more exotic, even whimsical. The child of an Indian man and an African woman was called a *lobo* (wolf), for example, an Indian man and a mestiza produced a *coyote*, while other pairings "down" the hierarchy bore labels such as *torna atrás* ("a backward step") and *ahí te estás* ("there you are"; essentially, "you deserve what you get from such a coupling"). The domestic social settings shown in the paintings portray decreasing affluence and somewhat less decorous behavior. Differentiations beneath "pure" Spanish and above "pure" Indian were based substantially on the degree of a person's African blood. There was a considerable degree of porosity between the groups, although mixing tended to occur mostly in the middle.

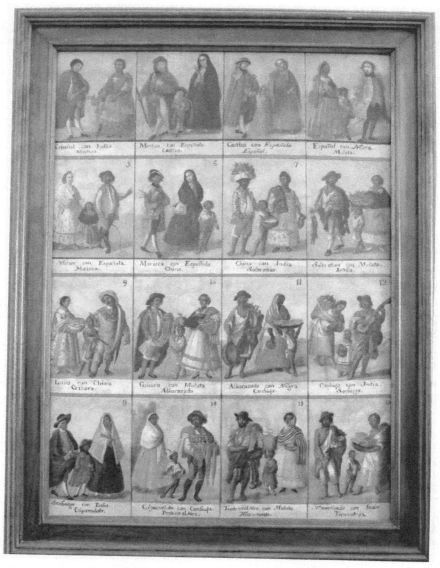

Figure 2.2. Typical casta painting of the late colonial period. Wikimedia Commons/Luis Alvaz.

It was much more likely for a mulatto or mestizo man (because men tended to "marry down" the racial hierarchy and women to "marry up") to marry an Indian woman than for a European Spaniard to marry an Indian, although there were always exceptions, unsanctified unions were frequent, and rates of illegitimacy were quite high. Outside the basic eight or so categories the descriptors were notional, rarely if ever used. So while it is fair to say that colonial Mexico was a racially stratified society, it is also true that the stratification was not rigid nor the borders between groups impermeable. Assignment to one category or another was a matter of ascription given in parish registers (records of births, deaths, and marriages kept by priests) at an individual's birth. After that it was largely subjective, dependent on who was making the assignment and the self-identification of the person being assigned, and influenced by the social situation of the moment.[5]

CITIES

What did the society of New Spain look like in the last half century or so of the colonial era? New Spain included not only what we know today as Mexico proper but also Central America and what is now the US Southwest. Although cities played a vital part in all aspects of life, the colony was over-whelmingly rural. On the eve of independence from Spain the urban popula-tion was perhaps 10 percent of the total. The colony-wide census of 1793 produced totals for the ten largest cities, amounting to about 5 percent of New Spain's population (see table 2.2).

By 1800 Mexico City's population was about 120,000 people. During the 1810–1821 insurgency it reached its highest point in 1813, nearly 170,000, as people fled the fighting and insecure conditions of the countryside. By way of comparison, in 1800 or so the populations of the world's largest cities,

Table 2.2. Population of the ten largest Mexican cities, 1793. *Source:* Eric Van Young, Hacienda and Market in Eighteenth-Century Mexico: The Rural Economy of the Guadalajara Region, *1675–1820*, second edition (Lanham, MD: Rowman & Littlefield, 2006), 35.

City	Population
Mexico City	112,926
Puebla	52,717
Guanajuato	32,098
Guadalajara	28,250
Zacatecas	24,495
Antequera (Oaxaca City)	19,069
Valladolid (Morelia)	17,093
Durango	11,027
San Luis Potosí	8,571
Tlaxcala	3,357
Total	309,063

London and Peking (modern Beijing), were about one million each, and Paris's half that size. By mid-century Mexico City counted around 180,000.

Much smaller than Mexico City at the start of the nineteenth century was the western city of Guadalajara, an administrative and commercial hub with a well-developed agricultural hinterland sharing many of the capital's characteristics; a look at it gives some idea of what major urban areas were like as colony gave way to nation. The official life of the city was dominated by a royal high court (*audiencia*) with the lawyers, notaries, and other officials orbiting around it, much as Mexico City centered in large measure on the royal government of an enormous and geographically diverse colony. Guadalajara's 500 or so merchants, fifty or more large wholesalers, and the important merchants' gild/court, the *consulado* (one of only three in the country, the others located in Veracruz and Mexico City), dominated the western part of the colony. By 1800 this city of around 35,000 inhabitants had a handsome urban center with a cathedral looming over the central square. It was made up of some 350 city blocks laid out in a grid pattern of rectilinear streets radiating out from the central plaza and a large suburban area; the finer structures were constructed of stone. The wealthier citizens lived as near the center of town as possible, their religious life revolving around the *sagrario* parish extending around the cathedral, a typical spatial arrangement that also prevailed in Mexico City. Where physical factors prevented the application of this famous "grid pattern" template, as in the great silver mining center at Guanajuato and other mountainous mining towns with their irregular topography, the grid pattern might peter out very close to the center of town. Increasing irregularity of layout and decreasing social status of the inhabitants corresponded directly to distance from the city center. Indians lived scattered throughout the urban landscape because in the city center they often worked as domestic servants and in the provision of essential services, such as water carrying and charcoal selling. Guadalajara grew to absorb several smaller Indigenous towns and villages that then lost their political identities but retained their heavily Indian character, as did the Indigenous *barrios* (neighborhoods) of Mexico City—Tlatelolco, Ixtapalapa, Coyocán, etc.

New Spain definitely demonstrated what has been called a "primate city pattern," with one great city—the capital—many times the size in population of the ones trailing it in the urban hierarchy, a layout replicated in most of the provinces (and later the states). To a great extent this is still the case. In 2010 greater Mexico City held a population of over twenty million while Mexico's second and third cities in size, Guadalajara and Monterrey, had around four million each. The disparity in size was therefore about the same in 2000 as it was around 1800, the capital being four or five times the size of Guadalajara.

New Spain's capital and other cities ate people, the rate of mortality outrunning that of natural reproduction so that a constant stream of immigrants from smaller towns and villages was required to maintain the stability of their populations, let alone provide for growth. Only after 1850 did urban mortality from outbreaks of epidemic disease began to ebb. The public health situation improved even more markedly toward the end of the century under the modernizing push of the Porfirio Díaz regime. Before the late nineteenth century public hygiene was primitive at best, nonexistent at worst. This is hardly surprising when one considers that in London, the avatar of modernization at the time, the modern sewer system was only constructed after 1856; before that the Thames River was described as an open sewer. Mexico City's streets were filled with trash and less pleasant things, including the occasional dead horse or donkey. Many homeowners there and elsewhere kept smaller livestock—chickens, pigs, goats—in the inner courtyards of their houses. This created more public health problems, and still did at least until recently, adding its own note in the form of dried, bacteria-bearing animal feces to the great city's famous vehicular and industrial air pollution. Around 1850, in the closing pages of his *Historia de Méjico*, in diagnosing the country's ills Lucas Alamán noted the contrast between private luxury, as exemplified by the many elegant homes in the wealthier zones of the city, and the public squalor of the garbage-filled streets, half-hearted measures of public hygiene, and other remediable but neglected public problems. Urban living conditions in Mexico around 1800 were simply unsanitary, although they may have been better in small towns and villages where the population densities were lower. Nor were police services in large cities very effective.

THE TWO REPUBLICS

Important though they were, Mexican cities at the end of the colonial era and early republican times were islands in a sea of country villages, hamlets, small towns, missions, and other forms of rural settlement. The great plains and rugged mountains of the Mexican North were home to a number of nomadic and semisedentary Indigenous groups known generically to the Aztecs, to their state-level neighbors, and to their Spanish conquerors as *Chichimecas*, essentially meaning "barbarians." Village-based Indigenous farmers were found in pockets in well-watered northern intermontane valleys and stretching up the Pacific coast to the Californias and beyond. Perpetually stretched for resources, the colonial government was hard pressed to "pacify" and dominate these northern peoples, a problem that would pose even greater difficulties for the empty treasuries of the newly independent Mexican state. So the Spanish crown, partly out of religious piety, partly out of military, fiscal, administrative, and geopolitical considerations, essentially off loaded the north as a field for Christian proselytization and the implanting of Spanish civilization onto male Catholic regular religious orders. These tasks fell most especially upon the Society of Jesus, founded only in 1540 and active in this missionary field in Mexico between 1683 and 1767. Scores of Jesuit missions dotted the northwest up into the Californias, generally near or paired with military posts called *presidios.*[6] When the Jesuit Order was abruptly expelled for political reasons from all the Spanish realms in 1767, the established missions passed into the care of the Franciscan Order, which would go on to found yet other missions in the north under the leadership of the famous Father Junípero Serra (1713–1784). But the most pious of missionary intentions weighed disastrously on the Indigenous peoples thus Christianized and "civilized," both in terms of culture loss and population decline from accidentally introduced diseases. The effective "pacification" of the Mexican North waned as fiscal resources to support the effort dried up and colonization programs fizzled. Also making pacification and control even harder to achieve in the desert north was the westward American colonization that pushed the fiercer nomadic peoples toward the south. In the 1830s the Mexican government took measures to secularize the missions, converting them into villages without connections to the missionary orders.

The central and southern areas of the country were the most densely settled. The major native state-level peoples in pre-Hispanic times were the Maya in the Yucatán Peninsula and on southward into Central America, the Aztecs in the Valley of Mexico, the Tarascans to the west, the Mixtecs and Zapotecs in the area of Oaxaca, the Otomí to the northeast of the Valley of Mexico, and the Tlaxcalans directly east.[7] Here the story was very different than in the north. The Spanish had by military and other means decapitated the upper political structures existing at their arrival and superimposed their own rule upon settled peasant societies, extracting labor and tribute from the natives, reorganizing political life, and doing them the dubious favor of converting them to Christianity. This was done by means of preaching, missionizing, and exemplary Christian behavior when possible, by force when thought necessary. Indigenous people were removed from the jurisdiction of the Spanish Inquisition by 1570 and thereafter tried for religious heterodoxy in regular ecclesiastical courts. By the late eighteenth and early nineteenth centuries thousands of native villages populated the rural landscape, most heavily in the valleys of Mexico, Cuernavaca, Toluca, west to the Pacific coast and east to the Gulf, and in the areas of Oaxaca and Yucatán. Even today the state of Oaxaca, a single state among the country's thirty-one federative entities (plus the Federal District), is thronged with Indigenous villages and boasts 570 municipalities (counties, basically), 25 percent of the nation's total, each of which may embrace several villages of varying sizes. The vast majority of such communities in colonial times were labeled as Indian, but such identifications could be fluid or ambiguous. At some points along the valley of the

Balsas River, for example, which runs for nearly 500 miles through several states in Mexico's south-central region, principally in the state of Guerrero, the mortality among Indigenous people in the early colonial period was as heavy as anywhere, leaving entire communities virtually depopulated. Due to certain oddities in regional demographics, several such village communities reconstituted themselves as nominally Indigenous during the seventeenth and eighteenth centuries but were in actuality mostly populated by Afro-mestizos. The official "Indian" status conferred access to communal lands and certain legal privileges and exemptions on the inhabitants, but some disadvantages as well, including tribute obligations.

On the eve of independence from Spain the doctrine of the *dos repúblicas*—two republics, one Indigenous, the other Spanish—still theoretically prevailed in Spanish America but had pretty much faded into a notional concept since its introduction in the sixteenth century. One of the "republics" in this sense was, broadly, a polity, a political society embracing all of Spanish society (including racially mixed groups), while the other republic comprised Indigenous society. The distinction was established by the Spanish crown to insulate Indigenous peoples as much as possible from the corrupting influence of non-Indian groups. Lest it be thought by readers that royal Spanish government was a deeply benign form of rule for native peoples, we should remember that the theoretical interest in protecting Indians was driven as much or more by crown concerns that colonial elites would extend unlimited social control and labor demands over the Indigenous masses, thereby threatening the domination of the Spanish monarchy over the colony, as it was by any humanitarian or religious motives. The concept of the two republics was built upon assumptions of the child-like, semirational nature of Indians, thought to require crown protections, as for example by officially restricting the ways in which they could dispose of land. This was a legal construct and therefore something of an abstraction, not a mechanism of spatial segregation, like Indian reservations in the United States, or even in colonial Nueva Granada, the mega-viceroyalty that would later fragment into Colombia, Venezuela, and Ecuador. It imposed no impervious barrier between "native" and "non-native" societies, especially in the economic sphere, because Indigenous people were deeply integrated into the non-Indian economy for purposes of labor, exchange, and the extraction of taxes from them.

The theoretical existence of the "two republics" doctrine, in fact, and the mixing of native and "Spanish" people more and more as time went on reflects an ongoing schizophrenia in Mexican society as old as the Spanish conquest itself. The issue was whether to encourage or even force the transformation of Indigenous people into "Mexicans" like everyone else, or to allow them to retain a strong native cultural tradition including language, religious customs, and lifeways. Some thinkers in the nineteenth century believed Indians to be a drag on the modernization they were seeking to accelerate, which implied that social and economic development could only move forward on a sort of dual society basis, with a modern sector and a "backward" sector. This tension has extended into the modern era, well past the Mexican Revolution of 1910, in central government policies toward Indian groups and in cultural debates about the very nature of Mexico itself, as I have suggested—whether its essence is Indigenous or Spanish/mestizo. Indigenous identity could not be stamped out, particularly in the young Mexican republic up to the mid-nineteenth century, and has survived into our own day nowhere completely intact, but in some places more robustly than others. The uprising of Maya-speaking people in the southeastern Mexican state of Chiapas in 1994 in the form of the Ejército Zapatista de Liberación Nacional (Zapatista National Liberation Army, or EZLN) especially targeted the North American Free Trade Agreement (NAFTA) as an instrument of neoliberal exploitation. In proclaiming for itself an anticolonial, antiglobalization, anarchist-libertarian ideology the movement also represented a resurgence in Indigenous cultural and political identity in an armed form. Where modernization is concerned, the dilemma of integration versus separation has resolved itself over time because the Indigenous population of Mexico is today only about 10 to 14 percent of the total.

THE INDIAN COUNTRYSIDE

A "typical" Indigenous village in Central Mexico would have been built around some sort of central plaza with a parish church. Some of these were very simple adobe structures, others much more elaborate. A modest building dedicated to the activities of the town council (*cabildo*) might also face the plaza. This structure might even have had a small jail in it, although these were notoriously rickety affairs from which prisoners frequently escaped. The village government was likely to be gerontocratic, the offices held by older men, *exclusively* men. Women were not allowed to vote or hold office so their opinions or activities would have slipped under the radar screen, but it seems likely that they expressed their opinions to their husbands or sons, in that way influencing political life. Sponsorship of religious celebrations was obligatory for men on the path to village office but could be so expensive that the villagers so honored might need to be compelled to sponsor festivities. Social status was earned through participation in what has been called the "civil-religious" hierarchy, or some approximation of it, in which men alternated back and forth between secular civic offices and lay positions in the local church. Office holders thus eventually climbed a "ladder" to a position of some authority in the community as elders or emeriti officials referred to as *principales*. Intertwined with this structure was that of a very localized Indigenous nobility presumably tracing its roots to the pre-Conquest period. Male members of the Indian nobility, sometimes called *caciques*, often functioned at the highest level of village politics, holding the office of *gobernador*, in some cases indefinitely. In some circumstances people who were not strictly Indigenous by "blood" (that is, by genetic heritage) might well come to occupy the *cacique* role and establish local political dynasties, although this could be disputed in the courts if there were counter-claimants to the distinction.

Village life revolved around the religious calendar—the marking of life's milestones (births, baptisms, marriages, deaths), regular attendance at mass and confession, and the rituals and celebrations of the general liturgical calendar (Christmas, Epiphany, Easter, Corpus Christi, etc.). Added to these were festivities celebrating the saint's name day of the village—San Pedro, San Pablo, San Juan, San José, Santa María, Santa Ana, etc., usually combined with a native place name, for example, Santa Ana Acatlán. If the village functioned as the head settlement in a district with other villages and hamlets, religious affairs might be officiated over by a resident priest or his assistant or by a priest from a neighboring community who rode circuit over a certain area. Still, thin as royal officials were on the ground, the local priest was in many cases the closest contact villagers had with any representative of Church or state authority on a regular basis. Geographic isolation, especially distancing the ministrations of the Catholic Church, might produce some interesting cultural effects at the village level. Around 1800, for instance, an episcopal inspection (that is, a tour of the diocese by the new bishop) of the Huasteca, a large region stretching along the Gulf coast and into the neighboring uplands, comprising parts of the modern states of Veracruz, Puebla, Hidalgo, San Luis Potosí, and Querétaro, produced a series of reports describing the life of villages in some of the less accessible zones. Church officials expressed alarm at the drunkenness of native people in several villages, not an uncommon complaint about Indians. They were drinking *pulque*, a fermented, agave-derived intoxicant, but adulterated with certain native herbs and roots to boost its potency. This produced a black, extremely strong beverage that induced delusions, bleeding from the mouth, and even blindness (so the inspecting officials said), although the physical risks in no way discouraged copious drinking. The same officials ascribed the religious backsliding and lapse almost into paganism in the area to the lack of priestly oversight due to these villages' isolation. They also lamented the absence of sacramental observation, the lack of legitimate marriage that resulted in "free" unions and high rates of illegitimacy among children, and other even more wildly unorthodox practices.

Rural priests occasionally grew desperate with the isolation of communities all over the viceroyalty, the villagers' recalcitrance to learn approved doctrine and practice, and the backsliding of their parishioners. Many of these men tried regularly to move up into parishes in larger communities nearer a town or a city where they could earn a better living from the collection of ecclesiastical fees for the administration of the sacraments and lead more "civilized" lives. Around 1770, for instance, one priest in the mountainous and thinly populated country of the present-day state of Guerrero, in a pueblo near the mining center of Taxco, wrote to another priest, his friend, living in an even more isolated village. He commiserated with him (not without a touch of *Schadenfreude*) about not having emerged successful from a competition to win a more desirable living:

> I do not know how I can accurately convey to you my feelings at seeing you stuck in that curacy, or to put it better, exile, or insufferable wasteland more desolate than Thebes, more insufferable even than a military prison. This truth has nothing of hyperbole in it, taking into consideration the circumstances of its heat, diseases, mountains, loneliness, and the intractable style of the natives, with their excessive drunkenness and detestable customs. There your sight has no other object [to occupy it] than the vegetable [realm], a mad [jumble] of mountains covered with wild trees, nor your mind other than those few semi-salamandrine Adams. Even your water well is thickened by a disgusting sediment of mud, frogs, and lizards.

Private homes in Indigenous communities typically consisted of a sleeping room (used by the entire family) doubling as a living room, a kitchen in an attached structure, and perhaps a storeroom for grain and farming implements, all very modest. Added to these would be a yard for chickens, pigs, and goats and a vegetable garden for family use. There were of course gradations of wealth, as in most human communities, but these were not large. More affluent families in the village might have larger homes, but they were basically just variations on a common template. Children tended to have a good amount of freedom to play on their own and wander about until they reached the age of seven or so, when the boys began to dedicate themselves to farm work with their fathers, elder brothers, or uncles. At this age the girls learned the domestic tasks that would occupy their lives as adults: cooking, making tortillas, collecting firewood, attending younger siblings, caring for the yard animals, and so forth. Farmlands in most places were owned communally by the village and worked in allotments by individual farming families, although there was also privately held land for farming acquired by purchase or inheritance and *cacique* families might have more land than the average. The modern form of this type of the communal landholding regimen was codified in the postrevolutionary Mexican Constitution of 1917 as the *ejido* system, although it has since been much modified in keeping with the neoliberal economic doctrines of the late twentieth century.

In most places the main cultivated cereal crop was maize, the essential ingredient (along with water, lime, and female muscle power) for tortillas, the staple of the family diet. Although for most village farmers maize production was mostly for family subsistence use, some surplus might be available for sale locally in a town market, along with some vegetable or fruit crops, a few eggs from the family chickens, or other small surpluses. Villages also might own common lands considered too sterile to produce maize crops, not well-enough watered, or hilly and too difficult of cultivation. These lands were vital to the community, however, and available to all village families for wood collection, clay digging, the pasturage of an animal or two, and other activities vital to the household. Even with the cultivation of maize, which required weeding and watering (although much maize farming was on *tierra de temporal*, rain-fed rather than irrigated land), there were slack periods in the growing season when family labor was available for other activities such as handicraft production. Indian family farmers also frequently sold their labor to nearby non-Indigenous landowners either on a seasonal basis or on a full-time basis during the entire year, living in their villages and working on neighboring estates.

The symbiotic, but also antagonistic, relationship between farming communities and large, privately owned estates was an enduring feature of the Mexican rural economy from the colonial period well into the twentieth century. Before waged labor became the norm earlier mechanisms of labor extraction depended at least in the last resort on the threat of physical coercion. The *encomienda*, carried in somewhat altered form from Spain to the Caribbean islands in the sixteenth century and thence to New Spain, was an arrangement by which certain groups of natives, typically villages or parts of them, were "allotted" by crown officers in grants to Spanish settlers called *encomenderos* (from the verb *encomendar*, to give something into the care of someone). The Indians distributed in this manner (they of course had no voice in the process) paid tribute to the *encomendero* in lieu of paying it to the crown, primarily in the form of labor service in exchange for nominal wages, food, and indoctrination into a Christian life. The size of the *encomienda* grant could vary from a few dozen natives to the enormous one granted to *conquistador* Fernando Cortés, embracing some 25,000 people. This system coexisted with Indian slavery, both extinguished by the Spanish crown by the mid-sixteenth century, but it was not slavery, although it has sometimes mistakenly been characterized as such. Encomienda grants generally conferred no judicial powers over the Indigenous people so granted. Extrajudicial and extralegal forms of control and coercion were always part of landowner-worker relationships, however, varying directly with distance from the oversight of royal officials. But the grants did give the *appearance* of being feudal in nature, which prompted some modern scholars to interpret colonial Mexican society as a "feudal system," which it never was (an issue discussed further in the following chapter). African slavery was never the major labor element in commercial agriculture as it was in the Caribbean sugar islands or the south of the United States. It coexisted alongside evolving labor relationships between Indigenous workers and non-Indigenous property owners, although it had become largely moribund as a source of labor power by the early nineteenth century and was abolished in 1829. Generally speaking, as native numbers rebounded and labor became more available coercion became less necessary so that earlier forms of labor extraction evolved into a waged labor system marked in some areas of the country by debt peonage.

EPIDEMIC DISEASE IN NEW SPAIN

In New Spain and early republican Mexico epidemic disease was a constant threat on the public horizon. The disastrous disease situation of the first 130 years or so of the colonial era, up to about 1650, has been well studied. Among the Old World pathogens to which native Americans had no immunity due to the long isolation of the New World from Eurasia were yellow fever, measles, typhus, cholera, possibly bubonic plague (still somewhat disputed), and above all smallpox. Under the impact of these diseases the Indigenous population of Mesoamerica fell by about 95 percent over the 130 years following contact with Europe. At the very end of the eighteenth century and the first years of the nineteenth the Spanish crown sponsored a scientific expedition to the colonies to vaccinate against smallpox using the techniques developed by the English physician Edward Jenner (1749–1823). This reduced the effects of smallpox epidemics in Mexico, although the disease was not entirely eradicated until the 1950s. The colonial period and the nineteenth century saw repeated deadly outbreaks of typhus and cholera in Mexico. The country experienced colony-wide epidemics of the bacterial disease typhus in 1714, 1736, and 1761. Another occurred in 1813 following the movement around the central parts of New Spain of large contingents of royalist and rebel troops carrying the disease with them and inflicting a mortality rate among those struck as high as 30 to 50 percent.[8] The other great epidemic killer was water-and food-born cholera, which struck deadly blows several times, most notably in 1833 and 1850, when hundreds of thousands died. In his unpublished memoirs Lucas Alamán alluded to the 1833 cholera epidemic, a local manifestation of a worldwide pandemic that struck Asia, Europe, and the Americas during the years 1826–1837. In 1833 Alamán was in a self-imposed, secret place of internal exile in Mexico City to evade prosecution by a congressional grand jury for alleged political crimes. He drew an explicit parallel between his own situation and that of the ten young women and men of Giovanni Boccaccio's *Decameron* (1353). These young maidens and cavaliers isolated themselves for a number of weeks in a villa outside Florence to avoid contact with the bubonic plague then raging in many parts of Europe, telling each other tales of love while they waited for the contagion to burn itself out. Alamán wrote that "the only thing that interrupted the silence of my asylum was news of the illness or death of persons dear to me, torn [from us] daily and in great numbers by the cruel epidemic suffered in that year [1833] [throughout] the Republic."

CHURCHMEN

The priests hurrying through the streets of Mexico City during these terrible epidemic episodes to succor the dying and help bury the dead represented one of the few institutions that all the people in this city and colony of ethnic distinctions had in common: their Catholic religion. For all his class prejudices Lucas Alamán in his writings is a good guide to the dynamics of Mexican national society during its first thirty or forty years. Lamenting about 1850 or so the weak bonds of national cohesion, he observed that even if the tenets of the Catholic faith were not self-evidently true, the presence of the Church and its institutions was essential as the one force that bound Mexicans together in the absence of a strong national sensibility among them. The tenets and practices of their Catholic faith were the same for all Mexicans—the central role of Jesus, the veneration of Mary, the doctrine of original sin, the miracle of transubstantiation, the sanctity of the Bible and the sacraments, and the concept of Purgatory. But they might emphasize different aspects of them, believe in somewhat different forms, and embody their beliefs in different styles. For example, public celebration of the liturgical calendar in Indigenous villages could be quite noisy, colorful, and expensive. These were aspects of popular religious life that crown reformers tried to suppress during the eighteenth century, as we shall see, in favor of the more "rational," sober, less resource-consuming practices often seen in cities toward the end of the colonial period. The gamut of practices ranged from the Catholicism mixed with pagan elements of older native traditions whose presence surprised priests like the ones we met in Toluca and the Huasteca around 1820 to the quieter, European-style, inward-looking piety among many people of the middling and elite groups.

The Mexican church was a highly complex hierarchical institution further segmented by ethnic, class, spatial, educational, and political variables. By

1800 New Spain had very few European-born clergymen, and most of these were in the highest ranks of the ecclesiastical structure. New Spain's archbishop Pedro José de Fonte (1777–1839), for example, was born in Spain and died there after playing a prominent role in Spanish political life following his return from Mexico. The bishop of the western province of Michoacán, Manuel Abad y Queipo (1751–1825), social reformer and excommunicator of Father Miguel Hidalgo y Costilla (1753–1811), progenitor of Mexican independence, was also born in Spain and died there; the same could be said of many other prelates. While there were few lower clergy clearly distinguishable as Indians, many were racially mixed. This was the case, for example, of Father José María Morelos y Pavón (1765–1815), a seminary student of Hidalgo's and the leader of the insurgent forces after the older man's death in 1811. Around 1810 there were some 7,300 ecclesiastical personnel in New Spain (a low estimate, probably), just over one tenth of one percent of the total colonial population. Of these, 3,100 men and women lived in monasteries, missions, and convents. The remaining 4,200 or so were parish clergy, priests who actually administered to their flocks in city and country parishes. Aside from any income a priest might garner from an endowment attached to his position, his living came chiefly from the collection of ecclesiastical fees. These were paid in cash by his parishioners for baptisms, marriages, burials, and other services and in any goods in kind or services they might be willing to provide or the priest to insist upon to maintain his household. Rural priests or their assistants might well acquire land or other productive resources, devoting themselves in part to their labors as private farmers or individual entrepreneurs; Father Miguel Hidalgo owned a hacienda, for example.

The life course and living situations of priests varied a good deal. Rural parish priests might spend their lives in one place or attempt to move up through a Church examination system to less isolated and more profitable appointments. Even though they experienced some difficulties, most priests were dedicated men of the cloth, devoted out of true religious vocation to the interests and souls of their mostly humble parishioners. Their problems included the failure of those parishioners to attend Mass regularly, backsliding among their flocks into vice and sin, complaints about their own reduced material circumstances and isolation, and their often frustrated career aspirations to move to better positions. These men were only human, however, and some gave in to fleshly temptation and loneliness despite their vows of chastity, taking mistresses who bore them illegitimate children apparently tolerated by the priest's flock. This was the case with Father Hidalgo himself, for example, who fathered eight children with three different women, and also with his student and successor Father Morelos, whose son, Juan Nepomuceno Almonte (1803–1869), later became a prominent military and political figure.[9] And although most rural priests had a minimal seminary education and were not worldly men, some were highly educated and intellectually sophisticated. A somewhat extreme but hardly unique example was Father Hidalgo, a highly educated man and former university rector, who read so much French Enlightenment literature (officially banned by the Church) that his parish of Dolores, in Central Mexico, became known as "little France." Some churchmen were much venerated and might well be the figures most closely associated with the colonial state whom villagers encountered in their lifetimes. By the end of the colonial era the lower clergy were in many instances more intimately embedded (no pun intended) among common people than the secular officials who represented royal authority at the most granular level. There had come to be if not an outright rift then at least a political, ideological, and social distance between the upper clergy in the cities of the realm—the bishops, cathedral canons, ecclesiastical bureaucracy—and the parish clergymen. It is therefore understandable that they assumed or were thrust by circumstances into leadership positions during the insurgency of 1810–1821, although the vast majority of their kind remained at least nominally loyal to the royalist regime.

But there could be stress in the priest-parishioner relationship, scaling up even to violent enmity. In the history of the country there has been an unmistakable strain of popular anticlericalism at the same time that Mexicans have always been among the most religious people in Latin America. This means that ordinary people might protest against their priests, or even visit violence upon them, while still maintaining their domestic shrines to the Virgin, following prescribed Church practices as they could, and keeping intact their inner piety; they may have been anticlerical, in other words, but not irreligious. Anticlericalism has come to the surface most broadly and vividly at moments of civil conflict. Among these have been the independence movement, the Wars of the Reform of the 1850s and 1860s just after the close of our period, and the Mexican Revolution of 1910 and its aftermath, most prominently in the Cristero rebellions of the 1920s and 1930s provoked by the official anticlerical policies of postrevolutionary governments. The insurgency of 1810–1821 aside, in the colonial period and into the early republican decades outbreaks of explicit anticlericalism may have been relatively unusual, but stresses there certainly were. For one thing, despite official certification to the contrary, many rural clergymen had at best an imperfect command of the Indigenous languages—Náhuatl, Otomí, Zapotec, the Maya dialects, etc.— still so pervasive in the countryside of New Spain, or none at all. This made difficult if not impossible the hearing of confession, the administration of ecclesiastical rites, or the giving of priestly counsel to humble people. Then there was the matter of the fees priests collected for their services. Often beyond the means of Indigenous peasants, such payments might be viewed as extortionate, although scales were set by the Church. Rural parishioners occasionally complained about priests administering corporal punishment for such sins as adultery and noncompliance with religious obligations.

A 1777 episode in the village of Tepoztlán, to the south of Mexico City near Cuernavaca, later made famous by the fieldwork there of the anthropologist Oscar Lewis, illustrates several strands that woven together might produce a tapestry of conflict. The local priest complained to higher Church authorities that the villagers were habitually drunken (a very common complaint whose accuracy is difficult to judge), resisted Church teachings, attended Mass very irregularly, and were "inclined to vice and superstition" of all kinds. They refused to support a village school, secretly buried their dead outside town to avoid paying fees to the priest, both sexes bathed together in the traditional *temescal* (a steam bath, basically), and couples cohabited without benefit of clergy. For their part, villagers complained that the local priest expropriated pueblo resources without license or payment, neglected the parishioners' spiritual needs, and administered public whippings of both sexes for minor infractions. As often occurs in such cases the documents reveal no resolution, but the same mutual complaints were repeated a decade later in the same place.

The independence movement kicked off on September 16, 1810, by Father Miguel Hidalgo y Costilla occasioned the expression of anticlerical sentiments as well as considerable abuse of rural priests and churches. In late 1810, for example, at the village of Amecameca, not far from Tepoztlán, one local rebel Indian leader was reported to have yelled, "War, war against the *gachupines* [that is, European-born Spaniards] . . . and against the fathers!" A good deal of anticlerical literature in the form of pamphlets and broadsides circulated at the hands of the insurgents, and on a number of occasions in the following years loyalist priests were roughed up by rebels or even killed. Churches were regularly profaned, damaged, or completely destroyed, their holy vessels and other sacred objects of silver stolen or melted down by the insurgents. This occurred in September 1812, for instance, at the Franciscan religious house in the town of Calpulalpan. The doors of the cells were broken down; everything usable was stolen; horses were stabled in the church; and books and papers were destroyed, ornaments looted, and windows smashed. It is difficult to know in most cases of such attacks whether they were motivated in part by local preinsurgency grievances against clerics, spurred by genuine anticlerical thinking and affective pressure, were purely circumstantial, or were intended as tactical acts to secure resources in support of the rebellion. What does seem clear is that the violent, disruptive conditions of the insurgency provided an opening for the emergence of anticlerical expressions, some of which were suppressed in everyday life but were already present and some of which emerged as a product of the insurgency itself.

CONCLUSION

The ethnic and class distinctions within the society of New Spain had porous boundaries despite their categorical complexity. Their application was often subjective and always influenced by the social context in which ethnic labels were assigned. Over time these boundaries would become more porous but still remain strong. Independence from Spain opened up the political sphere to men of color primarily through the door of military leadership, the wars of the Liberal Reform in the 1850s and 1860s pushed that door even further open, and the Mexican Revolution of 1910–1920 loosened social boundaries all the more. In the late colonial period some paths to upward mobility were accessible to humble people—racial "passing," marriage up the social hierarchy, the exercise of a rare talent, unusual service to the Spanish crown, or extraordinary personal application to a craft or commerce. Toward the close of the colonial period there even existed the formalized institution of the *gracias al sacar*, which applied exclusively to people of African ancestry or mixture who had enjoyed freedom for some generations. This was a mechanism whereby such individuals could, in exchange for a monetary payment, petition the royal authorities for certificates attesting their "whiteness." They were thus exempted from the disadvantages of their socioethnic status, such as prohibitions against exercising certain professions, attending universities, and occupying official posts. But despite the increasing "mesticization" of the population that I have pointed out, the paths to upward mobility were narrow and less traveled between 1750 and 1850 than after the mid-nineteenth century. Most mobility was probably downward, in fact, as bad judgment, ill luck, and inheritance practices dissipated some elite family fortunes and social status over time. This is effectively what happened to Lucas Alamán, although through natural talent, hard work, education, and early involvement in politics he managed to ascend the social pyramid to a position near the top. But most people knew their place: if you were born a village-dwelling Indian peasant you would almost certainly remain one. The ability of people occasionally to test the porosity of the socioethnic categories has sometimes been adduced as evidence that the society of New Spain was not as full of outright prejudice and exploitation of the powerless by the powerful as its detractors have made it out to be. But it was, even if not to the extremes sometimes painted. As Lucas Alamán was to suggest at the end of our period, one set of beliefs and practices that crossed the social and ethnic barriers separating groups was their Catholic religion, even if Mexicans sometimes dissented from the habits and demands of the institutional Church or exercised their religion in unorthodox ways.

One of the most interesting questions about Mexican history, no less for the period from 1750 to 1850 than for the 170 years since then, is the degree to which class and race reinforced each other. At the end of the colonial period it was quite likely that socioeconomic status mapped closely onto color; the poorer the person and the further down the social hierarchy she or he happened to be, the browner her or his skin. There were "white" Creoles, it is true, and nominally peninsular Spaniards of very little means among the working poor, and still others among the socially marginal. But the class system in New Spain was not well developed either by objective or subjective criteria. Along with the weak class structure, New Spain and republican Mexico were strongly regionalized. The project of the late colonial Bourbon Reforms to some degree, and more strongly of the republican regimes that followed it, was to replace the strong regional and weak class structures with weak regional and strong class structures. A weaker regional organization would have meant stronger national integration, both political and economic, a task definitively accomplished later by the railroad and telegraph. A stronger class system would have been the outcome of economic development, and especially of industrialization, which the Bourbon reformers flirted with but the republicans after them tried to accomplish with mixed success until the Porfirian era after 1875. Efforts at modernization were bent in this direction following independence from Spain, but endemic political instability and scarcity of means imposed severe limits on what could be accomplished, as we shall see.

NOTES

1. Average life span would only reach fifty years in Mexico by about 1950. I will use the names "Mexico" and "New Spain" interchangeably so as to avoid repetitiveness. Readers should also remember that after 1848 Mexico was half its previous size, about 50 percent of its territory shorn away by the United States as an outcome of the Mexican-American War (1846–1848). While in terms of population this was not a huge loss, in relation to territorial extension and resources it was. There will also be throughout the book many references to Mexico City and Guadalajara because the first was by far the most important city in the realm, and the western town of Guadalajara the fourth largest, just behind the great silver mining complex at Guanajuato; these are the cities I know best from my own research over the years; and what went on in them in the 1750–1850 period was in many ways representative of the rest of the country. Similarly, there will be a good many references to the life and work of the statesman-historian Lucas Alamán (1792–1853), of whom I recently completed a biography, *A Life Together*. While he was not "average" or "typical" of the Mexican elite in the first decades of the republican period, he may be seen to exemplify a certain important sector of Mexican society, was an acute observer of his

surroundings, and serves as an excellent guide to certain aspects of the century from 1750 to 1850.

2. The complex issue of race/ethnicity, and the ways in which racial assignment interacted with social position and what there was of class position, deserves extensive comment here because it was a major constitutive element in colonial society. Such ascriptions in large measure determined an individual's life chances and group identifications. Although the officially sanctioned handicaps associated with inclusion in certain racial groupings were abolished or softened over time, some prejudices remain alive even today.

3. The classic statement of the duality and tension between a "Westernized" and an Indigenous Mexico is Guillermo Bonfil Batalla, *México profundo. Una civilización negada* (Mexico City: Centro de Investigaciónes y Estudios Superiores en Antropología Social, 1987).

4. On linguistic change among Indigenous groups in colonial times, see James Lockhart, *The Nahuas after the Conquest: A Social and Cultural History of the Indians of Central Mexico, Sixteenth through Eighteenth Centuries* (Stanford: Stanford University Press, 1992).

5. For the racial hierarchy and "caste system," see María Elena Martínez, *Genealogical Fictions: Limpieza de Sangre, Religion, and Gender in Colonial Mexico* (Stanford: Stanford University Press, 2008).

6. As I write this, the site of the Presidio Real de San Diego, established in 1769 and whose mission was originally occupied by the Kumeyaay Indian people, lies no further than a mile or so from my study.

7. The proper historical term for the dominant Indigenous people of central Mexico is "Mexica," not "Aztecs." The term "Aztec" is derived from the mythological northern home of this group, Aztlán, but was little used before being taken up by nineteenth-century writers. I have used it throughout because that name has become the conventional usage.

8. At the very same moment, half a world away Emperor Napoleon's Grande Armée was suffering terrible mortality from typhus and hypothermia during the French invasion of Russia in 1812, a military misadventure that saw the French forces decimated as they later retreated westward from Moscow through the Russian winter.

9. His father's republican sympathies notwithstanding, Almonte was an ardent supporter in the 1860s of Mexico's return to monarchy in the form of the French-backed Austrian prince Maximilian von Habsburg, ending his life in European exile two years after the ignominious collapse of the Second Empire (1867).

Chapter 3

The Economy of New Spain
in the Age of Silver

The economy of New Spain on the eve of independence was relatively uncomplicated: it had few major production sectors, but regional identities within the colony were well defined and economic integration limited. The regions were linked to Mexico City by trade in certain commodities, by colonial administration and the remission of taxes, and by other strands, but only weakly connected to each other.[1] The federalism that became the ideology *du jour* among liberals after independence was meant to reduce the gravitational pull and predatory policies of the central government rather than to make horizontal relationships among the states more robust. The large distances and difficult geography of the country meant that in general only items of high value on the selling end relative to their bulk or weight could sustain the transport costs. In dire circumstances, as with a widespread harvest failure, maize might be shipped over long distances, but this was an exceptional occurrence. Furthermore, the economy was only partially monetized because silver was continually flowing out of the country as taxes to the Spanish crown, private remittances by individuals, and payment for imports. Much economic activity the colony produced, mostly in the form of subsistence agriculture, was unquantifiable. Such activity was neither traded nor taxed directly except for the ecclesiastical tithe on agricultural produce at a notional 10 percent, from which Indigenous people were exempt, and was therefore virtually invisible although vital to the colonial economy as a whole. One might think of the whole of the economy as like an iceberg, most of it under the water line, although perhaps not as much as 90 percent, the generally accepted percentage for submersion in icebergs. An important objective of modernization was to raise this hidden sector above the water line, as it were, to make it visible, tie it in fully with cash market relations, and make it more intelligible and accessible to counting and taxation. This would commoditize labor—make it a finitely divisible "thing" that could be valued by the market

41

at so much per task, per hour, per week, per month, etc.—and its products while also reducing the "friction of distance" by lowering transport costs. Before the railroads these were large orders under the conditions of the late colonial era and early nineteenth century.

By the time independence arrived, some thinkers in political economy believed that the path to modernization lay in complicating the economy, diversifying it from its heavy dependence upon the export of silver while strengthening its agricultural base, chiefly in the commercial sector resting upon large estates. Also essential were the improvement of communications over medium and long distances, the widening and deepening of consumer markets, and the stimulation of manufacturing. After 1821 the path to modernization was mapped differently by liberals and conservatives, their doctrines substantially the opposite of the ideas we associate with the two tendencies today. The liberals favored the play of the "invisible hand" of market forces, the conservatives active state intervention to jump-start and guide the economy. The Bourbon monarchy made halting efforts in this direction through state-directed initiatives. But these were contradicted by a push to extract more wealth from the colony by rationalizing the tax structure, closing gaps in the system of tribute collection from Indigenous people, and introducing new crown monopolies on tobacco and other domestically produced items of wide popular consumption. All these measures contributed to sucking capital out of the economy and therefore retarding development. Historical patterns of asymmetrical trade relations with Spain, and through it with the rest of Europe, were hard to break, and as New Spain became Mexico other powers moved in to fill the vacuum Spain had left behind. First Britain arrived on the scene, then briefly and violently France, and finally over the long term the United States, a relationship also punctuated by great violence.

SILVER MINING

What made New Spain so valuable to the Habsburg monarchy for the colony's first two hundred years, and then to the Bourbon dynasty for the last century of colonial rule, was the tremendous stream of silver (and some gold) that poured from its mines. This had begun as an important but relatively small trickle of precious metals, at first mainly gold, in the three decades during which Columbus and his successors perched on the Caribbean islands before Fernando Cortés undertook the conquest of the Aztec Empire in 1518–1521. It continued as minor silver strikes were made in New Spain after 1521, then broadened into a river with great silver finds in Zacatecas, in the near north, and Guanajuato and Pachuca, further to the south and east, as well as other *reales de minas* (mining camps), all a little before or after 1550.

Coincidentally, enormous mineral wealth was also discovered around the same time at Potosí, high in the Andes in what was then called Upper Peru, today's Bolivia. Until about 1690 the Peruvian treasure was much greater than that of New Spain, although by the close of the eighteenth century their positions had been reversed. During the three centuries of colonial rule, Mexico and Peru together produced about 100,000 tons of silver, 80 percent of the world's entire supply, much of which ended up in China in payment for goods desired by the Europeans. The economy of New Spain was driven in large measure by silver production because mining generated demand within the country for livestock, food, some equipment, and other goods to support its activities, thus fueling the agricultural economy in broad regions around the mining centers and even further afield. Silver was the chief exportable product of the colony, accounting in value for about 75 percent of all exports between 1796 and 1820, while around 65 percent of imports consisted of textiles in various forms. It was to reduce both these figures to less crushing proportions that economic reform efforts in newly independent Mexico were directed. It was hoped that more of the metal would be retained within the country to grease the wheels of the economy, to replace textile imports with domestic production of this consumer nondurable item for which there was always a high demand, and incidentally to make entrepreneurial fortunes and employ people.

Mexico is still the world's largest producer of silver and an important source of other minerals found in close proximity to it (lead, copper, zinc), but a major industrialized economy producing consumer and capital goods has grown up, reducing mining's relative importance. Silver output had declined during the seventeenth century for various reasons but recovered its upward trajectory in the eighteenth despite the jerky boom and bust pattern typical of individual mines. Over the long century from 1695 to 1810 silver production increased by 600 percent. Within this large overall picture production reached its peak during the 1790s, although the point of maximum returns on investment to mine owners came some decades earlier, suggesting a certain softening in the industry as the colonial era drew to a close. The mines in Guanajuato, chief among them the Valenciana and Rayas, produced about a quarter of all Mexican silver, and Mexico 60 percent of the world's silver supply during the most lucrative days of the industry. Lucas Alamán's family owned shares in the important Mellado and Cata mines in Guanajuato, the latter still in operation today. Although Guanajuato was the brightest star in this silver firmament, other areas—among them Pachuca (with the Real del Monte mine), Zacatecas, Bolaños, Chihuahua, and Taxco—also poured out silver and with it great family fortunes. By reducing the near-monopolistic profits exacted by large merchants, the Bourbon Reform policies loosening trade restrictions within the Spanish Empire beginning in 1789 stimulated the shift of capital into mining, fueling investment. Of the nearly fifty noble titles granted to wealthy Mexicans by the Spanish monarchs during the eighteenth century, sixteen went to owners of silver mines. Some enormous fortunes were dragged out of the earth in this way, such as that of Pedro Romero de Terreros (1710–1781), ennobled as the Conde de Regla and reckoned at one time one of the world's richest men thanks to his mining enterprises at Real del Monte in Pachuca.

Unlike the products of agriculture, silver is a nonrenewable resource; once it is exhausted it is gone, and there is no other remedy than the discovery of more ore deposits. Nor is mining significantly affected by weather cycles, although it is marked by unpredictable boom and bust periods. In colonial times the further the mine went down into the earth the more expensive the process became and the more the "sunk" capital of the enterprise (in this case, literally sunk because underground)—that is, the inert, unrecoverable investments in tunnels, shafts, and so forth—weighed against its profitability. The pursuit of silver-bearing ores worth the cost of digging them out of the ground and then refining them required increasing amounts of investment and labor, expertise in engineering and the chemical processes of refining, and efficient management of logistics. The silver mines of New Spain were not in general characterized by especially rich ores—that is, high-yielding rock from which much silver could be refined—but by many deposits of relatively low yield that could nonetheless be enormously profitable if refined at scale. The extraction of silver from most of the three thousand mines scattered around the colony was a deep shaft proposition, the main shafts going down hundreds of feet. The main shaft of the great Valenciana mine in Guanajuato, for example, had been pushed nearly two thousand feet straight down into the earth by 1810, making it the world's deepest mineshaft at the time, but shafts of 1,000 to 1,500 feet in other mines were hardly exceptional. And this was to say nothing of the long horizontal passages, called adits, extended more or less perpendicularly from the central shaft to provide drainage and access to the seams of ore as they wandered in odd directions beneath the surface.

Cave-ins, subterranean fires, and other mishaps could cause ghastly forms of injury and death to the mine workers, not to mention horrendous damage to the mine infrastructure. But flooding of the works was the worst problem for owners. As mines were driven deeper they required the excavation of drainage tunnels and the removal of water. This was accomplished primarily with the installation of winches at the mine head on the surface, using leather bags lifted up and down the shaft by animal power (think of the capstans used to raise anchors on old sailing ships). Steam power equipment for pumping and the crushing of ore for the refinement process, although known, admired, and experimented with by the 1820s or so, was simply not practical due to the lack of coal or wood for fuel in most mining areas. The transport of heavy items overland from the port of Veracruz to the mining zones in the highlands was prohibitively expensive. There was little technological innovation in Mexican silver mining until the Porfirian era in the later nineteenth century.

There were essentially two ways to get the mineral out of ore, the native rock. If the ore was rich enough for silver to be smelted out of the rock at high temperature, this could be done with a small-scale blast furnace. The other technique was the mercury amalgamation method, the so-called patio process suited to lower-yield ores, invented by the Spaniard Bartolomé de Medina (1497–1585) in the mid-sixteenth century. The patio process prevailed almost everywhere well into the nineteenth century, until the application of cyanide and other advanced methods of refining. The chemical reaction in the patio method involved the affinity between mercury and silver, a highly delicate operation requiring considerable technical expertise on the part of experienced masters of the process. Refining also depended upon access to strong streams of moving water to operate the large mills that crushed the ore into as fine a powder as possible to facilitate its amalgamation with mercury. Once crushed, the ore was then mixed with liquid mercury and spread out on a large brick surface (the patio) where other chemical agents were added to catalyze the amalgamation process. This mixture was stirred occasionally and allowed to sit for several weeks. The resulting sludge, an amalgam of mercury and silver mixed with baser elements, was baked in furnaces where the silver was precipitated out in a highly purified state, and the mercury evaporated, to be captured for reuse. The major mining zones each had dozens of these refineries, some owned and operated by the miners themselves, others operated independently. Lucas Alamán's father, a prosperous miner, owned a refinery called El Patrocinio downstream from the mines, which Alamán the son later inherited, lamenting that the mine in which his family owned shares was so worthless by the end of the 1830s or so that the refinery itself was worthless, as well.

Along with blasting powder and some other vital elements in the mining and refining operation, mercury was a crown monopoly supplied from Spain. Its cost heavily determined the profitability of silver mining, so the manipulation of its price was a way of subsidizing mining activity when it was in the doldrums or of encouraging new exploration. The major element here was the Spanish crown's royal fifth, the *quinto*, which could be collected at full value on mining production or reduced to a tenth to bring silver production costs down, stabilize profits, and encourage investment. The royal claim was predicated on the idea that subsoil rights pertained to the monarchy; the exploitation of a mine was thus basically an agreement in which the crown granted exploitation rights in return for a fee. This practice lapsed during the Porfirian era of the late nineteenth and early twentieth centuries. Revived and codified in modern form in the postrevolutionary Mexican Constitution of

1917, it is the basis for the Mexican state's ownership of oil deposits within the national territory.

Mining and refining operations required very large labor forces often involving hundreds of men, perhaps as many as a thousand or more at the larger mines; the Valenciana in Guanajuato employed about three thousand men at one point. Some of these workers lived with their families in nearby villages or in the settlements that developed around the mines themselves, while others were drawn from distant points. By 1810 there were perhaps 45,000 mine workers in New Spain. Relatively well remunerated for their labor and not especially oppressed, they were nonetheless a somewhat turbulent lot and could respond violently to negative changes in working conditions or pay arrangements. A longstanding form of additional pay for them was the *partido* system, in which individual mine workers took a designated amount of high-grade ore with them out of the mines during their shifts and sold it to refiners, in this way earning a sort of bonus above their wages. When mine owners began to eliminate this practice in the latter part of the eighteenth century in an effort to reduce production costs by lowering wages-in-kind, mine workers objected strenuously. In 1766 this and other grievances about workload and safety provoked a massive strike by miners in the fabulously wealthy mines at Real del Monte, near Pachuca to the northeast of Mexico City, owned by Pedro Romero de Terreros, the Count of Regla. By the close of the colonial period mine laborers, with their reasonably specialized skills, comparatively high wages (in contrast to agricultural laborers or even independent peasant cultivators), and unhindered physical mobility constituted a relatively privileged sector of the labor force in New Spain. If "modern" forms of labor organization existed any place in the country as it lurched into independence it was in the mining sector. But even in this industry the heavy traces of paternalism infusing the economic connection between capital and labor added the element of a father-to-children bond to that of the employer-employee economic one.

LABOR AND LIVELIHOOD

Whatever the nature of the relationship between working people and their bosses, *novohispanos* (inhabitants of New Spain) working for wages were at the mercy of market forces. Late colonial Mexico saw only a trickle of in-migration, so one of the main factors determining the relationship of owners to workers was domestic population change. There was significant demographic pressure on the labor market of New Spain in the last decades of the colonial era. As the Indigenous population recovered from the catastrophic disease-induced fall of the first 150 years, the mixed-blood population also grew, and more and more farming land was appropriated by large landowners for commercial agriculture through fair means or foul. This undermined peasant farming, forced humble people into the wage labor market, and put a palpable downward pressure on wages in the countryside. Some form of rations in lieu of part of the agreed-upon money wage was very common throughout the century from 1750 to 1850, with wide regional variation as to amount and composition, but for the most part it would have consisted of maize, the staple of the rural diet. Because the maize ration was typically insufficient for the support of a family, working people needed to purchase the prime necessities of the family "market basket" for cash or on credit. They might supplement the ration with the produce of their own small plots of land, if they were lucky, thus reducing pressure on the family cash income somewhat. They might also purchase food, perhaps on the very estates where they worked. Prices for maize and most other items of popular consumption rose in the last three decades of colonial rule, while nominal wages—the cash wages paid to workers—for the most part remained stable, thus failing to keep pace with the rising cost of living.

The result of these pressures was that real wages, what people's money could actually buy, fell by something like 25 percent between about 1775 and 1810, effectively reducing the living standard for a very large segment of the population. On top of this, the later eighteenth century saw periodic failures of the maize harvest, conditions of extreme dearth recurring roughly in a ten-year cycle: 1741, 1750, 1761–1762, 1770, and 1785–1786. Particularly bad was the 1785–1786 episode, known as the *año de hambre* (year of hunger), caused by an early frost affecting the maize crop over many central parts of the country. There was actual starvation and spread of disease among a nutritionally weakened population ravaged by a possible combination of typhoid, dysentery, pneumonia, and influenza. The burial rate in León, for example, an important town in the Bajío region, the country's traditional breadbasket to the north of the capital, was four times the normal in 1786. In Guadalajara perhaps a fifth to a quarter of the population died as starving people flocked from the countryside into the city seeking relief, creating conditions of overcrowding and terrible sanitation even more conducive to the spread of disease. Another such episode occurred in 1810, when the movement for independence from Spain began. While an increase in poverty or even a sudden sharp episode of starvation and economic dislocation do not necessarily directly produce massive political violence like that heralding the end of the colonial regime in Mexico, they are certainly conducive to it.

THE FARMING ECONOMY

Most Mexicans in the late eighteenth century resided in the countryside, or at least not in cities—they lived on isolated ranches, large agricultural estates called haciendas, small hamlets, larger villages, or small towns. Despite a few earlier efforts to jump-start manufacturing and some promising beginnings, the country would not industrialize significantly until the late nineteenth and early twentieth centuries. So it was an overwhelmingly agrarian society in which at least 80 percent of the economically active population got their living directly from the land as peasant cultivators, laborers, middle-sized farmers, large land owners, rural middlemen, and so forth. According to the World Bank, the corresponding figure today in Mexico is 13 percent, about half what it was as recently as three decades ago. Thus, while silver—with a few other items trailing far behind, such as the dye products cochineal and indigo, cattle hides, and some sugar—was the dominant exportable product by a large margin, the annual value of agricultural production, mostly for domestic consumption within New Spain, was certainly many times that of the mineral. The picture became more diversified after 1850, when henequen (a hard fiber for cordage) began to be exported at scale, mostly to the wheat farms of the US Midwest, to be used as binding twine in wheat harvested mechanically by the newly introduced McCormick reapers. Coffee, vanilla, and other products later joined henequen in foreign markets. Where exports are concerned, however, Mexico has always been at something of a disadvantage due to its distance from European markets. A partial solution to this problem of transportation costs was of course the railroad, which came much later but gave Mexico virtually unlimited access to the closest and most robust market to be found. The United States, despite political ups and downs in the two countries' relationship, quickly grew to be Mexico's dominant trading partner. Today about 75 percent of the country's exports by value go to the United States, the second-place trading partner being Canada, with less than 3 percent.

Around 1800 the basic elements of the peasant and Indian diet (not all peasants were Indigenous people, and not all Indigenous people peasants) remained, as they had been for millennia, maize, beans, squash, and chilies, with only occasional additions of animal protein. Maize as a staple grain crop has a fairly wide geographical growing range, although it is highly susceptible to frost. Modern genetic experiments, products of the "Green Revolution," have greatly expanded its cultivable range, the conditions under which it may be produced, and crop yields. The crop was gown chiefly in the central and southern parts of Mexico, where the Indigenous population was densest, and wheat, the other major grain, a European introduction, in the more northerly areas of the country. This is reflected in regional cuisines even today—corn tortillas in the center and south, wheat tortillas in the north. Many orchard and vegetable crops were European introductions, along with wine grapes, and might be found in small kitchen gardens on peasant farms or on a larger scale on rural estates.

Old World livestock introductions—cattle, horses, mules, goats, sheep, and pigs, along with chickens—did well everywhere in New Spain, but their distribution tended to vary directly with access to capital and land. Used for both work and food, the large grazing animals required extensive grasslands to support them, so they tended to show up on the typically non-Indian-owned rural estates known as ranchos and haciendas, sometimes in huge numbers. The herds increased in size the farther north one ventured, the only constraining factor being the availability of water for pasturage. In some areas of the country patterns of transhumance were adapted from the Old World—the seasonal migration of herds of cattle and sheep from one zone to another in search of pasturage. From the moment the Spanish were able to extend their control over large territories outside the immediate area of Aztec political hegemony, sheep and cattle estates were established in many areas of the country, sending their products to Mexico City, other urban markets, and mining districts. Although herds might suffer losses en route and the animals might lose weight, they were still considered sufficiently valuable at their destination to sustain the losses and could be refattened for the market. The risks involved in the long-distance livestock trade are illustrated by the account of a cattle drive from a hacienda on the mid-western coast of New Spain to Mexico City in 1783. The drive over several hundred miles took more than a hundred days. While 1,360 animals left the hacienda on July 30, only about a thousand reached Mexico City by mid-November, making for a loss in numbers alone of about 25 percent, not to mention the loss of weight of the surviving cattle, and therefore a fall in their selling price at the destination point. Twenty years later an estate administrator in the Guadalajara area wrote to a friend, advising him to stay out of the cattle trade: "Unless the cattle are three years or older, fat and healthy, and managed by a man who is honest and knows what he is doing, don't become involved in the cattle trade, because in one stampede you will lose everything." Where humble rural folk were concerned, goats, pigs, and chickens might be kept in small numbers because they are foragers and require much less land than the large grass eaters.

The economic landscape of rural New Spain was a mosaic of different forms of productive and social units—large estates, ranches, middle-sized farms, and peasant holdings—and within these categories there was a wide gamut of variation and arrangements for working the land. The "rancho" is notoriously hard to define for the period from 1750 to 1850, and as with all rural property types there was a certain arbitrary element involved in the categorization.[2] For example, in a famous Mexican novel about rural life and banditry around the middle of the nineteenth century, one of the minor characters, the socially ambitious don Espiridión, simply upgraded the name of his property overnight from a Rancho Such-and-Such to a Hacienda de Such-and-Such, thereby awarding himself the prestige of an estate owner, a *hacendado*, in place of the more modest designation of *ranchero*. A rancho could be a family-run farm, a moderate-sized livestock estate, an enormous tract of land for raising cattle, or even a small settlement known more typically as a *ranchería*, more or less like a hamlet. The balance of property types, what they produced, and the technologies employed changed over time, the technology least of all. On large estates crop rotation (the yearly alternation of one crop with another—say, maize with alfalfa—to maintain or restore fertility by putting back into the soil the nitrogen depleted by grain crops) was not widespread, and the application of steam to such processes as sugar refining unknown until much later in the nineteenth century. The use of organic fertilizers, either directly applied or from the manure of grazing animals, although common in western Europe was virtually unknown because it was too expensive and required too much management in relation to the value of the crops harvested.

Haciendas in the arid and semiarid north of the country tended to be quite large, extending to tens or hundreds of thousands of acres. Those within easy transport range of big cities or near mining centers were typically smaller, better irrigated, more intensely farmed, and possibly produced horticultural crops or even dairy products impossible to transport over long distances due to spoilage. As urban populations grew during the eighteenth century, and with them the profitability of commercial agriculture, the value of haciendas reflected this and the factors of production (that is, what they used to produce whatever it was that they sent to market) changed. For example, the Hacienda de Huejotitán, owned by the prominent Villaseñor family near Lake Chapala, south of Guadalajara, more than tripled in value over the half-century before the outbreak of the independence movement. The value of its livestock declined from nearly two-thirds of the estate's total value to about a fifth, most of it accounted for by plow animals (oxen), and this was true of many other estates in the region as well. Irrigation, fencing, and sown lands nearly tripled in value, as did the estate's buildings, all reflecting a transition from producing livestock to producing grain for the urban market—less profitable on a per unit basis but much less risky than exporting livestock over long distances. Meanwhile, in the Guadalajara region and elsewhere, as grain-producing estates tended to dominate areas closest to their urban consumers, livestock-producing estates were pushed farther away.

Large estates were typically owned by families, but not necessarily over many generations. Inheritance practices, the burdens of debt, very often to entities within the Catholic Church (convents and monasteries, for example), and the inevitable influence of weather and/or market variations might drive estates into bankruptcy or sale. One very common source of debt that could accumulate on haciendas and eventually drag them down was the owners' practice, and perhaps that of several generations of owners, of establishing liens (mortgages, basically) on a certain percentage of a property's value, the income of which, at 5 percent annually, partially supported a parish priest who said masses for the soul of the patron to speed it through Purgatory. This constituted a sort of endowment of a parish "living" managed by Church authorities. For example, the owner of the Hacienda de Sutano wanted to support a nephew, Father Fulano, who had taken holy orders, so he imposed a lien on 10,000 pesos worth of an estate valued at 50,000 pesos, which would exist in perpetuity unless paid off. The income of the 10,000 pesos at 5 percent annually (which by Church law it could not exceed) would amount to 500 pesos paid to the priest to say 500 masses valued at a peso each, supporting the priest in the meantime. While the property might be sold, unless the lien was paid off it stayed with the estate as it passed from one owner to the next. There is some evidence that over the course of the eighteenth century large estates changed hands less rapidly, and the land market therefore became more stable because haciendas became more profitable and incidentally more capable of paying the interest on these mortgages without consuming all the profits of the enterprise. On the other hand, relatively few of the greatest family fortunes or titles of nobility were based in landholding alone because mining and large-scale commerce, if riskier, were more profitable. One commonly adopted economic strategy to smooth out the ups and downs of mining and commercial enterprises was diversification in the family portfolio through the ownership of shares in a mine, for example, or of a large mercantile establishment *along with* a rural estate. Proprietorship of a hacienda might provide a family with certain useful amenities—for example, horses for riding or some foods for household use and a rural family retreat. Some of the land might also be rented out on a cash or sharecropping basis to tenants, while some might be retained by the owner as a home farm under direct management. It might also serve as collateral in securing loans and support the still considerable prestige of large-scale land ownership. The social prestige factor was undoubtedly present, but what about the business side of things?

This is an opportune moment to look more closely at the widely held belief that the traditional Mexican landed estate was somehow "feudal" rather than run on a profit model, or had enough feudal characteristics to tip the balance in that direction. Although much discredited by the historical research of the past fifty or sixty years, the enduring generalization or trope that Mexico for much of its history was somehow "feudal" still pervades much popular thinking about the country, and even some scholarship, so it is worth examining. In this model, the hacienda was only minimally commercial, if at all; owned primarily for prestige; and based on the labor of some sort of enserfed laborers. The hacienda dominated the Mexican countryside for most of our period, and really up to the revolutionary constitution of 1917 and the massive agrarian reform in its aftermath. The corollary of this dominance is that because the countryside was where most people lived, if rural Mexico was feudal it was necessary by extension to apply the label to the society as a whole and to see it as therefore peculiarly resistant to modernization. Or at the very least, the country was said to have a dual socioeconomic organization, most of it—the rural areas—"feudal" and the urban areas more modern. In an influential book published in 1909, on the eve of the 1910 Revolution, the Mexican sociologist, public intellectual, and agrarian reformer Andrés Molina Enríquez offered the famous, somewhat Delphic statement that "La hacienda no es negocio" (The hacienda is not a business).[3] By this he meant that large Mexican landed estates had for the most part never been profit oriented but "feudal" enterprises. It followed that they were intended at best to produce the subsistence of the owner's family and perhaps a dribble of cash income, but even more to confer the prestige and power over other people growing from large-scale land ownership, a cultural value carried to the New World from the Old. Mexico was therefore only partially capitalistic if at all, in his view, and the country was in some respect backward while the Atlantic world had plunged fully into capitalist modernity.

Central to the historical understanding of Latin America in general and Mexico in particular, this issue has been argued over for several generations within the framework of classic European feudalism. Given the key role the hacienda has played in Mexican life, it came to be one of the most mulled-over questions in the historical literature, the perspective of the commentator often shaped by her or his political orientation. The general conclusion of modern scholarship has come to be that although feudal elements were present in the countryside, Mexico was never feudal but always embryonically capitalist, or at least in transition from a nonfeudal form of precapitalist socioeconomic system. This is hardly a dead horse, however, because one still sees references in textbooks, popular writings, and even the work of some historians to the "feudal" structure of Mexican society in the pre–Mexican Revolution era.[4] While the types "capitalist" and "feudal" were hardly ever pure themselves, the resolution of the debate lies between the two models depending upon where and when one is looking. The question of whether the "traditional" Mexican landed estate was "feudal" or "capitalistic" is more than just a historical curiosity, however, because the answer is thought to help explain the broad nature of the society, the developmental problems it has faced over the course of its history, and the reform policies recommended and enacted at various times to meet those problems. Was the colonial period an extension of late European feudalism, its institutions and practices transferred to the New World even while much of western Europe was experiencing the Low (that is, Late) Renaissance and already launched into modernization, with its growing domestic markets, emerging bourgeoisie, banking houses, international trade, global expansion, and so forth? If so, how far behind were New Spain and the other Iberian colonies, and how would their independent succession states close the gap? What did the civil chaos of the early nineteenth century in most of the former Spanish colonies, and Mexico in particular, owe to an incipient transition from feudalism into the modern world?

One way to test Molina Enríquez's famous formulation, and by extension assess whether Mexican society was "feudal" as a whole, is to compare the great landed estate of the colonial period and the nineteenth century to the quintessential institution of medieval Europe, the feudal manor. This is done in a very schematic way in table 3.1, which also includes the "rancho" and "plantation" types to sharpen the comparison.

Of the types of nonvillage agrosocial units ("agrosocial" meaning that the labor force tended to live where it worked) found in New Spain/Mexico, the hacienda shared with the European feudal manor four of the seven listed variables, the rancho two, and the plantation one. Let me mention some of the more obvious differences among the four types without unduly belaboring the issue. The New World tropical plantation produced a single product

Table 3.1. The Mexican hacienda in a comparative context. Note: The variables in the table are derived from Eric R. Wolf and Sidney W. Mintz, "Haciendas and Plantations in Middle America and the Antilles," *Social and Economic Studies* 6, no. 3 (September 1957): 380–412.

Variable	Hacienda	Rancho	Plantation	Feudal Manor
Production mix	mixed	livestock	single crop	mixed
Capital investment	low to moderate	low	high	low
Technology level	low	low	high	low
Labor relations	free waged; debt peonage; share-cropping; renters	free waged; peonage	waged; African slavery	serfdom
Market connection	moderate	high	high	low
Owner control over labor force	moderate	low to moderate	high	high
Environment	temperate	arid/steppe	tropical	temperate

(typically sugar, tobacco, or some other tradeable commodity—think of the southern United States or the Caribbean islands) for a domestic urban or world market upon which it was totally dependent for its income. The manor might produce a mix of things including grain and livestock for the consumption of its own inhabitants, the support of the lord's armed retainers, and perhaps a small surplus marketed locally. The arid-zone rancho, often a livestock estate of considerable extension due to the need for grazing lands in a semiarid landscape, and therefore in the Mexican case most likely to occur in the north, also produced a single item, livestock: cattle, sheep, or horses, or typically a mix of these, which could walk themselves to market. Because of its low technological levels, the capital requirements of the rancho were also relatively low, and those of the hacienda only moderate—irrigation works, storage facilities, and perhaps modest houses for the resident workers.

Let us concentrate on the hacienda/feudal manor comparison because this is the point upon which the characterization of Mexico as "feudal" primarily turns. Relationship to a market was of course extremely important, especially as the colonial era drew to a close. The Mexican hacienda was a commercial enterprise geared to sell much of what it produced and buy as little of what it needed as possible from outside—farming implements, additional work animals, etc. The optimal situation would have been for the estate to be as self-sufficient as possible so that income exceeded expenditure by a large margin, but this was not always possible, and profit margins varied considerably. One implication of this was that haciendas in the more central parts of the country, geography allowing, tended to embrace large areas of land that was not necessarily cultivatable, reserved for purposes of clay digging, wood cutting, livestock grazing, etc., a strategy that brought haciendas into continual conflict with Indigenous villages and other estates that also valued access to such marginal lands. The records of litigation in the colonial courts (there was a rigorous, somewhat efficient legal system that often actually delivered justice) are replete with suits over the ownership of land among haciendas, between them and Indian communities, and pitting one village against another. Historians who have looked at the surviving account books of landed estates in the later colonial decades and early nineteenth century have concluded that whether properties were run by a religious order—say, the Jesuits before their expulsion from the Spanish realms in 1767—or a secular proprietor, they were managed with a keen eye for profit over and above the prestige such ownership conferred. The average rate of profit for estates in the Guadalajara region and many others has been calculated at about 6 percent or so.

As for the other variables, for present purposes we may collapse "production mix" and "environment" into one. The reasoning here is that while Mexico lies completely in the world's tropical zone, the

Figure 3.1. Painting of a typical late-nineteenth century hacienda, by the Mexican artist José María Velasco Gómez. Public Domain.

altitude of its most densely populated central areas, the presence of water there, and the most promising farming soils make those areas essentially temperate; in other words, altitude compensates for latitude. Almost all of Europe is in the temperate, wheat-growing zone, so the colonizing Europeans in Mexico tended to favor the populous, temperate upland areas for much of their agriculture, such as the valleys of Puebla, Mexico, and Toluca, where they reproduced much of what they had had in Europe. Of the two remaining variables, that of technology was at a fairly low level in the grain-and livestock-producing hacienda and would have been readily recognizable to a medieval manorial lord or a peasant; later developments in western European farming far outstripped what was happening in Mexico. The other variable accounting for the greatest typological distance between the European feudal manor and the Mexican hacienda was the relationship of the owner to the labor force, which determined the degree of control the owner exercised over the laborers. Along with market involvement, this is the key factor differentiating the two forms. In the last third of the nineteenth century Karl Marx's analysis of economic systems proposed the labor theory of value. This notion was predicated on the extraction of labor power from workers in capitalist enterprises provided the workers are laboring for wages in a monetized labor market. This concept has become foundational to understandings of the way economies work. The labor force on the notional European feudal manor was made up of enserfed peasants who owed their labor, part of their own farming production, a variety of fees, and other services and goods to the lord of the manor, who in turn owed knightly service to a higher lord, and he on upward to the monarch, an ascending chain of obligation the very essence of feudalism. The lords owed their serfs protection in time of war and against bandits, access to the manorial legal apparatus, and probably some protective aid against gross famine and economic catastrophe, but they took more than they gave back. The typical European serf had little personal freedom and no civil rights because the lord exercised a high degree of control over the work force. The serf was prohibited to leave the manorial territory, to travel, to marry, to grind his grain in any but the lord's mill, or to engage in any number of other mundane human activities without the lord's permission. He might even be required to render up his bride on her wedding night for the lord's pleasure under the custom of the *droit du seigneur*.[5]

It is often still written in textbooks and general works that the Indigenous population of Mexico was "enslaved" during the colonial period; this is not correct. For one thing, royal law as developed within the Spanish Empire forbade this except in certain very specific and limited circumstances. The practice of enslaving Indians had disappeared in New Spain by the end of the eighteenth century except as applied to those Indigenous people who took up armed rebellion against the Spanish crown, as for example some tribal peoples of the northern lands fiercely resistant to Spanish efforts to "pacify" the region up to 1810 and beyond. For another thing, the idea that all Indians were enslaved trivializes the brutalizing experience of actual bondage for Africans brought to the New World and the condition of one human being as the property of another. A variety of labor and rental arrangements existed for Indigenous and other workers on landed estates. Among them was rental of lands, an indirect form of labor, after all, mediated by rent payments from the farmer to the owner of the land; there also existed sharecropping and service tenantry. But the prevailing form was that of free waged labor—people (men) working for wages in a labor market at least nominally free, although this took time to become the dominant form. The encomienda was outlawed and mostly disappeared in the mid-sixteenth century. It was succeeded by the *repartimiento*, a forced, rotating wage labor system in use until quite late in colonial times and occasionally called into play in the mining economy until the eve of independence. By 1700 legal documents and estate accounts are full of references to free laborers working for wages, food rations (maize and other items), and other privileges, including some grazing rights for their own animals on the estate. As the Indigenous population recovered the potential work force grew and waged labor became increasingly common.

Worker indebtedness was originated in credit extended by owners to workers against the wages to be earned, effectively fixing them to the estate. Often referred to as debt peonage, this played an important role in securing and keeping a rural labor force. While it is quite clear that debt peonage existed in colonial times and was widespread in the nineteenth century, the degree of its prevalence has been debated by historians. In general, we can say that in the face of Indigenous population decline it developed from around 1600 as a way to attract and secure laborers in a labor-scarce situation. One witness in a court case around 1750 testified that "it is just as incredible that laborers work without advances [of credit] as to catch a star in your hand." Indicating laborers' leverage rather than their weakness, credit was provided to workers through an estate store often called a *tienda de raya* after the lines, *rayas*, marked down in account books indicating days worked. Here they could purchase various necessities of living that would have been difficult or even impossible to buy in village or town shops, depending upon where the hacienda was located. An example is the account of an Indigenous laborer named Nasario on a hacienda in the Guadalajara area during the two years 1785–1786. Against his days worked he received altogether in various forms 101 pesos: 41 pesos in cash for his actual wages, 30 pesos' worth of unspecified goods, 6 pesos for the value of an ox he purchased from the estate, and 5 pesos for tribute for the two years, a royal head tax leveled upon Indigenous people. The most striking and humanly revealing item in the account was 13 pesos paid by the hacendado to a priest for the burial rites of two of Nasario's children. The things he received on credit he was expected to pay off through his work on the estate. While there was always temporary, seasonal waged labor present in the countryside, there is evidence that it increased along with the rural population in the last colonial decades, reducing the need for owners to advance credit to workers. Wages for most sorts of farming labor seem to have remained more or less level from 1650 or so. By the logic of the hacienda economy, moreover, it made perfect sense to acquire as much land as possible for two reasons. First, with more land available production could be expanded should market conditions warrant doing so. Second, the acquisition of more land served to undercut the subsistence farming basis of the village peasant economy, making more labor available at a lower price.

So the question is: Was the debt peon on a Mexican hacienda in the same position as the serf on a medieval manor? The answer is no. This is not to say that there were no nonmarket constraints on the mobility of labor. What was likely to hold rural laborers to a landed estate? For one thing, the life circumstances of workers and the degree to which residence on a hacienda might mimic life in an autonomous peasant village played their roles here. Communities of resident laborers and their families sometimes embraced hundreds of people and featured an estate chapel where the all-important rituals of religious life were performed by itinerant priests. These were hard bonds to break. The protection that owners offered their resident workers was another valuable perquisite, although not directly an economic one. Physical restraint and coercion of laborers were hardly unknown and were complained of by workers to local authorities. The strongest constraint would be the debts owed by workers to the estate owner, which probably declined on a per capita basis toward the end of the eighteenth century. The question here would be whether the repayment of these debts by laborers was enforceable by law and repayable exclusively on the hacienda where they were contracted, whether the structure of laborer debt constrained the physical mobility of rural people, and the role of the colonial state in enforcing payment. In most cases repayment of credit advances never came into question because both owners and workers expected the latter to remain on estates in a continual condition of indebtedness, paying with their labor as they went. In 1785 the viceroy of New Spain issued regulations setting a ceiling for individual worker debt at 5 pesos and mandating free worker mobility despite debt, but in many areas of the colony these measures may have been honored more in the breach than the observance. Whether this amounted to "debt servitude" depends less on technical criteria than one's point of view and upon local conditions (for example, how far from centers of royal authority the estate lay, how much labor power was available in the market, etc.): there was debt, certainly, and there was service (that is, labor). The dictionary definition of "servitude" is "the state of being a slave or completely subject to someone more powerful"; the first condition did not generally obtain in late colonial Mexico. Neither resident nor temporary laborers owed estate owners fees or personal service *by feudal right* as was common in medieval Europe, although they might be required to perform domestic tasks as part of wage agreements. Rural laborers were free to marry, own property outside the bounds of the hacienda, and so forth. So while at the extremes the condition of estate laborers might approach that of medieval serfs, generally it fell far short. The hacienda owner's control over the labor force was moderate to weak, dependent substantially on the market forces of supply and demand rather than time-honored legal arrangements (the feudal system), and was monitored by the colonial state.

A reasonable summary of the situation comes from earlier work of my own on the Guadalajara area at the end of the colonial era:

> The real question [was] not so much the sanctity of the debt per se, but the kind of coercion which could be used in enforcing it. The principle was widely accepted by colonial authorities . . . that physical force was not admissible in insuring that workers paid off what they had borrowed. Physical punishment to discourage laziness or to enforce discipline in work situations . . . was apparently seen as inevitable and justified as long as it was not excessive. But beating or incarcerating [laborers] for debt was consistently disallowed by the [colonial authorities] in the cases [they heard], most of which arose from attempts by

Indian laborers with extant debts to leave estates. Nor was the retention of laborers for the . . . debts of their fathers or other relations legitimate. . . . On occasion hacendados sought and obtained orders from the [authorities] that legally forced workers who had fled without justification or without making alternative arrangements to return to haciendas and liquidate their debts. [The royal authorities upheld] the absolute principle of the physical freedom of Indian laborers and probably of laborers in general, [which] prompted landowners to complain even when the validity of the debt itself was never called into question. . . . [T] he implicit attitude of landowners [was] that they should be absolute masters of their retainers. [Nonetheless], many haciendas perennially carried on their books large numbers of laborers and other workers who had fled or temporarily absented themselves.[6]

The oft-commented unhappy condition of hacienda debt peons in the latter part of the nineteenth century, especially during the Porfirio Díaz regime up to 1910, was due to the laissez-faire attitude of the "liberal" state, which seems to have paid considerably less attention to the welfare of its citizens than the colonial state had paid to that of its subjects.

A COLONIAL MURDER CASE: A TALE OF FOUR JOSÉS[7]

Readers may think that my effort to dismantle the "feudal" idea about rural New Spain/Mexico and to emphasize the role of free waged labor in the way haciendas were operated tends toward an excessively rosy picture of things. But it should be acknowledged that there might well be a subsurface current of resentment and potential violence in the relations between landowners and laborers on their estates. Although there were estate owners and their foremen who treated workers benignly and might develop personal bonds with them, judged by our modern standards this tended toward an abusive and exploitative relationship into which lethal anger could occasionally erupt, as the following episode illustrates.

I have devoted a good deal of space to the colonial landed estate because along with the mining industry, Catholic Church, royal government, and the Indigenous community it was a key institution of life in New Spain with millions of people living within its sphere of power and influence. It seems to have altered little during the early republican decades until the importation of new farming technologies from the United States, and above all the coming of the railroad and therefore the expansion of commercial possibilities changed things in the latter part of the nineteenth century. The Mexican hacienda was certainly paternalistic in its characteristics, but that is not the same as "feudal." What can be said of most haciendas is that they were profit-oriented or even capitalist economically but demonstrated feudal or paternalistic social

BOX 3.1

In the middle of a fresh summer's morning on August 21, 1752, the Spanish magistrate of the district of Etzatlán and La Magdalena, in New Spain, was called to the rural estate Labor de Rivera near the town of Ahualulco, forty miles west of Guadalajara. At about five o'clock that same morning the estate administrator, don José Leandro de Siordia, also the owner's brother, had been brutally murdered. The magistrate duly took testimony from a number of witnesses, sent four laborers to the ramshackle little jail in the town of Ahualulco as material witnesses and possible accessories (later cleared) to the crime, and eventually made his determination in the case: homicide. But by that time the killer was nowhere to be found, having added insult to injury by stealing his victim's horse and riding off into the morning.

In 1752 Ahualulco was a sleepy little village of a few hundred souls not far from the town of Tequila, later famous for its eponymous agave-derived liquor. The death of José Leandro de Siordia must have been a topic of conversation and gossip for some months after the event because there simply was not much else to talk about except the weather and the state of the crops and livestock. The entire parish of Ahualulco contained perhaps two thousand people, mainly Spanish (that is, Creole) and mestizo, mostly living on the rural estates, smaller ranchos, and hamlets scattered about the jurisdiction. A good part of the area's inhabitants, probably including the four hundred or so Indigenous people living there, were resident laborers on the half-dozen haciendas that dominated its economy. The estates and ranches in the district, including the hacienda Labor de Rivera, produced cattle, maize, and a little wheat. In the general agricultural expansion of the late eighteenth century the hacienda's population was to rise to about two hundred permanent laborers and their families, but in 1752 there were a few dozen laboring families at most. In Ahualulco and the surrounding hamlets, a good deal of simple weaving of textiles was done on hand looms, and the town was famous for the quality of the saddles produced by its few resident artisans. There was still a little desultory open pit silver mining activity in the neighborhood, a holdover from palmier days. Even as late as 1800 the area was known for the quality and extent of its wooded lands, which boasted abundant stands of pine, oak, and cedar. Just a few miles to the northeast, the wooded hills around Tequila were already becoming denuded because the distilling industry there required enormous amounts of firewood and charcoal to keep its stills producing the local firewater. Agriculture was the lifeblood of the entire area, and the wealthiest men and families were those who owned the land.

On that August morning, after a two-hour horseback ride over a sinuous road through a landscape roughened by wooded hillsides and deep canyons, the magistrate reached the Labor de Rivera, where he had been summoned by the victim's sister. He arrived to find José Leandro's body stretched out on a reed mat (*petate*) in the one-room house of Tomás Aquino, one of the estate's resident laborers, with a large crowd of people gathered around talking in hushed tones of the sudden and tragic events of the morning. José Leandro's elder brother José Luis (José was the most common male name at the time), the actual owner of the Labor de Rivera, was absent that day on one of his other rural properties and did not arrive in time for his brother's funeral. The victim's body was wrapped in a blue cloak with a hand-kerchief draped over the face and was found upon inspection to have several deep stab wounds. From the highly detailed but kaleidoscopic testimony of several witnesses, it is possible to piece together in some detail the circumstances of the crime.

At about five in the morning, while it was still dark, don José Leandro had arrived during his rounds of the estate laborers' homes at the dwelling of José Clemente Lorea to wake him and summon him to work. José Clemente's wife, Juana Isabel, told the administrator that her husband had already left for the fields. José Leandro then went to the kitchen of the house, in a separate structure at the back, to light a cigarette at the stove, and shortly returned to ask Juana Isabel who it was that was sleeping, wrapped up in a blanket or cloak, by the still-warm stove. She replied that it was José Tomás, a laborer often employed during the preceding two years on the estate, a bachelor who had lived for much of that time in the home of José Clemente and his wife. For unspecified reasons Don José Leandro had discharged the man from the estate's employ about a week earlier and was clearly displeased to find him back again. He went back to the kitchen and woke José Tomás, probably none too gently, challenging him brusquely with the words, "Didn't I kick you off the place and settle our accounts?"

The man jumped up from his place on the floor, answered, "I came back because the boss sent for me!" and without so much as another word drew from his clothing a long dagger (*terciado*) and stabbed his interlocutor repeatedly. Threatening to kill Juana Isabel if she ran for help, José Tomás made good his escape on the victim's horse. In the meantime, don José Leandro—mortally wounded—stumbled into the patio of the neighboring house of Tomás Aquino, another estate laborer, Juana Isabel's brother, where he sat down heavily on the ground and was described in his death agony by Tomás Aquino as slipping first to one side, then the other. Another man, summoned by the shouting, was sent up to the owner's house (*la casa grande*) to fetch help, but the younger Siordia brother died in the meantime. José Tomás's motive for the crime was never actually made clear, though presumably it was anger over his firing. The records of the case do not indicate if he was ever brought to justice.

features. Large landed estates were definitely linked to urban and mining markets when circumstances allowed it but could also fold in upon themselves when local market conditions or other situations dictated that they do so. It was primarily this ability to turn inward, and in a sense hibernate or reduce their metabolic processes from commercial to subsistence levels, that led them to be described as feudal. Their centrality to economy and society in the period from 1750 to 1850 seemed to justify extending that description to the society as a whole.

COMMERCE AND MANUFACTURES

I have said little about commerce or manufacturing in all their many forms. Commerce stretched to even the remotest corner of the colony, carried there by itinerant merchants—the capillaries of empire—whose commercial goods were probably supplied by larger merchants, these merchants by yet larger ones, and on up a commercial and credit chain. The important constraint to the volume of interprovincial commerce was the friction of distance, the necessity of dealing in goods of a sufficiently high unit value to offset the transport costs; the same economic logic applied to manufactured or artisan-produced goods as to agricultural products. The primary entrepôt of foreign goods was the city and port of Veracruz on the Gulf coast. Under the mercantilist assumptions of the Spanish colonial system, peninsular Spanish merchants and their collaborators in New Spain maintained a monopoly on trans-Atlantic trade with the backing of law and force from the Spanish colonial state. This meant that foreign-made goods not manufactured in Spain itself leaked into Spanish hands from France, Britain, and the Low Countries and came to New Spain as ostensibly made in Spain. There was also a good deal of contraband into the ports of the colony. Trading arrangements were partially liberalized in the last colonial decades but "free trade" to and from the colonies was never on the books. Customs and tariff policy by the governments of independent Mexico allowed more open or more closed trading depending upon the fiscal policies of the always-needy government and whether domestic manufacturing was being encouraged and therefore protected from foreign competition. From Veracruz imported textiles and other manufactured items were distributed through great annual trade fairs at Jalapa, near Veracruz, and at San Juan de los Lagos, in the western part of the country. There were even several noble titles linked to large commercial fortunes. Wealth acquired in trade was overshadowed by that based on large-scale land ownership and mining, although these activities overlapped in the portfolios of wealthy individuals and families. As writers even in the ancient world insisted, trade was the activity that knitted society together, not only embracing the buying, selling, and transportation of goods but also providing for the movement of information, rumor, ideas, and even subversion of the colonial order. The role of *arrieros*—mule skinners, the masters of commercial mule trains whether employees or owners—in propagating information and propaganda in favor of the insurgency of 1810 has often been noted. Father José María Morelos, who inherited the mantle of insurgent leader after the death of his former teacher and distant relative Father Miguel Hidalgo y Costilla, worked for a time as an *arriero*.[8]

Manufacturing enterprises formed a tiny sector of the colonial economy. Textiles, many metal products, luxury goods, books, and other items were imported from Spain, and in turn into Spain from the more industrialized parts of Europe. Certain items were actually prohibited from manufacture in New Spain, thereby preserving profitable monopolies for small groups of privileged merchants. The biggest of what we would think of as industrial concerns were the silver mines and sugar estates, but these were really processing rather than manufacturing activities. Domestic textile production in cottons and woolens was the largest in scale and most widespread of industrial enterprises in the form of *obrajes*, textile workshops that might employ up to 200 workers or so. The major centers for this industry were the cities of Puebla, Querétaro, and Guadalajara and remained so into the republican era even as the textile industry became more mechanized along modern lines. The manufacture of this consumer nondurable item—clothing being an item required by everyone and needing to be renewed periodically—was of course at the leading edge of industrialization in Europe and would come to be seen in the same way in independent Mexico. As a central government minister in the early 1830s, Lucas Alamán would found and direct a development bank to spur textile manufacture in particular and years later establish an enormous textile factory in partnership with other men; the first initiative enjoyed mixed success while the second went bankrupt. Of other manufacturing activities, in Mexico City the royal tobacco manufactory employed hundreds of workers, primarily women. But most fabrication of articles of daily use—crockery, for example, or tools—was done locally by craftsmen or even by their own users.

CONCLUSION

At a guess, perhaps 80 percent of New Spain's population got its living directly or at a small remove from the land, as I mentioned earlier. Within the farming economy the largest segment was unquestionably made up of Indigenous villagers—peasants producing at the subsistence level to support their own families, with perhaps small surpluses that they sold in local markets. Allowing for natural resource endowments, social structure, and other variables, there was a rough equivalence between how the major part of the population labored and lived and the way rural people labored and lived in France, Russia, on the *junker* estates of east Prussia, or other parts of continental Europe around the same time. On the whole rural people in New Spain may have been slightly better off than Andean peasants. The hacienda sector was the primary supplier of food to the cities of the realm. While it would be incorrect to call this part of the rural economy "backward," nor was it "modern" in the way that English commercial farms were becoming modern around the same time. "Premodern" is an awkward description of hacienda agriculture, so perhaps something like "traditional" describes it less inaccurately. In general, the hacienda as an enterprise was not especially resistant to technological change, but the cost/productivity ratio of such innovation was typically too high to warrant investment in such change even were it readily available. Any growth in production was therefore vegetative, resulting from putting more of the same factors into production—more labor, more land, more draft animals—rather than introducing anything new. One subsector of this economy, the sugar industry, was industrialized and nearly on a footing with production units in the Caribbean area. This was highly capitalized and if not technologically advanced, then at least on a par with sugar plantations elsewhere in the Western Hemisphere. The introduction of steam power and innovations in the way sugar milling equipment functioned would make a positive difference in productivity, but not until later in the nineteenth century. The market for the sugar estates' products (sugar of various grades, molasses, and rum) was domestic, supplying nearby Mexico City. The major zone of its activity was around Cuernavaca, to the south of the capital, although sugar production was scattered all around the colony wherever environmental conditions permitted the cultivation of sugar cane. There was a type of rural production unit between the large estate and Indian subsistence farming represented by the *rancho*, a family-farmed, mixed-production landholding worked primarily with family labor and linked to local urban or town markets. But we don't know much about this stratum of the rural economy during the colonial period. The fact that a small family-owned farm in central New Spain and a large livestock estate in the northern part of the country could both be called "ranchos" makes things confusing.

Silver mining was the engine that drove most of the monetized economic sector of New Spain. The metal proved remarkably durable by a large margin as the colony's most important export and was therefore the raison d'être of the colonial arrangement as far as the mother country was concerned. As with an iceberg, however, this was the part of the economy above the water line, while most small-scale enterprise, whether in craft production or farming, was situated below the surface of the money economy. Mining was a heavily capital-intensive, industrialized activity, although it was slow to change technologically until the later nineteenth century. Because of its geographical and economic concentration silver mining could be manipulated by the Spanish crown through taxation and other means; this also applied to large-scale commerce, but not to agriculture. By the same token, because of its concentration and heavy capital costs silver mining produced some of the colony's largest fortunes.

So how might we characterize the economy of late colonial New Spain into the first decade of the nineteenth century and the transition to independent national life? In comparison to any plausible model of modernization in that era it was definitely mixed. We noted earlier that in terms of national and per capita income its position around 1800 vis-à-vis the fledgling United States was not as unfavorable as one might have supposed, but the gap would widen quickly during the nineteenth century. The proportion of the working population involved in activities other than subsistence agriculture was relatively low and the scale of most manufacturing small. Market integration across the long and geographically difficult distances of the country was constrained by the growing but limited urbanization, by most people's low disposable incomes, and by high transportation costs. So while New Spain was quite advanced economically in comparison with some place like Albania, it was far behind most of western Europe and even its sister republic to the north.

NOTES

1. As with many other questions, there are still differences of opinion among scholars as to the degree of spatial integration of New Spain's economy in the late colonial period and of the linkages of one region to another. For the view that there was a high degree of integration between the regions and Mexico City, and among the regions, see Antonio Ibarra Romero, *La organización regional del mercado interno novohispano: La economía colonial de Guadalajara, 1770–1804* (Puebla: Benemérito Universidad Autónoma de Puebla/Universidad Nacional Autónoma de México, 2000); for the view that such interregional integration was relatively weak, see Eric Van Young, "Doing Regional History: A Theoretical Discussion and Some Mexican Cases," in Van Young, *Writing Mexican History* (Stanford: Stanford University Press, 2012), 167–98.

2. I once spent much of an agreeable evening drinking beer in a noisy café with the late distinguished historian of Mexico Paul Vanderwood, puzzling out what the term "rancho" meant in the nineteenth century without really coming to any firm conclusion. Such is the scholar's life.

3. Andrés Molina Enríquez, *Los grandes problemas nacionales* (1909; Mexico City: Ediciones del Instituto Nacional de la Juventud Mexicana, 1964). For a discussion of Molina Enriquez's thinking and its influence on Mexican agrarian reform after the Revolution of 1910, see Emilio Kourí, "Los pueblos y sus tierras en el México porfiriano: Una legada inexplorada de Andrés Molina Enríquez," in *En busca de Molina Enríquez: Cien años de Los grandes problemas nacionales*, ed. Emilio Kourí (Mexico City: El Colegio de México, 2009), 253–330.

4. For something of this view, see Alan Knight, *Mexico: The Colonial Era* (Cambridge: Cambridge University Press, 2002); by contrast, Eric Van Young, *Hacienda and Market in Eighteenth-Century Mexico: The Rural Economy of the Guadalajara Region, 1680–1820* (Berkeley: University of California Press, 1981).

5. In Latin this was *primae noctis* or *jus primae noctis*; there has been some scholarly controversy as to whether this was actually practiced widely in medieval Europe.

6. Van Young, *Hacienda and Market*, 260–61.

7. My account of the Siordia murder case is drawn from a longer essay, Eric Van Young, "Material Life," in *Rural Society in Colonial Latin America*, ed. Louisa Schell Hoberman and Susan Migden Socolow (Albuquerque: University of New Mexico Press, 1996), 49–74, and based upon the archival sources cited there.

8. The word *arriero* is derived, via the Spanish verb *arrear*, from the call used by muleteers to urge their mules (or burros) forward: "Arre, burro, arre!"

Chapter 4

Signs of Stress, Efforts at Reform

At first glance it would seem reasonably clear how to infer from the historical record the recipe that produced Mexico's independence from Spain. Start with a cup or so of Enlightenment political thinking about the self-determination of peoples, sovereignty, republicanism, and the limits of despotism; throw in a lump of the demonstration and disruptive effects of the American and French revolutions and the seasoning of international warfare; add a large handful of internal structural strain, social conflict, and the Bourbon Reforms within New Spain itself; and stir in a generous dollop of Napoleon Bonaparte. We may finish the dish with a skosh of historical contingency: What if La Corregidora had been abed with a debilitating case of the flu so the conspirators of Querétaro were all arrested in mid-September 1810 by the viceregal authorities before being warned that their conspiracy had been exposed to the authorities and before they could act to kick off the rebellion? Or if Father Miguel Hidalgo had fallen down a flight of stairs and been knocked unconscious by a concussion in the early morning hours of September 16? The situation in New Spain before 1810 was of course very much more complicated than this list of ingredients suggests, as the antecedents of epochal events like the Mexican independence movement always are. Here let me again invoke Lucas Alamán, the great statesman-historian whose own life was touched directly by the initial outbreak of the insurgency and who was an eye witness to the first years of the rebellion and its aftermath. He wrote that had events in Europe not triggered the rebellion when they did, between 1808 and 1810, independence would inevitably have come to Mexico anyway as the result of a social and political maturation that sent the colony down a path diverging from that of the metropolitan power. This is a reasonable hypothesis that throws into even sharper relief the benefit of looking at the century from 1750 to 1850 as in many respects a unit. As a historian who has spent some years trying to understand the century from 1750 to 1850 in order to arrive at some plausible set of propositions about the antecedents, course, and aftermath of the independence movement(s), I cannot claim to offer a definitive explanation here for the route New Spain followed to become Mexico but only something like an inventory of contributing factors, albeit placing greater weight on certain ones than on others.

Within the scholarly disciplines of economics and political science a set of theories has developed to emphasize institutional life, particularly in the sphere of politics, as a key variable in the "success" or "failure" of nations to prosper economically. The idea that political arrangements in large measure determine institutional ones and therefore economic performance would seem almost too obvious to warrant comment were it not for the fact that conventional wisdom has generally pointed the stronger causal arrow in the opposite direction, from economics to political and institutional life. The traditional idea here follows Karl Marx's notion that power over the means of production—wealth in its many forms—determines political power and therefore the capacity to shape institutions. Lucas Alamán was not alone in describing the political life of the young republic as "anarchic," ascribing this condition to the way in which independence had been won. In early republican Mexico it was not a question of the failure of a weak state to direct or stimulate economic development from above but of a fragile state in a violently contested political terrain finding itself unable to assure the minimal conditions of stability in which development might thrive. Alamán's ideas and activities run through this book as a narrative and organizational thread. He attempted to impose political stability on the country during his periods as chief minister in the national government. He did so not out of an inherently authoritarian personality, or cruelty, nor solely out of a desire to preserve class privileges but from the belief that political stability was a predicate to economic development, and economic development the preeminent element of modernization. Digging even below institutions, however, at bottom the persistent contention and civil conflict of the young republic arose from the failure of political actors to invent a principle of legitimacy to which all political men could subscribe and at least grudgingly subordinate their interests after the Spanish monarchy was swept away. In other words, not only the right to enjoy triumph in the political sphere but also the grace to accept frustration or defeat needed to be seen as rules of the game on the assumption that the institutional arrangements—political parties, congress, the court system, the presidency, the army, even the republic itself—were essentially "right" and legitimate and would not turn against losers in an arbitrary or vindictive way. With these considerations in mind, let us look at the situation within the colonial and wider Atlantic worlds as it stood up to 1810.

DISTURBANCES

New Spain was anything but a peaceable kingdom in the late eighteenth century. The Anglo-American colonies had their share of tax rebellions and other forms of violent protest against this or that measure of "oppression" by the British metropolis, and such incidents continued after American independence (for example, the Whiskey Rebellion in western Pennsylvania, 1791–1794). Massive political violence also occurred elsewhere in the Spanish overseas realms, as in what later became the independent nations of Peru, Bolivia, and Colombia in the early 1780s in the Tupac Amaru, Tupac Katari, and Comunero uprisings, respectively. But for sheer numbers and intensity of violence New Spain took a back seat to no other colony, especially in the violent episodes involving Indigenous people that were the most frequent by far. The occurrence of uprisings after 1821, furthermore—some genuinely popular rebellions, many more in the form of the ubiquitous *pronunciamientos* staged by military men—was only to escalate up to 1850. Few of these incidents attained a regional scope. In the colonial era riots or insurrections could be triggered by discontent among Indigenous people about taxes, by conditions of scarcity, or by political interference from royal officials in local political affairs and other grievances. The larger rebellions might last for weeks, entail a number of deaths among rebels as well as among the forces of "order," and leave lasting memories in the countryside where they mostly took place. A few had religious overtones, and a handful demonstrated messianic elements. One or two put forth claims that the legitimate monarch of New Spain was actually an Indian who was present in the colony to redress the injustices being perpetrated upon the crown's native subjects, such as in the so-called Indio Mariano uprising along New Spain's west coast around 1801.

One of the larger such episodes was a widespread and quite violent uprising in 1767 that touched many regions of New Spain, especially the mining areas in the near north, and involved other people besides Indians. The conflict was set off by the overnight expulsion of the Jesuit Order from the Spanish realms by royal edict, ostensibly an outgrowth of the Motín de Esquilache (Esquilache Riot) in Madrid the previous year. This had been a somewhat peculiar, violent mass urban riot directed at a royal edict prohibiting, in the name of adjusting to modern styles, the wearing of some traditional items of male clothing, condemning the crown minister (Esquilache; a Sicilian, the Italian version of his name was Squillace) whose policy it embodied, and protesting the high prices in Madrid for articles of prime necessity, chiefly bread. The Jesuits were thought by royal authorities to have conspired to raise the disturbance, or at least were expediently blamed for it, and were banned from the Spanish Empire on January 1, 1767. But as typically occurred in

large-scale movements, in New Spain other simmering issues—labor problems, taxes, resentments at measures of imperial reform—contributed to the
energy and social depth of this incident. The viceregal government's suppression of the simultaneous but uncoordinated uprisings was extremely harsh,
entailing hundreds of hangings, jailings, and exilings. The government's
response was led by José de Gálvez (1720–1787), whom we shall meet again,
a Spanish imperial official sent to New Spain as inspector general between
1764 and 1772 to impose various reforms (see figure 4.1).

Rebellions were in general almost exclusively rural, however. They
erupted suddenly, were quite localized, and rarely embraced more than a
single village or two, eventually to sputter out in the face of local repressive
measures. Such incidents were mostly characterized by colonial authorities as
tumultos (riots). They could be occasioned by villagers' conflicts with local
non-Indigenous officials or priests over harsh treatment or excessive taxation.
Conflicting claims between villagers and neighboring landowners or other
villages over the ownership of land, complaints of local people regarding
their own Indian officials, or other points of tension could also kick them off.
On occasion the disturbances were led by women. One scholar has described
this behavior as "bargaining by riot," one of a number of instruments in the
common people's political repertoire to make their voices heard by colonial
officialdom. They could involve anything from just a handful of people to
several hundred. And although the count of 150 such episodes during the
eighteenth century given here is certainly too low, it should also be acknowledged that nonvillage authorities could be rather hysterical about them and
might characterize a shoving match or a brawl among four inebriated men in
a village plaza as a "riot." Although such movements could occasion much
loss of life, they could also result in compromise solutions to local problems
such as the removal of an irksome priest to a different posting, for example,
or an adjustment in the level of the tribute tax owed by a village.[1] In the 120
years between 1700 and 1820 there were at least 150 village riots in the more
central parts of New Spain. While they varied a great deal over time and
space, there were some common characteristics in scope. What is interesting
for our purposes here is that the frequency of these small-scale eruptions of
popular violence increased notably after about 1765 or so, precisely during the period when imperial inspector general Gálvez was carrying out his
reform measures in New Spain. The incidents rose to a peak in the quinquennium from 1806 to 1810, when there were twenty of them. From 1811 on the
number dropped sharply as local episodes were masked by insurgent violence
or subsumed into it.

The riotous outbreaks pointed toward the massive eruption of popular
violence in 1810, and in some cases even contributed to it. What, then, was
behind this ascending trend and the social pressures it reflected among both

Figure 4.1. José de Gálvez (1720–1787), visitador of New Spain and later Minister of the Indies. agefotostock/Alamy Stock Photo.

elite groups and common people? There were several factors at work here, some of which illuminate the Bourbon state's efforts at reform within the implicit framework of "enlightened despotism." The economic pressures at work differed in their impacts on different sectors of the population, not all of them encouraging violent protest in the form of riots but cumulatively fueling what later became the independence movement. Among these were increased rates of fiscal extraction by the colonial state in the form of forced loans to support Spain's war efforts in continental Europe and the Atlantic world during the Napoleonic period, although such taxation was unlikely to affect people without much property, who made up the vast majority of the populace. Furthermore, a war measure enacted by the Spanish crown during the years from 1804 to 1808, the Consolidación de Vales Reales, mandated the seizure and liquidation (paying off) of outstanding mortgages held by the Church that had originated as loans from pious establishments to owners of real estate or as liens established by the owners, primarily as endowments to support secular clergy. This had a significantly negative effect on estate owners, many of whom could not come up with the cash to pay off the obligations. Father Miguel Hidalgo himself was caught by this policy because he owned a hacienda, as was his coinsurgent leader Ignacio Allende. Among other belt-tightening responses such people were forced to discharge laborers or suspend wages to them or to sell off their properties entirely, so that the effects of the measures rippled up and down the social hierarchy.

Where common people were concerned, the impact of a number of policies and economic forces helped spur them to intermittent political violence. The closing of loopholes in the structure of Indian tribute payments and the establishment of royal monopolies on tobacco and other items of wide popular consumption, along with other reforms essentially constituting taxation measures, had a directly negative impact on the pocketbooks of ordinary people. I have already pointed to the decline in real wages for working people of something like 25 percent in the last thirty years or so of the colonial regime. This combined with demand-driven inflation to increase rural poverty if not exactly to create immiseration. Demographic pressure on farming land was an extremely important factor as well: increasing numbers of humble people needed to be supported by a relatively inelastic amount of agricultural land. A reflection of this is the upward tick in the litigation over land in the courts in the latter part of the eighteenth century. Added to this, and a major cause of it, was the notable development of commercial, hacienda-based agriculture to feed the cities and mining areas. This entailed major shifts in favor of large landowners in access to farming land as haciendas expanded, legally or illegally, to accommodate increased production.

Then there were noneconomic factors in the cultural and political spheres that were at points intimately intertwined. One element was the Bourbon policy of suppressing the more florid religious cults and observances supported by common people in the tradition of popular piety, which especially created tensions in the countryside. These practices consisted of religious celebrations, processions of various kinds associated with the liturgical calendar, the veneration of local icons, and the spontaneous cults and chapels that one still sees in Mexico today. For example, the "folk saints" El Niño Fidencio and Juan Soldado have had popular cults developed around them in northern Mexico in the twentieth century.[2]

Before about the last third of the eighteenth century such manifestations of popular piety, for the most part quite Catholic in content but only loosely if at all under the control of the Church, had been tolerated or even encouraged in keeping with the baroque exuberance of Catholicism at the hands of common people. After that turning point, however, the Mexican church shifted its position in keeping with the tenor of the Bourbon Reforms issuing from the authorities in Spain. Popular forms of piety were thenceforth sanitized, restricted, or suppressed outright, provoking sometimes violent resistance on the part of Indigenous villagers in particular. Repeated viceregal decrees also condemned "abuses" by Indigenous and non-Indigenous people, including excessive spending, gambling, drinking, and commercial activities carried on in conjunction with the celebrations that marked the liturgical calendar, such as Holy Week. Deviations from officially sanctioned theology and practice drew the negative attention of Church authorities. In the last decades of the century, royal officials regularly refused licenses to Indians for the establishment of popular chapels in country villages. Several of the village riots or uprisings that erupted in connection with the Hidalgo rebellion in 1810 occurred in villages that already had a history of such disturbances or were linked to popular frustrations with clerical attempts to suppress religious celebrations, especially those of All Saints and All Souls Days. Certain forms of popular religious piety identified as noxious by the enlightened Mexican church—seen as economically wasteful, theologically unorthodox, and unseemly: unmodern, in other words—thus entered a sort of collective unconscious that nourished unorthodox religious belief and practice along with a habit of resistance to the power of the colonial regime that sought to tame or suppress such practices. While it is impossible except in a few instances to draw a straight line connecting discontent with these policies, local violence, and the insurgency in 1810, the links can be strongly inferred.

Another major social and political stressor for the thousands of Indigenous communities that dotted the countryside was the feeling among villagers, demonstrated more by collective action than explicitly articulated in written forms, that their way of life was under siege. In other works of my own I have suggested that this was demonstrated in a stubborn drive for political autonomy, the control of their own affairs and the often violent rejection of outside official, ecclesiastical, or private authority on the part of villagers and village elites in the latter part of the eighteenth century. The ethnic identity of the Indigenous people who made up the large majority of rural dwellers was intimately tied to the coherence of their communities, and the coherence and identity of communities in turn to their celebratory religious life. This was the double helix of politics and religion in village life. The well-established independence of village communities as political entities rested on control of their own internal affairs, including elections, relations with other communities, allotment of communal lands for farming, and the use of other local resources. This autonomy was reinforced by the community's public manifestations of its spiritual life, and both of these marked off from the outside by the personal identity of villagers as citizens of a small community and *as Indigenous people*. This age-old tradition of localism at the community level is still much in evidence in Mexico today, even as the element of ethnic distinction from non-Indigenous society has tended to fade over time. What anthropologists sometimes have called "localocentrism" explains in large measure the failure of colonial-era disturbances to coalesce into larger movements because the vision of local power holders and common citizens was focused more inward than outward. During the independence movement Creole elites were at first interested in claiming greater political autonomy for New Spain within the Spanish Empire and then in independent nationhood. Indigenous rebels, on the other hand—not all, perhaps, but most of them— were more interested in preserving the integrity of local communities against the intrusions of the Bourbon state, in the form of whatever agents, in their political and religious lives. The Creole and mestizo insurgent leadership, therefore, had different goals in mind from those of the Indigenous people who fought in the rebel ranks. The two groups were in essence moving in opposite directions, the insurgent leaders toward nationhood, the Indigenous villagers toward the preservation of community autonomy. This schism accounts in part for the fragility of the new nation-state when it came into being in 1821. To it can be ascribed the often negative, racialist attitude of non-Indian elites toward the "backward" Indigenous masses of the country, the difficulties of enacting republican citizenship in a meaningful way, and the halting process of modernization in Mexico.

The violent contention over the possession of the statue in the following episode was only the most visible provocation for local conflict. The judicial documentation on the incident includes a great deal of detail about the conflict itself and the local power structure. The gist of it is that the confrontation also involved shifts over a generation or so in favor of local non-Indigenous farmers in the access to land resources. Within the Indigenous community parallel shifts from the humbler to the more privileged stratum had occurred. These alterations in wealth and power were facilitated by collusion between

BOX 4.1. A VILLAGE RIOT

Here I offer a brief account of a village riot over the possession of a religious icon in the important pueblo of Cuauhtitlán, a short distance to the north of Mexico City, with a mixed Indian/non-Indian population. The peculiarly strong, knotted relationship of individual, communal, and cultural identity I have just sketched is well illustrated by the Cuauhtitlán incident. This area was to see at least one invasion by rebel forces in the early years of the insurgency of 1810, along with continuing antiroyalist guerrilla activity and the intermittent but substantial participation of local Indians in the uprising.

On the evening of Thursday, December 7, 1785, a large group of Indigenous parishioners in the town of Cuauhtitlán exploded in a riot during which the houses of the local priest, the tithe collector, and at least two Spanish merchants were broken into, the windows smashed, and the contents partially looted. The priest himself climbed down a ladder from the upper floor in one of the merchant's homes and fled through the patio, claiming later that he had escaped the rioters with his life only through the miraculous intervention of God and the Virgin. The violence was occasioned by a rumor rapidly circulating among the Indigenous parishioners gathered at the town church earlier that evening for a religious procession and Mass. The reluctance of the parish priest to bring a locally venerated effigy of the Virgin Mary out of the church, so the rumor ran, was due to the replacement of the original statue by a new, less holy one. This had been done with the priest's connivance under the patronage of a local Spanish woman of means against the strong objections of the town's Indians and in defiance of an order from the authorities in Mexico City blocking the action, issued just two days previously. In their petition to the viceroy the Indigenous citizens of Cuauhtitlán had praised the effigy for its "singular beauty," the "innumerable prodigies" recommending it to the "tender affection" of the town, and its wide veneration outside the parish itself. The planned repairs to the statue threatened to alter not just the body but the face, the petitioners alleged, "without acknowledging that the said image belongs to no Spaniard, but only the Indians." In defending his actions after the event, the priest claimed that the body of the statue was desperately in need of repair because it was full of holes serving for rats' nests, and the rodent tenants were gnawing the Virgin's clothes to bits from the inside.[3] And the priest averred that "although the origins [of the effigy] are unknown, there are ample grounds for believing that it belongs to the Spaniards, not to the Indians."

some native officials and local non-Indian powerholders, so that the integrity and cohesion of the Indigenous political structure was also openly challenged. Whatever the original ownership of the statue, a major element in the conflict was a struggle between contending groups, set off from each other by ethnic and loose class boundaries, each attempting to appropriate for purposes of self-definition and political leverage a symbolic object common to both. It encapsulates the cultural gulf dividing Creole and Indian cultures during the period, especially during the insurgency of 1810–1821, further explored in the following chapter.

DYNASTIC CHANGE: THE ARRIVAL OF THE BOURBONS

Outside New Spain, peninsular Spain itself and its other trans-Atlantic realms were thrust into a period of internal ferment and war in the eighteenth century. The ascent of the Bourbon family to the throne of the Spanish Empire in 1700 in place of the Habsburgs, who had ruled for two centuries, is an extremely complicated tale of European royal bedrooms, dynastic politics, diplomacy, and warfare whose details would bog us down here. But a brief rendering of this backstory of the Spanish imperial reforms of the later eighteenth century, for it was the Bourbon monarchs who undertook them, will be useful in establishing the context for the century from 1750 to 1850. This stream of events in the realm of international high politics, warfare, and royal dynasties also serves to remind us that the European and colonial worlds of the eighteenth century were deeply interconnected, that political happenings and dates matter despite our tendency to dismiss them as "old-fashioned history," and that large-scale accidents have important implications in smaller landscapes. To cite but one example, had Spanish King Felipe V not acceded to the Spanish crown the Bourbon Reforms might not have come to New Spain because they were modeled on French measures; the ripples they created would not have contributed to the turbulence of the late eighteenth century; and the independence movement might have been delayed significantly. To help unscramble the dynastic tangle a bit I have provided here a listing of the

Bourbon monarchs of Spain (but including one Habsburg and one usurper) with the dates of their lives and reigns during our period:

- Carlos II (1661–1700), r. 1665–1700 (a Habsburg, as a child he reigned under a regency)
- Felipe V (1683–1746), r. 1700–1724 (abdicated in favor of his son, Louis I)
- Louis I (1707–1724), r. 1724 (died of smallpox after six months on the throne)
- Felipe V, r. 1725–1746 (reassumed the throne after the death of his son Louis)
- Ferdinand VI (1713–1759), r. 1746–1759
- Carlos III (1716–1788), r. 1759–1788 (followed his half-brother Ferdinand to the throne)
- Carlos IV (1748–1819), r. 1788–1808 (abdicated in favor of his son Ferdinand)
- Ferdinand VII (1784–1833), r. 1808 (abdicated in favor of Joseph Bonaparte)
- José Bonaparte (1768–1844), r. 1808–1813 (ejected by armed struggle)
- Ferdinand VII, r. 1813–1833 (returned to throne after French were ejected from Spain)
- Isabel II (1830–1904), r. 1833–1868 (overthrown)

The Bourbon family still rules Spain at least nominally, now in the person of King Felipe VI de Borbón (that is, Bourbon) y de Grecia (his mother is Greek). The previous King Felipe (1683–1746), a French prince, was a grandson of Louis XIV of France and thus first in the line of succession to the French throne. The king of Spain and its overseas dominions at the time, Carlos II, related through marriage to the French ruling dynasty of the Bourbons, was a Habsburg (the ancient dynasty extinguished with the fall of the Austro-Hungarian Empire at the end of World War I) who died childless in November 1700. In his will King Carlos designated as his heir and successor to the Spanish throne Philip of France, this grandson of the Sun King, Louis XIV. But there was a Habsburg claimant to the Spanish kingdoms as well, also linked by dynastic descent to the Spanish monarchy, which complicated things considerably. Philip was duly declared king of Spain as Felipe V on November 16, 1700, eventually renouncing any claim he might have to the French throne. But until that renunciation, the prospect that the Spanish Empire and the French kingdom might be conjoined on a single throne upset the complicated balance of power among the European monarchies, setting off the War of the Spanish Succession (1701–1714), a nearly European-wide conflagration.

The main contenders in the war were Spain, with its ally France supporting its claimant to the throne of the Spanish Empire. This combination was
faced by the Grand Alliance, embracing the Habsburg-ruled Holy Roman
Empire of central Europe, based principally on the German-speaking lands,
aided by its sometime allies Britain, the Dutch Republic, and Savoy (much
later the nucleus of Italy). The fighting raged for a dozen years, the joint
forces of the Grand Alliance commanded by John Churchill (1650–1722),
later (1689) ennobled as the Duke of Marlborough, the direct ancestor of
Winston Churchill. The war came finally to an end through diplomatic means
with the multiparty Treaty of Utrecht in 1713. In exchange for consolidating
his accession to the kingship of Spain and its empire and his renunciation of
any claim to the French throne, Felipe V ceded various European territories
to the opposing parties.

Spain ceded the Spanish Netherlands, the Kingdom of Naples, the Duchy
of Milan, and the island of Sardinia to the Habsburgs; Sicily to the Duchy
of Savoy; Gibraltar and the island of Menorca to the British; and to the
Portuguese, the Colonia del Sacramento, on the east side of the Rio de la
Plata, in a region first known as the Banda Oriental (the Eastern Shore)
that would later become Uruguay. The Spanish Atlantic empire remained
intact but commercial access to it, including the trade in African slaves to
the Spanish colonies, was granted to the British, who really emerged the
big winners in the conflict. Commercial privileges were a key issue because
under the prevailing doctrines of mercantilism international trade was basically seen as a zero-sum game in which one nation's gain was another's loss.
The British acquisition of Gibraltar, at the southern tip of Spain, provided a
military foothold the British have maintained to this day, giving them strategic naval dominance over the western Mediterranean. Britain also emerged
the preeminent global naval power, a position that underwrote its prosperity
and military hegemony during the eighteenth and nineteenth centuries. This
ensured its eventual supremacy over its rival France, the final test of which
would be the defeat of Napoleon in 1815 after his brief return from exile.
Another important provision of the Treaty of Utrecht was France's abandon-
ment of its support for the Stuart dynasty in its claims to the British throne,
eventually clearing away ambiguities in the line of succession in favor of
the Dutchman William of Orange and thus ensuring a Protestant succession
in Britain.[4] The war also marked the decline of the Dutch Republic, a strong
military and commercial competitor of the British during the seventeenth
century, virtually bankrupted by the debts accrued from the military effort
of the war.

As the first of the Spanish Bourbon line Felipe V turned out to be less than
an outstanding monarch. By all accounts he was a manic depressive who
during the last decade of his life could only be brought out of the melancholy

phase of his cycles by the brilliant singing of the court favorite, the famous Italian *castrato* Farinelli (1705–1782).[5] Felipe was totally dominated by his queen, Elizabeth Farnese, although he was not so passive that he was unable to procreate several sons with her. One of these later succeeded to the throne as Charles III (1716–1788), a remarkably homely man as portrayed in a famous portrait by Francisco Goya but an effective monarch under whose reign most of the Bourbon Reforms were carried out. King Felipe did edge toward the improvement of Spain's government, strengthening the central authority and undertaking some other reform measures, a program carried forward and much expanded by King Charles III.

THE INTERNATIONAL CONTEXT: RIVALRY AND WAR

No century in modern times has been free of national or imperial rivalries and warfare, but the eighteenth century was particularly fraught with massive armed conflict between nations. The growth of the absolutist regimes in Europe was both a cause and effect of the need to field great armies because large-scale warfare called forth enormous fiscal, organizational, and logistical efforts by governments that in turn reinforced the power of the state.[6] All the major seafaring nations of the continent—the British, French, Dutch, Spanish, and Portuguese—had colonial possessions they strove to exploit and protect. The Habsburg, Russian, and Ottoman empires were largely land-based but had their own territorial ambitions. The two major contenders for dominance in continental Europe, the Middle East, Asia, and the Americas were Britain and France. Later, new aspirants such as Belgium and Germany also joined the scramble for colonies. By the close of the Napoleonic Wars in 1815, however, the British-French rivalry had been largely resolved in favor of Great Britain, which embarked on a century of unrivalled development and prosperity, building on its dominance of the world's oceans established around the time of the War of the Spanish Succession. But while this struggle was unfolding in Europe during the eighteenth century, the seas themselves and the colonies became theaters of warfare by extension. Spain was sometimes drawn in as a French ally on the basis of the Bourbon family connection, the so-called *Pacte de Famille*, formalized by treaties between the two powers in 1733, 1743, 1761, 1779, and 1796. This alignment changed radically after Napoleon Bonaparte's rise to power, the new antagonism between France and Spain coming to a head in the Peninsular War of 1808–1814. Spain gained very little from their joint military engagements, and as in the War of the Spanish Succession Britain was the major beneficiary of the conflicts.

International armed conflicts, some larger and some smaller, raged almost constantly during the century. Spain invested financial and human resources with little to show for them: Queen Anne's War (1702–1713), the Ottoman-Venetian War (1714–1718), the War of the Polish Succession (1733–1738), and the War of the Spanish Succession; and so it went. The real shock to the aging Spanish Empire occurred with the Seven Years War (1756–1763), also known as the French and Indian War, in which Spain was allied with the French against Great Britain and its client state, Portugal. Aside from its importance in the prehistory of the United States (George Washington commanded militia forces against the French and Indians, for example), this long engagement, which ended with the Treaty of Paris in 1763, saw war in continental Europe fully erupt into the contenders' extra-European colonies. The outcome for Spain was mixed because in the peace settlement of 1763 it acquired Louisiana from France but did not hold it long. This enormous territory later reverted to France again and was sold by Napoleon to the United States in 1803 as Thomas Jefferson's Louisiana Purchase, nearly doubling the size of the United States. During the war the British captured both Havana, Spain's strategic stronghold in the Caribbean, and Manila, in the Philippines. By the terms of the 1763 treaty Spain ceded Florida to the British in exchange for the return of Havana and Manila. But the capture of Havana, held for a year by British forces, proved a terrible wound to the Spanish militarily, commercially, and to national honor. These engagements took a huge toll on the Spanish navy. In the year the British held Havana, shipping through the port increased many times over under their system of substantially free trade; the demonstration effect of this was one of the strongest motives behind the Spanish policy of loosening trade restrictions with its American colonies some years later. The relative ease with which the British forces besieged and captured Havana, the spurt in prosperity of the island of Cuba while they held it, and the damage inflicted on the Spanish navy made Spain starkly aware of the vulnerability of her overseas empire, spurring the heroic effort at defensive modernization and national regeneration embodied in the Bourbon Reforms.

The return engagement some fifteen years later produced a more positive outcome for Spain but on the whole would better have been avoided. Spain was drawn into the American Revolution not only out of a desire to avenge itself for the humiliations suffered at the hands of the British in the Seven Years War but also by the *Pacte de Famille* as an ally of the French, a vital European supporter of the British colonists' strike for independence. The Anglo-Spanish War of 1779–1783 was really an aspect of the British and French conflict over the English colonies in America, yet another episode in a still larger struggle over hegemony in Europe and colonial domination on a global basis that also embraced the Indian subcontinent. The theater of this engagement, primarily a naval encounter, included the English Channel, the Strait of Gibraltar, the Atlantic, the Caribbean, Central America, Louisiana, and other areas. Spain primarily provided logistical support and supplies for the American revolutionaries. By the terms of the Treaty of Paris in 1783 Britain's American colonies gained their independence, but there were other territorial adjustments, including the return to Spain of East and West Florida and Minorca and of the Bahamas to the British. But for Spain the long-term costs of her fight with the British were enormous. In the first place, the war gave birth to a republican polity, soon to become a continental power at the very expense of Spain herself. The advent of the American republic was an open contradiction of Spain's own institutions of governance and the doctrines of enlightened absolutism. Second, it provided the model of an anticolonial struggle for national liberation that inspired the independence movements in Spain's New World colonies in the early nineteenth century. Finally, messing about with another empire's colonies proved an unfortunate precedent followed by the British when Spanish American independence movements appeared on the horizon in the second decade of the new century.

ENLIGHTENED REFORMERS: THE TRATADISTAS

It was against this background of international rivalry and warfare that the Spanish imperial state undertook a series of political and economic measures to arrest the weakening of the empire's international position, make the New World colonies more profitable for the mother country, and reverse economic stagnation in Spain itself.[7] Known collectively as the Bourbon Reforms, this series of policies, laws, and regulations was not really planned as a single coherent program. It was enacted, rather, in an almost haphazard way by the crown and its ministers as situations arose, reformist ideas took hold, or particularly dynamic personalities in the ministries held the reins of government. The reforms were put in place in piecemeal fashion between mid-century and about 1790, modeled on governmental practices the Bourbon dynasty had brought with it from France. But the reforms did have a discernible philosophical underpinning from the Spanish side in the writings on political economy of a group of men, mostly trained lawyers and high royal officials of intellectual and scholarly inclinations, sometimes known collectively as the *tratadistas* (from the *tratados*, or treatises, they wrote proposing reforms). Few of their concrete recommendations were actually put into practice aside from a loosening of trade restrictions within the empire. The influence of their thinking, however, deeply affected royal policy and the action of crown ministers, those high officials who headed the various departments of government. The implicit framework was "enlightened despotism," or less ominously, "enlightened absolutism," the philosophy of kingship in most of Western Europe. This political doctrine extended even to the Russia of

Catherine the Great (1729–1796) and the Habsburg Empire (Austria-Hungary and annexed lands) of Emperor Joseph II (1741–1790), brother of the ill-fated French queen Marie Antoinette.

Much of what we know as the modern European nation took shape during the eighteenth century, with roles played in the process by virtually constant warfare and the need this created for increased taxation and rationalized systems of collection, by large standing armies, the establishment and management (and loss) of colonies, and by technological change. The "absolutism" part of the formula meant an ever-increasing concentration of political power in the central state, in almost all cases hereditary "divine right" monarchies save for Switzerland, some of the Italian city-states, and across the Atlantic the United States. Although it seems anachronistic to many people, a number of European monarchies survive today, the most important among them Great Britain, followed by Belgium, Denmark, the Netherlands, Norway, Sweden, Greece, and of course Spain, although this form of state is widespread in the Middle East and East Asia. With the drive toward centralization and more powerful executive authority in the eighteenth century came the development not only of large, systematized bureaucracies and armies but also the reduction of aristocratic power competitive with royal authority, the increasing acceptance of experimental science, and the rise of popular nationalistic sensibilities. As for the "enlightened" element of the formula, although Spain itself was not lacking in a long tradition of political philosophy, the Spanish reformers read widely in the thought of other European writers, among them the French legal scholar and political philosopher Charles-Louis de Montesquieu (1689–1755) and the *philosophes*, the Scotsman David Hume (1711–1776), and another Scot, Adam Smith (1723–1790), whose *Wealth of Nations* was very influential. For those Spanish thinkers who outlived the first years of the French Revolution and could read his conservative manifesto, the Irish parliamentarian Edmund Burke's (1729–1797) *Reflections on the Revolution in France* (1790) was deeply influential, as it has continued to be on modern conservative political thought. The Spanish *tratadistas* believed, in general, in the historical groundedness, social value, and political necessity of monarchy. They were very practical politicians, rejecting abstract political thinking or radical projects. For the most part they thought that given the inherently conservative nature of Spanish society, incremental changes rather than sharp breaks with tradition were the way to get Spain moving in the direction they felt it should go. I have devoted several pages to the Spanish reformers because while it is vital to know the nature of the concrete reforms applied to the Spanish New World colonies and their effects, it is equally or more important to consider something of the intellectual atmosphere in Spain and Europe in the latter half of the eighteenth century. These ideas in many ways charted the course of modernization in Mexico and elsewhere but also opened the door to new thinking about forms of governance and nationhood.

The three most significant of these men (although there were other important figures) in order of birth were José del Campillo y Cossío (1695–1743); Pedro Rodríguez, Count of Campomanes (1723–1802); and Gaspar Melchor de Jovellanos (1744–1811)—the last, looking thoughtfully melancholy, the subject of a well-known portrait by Goya (see figure 4.2). They were thus a generation apart from each other, their lives spanning more than a century, suggesting that their ideas had long gestated even before the Bourbon Reforms were enacted. They were preceded by other reformist writers who suggested remedies for the "decadence and annihilation of this monarchy," but they are the three principally associated with the late century reforms in Spain and its overseas dominions. All three occupied high government positions at one time or another, sometimes more than once. Campillo was simultaneously secretary of the navy and of the Indies (basically the colonial office) during the last years of King Felipe V, and Campomanes minister of finance from 1788 to 1793 under King Charles III, Felipe's second son, and then King Carlos IV. These were highly accomplished men whose relatively modest backgrounds and rapid rise sometimes provoked jealousies and resistance to the implementation of their ideas from established, more traditionalist power holders. Jovellanos, for example, was a lawyer of humble origins who wrote in a number of fields besides political economy and had been a magistrate in Seville before rising to the royal ministry. He incurred the disfavor of Manuel de Godoy (1767–1851), a handsome *arriviste* guardsman of the royal household. Elevated to the position of prime minister at the age of twenty-five and heaped with titles and honors over the next years, Godoy was long the court favorite of King Carlos IV. The king was an easygoing man who preferred to hunt rather than govern and was happy to hand off his governing duties (and reputedly his husbandly obligations to his queen) to the ambitious young officer. Banished to the island of Mallorca by Godoy for nearly a decade, Jovellanos later refused the offer of a cabinet post from King José I (and last), Napoleon Bonaparte's older brother, opting instead to serve the nationalist government resisting the French usurpation between 1808 and 1814.

European thinkers of the age sometimes cited the Spanish and Ottoman empires as examples of what an empire should *not* be: inflexible, illiberal, and tyrannous; and, it might be added, inefficient and overextended. The remedy for these imperial ills was to strengthen the monarchy, it was thought, through promoting exports and imports to and from America and raising more revenue. The three reformers set themselves to encourage this policy but also to revitalize Spain itself; their proposed solutions were therefore chiefly economic in nature. The "decadence" of the country vis-à-vis the rest of

Figure 4.2. Portrait of Gaspar Melchor de Jovellanos (1744–1811), lawyer, statesman, and tratadista, by Francisco José de Goya y Lucientes. Wikimedia Commons/Public Domain.

western Europe (primarily the British, the French, and the Dutch), despite the potential wealth of the far-flung colonies, was reflected in Spain's decline as a world power during the seventeenth and eighteenth centuries. Domestically, the country's relatively slow population increase, the backwardness of its agriculture relative to the rest of western Europe, the constricted nature of its commerce, and the weakness of its industrial capacity except in certain peripheral regions, such as Catalonia, in the northeast, put it at a disadvantage relative to the other powers. Some of the natural determinants of this "backwardness" could not be counteracted even by the wisest policy measures. Among these handicaps were the lack of navigable rivers in Spain, the sparseness of population (although both pro-and antinatalist policies in many societies have enjoyed some success in modern times), the absence of coal and iron deposits, and so forth. Being practical men rather than radical ideologues they favored moderate reforms instead of attempts at the radical reshaping of society represented by the French revolutionary regimes. Among the proposals they all seemed to favor were the encouragement of population growth (an article of faith among eighteenth-century Atlantic polities), commerce, and technical education.

All three thinkers acknowledged the paradox that Spain's riches in the form of silver from the New World had actually retarded the country's economic development over the long run beginning with King Philip II (r. 1556–1598). The influx of mineral wealth periodically created high rates of inflation as the money supply expanded but wages and other forms of income for ordinary people lagged behind, as they typically do in such situations. With all the treasure coming into the country beginning about the middle of the sixteenth century, Spain bought what it needed from Britain, France, and the Netherlands rather than producing it domestically. Those countries, especially Britain and the Netherlands, diversified their economies partially on the basis of American silver. In the meantime, Spanish industry languished while Spain itself subsisted on that silver and poured money into warfare defending European Catholicism against the Protestant onslaught that began with Martin Luther at almost exactly the same time that Fernando Cortés was conquering the Aztecs. By the early decades of the eighteenth century Campillo was writing that the silver of the empire was a curse, while Campomanes suggested that the treasure had made Spain into a "canal through which the products of her mines and the wealth of the Indies [that is, Spanish America] has been emptied over the whole of Europe." Interestingly, Lucas Alamán was to employ very similar language nearly a century later, suggesting in 1844 that Mexico should diversify away from its centuries-long dependence on silver as its major economic prop:

> To be rich and happy, the republic must have manufacturing, for without it
> her agriculture will remain reduced to a state of languor and poverty, and the
> treasures torn form the bowels of the earth, passing immediately from the
> mines . . . to the ports from which they are embarked, will only serve to demon-
> strate with this rapid and unproductive passage, that the wealth does not belong
> to the peoples to whom nature conceded it . . . but rather to those who know how
> to utilize our precious metals and increase their value.[8]

Where the New World colonies were concerned, it has also been suggested
that the value of their silver exports to Spain induced the mother country to
hug them to her bosom more closely than the British or French did their colonies. For most of the colonial period the Spanish government discouraged
manufactures in the Americas through monopolistic and exclusionary trading
practices meant to keep the colonies tightly subordinated in an asymmetrical
relationship to Spain.

The three *tratadistas* were on the whole less concerned with the welfare
of Spain's colonial dominions than with that of Spain itself. The chief remedy they proposed for jolting the home economy out of its lassitude was to
embrace some degree of free trade with the trans-Atlantic realms. This policy
made its way through the imperial bureaucracy and entrenched interests to
emerge in the last two decades of colonial rule as one of the most important
features of the Bourbon Reforms. In part this was due to the fact that trade
could be liberalized by royal decrees relatively quickly, while other suggested reform policies would take much longer and would alienate more
special interest groups and large sectors of the population. Writing in the
1760s, Campomanes launched a full-frontal assault upon mercantilist political economy, condemning protective tariffs, the craze for accumulating silver
bullion, and closed trading systems, insisting that "all nations now believe
that wealth through commerce, navigation and industry is the only source of
public happiness." Two decades earlier Campillo had argued for the opening
of ports in Spain and the Americas to trade with each other and for the abolition of the expensive, slow, and ponderous convoy system of trans-Atlantic
shipping, a practice dictated by concern to protect fleets bearing New World
silver to Spain. Campillo also advocated the establishment of royal monopolies in tobacco and brandy to compensate revenue lost from foregone taxes,
policies that came to be important later in the century. Where the structures
of governance in the colonies were concerned, Campomanes insisted that too
many high offices there, both secular and ecclesiastic, had been allowed to
fall into the hands of Creoles during the seventeenth century. This practice
weakened royal control over the overseas dominions because these officials
looked more to their own benefit and that of their families and social networks

than those of the Spanish crown. It also entrenched local power groups and allowed the leakage of royal revenues en route to Madrid.

Among weaknesses in Spanish society the reformers identified the political strength of the Church, its counterclaim upon the loyalties of the king's subjects, and its tremendous wealth. All of this would later be tackled through the policy of regalism, which established the clear dominance of royal power over ecclesiastical institutions. A target of Jovellanos, especially, were the "excesses" of popular religious practice in Spain, with its "stupid superstitions," a complaint we have seen crop up in New Spain as well. Another major problem identified by the *tratadistas* was the enormous (largely unproductive) concentration of land ownership in Spain, by both aristocrats and the Church, which they felt impeded the free functioning of the market and the optimal employment of productive resources. This economic and social critique was echoed by some advanced thinkers in the colonies, among them the churchman Manuel Abad y Queipo (1751–1825), bishop-designate (unconfirmed) of the important western Mexican city of Valladolid (later Morelia). At the end of the colonial period Abad y Queipo argued for the radical idea of land reform: the breakup of large, underproductive landed estates and their redistribution in smaller plots. Despite his progressive beliefs on many questions, however, the bishop-designate was a church-and-crown man who supported the Spanish monarchy and would later excommunicate his fellow churchman Father Miguel Hidalgo, the progenitor of Mexican independence. Reform should be incremental rather than radical, the *tratadistas* suggested, so as not to destroy the institutional foundations of Spanish state and society. As historian David Brading has summarized Jovellanos's thinking, "In effect, Jovellanos reiterated Montesquieu's principles that laws should fit the character, climate and history of a people and hence should vary from country to country, the very opposite of Rousseau's conviction that governments through wise laws should strive to change and improve the character and morals of the people."[9] This incremental and minimalist approach to politics and law making underlay the ideas of Lucas Alamán and other Mexican conservatives in the young republic and is very much at the heart of conservatism today.

One deeply embedded characteristic of Spanish and Spanish colonial society for which the reformers could offer few short-term concrete solutions was the "spirit of conquest," and with it the shadow of feudalism that Campillo and others identified as holding Spain back. The country had clung to an anachronistic ethos of domination through military might, he thought, that had grown out of the reconquest (*Reconquista*) of the Iberian Peninsula from the Muslim kingdoms between the eighth and fifteenth centuries and had carried over into the Spanish conquests in the New World. This was a crusading, military-feudal ethic that had outlived its usefulness and was no longer adaptive in a world based on international commerce, burgeoning ideas of

economic development, and bureaucratic rationality. The prescription suggested by Campillo was to open Spain and its New World dominions not
only to trade but also to a controlled but more liberal inflow of new ideas and
even foreigners. He hoped that the Spanish mind and Spanish society would
open but not tumble into an abyss of political chaos, war, and utopian projects
as France had done in 1789. To put this in another way: How much change/
modernization was tolerable or advisable? The question became how to liberalize the colonial regime enough to make the colonials happy and to stimulate
prosperity on both sides of the Atlantic, but not so much as to loosen the grip
of the mother country on its overseas realms or to forego for it the benefits of
reforms. The men who steered the Spanish Empire were never able to solve
this conundrum. It is difficult to draw a straight line between the thinking
of the reformers and the Bourbon Reforms themselves, but the ideas were
in the air and the influences were there. While King Philip V had begun to
take some steps in this direction, and his second son and successor Ferdinand
VI continued modestly in the same direction, Ferdinand's half-brother King
Charles III took even bolder ones. Such changes were anathema to Charles's
grandson, King Ferdinand VII, so that reform in the direction of a more accelerated modernization was slowed considerably if not completely stopped in
its tracks. The intervention of Napoleon Bonaparte in capturing the Spanish
throne in 1808 had a great deal to do with this because there were those colonials who wanted to seize the opportunity to strike for independence. But had
King Ferdinand VII been less a dyed-in-the-wool reactionary, had he assumed
a more conciliatory attitude toward the Spanish American dominions upon his
return to the throne in 1814, and had he continued the program of incremental
reform, independence might have been delayed for a generation or so, or at
least this is what Lucas Alamán believed.

THE BOURBON REFORMS

The defensive modernization undertaken by Spain at home and abroad aimed
at the reorganization of the military, political, commercial, fiscal, and to some
extent religious structures of the Spanish realms. These were not altruistic
efforts putting the welfare of Spanish and colonial subjects first but were
intended to strengthen Spain against the actual or feared depredations of other
European states, in particular the rising power of Britain. Should the reforms
increase the productivity and prosperity of the people, so much the better
because that would inevitably strengthen the empire's fiscal base and dampen
any potential discontent fueled by the underperforming economy. The goals
were to improve Spain's military capabilities, strengthen and centralize royal
government, bring the commercial system to some measure of parity with the

other states of western Europe, and make the taxation system more efficient and productive. Where the Catholic Church was concerned, the reformers also sought to assert the Gallicanist doctrine, the view of Catholic authority in which national interests might well trump papal interests; to assert the ascendancy of secular monarchical authority over the Church; and to purge popular religious practices of their more heterodox and riotous elements. The reforms amounted less to a planned, coherent program than to a halting series of policies requiring nearly a century to implement even incompletely. They began under King Philip V and King Ferdinand VI, found their fullest expression under King Charles III, continued somewhat languidly under King Charles IV, and were choked off by the French invasion of Spain in 1808. The models of the reform measures were the changes instituted by King Louis XIV in France, the greatest continental power in Europe, and brought into Spain by the Sun King's Bourbon grandson. Instituted from above, they represented a sort of social engineering aiming at functional improvement rather than fundamental change. In the end the measures did produce short-term gains but eroded the bonds between Spain and its colonies. Less than fundamental though they may have been, the policies of political reorganization and centralization, the increased rates of fiscal extraction, and the attacks on traditional forms of religious practice did provoke riots and rebellions in New Spain suppressed more harshly under Bourbon than Habsburg rule. As a modern historian of Mexico has written, the Bourbon "project"

> was premised on notions of the free market but involving a growing and costly bureaucracy, hefty taxation, elaborate regulation of trade and manufacture, and the establishment of powerful monopolies. The Bourbons took upon themselves the paradoxical task of pounding civil society into an acceptance of laissez-faire capitalism and rational-legal political authority. Their subjects would be forced to be economically free and cuffed into an acceptance of centralized state authority. . . . By the 1800s Mexico was—certainly compared with its past—an over-taxed and over-governed society. Fiscal oppression became a staple complaint of the rebels of 1810. By squeezing New Spain as never before . . . the Bourbons "gained a revenue and lost an empire."[10]

Perhaps furthest from the lives of ordinary Mexicans were the administrative changes undertaken toward the beginning of the eighteenth century. In 1721 the primary responsibility for governance of the colonies was conferred upon a newly established ministry of the Indies and navy. This shift from conciliar forms of administration and political decision making to ministerial forms was characteristic of the Bourbons in other areas of government as well. It meant that eventually the committee structure dominated by Spanish aristocrats was replaced by modern ministerial forms (state, treasury, justice, war, etc.) that made administrative accountability by professional salaried bureaucrats clearer, functional borders and lines of authority less blurry, and processes more streamlined. New, larger territorial-administrative units were created in the empire primarily for the sake of defense and the regulation of trade, especially the suppression of contraband in the circum-Caribbean and South Atlantic zones. Other territorial rearrangements were undertaken in northern New Spain to make defense against hostile Indigenous groups more agile. Within the viceroyalties the intendancy system was introduced, each with its own bureaucracy and treasury, corresponding fairly closely to the modern states in the Mexican federation. Much of the power of the viceroys devolved upon the new intendants whose spheres of responsibility included local government and regional activities such as road building, public sanitation, and tax collection.

Closer to the lives of the colonial elite were the changes in governing structures and access to office introduced by the Bourbons. During the seventeenth century, as Spain had become weaker and more than ever desperately in need of funds to support its European adventures, the sale of royal office in New Spain up to the highest levels had become a common practice. Under the more lax rule of the Habsburgs this had allowed the Creole elite of the colony to insinuate itself into the government despite royal injunctions to the contrary that were obviously incompatible with the sale of offices. The process made for an increasing degree of colonial autonomy in political and economic matters. Starting in 1750 the sale of judgeships on the highest royal courts in New Spain was barred, along with the sale of posts at other levels of government. As the century drew on Creole officials at any but the most local level were steadily pushed out in favor of Spanish-born candidates. Royal Visitor (inspector general, basically) José de Gálvez was one instrument of this change during his years in New Spain (1764–1772) and later as minister for the Indies (1775–1787). In the 1770s the ratio of Creole to Spanish-born judges had been eight to three, respectively; by the 1780s it had been reversed to a ratio of ten Spaniards for every four Creoles. Of the dozen newly installed intendants in New Spain most were recruited from the ranks of peninsular (Spanish-born) military and fiscal officials, and the same was true of lower levels in the government as well. This tendency provoked one of the major grievances of the Creoles to emerge in the insurgency of 1810—their exclusion from high office in church and state in favor of men from the peninsula. It has sometimes been asserted by historians that this was the major grievance behind the movement for independence from Spain, but although its importance as an irritant is undeniable, it was only one factor among many.

Another longstanding practice associated with the older administrative structures ostensibly replaced by the intendancy system, particularly revealing of how the Bourbon Reforms worked or did not work, was specifically irksome to New Spain's Indigenous subjects. The attempt of the Bourbon reformers to do away with it in the name of bureaucratic modernization illustrates how resistant to change the arrangements of colonial governance were. This institution was the *reparto de comercio* (also known as the *reparto de mercancías*), an arrangement in which district governors in heavily Indian districts forced upon the Indians within their districts the sale of goods at highly inflated prices on pain of imprisonment or other sorts of coercion of noncompliant villagers. Among these goods were textiles, farming implements, domestic animals, and other goods, some of which were luxury items that the Indians could ill afford and neither needed nor wanted. Although the practice could reach abusive levels, if kept within accepted limits it was considered less an abuse than a perquisite of office, a form of payment for officials whose salaries were risibly low. This commerce was deeply entrenched in the system of colonial governance, serving to shift the administrative costs of empire from the crown to its subjects. The practice could weigh heavily upon Indigenous household budgets. The supervising officials generally had business relationships with merchants in towns or cities who posted the bonds required of them as surety against defalcation in the collection of tributes from the crown's Indigenous subjects. This custom reached such a noxious level in the Andean area that it contributed in large measure to a major Indigenous uprising against Spanish rule in the early 1780s, known as the Tupac Amaru rebellion. Resistance to it remained more localized and episodic in New Spain, never achieving the level of a great insurgency. The practice of the *reparto de comercio* was officially outlawed with the establishment of the intendancy system mandated by royal ordinance in 1786 but hung on anyway at the margins of legality. The new arrangements for paying officials produced salaries completely inadequate to attract good candidates for the posts under the new system, the exigencies of warfare in Europe and overseas put severe constraints on crown resources, and bureaucratic infighting within New Spain proved an obstacle to the clean application of the reform.

The efforts of the Spanish crown and its ministers to govern the overseas colonies with as little overhead cost as possible contributed to breed a disrespect for law and centralized authority. Most colonial officials had bought their posts and expected to recoup the costs as well as make a profit on the investment. The victims here, of course, as in so many other arrangements in the history of Mexico, were the Indigenous people. The interest groups primarily defending the *reparto* system, officials and their merchant backers, had much to lose in the application of the prohibitions of the 1780s against coercion of Indians, whether by debt, physical abuse, or imprisonment. What we might see as corruption, the deployment of state means to realize illegitimate private ends, beneficiaries of this system saw as the normal overhead costs of governance. This made for a porous border between the legal and the illegal and between private and public interests. All parties to this arrangement, the exploited and the exploiters, assumed that a degree of nonmarket extraction of resources was tolerable as long as it remained within certain bounds, whether or not technically illegal or proscribed. Should the extraction exceed consensual limits, legal or even violent resistance might result. This culture of impunity, evasion, and what we might call "extralegal legal practices" carried over into independent Mexico.

The Spanish crown and its agents undertook to increase the efficiency of tax collections of all kinds. Loopholes were closed in the system of Indian tributes and extended to include those *novohispanos* of pure or partial African descent. This head tax was not an insignificant element in royal income, making up about 15 percent of tax remittances from New Spain by 1780 or so. The Spanish colonial state collected this tax simply because it could do so and had done so for three centuries. The collection of sales and other sorts of taxes on the general population had long been farmed out (that is, ceded by contract from the crown for specified time periods for a lump sum) to wealthy individuals and merchant guilds. In this way the crown was purposely renting out its right to tax in exchange for a less risky and troublesome form of payment in which the tax farmer's interest was to extract as much as he could over the rental price, a common practice among European powers of the time. As part of the reforms, these taxes were reclaimed for direct collection by crown officials, while the number and rate of taxes increased. A number of quite lucrative royal monopolies were established, such as those on tobacco, pulque (the mildly intoxicating drink especially favored by Indians), brandy, playing cards, salt, cockfights, and mercury (for silver refining), among other items. Because of the wide consumption of the product, the most profitable of these was the tobacco monopoly, established in Cuba in 1715 and in New Spain in 1765. Revenues from this source came to make up about 20 percent of all fiscal receipts from the colony. The tobacco monopoly provoked evasion and smuggling, encouraging disrespect for law and spurring criminality, especially in the form of banditry; many tobacco smugglers were found among the ranks of insurgents after 1810. The most notable effect of these and other fiscal measures, making some allowance for population growth, was to increase crown revenues from New Spain from about 5,000,000 pesos in 1700 to 36,000,000 in 1790, the Mexican colony being the most profitable of all the Spanish American realms.

While the Bourbon Reforms reduced the power and wealth of the Catholic Church, they increased the capacity of the military. A large proportion of the increased fiscal revenues squeezed out of New Spain went to subsidize Spanish military presence in Europe, the Philippines, the Caribbean (especially Cuba), and the colony's enormous northern frontier, stretching from Upper California to the Mississippi. Previously there had been no standing army in New Spain, but this changed in the early 1760s. The military was professionalized through training and the dedication of more resources to it, and the militias were reorganized. It is worth noting in relation to the militia that a number of insurgent leaders in 1810 and after were officers in the militia before the outbreak of the independence movement and could therefore boast some basic elements of military training. The suppression of banditry and even urban crime was taken out of the hands of an older constabulary body called the Acordada and assigned to the army. The protection along the northern frontier in response to the threats from nonsedentary Indigenous groups, a continual problem extending well into the republican period, was significantly increased through the presidio system. In the wider empire fortified strong points were established or improved, and Spain's navy was rebuilt. None of this would have been possible without the revenues harvested from New Spain. The general militarization of the colony during the decade-long insurgency carried over into the republican period, in fact, when many of the major public figures were political generals who had fought in the independence struggle on one side or the other, and often both in succession. Among them were presidents Antonio López de Santa Anna, Vicente Guerrero, Nicolás Bravo, José Joaquín de Herrera, and Miguel Barragán, as well as Emperor Agustín de Iturbide (many of whom we will meet in the following chapters), and the list goes on.

While the military was on the ascendant in New Spain and the empire, the Bourbon reformers applied themselves to bringing the institutional Catholic Church to heel under the doctrine of regalism—that the secular state, in the person of the Spanish monarch, should wield the ultimate authority within the empire, with no interference from the Church or the pope and no competition for the loyalty of subjects. The reforms involving the Church were not anticlerical as such but political in nature. One of the most explicit and far-reaching moves to corral the power and wealth of the Church was the expulsion of the Jesuits from the Spanish realms at a single moment in 1767, an act whose immediate circumstances I mentioned earlier. The Jesuit Order was singled out for its independence and its direct loyalty and accountability to the pope in Rome rather than to the Church hierarchy in New Spain. Six hundred and eighty Jesuits were expelled from the country literally overnight, of whom 450 were Creoles, provoking a diaspora that took many of them to Italy, while secular clergy (priests not belonging to a clerical order) took over their parishes. Because the Jesuits had taken a very prominent role in educating the children of the Mexican elite (Lucas Alamán's early schooling had been at the hands of the Jesuits), the Creoles were particularly angered by what they regarded as a high-handed maneuver arising in the court politics of

Madrid. On the other hand, this same group of wealthy Creoles was the beneficiary of the sell-off of Jesuit rural properties for which the crown received
the purchase price. Other measures restricting the powers of the Church
followed, such as the abolition of the ecclesiastical *fuero*, the exemption of
churchmen from the legal jurisdiction of the secular authorities. Furthermore,
many forms of popular piety that existed at the margins of the official church
were purged by the ecclesiastical hierarchy in the late eighteenth century. But
the populace of New Spain, and after it Mexico, remained extremely pious
despite the puritanical interventions of the Bourbon state and its ecclesiastical agents, so that Mexico is still today regarded as among the most deeply
religious of Latin American nations.

Finally, the Bourbon Reforms carried out a number of changes in the commercial sphere that in one way or another would have affected everyone in
New Spain—merchants, royal officials, churchmen, and consumers all the
way from titled aristocrats and silver magnates in their near-palatial Mexico
City homes down to the level of village Indians. In the 1730s reforms recommended by Campillo reduced the monopolistic trading powers of the
merchant guild (*consulado*) of Cádiz, downriver from Sevilla, the country's
great southwestern port long the exclusive terminus of the New World trade.
The clumsy and expensive fleet system was eventually abolished in favor of
what were known as "register ships" (licensed vessels) that plied the Atlantic
singly. The recovery of Havana from the British led in 1765 to the opening
of trade from Cuba to all the ports in Spain. More expansive measures followed, culminating in the decree of free trade of 1778, not fully implemented
in New Spain until 1789, which opened most American ports to trade with
Spanish ones, although other European nations were still excluded from the
colonial trade of Spain. Under cover of Spanish shipping Spanish American
markets quickly became saturated with European goods, prices fell, increased
amounts of silver left New Spain to pay for the imported goods, and much
capital migrated from the commercial sector into large-scale agriculture
(haciendas) and silver mining, on the whole a salutary shift. Other reforms of
commercial policies followed.

A host of other changes were introduced in the last two or three decades
of the colonial regime that either reformed existing institutions or established
new ones. A new university was founded in Guadalajara in 1792, today an
enormous institution with more than 250,000 students and fifteen campuses.
Several scientific expeditions were sent to the Spanish American colonies,
some of which embraced New Spain, as well as an antismallpox vaccina-
tion expedition. The renowned German scientific polymath Alexander von
Humboldt visited the country at length in 1803 and several years later published an encyclopedic study of the colony, *Political Essay on the Kingdom
of New Spain* (1811). This canonical work made its way into the scientific

and historiographical literature of Mexico, providing a somewhat mixed but generally favorable, even celebratory view of the country that essentially became an advertisement for republican Mexico. The book was carried as a reference work by the fatally destined Austrian prince Maximilian von Habsburg when he came with his Belgian wife Carlota to rule Mexico briefly as emperor in the 1860s and is still much in use by historians today as a primary source. Measures were also undertaken to improve the mining industry with subsidized prices for mercury and blasting powder, the establishment of the Real Colegio de Minas in 1791 (where Lucas Alamán studied engineering and chemistry as a young man), and the foundation of a miners' guild with judicial functions in 1777. Serious infrastructural improvements were undertaken on roads and bridges, and the royal mail service improved. And these initiatives only begin to complete the list of improvements undertaken under the aegis of the Bourbon reformers.

JOSÉ DE GÁLVEZ AND REFORM IN NEW SPAIN

Ideas and projects may circulate among educated people and politicians, but even diffuse projects like the Bourbon Reforms, implanted over a century or so, need people to put them in place. The single most important figure in applying the measures coming out of Madrid to New Spain was the Spanish royal official José de Gálvez (1720–1787), whom we have already met suppressing the 1767 rebellion with exemplary harshness. A brief review of his career illuminates the human dimension of the Bourbon Reforms. Between 1765 and 1771 he was in New Spain as *visitador*—basically inspector general with plenary powers granted by King Charles III to carry out a number of reforms in Spain's richest colony.[11] Born in the Andalusian pueblo of Macharaviaya, today a lovely, quaint village in the far south of Spain with about five hundred inhabitants, he, his brothers, and his nephew all became very high officials in that part of the Spanish government devoted to colonial affairs. Gálvez unquestionably rose to be the most powerful crown official dealing with overseas matters during the decade from 1776 to 1787, when he served as chief of the colonial ministry, his authority embracing New Spain and the rest of the Spanish overseas realms. Trained as a lawyer in his youth, he occupied a number of minor posts in the government in Madrid before coming to the notice of high officials there. In his mid-forties he was sent to New Spain to improve the military capability of the colony in the face of possible Russian encroachments in Upper California, endemic Indian rebellion in the northwest, and the constant European warfare that had already spilled over into the colonial world. He was also tasked with improving the collection of royal revenues, most of which went to subsidize Spanish military forces in the Caribbean. After his extended experience in New Spain he ascended to head the colonial ministry in Madrid, along the way amassing a large personal fortune from his official salary and other sources within the field of his office.

Although in the words of his biographer Zepeda Cortés he enjoyed in his final years a brilliant career as "Spain's top imperial modernizer," Gálvez faced oppositional headwinds and sharp criticism along the way from more traditionalist, entrenched figures and interest groups both in the Spanish government and in the New World. These reactions were provoked by administrative reforms, commercial reforms, fiscal reforms, and efforts to reduce the power and wealth of the Church. The royal bureaucracy tended to move ponderously, slow to acknowledge problems, slow to develop solutions, and slow to apply remedies. Although in theory bureaucracies are supposed to be non- or postpolitical, the Bourbon bureaucracy, and particularly that part of it dealing with the Spanish colonial world, was highly political. Interest groups from the outside—merchants, for example—and bureaucrats themselves developed material interests that they furthered purposefully and defended ardently. This was one of the limits to Bourbon modernization efforts, and more specifically of José de Gálvez's work to apply the reforms mandated by his royal master. There is irony in this because bureaucracy, with its rationalized routines, clear lines of authority, and so forth, is one of the hallmarks of modernization. In part as a workaround in the face of such resistance and criticism, Gálvez deployed some methods that can be seen as *unmodern* and that certainly brought down much criticism and complaint upon his head during his career. The age-old practice of nepotism, for example, was a major weapon in his arsenal. He was notorious for giving preferment in the form of jobs or other material benefits to his younger relatives and his friends rather than awarding posts strictly on the basis of merit because he felt that he knew these men, could trust them, and enjoyed some control over them as the senior male in a kinship network. And of course the men he favored were peninsular Spaniards, adding fuel to the smoldering embers of Creole resentment.

Despite the political headwinds he faced, Gálvez was a forceful personality and fortunately for him had protectors in court and ministerial circles. His accomplishments during his inspector generalship of New Spain continued when he became minister of the Indies in the last decade of his life. In New Spain he encouraged the exploration of the California coast and the establishment of pueblos, missions, and presidios; his measures stimulated the silver mining industry; he made advances in "peninsularizing" the colonial government; he tightened the tax structure, thus improving the fiscal situation of the monarchy; and he put the army in New Spain on a regular footing. In accomplishing these reforms and a number of others, including the introduction of the Comercio Libre law of 1772, he was clearly following the lines of thinking laid out by the *tratadistas*. He published his own extended essay on imperial reform as early as 1759, the *Discurso y reflexiones de un vasallo* (*Discourse and Reflections of a Subject*), while still relatively young and on the rise politically. While his proposals and policies echoed those of Campillo and Campomanes, drawing a direct line between their works and his career is difficult. He did belong to the same government circles and social networks as the relatively progressive thinkers of the time and had in his library a number of the published works of his remarkably prolific contemporary, the Conde de Campomanes, including histories and translations. In the early 1770s Campomanes and another powerful politician, the Conde de Floridablanca (1728–1808), intervened in questions that had been raised about Gálvez's actions in New Spain, saving him from political ruin and paving the way for his rise to the top of the colonial bureaucracy.

CONCLUSION

Let us leave José de Gálvez to his delusions, then, and close this chapter considering the questions of what the Bourbon Reforms were intended to accomplish and to what degree they achieved the goals set for them. We must take into account the piecemeal and even ad hoc nature of the measures, initiated under different monarchs, executed by different servants of the crown, and strung out over most of a century. They were subject to changing crosswinds and headwinds—the fortunes of war, international diplomacy, and political events in other European nations. There was little overall coherence to the reforms in the sense of their having been planned out as a set of interlocking measures with a clear goal in mind, but there was nonetheless a sort of unity. The impulse for the reforms grew out of a sense that Spain had become militarily weak and was therefore not the armed political juggernaut it had been in the sixteenth century, when it defended Catholicism in Europe against the advances of Protestantism, launched the ultimately disastrous but tremendously ambitious Spanish Armada to conquer England, and reached out to extend its dominance over much of the New World. Absent significant rethinking of economic and fiscal arrangements to increase crown income, the empire's military capabilities would never be recovered except through the mobilization of colonial resources, of which New Spain was now the centerpiece. But the condition of Spain itself was also an object of grave concern and reform. It was definitely lagging behind in population dynamics, industrialization, commerce, entrepreneurial spirit, and overall living standards for the mass of the population. The solution to this "catch-up" problem was state-sponsored modernization from the top down and from the peninsular center

BOX 4.2. JOSÉ DE GÁLVEZ AND
THE ARMY OF MONKEYS

A curious episode marked Gálvez's life while he was acting as visitor general in New Spain. In October 1769 he reached the presidio (a fortified military settlement) of Pitic (today's Hermosillo, the state capital), in Sonora, in the semidesertic north of the country, commanding an armed force that he intended to throw against some Indigenous rebels in the area. He had suffered intermittent fevers since June, the medical nature of which has never been determined but which may have been aggravated by the difficult living conditions of the expedition and the inspector general's tendency to drive himself with overwork. Whatever the case, he awoke on the morning of October 13 claiming that during the night he had had a conversation with Saint Francis of Assisi, who had given him certain documents attesting without doubt to the military incompetence of the officers in the expedition. The saint told the visitor general that he would quell the Indian uprising by sending from Guatemala an army of six hundred monkeys, all kitted out in military uniforms. As far as we know the promised simian reinforcements never arrived, or if they did, it was only in Gálvez's disordered imagination. As the days passed, he seemed to grow more and more mentally agitated. The members of the expedition took him to Ures, about fifty miles to the northeast, where they locked him in a room, naked. From here, through an open window, he preached to the local Indians, who must have been puzzled by the Spaniard's florid mental disturbance, and even more so by his claiming to be the Aztec emperor, Moctezuma. His keepers then removed him to another Sonora town, Arizpe, where he declared himself king of Prussia, then elevating himself to the position of "Eternal Father," presiding over the Last Judgment. While in this disturbed condition Gálvez authored hundreds of decrees ordering implausible or frankly impossible things, such as the construction of a navigable canal joining Mexico City to the Pacific port town of Guaymas, Sonora, a distance of about a thousand miles. After several months Gálvez recovered his sanity and went on to a stellar career in Spanish politics and colonial affairs; his illness had lasted about six months, from October 1769 to April 1770. His political enemies both in Old and New Spain made hay from the episode, questioning his sanity even after the disturbance had passed. After all, if it had happened once, might it not recur? And even if it did not seize him again, what might the illness have said about his general mental stability and judgment? One witness compared the madness of José de Gálvez to that of Cervantes's Don Quijote.

It is quite common for people in the grip of a psychotic break to have their delusions informed by events or figures in their environment in exaggerated or distorted form, as though seen in a funhouse mirror, and so it was with Gálvez. Some of the references in his delusional repertoire are fairly obvious. The army of monkeys, for example, may well reflect the inspector general's worries about the capability of the armed force he brought with him to Sonora to overcome the Indian uprising—they were military reinforcements, although why they came from Guatemala is not clear. Imagining that he was the reincarnation of the Aztec emperor Moctezuma, however, may seem particularly odd, but it did tap into a sort of Indigenous shadow world of messianic expectation that popped to the surface in other Indian uprisings of the time. If not exactly a common trope for the reassertion of Indian political power against the Spanish conquerors, it was at least a known one, although how Gálvez had become aware of it has not been discovered. King Frederick the Great of Prussia was one of the most notable enlightened absolutist monarchs of the time; he brought Prussia to great power status in Europe, patronized the arts (he was a famously accomplished flautist and composer), and corresponded with some of the great literary figures of the age, such as Voltaire. Gálvez was, after all, a reformer, so what better model to which to aspire, or actually become, than Frederick the Great? And as for the one-thousand-mile canal from Mexico City to Guaymas, on the Pacific coast, in the words of Zepeda Cortés, Gálvez's disordered mind may well have been projecting "an aggrandized expression of the canal craze that riveted the imaginations of European modernizers at the time." Such a canal project, the Canal de Castilla, intended to move grain to a northern port in Spain, had in fact been initiated by King Fernando VI and was under construction during Gálvez's public life but took a century to be finished and never reached the planned length; it still exists today, and parts of it are still in use locally.

out into the colonies. In England this had been accomplished largely from the bottom (or perhaps from the middle) up, with the tracks greased by the Glorious Revolution of 1688, the political empowerment of nonstate actors, and the resulting capacity of society to undertake capitalist development. Granted, the English state did intervene in certain aspects of the economy—in building a navy, in encouraging canal development, in facilitating the enclosure movement and therefore the further development of commercial agriculture through parliamentary action, and in other ways. Spain did a little of this, but its sluggish economy could not furnish the capital and human capacities required. More importantly Spain lacked the institutional structures such as a functioning national representative body to jump-start major entrepreneurial activity, generate technological innovation, or encourage industrialization except in limited areas (Catalonia is the outstanding case). These were among the hallmarks of modernization, and the models most notably presented by Britain.

The Bourbon Reforms were undeniably significant for New Spain and the other Spanish American colonies, especially in the areas of fiscal productivity, administrative rearrangement, and commerce. But they were not sufficient to achieve the sort of changes the *tratadistas* had begun to envision and to which devoted and essentially conservative servants of the crown like José de Gálvez might have lent their energies. When one looks at the reforms from a certain angle most of them appear to be extractive in nature—the creation of monopolies, for example, to increase levels of fiscal income; of the intendancy system to foster administrative efficiency and thereby reduce colonial overhead costs; and the limited freeing up of commerce to stimulate supply and demand, and with them more taxes. Moreover, rather than tamper with more basic elements such as the structure of land ownership, as several of the Spanish thinkers and colonial figures such as Bishop-designate Abad y Queipo had recommended, most of the reforms were negative. They removed restrictions on the assumption that nonstate actors would immediately take advantage of the more open economy, but for the most part this did not happen. Even given this political timidity the reforms might still have realized important changes in the long run, and political compromises concerning the status of the colonies might have been reached. But all the arrangements were run off the tracks, first by the American and French revolutions and the reverberations they set off, then by Napoleon's invasion of the Iberian Peninsula in 1808 and the trans-Atlantic political maelstrom it created. Even by the most charitable interpretation the results of the Bourbon Reforms were decidedly mixed. The increased revenues were squandered on the military (although there appeared to be little alternative at the time if Spain were to defend her empire), and the introduction of the intendancy system created stresses in New Spain while it failed to root out old practices. In reducing the monopolistic mercantile profits associated with the old system, the freeing of commerce pushed much domestic capital into the mining sector rather than trade. The religious reforms alienated much of the population, while the clawing back of offices from Creoles to peninsular Spaniards created much resentment among native "white" Mexicans. On the whole, despite some minor positive effects in New Spain, the Bourbon Reforms disturbed social, economic, and political life just enough to make trouble but not enough to effect fundamental changes. The efforts at top-down modernization were stymied even if changes seeped into the colony through osmosis. Mexican independence from Spain seemed to many of its champions to promise the positive change that state-directed measures of modernization had attempted, but the exact nature of that change remained to be seen, most especially where the form of the state was concerned.

NOTES

1. For a full discussion of village riots during the last century of colonial rule and insurgency period, see Van Young, *The Other Rebellion*, 351–452. The apt expression "bargaining by riot" is that of William B. Taylor, *Drinking, Homicide, and Rebellion in Colonial Mexican Villages* (Stanford: Stanford University Press, 1979).

2. Juan Soldado ("Juan the Soldier"), whose name in life was Juan Castillo Morales (1918–1938), was a young Mexican soldier convicted and executed for the rape-murder of an eight-year-old girl in the Tijuana area in 1938. Many pious people believed he had been wrongly punished and was therefore a martyr. Immediately after his death a number of inexplicable events, among them blood boiling up out of his gravesite, suggested the miraculous and otherworldly powers of his spirit, unjustly martyred and therefore enjoying a special capacity to intervene between the unseen divine world and that of men. These and other such figures still attract thousands of devotees yearly to pray, be cured of medical ailments, and beg saintly intervention to resolve situations in their lives. They often leave behind them touching *ex-votos*, paintings done on sheets of metal in a "primitive" or folk style portraying the episode—injury in a car accident, for example, or the illness of a loved one—for which they are beseeching help in the form of a sympathetic intervention from the forces of divinity mediated by the venerated figure to whom the shrine is devoted. See Paul J. Vanderwood, *Juan Soldado: Rapist, Murderer, Martyr, Saint* (Durham, NC: Duke University Press, 2004).

3. Like many such icons of the Virgin at the time, the face and hands were most likely fashioned of wood, while the body consisted of a richly worked textile gown laid over a wicker or wooden framework stuffed with straw or some other vegetable fiber, and thus an ideal nest for rodents.

4. William of Orange (1650–1702), the *stadtholder* (effectively a hereditary monarch in all but title) of the Dutch Republic, reigned (1689–1702) as William III of England, Ireland, and Scotland. His claim to the British throne came to him from his grandfather, Charles I of England, and through the death of his English father-in-law,

the Catholic sovereign Charles II. An ardent defender of Protestantism in Europe, William invaded England in 1688 in conjunction with the "Glorious Revolution" of that year, which saw the dethroning of Charles and William's ascent to the throne.

5. Credited by some as one of the greatest operatic singers in history, Farinelli was born Carlo Maria Michelangelo Nicola Broschi. By preventing sexual maturation, surgical castration prevented the child-like vocal chords of the singer from developing, generally producing soprano singing voices of great range. The practice began to fade in the late eighteenth century and was outlawed in the nineteenth.

6. Eighteenth-century international warfare was also the origin of modern constitutions, according to Linda Colley, *The Gun, the Ship, and the Pen: Warfare, Constitutions, and the Making of the Modern World* (New York: Liveright, 2021).

7. Some readers will have noticed the apparent anomaly of the Spanish realms being collectively called an "empire," while the Spanish monarch was not referred to as an emperor but a king (*rey* in Spanish). The reason for this may be that each unit of the Spanish realms was technically a separate kingdom (for example, the Kingdom of New Spain, the Kingdom of Peru) of which the Spanish monarch was king. The application of the concept "empire" is simply a modern conventional usage due to the extent of the Spanish dominions.

8. Lucas Alamán, *Representación dirigida al Exmo. Señor Presidente Provisional de la República por la Junta General Directiva de la Industria Nacional, sobre la importancia de ésta, necesidad de su fomento, y medios de dispensarselo* (Mexico City: Imprenta de J. M. Lara, 1844).

9. David A. Brading, *The First America: The Spanish Monarchy, Creole Patriots, and the Liberal State, 1492–1867* (Cambridge: Cambridge University Press, 1991), 542.

10. Knight, *Mexico: The Colonial Period*, 246–49.

11. My brief treatment of Gálvez is based largely upon María Bárbara Zepeda Cortés's book *Minister, Madman, Mastermind: José de Gálvez and the Transformation of the Spanish Empire* (Yale University Press, forthcoming), and personal communication with the author, November 9, 2018.

PART II

The Tempest
Arrives: Independence

Chapter 5

The Storm Breaks

Should the Mexican struggle for independence (1810–1821) be viewed as the end of the colonial period or the beginning of independent nationhood?[1] It was both, of course, and as an epochal point of inflection its doubleness straddles the course of the country's history. The traditional way of teaching and writing about Mexican history, about Latin America more generally, and even about United States history breaks that account into colonial and national eras, typically allotting the independence struggle to the beginning of nationhood. While there is much to be said for this chronology, in the Mexican case by disaggregating the flow of historical events at 1821 much is also lost. In the early nineteenth century Mexican liberal writers, many of whom were themselves involved in high-level national politics, tended to see the achievement of independence from Spain as a new beginning, an opening into the future. They depicted the insurgency of 1810 as the active casting off of the violently imposed colonial arrangement, and with it the dark and brutal heritage of the Spanish conquest and three centuries of oppression and exploitation. The most optimistic liberals believed that independence had opened the door to a refashioning of society through enlightened governance, the development of a market economy, and forms of at least attenuated equality for all Mexicans within the framework of republican citizenship. The movement changed New Spain into Mexico, elevating the country into the rank of a sovereign nation-state, an order of polity still relatively new at the time. In the view of at least one influential modern scholar the nation and nationalism as universal phenomena arose largely from those very Spanish American independence struggles of which Mexico's was one of the most prominent—a large and debatable claim, but one worth thinking about.[2] Conservative writers about independence, among whom Lucas Alamán was the most prominent and articulate, mourned the passing of the Spanish colonial order even if not the destruction of colonial subordination itself. They insisted that there was more Spain in Mexico than the ardent supporters of independence were willing to admit and that it had great value. Mexico's tearing away from the colonial metropolis represented a sort of self-abnegation, they believed, the violence of the independence movement sending the country staggering down a blood-soaked path of anarchy and weakness. For Mexican public men following 1821, whether liberal or conservative, the consummation of independence in itself was not the problem because that was now a *fait accompli* unlikely to be reversed under any plausible circumstances. The object of discussion and conflict, rather, was the nature of the process that led to independent nationhood, the way that process illuminated the country's past and shaped its future, what form an independent national state should take, and what would happen to Mexican society along the way. Yet none but the most dyed-in-the-wool apologist for the Spanish imperial system would have denied that decolonization was a major milestone along the road to modernization.

CHANGE OR CONTINUITY?

There is no question that many things had changed with independence, although a number of Spanish colonial institutions and lifeways survived the separation, none absolutely intact. Recalling the several metrics mentioned in chapter 1 by which to assess the progress of decolonization—the political, social, economic, and cultural spheres—it is relatively easy to see that the most radically changed of these fields was that of political life. The severing of the political bonds with Spain produced a new nation-state with fixed territorial limits to be mapped and defended, although Central America struck out on its own within a few years and the northern half of Mexico was later forfeited to an aggressive neighboring republic as a prize of war. The political control of the national territory, the sovereignty of the nation, the country's at least nominal freedom of action in the international theater, and its command over domestic policies now resided within it, in the national government and its legislative powers, rather than outside it in a "foreign" capital. Where they had been nonexistent before, the practice of diplomacy and the power to form alliances became important instruments of national self-definition, defense, and strategy within the international order. Virtually overnight the subjects of the Spanish king became the citizens of Mexico, although what exactly that meant—for example, how far into the population citizenship extended, who were "active" and who "passive" citizens, and what the criteria for the electoral franchise should be—remained in dispute even as Mexico followed the Spanish Constitution of 1812 in its initial years. One of the most essential attributes of any nation-state, the power to tax, was now under the control of the national government, although this would change with the advent of the federalist constitution of 1824. The distribution of fiscal resources between the government in Mexico City and the states remained a major bone of contention, however, under the on-again off-again federal organization of the country, even while the organs of the central government were progressively strengthened after the mid-nineteenth century. Customs duties collected at ports of entry underwrote most of the national budget, serving to guarantee the service and repayment of the foreign loans that the central government contracted in abundance from British investors in the 1820s. There was now a national army, and with independence most states of the Mexican Federation developed militias that often fell into conflict with national political and armed forces. Finally, a massive alteration in political culture occurred. Monarchical rule sanctified by the Catholic Church, ancient habits of loyalty, rituals, and policies were major elements in the legitimacy of the colonial regime. When the universal Spanish monarchy was swept away in Mexico, what might have replaced it as the locus of political loyalty and legitimacy (after the very brief revival of the monarchy under Agustín de Iturbide) was the national charter on paper and the institutions of the republic, but they largely failed to do so. The militarization of society during the decade of fighting and the advent of classical liberal doctrines that introduced a certain relativistic point of view in political life, acted to undermine consensus around a new principle of legitimacy.

There were important continuities in political life, however, some longer lasting, others quite transient. During the three years or so before the promulgation of the national constitution of 1824 the Spanish Constitution of 1812 was more or less the ruling political and legal framework in Mexico. Fray Servando Teresa de Mier (1765–1827), among the most astute of early republican politicians, put things this way in 1823:

> The United States was not constituted until after the war with Great Britain ended. . . . And how did they govern themselves in the meantime? With the rules they inherited from their fathers. Even the Constitution which they later promulgated was no more than a collection of those [laws]. . . . And in the meantime with what do we govern ourselves? With the same laws that we have had until now. With the Spanish Constitution, the laws in our code books that have not been derogated, with the decrees of the Spanish Cortes until the year 1820 and those which the [Mexican] Congress has introduced and will continue to enact in accordance to our present system [of government] and our circumstances.[3]

The provincial deputations endured a long time in regional political arrangements, as did the constitutional *ayuntamientos* (city and town councils) introduced under the 1812 Constitution and built upon the model introduced by the Spanish in the sixteenth century. The legal system evolved over time with the addition of a supreme court as the final arbiter in matters of law and of increasingly elaborate legal codes to supplant Spanish laws. But while these took some time to appear, the court system of the Spanish colonial period and its legal terminologies and practices remained in place for many years. As a political force in national life the Catholic Church lost much of its leverage with independence even while Catholicism continued as the established religion of the country, but the Church remained the most widely and deeply venerated institution among Mexicans. Alamán asserted that as late as 1850, in lieu of strong national loyalties among the population, the Church and Catholic belief were the only things that went some way toward unifying the country.

The new nation's social structure, much more stubborn and harder to alter than the political because changing it was not primarily a matter of written laws but of custom and practice, does not seem to have changed a great deal with independence, although there were some adjustments. In the wake of independence ancient forms of hierarchy and compulsion were abolished: Indian tribute immediately, Spanish titles of nobility in 1826, and African slavery (already moribund) in 1829. One thing that did change with independence was the opening of some paths to upward social mobility for men of color. Much of this was a product of the independence movement itself as leaders of mixed ethnosocial background emerged from the insurgent ranks during the decade of military conflict. Vicente Guerrero (1782–1831) was the poster boy for this, with his Indigenous and African antecedents. His mixed ethnicity was a major factor in arraying Creole politicians against him and explaining his judicial murder early in 1831. But there were other men who also became politically prominent; had Father José María Morelos (1765–1815) survived the insurgency he would have been another. Men officially and phenotypically Creole still dominated the upper reaches of political life, but there were now cracks through which national political figures emerged later in the century, men of color such as presidents Benito Juárez and Porfirio Díaz. There was also by the 1820s a more visible if still small middle class composed primarily of educated professional men, industrialists and entrepreneurs, and lesser property owners.

The whole socioethnic structure remained basically stable, however. It is a misnomer to speak of "class" structure as the major determinant of where people fit into society because race played such a prominent role. Roughly speaking those individuals and families of unmixed European antecedents were on top, mestizos in the middle, and humble people of color on the bottom, with ownership of the means of production and wealth distributed accordingly. Family life, gender roles, child-rearing practices, and other aspects of the social *habitus* remained recognizable over the period of political transition from colony to nation and well into the republican era. There was no great demographic surge, and the population of the country grew

Figure 5.1. Vicente Guerrero (1782–1831), anticolonial insurgent fighter and later president of Mexico. Wikimedia Commons/Public Domain.

relatively slowly until the latter part of the century. It scarcely doubled over a hundred years, from about 6,000,000 in 1810 to about 15,000,000 in 1910, and around 1850 amounted to some 8,000,000 souls. The population of the United States, by comparison, increased from about 7,000,000 to over 90,000,000 between 1810 and 1910, granted that much of this was from European immigration. Urbanization continued to increase in Mexico but only slowly in comparison with the United States.

Change in economic life in newly independent Mexico was slower still. The weakness of the national state, the scarcity of domestic capital, and the

Figure 5.2. Father José María Morelos y Pavón (1765–1815), priest, disciple of Miguel Hidalgo, and anticolonial insurgent leader. Wikimedia Commons/Public Domain.

limited capacity for consumption among the majority of the population were important factors. Silver continued to be the chief tradeable good of the country (along with some tropical products), although at reduced levels due to the damages suffered by the industry during the decade-long insurgency. Massive British capital investment in the industry during the late 1820s did little to reverse this situation. Mexico now controlled its ports of entry, allowing at certain periods for the legitimate massive influx of British-manufactured textiles and other goods; at other times tariffs reached exclusionary levels to encourage domestic manufactures while simultaneously offering incentives for smuggling. The state could now consider intervening to stimulate the economy on a larger scale than the Bourbon regime had contemplated, albeit still within narrow limits. The attempt to do this during the 1830s with the Banco de Avío, a government-funded industrial development bank initially headed by Lucas Alamán, enjoyed only limited success, however, even though it had some positive effect in capitalizing the textile industry. There was more space for the play of individual entrepreneurship in the economy, but the unsettled political conditions until well past mid-century discouraged foreign investment and made lending (*agiotismo*) by a few wealthy Mexicans to a perennially cash-strapped government a major outlet for what domestic capital existed.

The Mexican economy was marked much more by continuity than change, however. The country remained largely peasant in its productive arrangements. As late as 1910 at least two-thirds of the economically active population was still peasant, including the rural laborers without access to independent landholdings, while the industrial labor force remained quite small. What Mexicans consumed apart from food was either produced by the artisan sector or was imported, and those very imports undermined artisanal production by undercutting it in price even with transoceanic shipping costs added in. The Mexican hacienda still retained its place as the dominant agrosocial unit in the countryside. With the enactment by individual states of disamortization laws seeking to dismantle collective ownership of land by Indigenous communities in favor of individual private ownership along more "liberal" lines, land continued moving from the family farming to the estate sector as it had during the last decades of colonial rule. The country's infrastructure saw little if any improvement until the advent of the railroads in the last two decades or so of the century, so the transportation of goods and people remained slow and expensive. National spatial and market integration therefore remained highly imperfect and regional identities strong. What little technological innovation there was came principally from outside the country. By 1860 there were several hundred miles of recently installed electrical telegraph lines in the country, for example, but the system had fallen into disrepair because of continual political and military disturbances. Widespread technological advance thus awaited the last decades of the century.

Finally, where cultural life was concerned change was perhaps hardest to track and paradoxically was both slow and fast; social status made a large difference here. After colonial restrictions were eliminated patterns of consumption for the well-off broadened with the importation of luxury goods from England and France. Our episodic guide to early republican life, Lucas Alamán, noted about mid-century that increasing differentiation in wealth within Mexico had led to a rampant materialism in the upper social reaches that he felt undermined the moral and spiritual bases of society:

> This accumulation of wealth . . . and the occasion presented by French dressmakers, tailors, and cooks have introduced a luxury so excessive that [they] . . . are the cause of frequent commercial bankruptcies. There is no city in Europe or the United States in which, proportionally to the population, there are so many private coaches as in Mexico City, and those for rent in public sites are three times more numerous than before independence.[4]

The very idea of modernization itself accelerated as the country opened up. The flow of foreign literature was no longer strictly controlled, and foreign newspapers might be within reach if one had the economic means. There certainly was an immense flowering of the domestic press, especially in the capital, with many newspapers in circulation at any given moment spanning the range of political viewpoints from radically liberal to extremely conservative.

But cultural continuity was strong between the late colonial and early republican eras. Especially for Mexicans in the countryside material life remained essentially the same over the century from 1750 to 1850. There was considerable difference here between popular and elite groups and between Indigenous rural dwellers and everyone else. The sense of Mexican nationalism was slow to take hold over the population as a whole until a plausible national mythology began to form around the heroes of independence. This progressed further still with the grafting of liberal political belief onto nationalism after the Reforma of the mid-1850s and the expulsion by force of arms of the French-backed Mexican Empire of Maximilian and Carlota a decade later. The hold of the Catholic religion across social and ethnic boundaries remained extremely strong even as more personalized, slightly less rigid forms of worship and thought crept into Mexican religious life at the upper levels of the social hierarchy. The cult of the Virgin of Guadalupe, however, maintained its sway, particularly over humble Mexicans. Gender norms changed slowly, if at all, until late in the century. Popular amusements—street dances, theater for those who could afford it, urban drinking establishments, and other pastimes—ran in the same channels they had carved in the later eighteenth century. Forms of social deference and ethnic hierarchy persisted despite some opening up of political life to men of color; there were some quirky examples of this stubbornness. Alamán noted around mid-century that after the winning of independence the attempts by radical liberals to supplant traditional Spanish forms of honorific address such as *don* and *doña* with the term "citizen," modeled on postrevolutionary France, or to institute the dating of the secular calendar from "the second [or third or fourth] year of independence" were quickly cast off in favor of traditional forms of address and calendrical calculation.

But what of the long decade of the independence struggle itself? Was it a true "revolution" as we have come to understand the earlier upheaval in France or the much later social upheavals in twentieth-century Russia and China? And what of the American Revolution compared to what happened in Mexico? Did the Mexican movement not only entail the violent destruction of a political regime and the building of a new one but also a more or less deep restructuring of society, an upending of prevailing class relations, the downward redistribution of wealth?[5] Or was it simply an enormous, sustained riot, a peasant *jacquerie*? Or something in between? It is safe to say that while the outcomes in Mexico were ambiguous—change in some aspects of society, continuity in others—the struggle for independence was also riddled with ambiguities. Revolutions are complicated social phenomena in which different groups may engage in armed political struggle for different reasons and in which the eventual outcomes may not be aligned with the goals of all the parties involved. I have for the most part used the terms "insurgency" or "rebellion" in this book to differentiate events in Mexico from the revolutions in Russia and China that have proved the modern paradigmatic cases and to which the Mexican Revolution of 1910 conformed more closely if still imperfectly.

NAPOLEON AND THE "RUNNING SORE"

But before New Spain, let us return to see something of Old Spain and European politics. Had there been no revolution in France in 1789, therefore no European-wide warfare between 1789 and 1815 and no Napoleon Bonaparte, the outbreak of the independence movement in New Spain in 1810 would not have occurred when it did or assumed the form it did; the same may be said of the American Revolution as a necessary (if by itself insufficient) cause of the upheaval in France. Counterfactual historical thought problems are typically constructed in terms of subtractions—that is, to suggest for example that had factors w and x not been present, events y and z would never have taken place. It is virtually impossible to imagine, however, that the Atlantic world's Age of Revolution, spanning from the American Revolution in 1775 to the European upheavals of 1848, would not have produced the fall of the colonial order in Mexico by some point early in the nineteenth century.

The geopolitical and military situation in Europe spawned by the French Revolution prompted Napoleon Bonaparte to invade Portugal through Spain in 1807. Then, turning upon France's traditional Spanish ally, yoked to France by the *Pacte de Famille*, the dynastic linkage across the Pyrenees of the Bourbon royal clan, Napoleon's forces occupied most of Spain itself through the course of 1808. Spanish King Carlos IV (1748–1819) abdicated the throne in 1808 in favor of his son Fernando (Ferdinand) (1784–1833), who thus became King Fernando VII. Napoleon then forced King Fernando to abdicate in favor of Joseph Bonaparte (1768–1844), Napoleon's older brother, who ruled Spain as King José I between 1808 and 1814, supported by pro-French Spanish politicians and a large French invasion force. The group of *afrancesados*, "Frenchified" intellectuals and politicians, supported the usurping Bonaparte regime in the hope that the political and other reforms introduced into those parts of Europe under Napoleonic hegemony would liberalize still-traditional and relatively backward Spanish society; thus does politics make for strange bedfellows. Large elements of the Spanish people had meanwhile risen against the French intruders, and alongside a British expeditionary force under the command of Arthur Wellesley (1769–1852), later the Duke of Wellington and a prominent conservative (Tory) figure in British politics, carried on a guerrilla struggle against the Bonapartist regime during the Peninsular War (1808–1814). Napoleon Bonaparte himself referred to this military-political struggle as "a running sore" for the resources in men and treasure it drained from France and his regime. For several years the object of ardent hope by his subjects on both sides of the Atlantic while held in captivity by Napoleon in France, Fernando became known as "El Deseado" ("The Longed-for One"). He proved a dedicated and nasty reactionary, however, when restored to the throne in 1814 after the defeat of the French in Spain; shortly thereafter that same Duke of Wellington defeated Napoleon's army at Waterloo.

The six-year forced leave of Fernando VII from the throne posed a grave question for Spanish political men on both sides of the Atlantic: What to do in the absence of the legitimate Spanish monarch? Despite other experiments in European history with republicanism as a replacement for divine right monarchy—the brief English republican regime under Oliver Cromwell in the 1650s, the First French Republic of 1792–1804—the establishment of a republic in Spain was never seriously contemplated at this time but rather the restoration of the Bourbon dynasty within a reformed, nonabsolutist political structure. Several bodies successively claimed King Fernando's authority in his stead, beginning with the Junta Suprema Central, a supreme governing council formed of Spanish patriots in resistance to French rule, succeeded in 1810 by the Junta de Regencia, a regency council. Authority finally devolved upon the revived Cortes (imperial parliament), seated in the fall of 1810 near the southwestern port city of Cádiz, on the Isla de León, protected by elements of British naval power. It included elected delegates from both Spain and its New World realms (technically known as kingdoms, not colonies), the former eventually outnumbering the latter by a ratio of nearly ten to one. What they lacked in numbers, however, the minority New World delegates made up for in talent and loquacity. During the eighteen months or so of intense debate in Cádiz there emerged a basic schism between liberal and conservative tendencies that would be carried through subsequent meetings of the parliament in the early 1820s. The liberals claimed for the parliament national sovereignty and political authority in the name of the Spanish people on both sides of the Atlantic and sought to refashion the absolutist regime into a constitutional monarchy. The conservatives, drawn almost exclusively from among the European Spanish delegates, were ready to concede some political reforms but desired to keep traditional forms of royal power, aristocratic privilege, and a limited popular voice in political life. The end product of the debates about the fate of the monarchy and the empire was a national constitution, finally promulgated in 1812.

The Constitution of Cádiz (more formally the Political Constitution of the Spanish Monarchy) proved one of the earliest and most liberal national charters but was applied only episodically because of the chaotic political situation in Spain and the Americas. Eventually it became a model for national constitutions in places as diverse as Norway, Portugal, and several Italian city-states, not to mention the Mexican federal constitution of 1824. Along with the French constitution of 1792 and the American of 1789, it threw a long political shadow over the nineteenth century. Legal scholars, political scientists, and historians have long debated the origins of the Constitution of Cádiz and the influences acting upon its construction. Karl Marx believed it totally original to Spain, showing very little influence from either the American or revolutionary French constitutions, which has come to be the consensus of many modern scholars. By its provisions sovereignty was established as inhering in the nation rather than the monarch, who became in effect the hereditary chief executive; there was to be an elected parliament based upon universal male suffrage, a royal ministry responsible to that parliament, a homogenized national (really imperial) state administered by a civil service, absolute rights to private property, freedom of the press, and other features of a modern constitutional nation-state. Roman Catholicism was established as the sole permissible religion within the Spanish state. Two paramount questions proved trickier to legislate about: the question of citizenship and the political status of the overseas realms in North, Central, and South America, the Caribbean, and the Philippines. Universal male citizenship was enacted throughout the European and extra-European territories of Spain, including Indigenous men in the New World colonies, but excluding women, slaves, and some racially mixed free men of African blood, who although they enjoyed civil rights were not citizens as such. Citizenship was a contentious issue because the total population of the overseas realms was estimated to be about 50 percent greater than that of European Spain. The exclusion of certain mixed-race groups according to the shaky ethnic assignments and population counts of the time therefore approximately equalized the base for parliamentary representation of the two hemispheres. This somewhat assuaged both the metropolitan Spaniards' fears of being outnumbered and the apprehensions of Spanish American whites (Creoles) that they might lose control in their home territories to people of color.

Where the question of the political status of the overseas kingdoms was concerned—the degree of autonomy they might enjoy within the imperial structure—the European deputies, after 1814 the restored King Fernando, and his royal ministers staunchly resisted any diffusion of political power from the center outward in the name of efficiency, flexibility, and the recognition of the rights of Spanish American citizens. In any case the issue was hardly under discussion in the 1810–1812 debates in Cádiz. When the Cortes met again in 1820–1822 a number of the Mexican deputies advocated the revival of a 1783 proposal that would have established three large, semiautonomous kingdoms—New Spain, Peru, and Costa Firme (northern South America)—each to be ruled by a Spanish Bourbon prince, each with its own parliament, fiscal authority, and so forth. All would ultimately be under the authority of the King of Spain in a sort of compound, federative monarchy or commonwealth. The plan did not get very far, but it reflected the underlying problem of what to do about the Spanish overseas realms, a critical issue by then because all were in active rebellion and rapidly gaining ground toward throwing off royal authority. The enactment of any such plan for restructuring the imperial realms would have constituted the grant of political freedoms to Spanish Americans that the king and even liberal metropolitan Spaniards were not prepared to concede. The French armies once expelled by the combined British expeditionary force and patriotic Spanish irregulars, King Fernando returned to the throne in 1814, immediately abrogating the Cádiz charter and imprisoning or forcing into exile the supporters of King José I, considered both dangerous liberals and perfidious traitors. He even reinstated the Spanish Inquisition, which had been abolished in 1812. For the next several years Ferdinand ruled as an absolutist prince.

POLITICAL ORIGINS OF THE MEXICAN INSURGENCY

Let us now jump back to the other side of the Atlantic, where things were moving quickly. The events of 1808–1810 in Spain created an open political space from which paths of plausible decisions led in several different directions. The news of the abdication by Kings Carlos and Fernando, the relatively quick French military seizure of virtually the entire Iberian Peninsula, and the elevation to the Spanish throne of Joseph Bonaparte by his kid brother Napoleon reached Spanish America rapidly. A number of *juntas* (political councils) sprang up, as in Spain anchored in major provincial capitals (Buenos Aires, Bogotá, Caracas, and Quito, for example), claiming that in the absence of a king sovereignty had "retroverted" to the political notables in these improvised bodies in the name of the people of their respective kingdoms. The question among men of the political class was where the locus of sovereignty and therefore of loyalty resided. Did Spanish Americans owe a sort of mystical allegiance to Spain itself, controlled for the moment by a usurping regime under the reign of "*el rey intruso*," whose dominance was disputed by several Spanish patriot juntas, or to the imprisoned but dynastically legitimate King Fernando VII, in an ancient, implicit pact between monarch and subjects? While there was genuine ideological and affective loyalty to the Spanish fatherland and/or to the monarchy among many of the men who assumed power in the New World juntas, there were also those who saw in the political limbo in Spain an opportunity to strike for the complete independence of their respective colonies should objective conditions permit it. Between these two extremes there ranged a variety of opinions, the politico-military situation working out differently in distinct areas depending upon the array of forces involved, the inclinations of the local populations, and the resources available to the contending parties.

In New Spain the situation evolved in fits and starts from a relatively contained proroyalist political coup in the capital in 1808 to a mixture of civil war, a war of national liberation, and a violent class conflict suffused with ethnic antagonisms. A rough narrative will take us up to the actual outbreak of the armed independence struggle on September 15/16, 1810. Viceroy of New Spain in 1808 when the news of upheavals in the metropolis reached the country in June, José de Iturrigaray (1742–1815) had previously been governor of the province of Cádiz and was a Spanish-born military official married to the daughter of the Peruvian viceroy. The political divisions unfolding in this critical situation echoed those in Spain between reform-minded liberals and tradition-anchored conservatives, but with the additional complicating element of differences over the colonial status of the country. The political redoubt of the Creoles favoring greater autonomy for New Spain within the Spanish imperial structure was the *ayuntamiento* (city council) of Mexico City, populated primarily by lawyers and what we would call professional men. The colony's high court, the *audiencia*, was dominated by conservative Spanish-born magistrates and lawyers, allied with other functionaries in the colonial bureaucracy loyal to the absolutist regime of the deposed King Fernando and those who claimed to rule in his name, supported by wealthy merchants and others benefiting most from the colonial relationship.

In the months of considerable political flux during the summer of 1808 the Creole-dominated *ayuntamiento* proposed the formation of a provisional government for New Spain headed by the viceroy, a plan vehemently opposed by the *audiencia* and other staunch royalists. The Creoles further proposed that a colony-wide congress be convened to decide the political fate of New Spain, arguing that in the absence of the king political sovereignty had devolved upon the people, a position endorsed by Viceroy Iturrigaray, who therefore came to be viewed by the *audiencia* as disloyal and subversive.

On September 15, 1808, Iturrigaray was deposed in a preemptive coup led by the wealthy Spanish-born merchant-landowner Gabriel de Yermo (1753–1813), who saw him as suspiciously sympathetic to Creole autonomists. Along with many large estate owners, Yermo had also been adversely affected by the calling in of mortgages under the Consolidación. Accused of embezzling government funds, Iturrigaray was bundled off to Spain. The plotters replaced him as viceroy with the nearly octogenarian Spanish field marshal Pedro de Garibay (1729–1815), who governed for less than a year before being replaced in turn by another Spanish-born loyalist, the canon lawyer, former professor, and archbishop of Mexico, Francisco Javier Lizana y Beaumont (1750–1811). During his scant ten months as viceroy Lizana y Beaumont strengthened the colony's military defenses, and by embargoing several estates in New Spain whose owners had expressed *afrancesado* (pro-French) political sympathies, he remitted considerable sums to the loyalists in Spain to prosecute the war against the French invaders. The major loyalist junta in Spain deposed Lizana in the summer of 1810 for alleged pro-Creole sympathies. Over the next decade he was followed successively onto the viceregal throne by three tough Spanish military men, initially appointed by the central junta and regency in Spain, then from 1814 by the restored King Fernando. These highly capable men put the Kingdom of New Spain on a war footing, marshalling human and fiscal resources aimed at suppressing a rebellion constantly mutating in goals, shape, and intensity but which they could never suppress. It must be clear from all this rapid change at the top of the colonial government that the office of viceroy and its powers were controlled by whichever political faction had for the moment gained the ascendancy in Mexico City. This undermined the legitimacy of the ruling structures in New Spain even beyond what Napoleon had managed to achieve in Old Spain and undoubtedly contributed to the sharpness of the colony's political crisis. In the longer term it also contributed to the instability of the early republican period that followed independence because it made leadership the tool of whatever faction could assert its military and political dominance at a given moment.

Meanwhile, the provinces of New Spain had begun to boil with political conspiracy. The most significant of these plots before the outbreak of the insurgency itself occurred at the end of 1809 in the western city of Valladolid (modern Morelia, named after insurgent leader Father José María Morelos y Pavón). A group of independence-minded Creole military men, priests, and lawyers, potentially supported by many Indigenous villagers of the area, plotted to overthrow the royalist government and establish a junta or congress in the city, ostensibly to keep the colony from falling into the hands of the godless French through the perfidy of pro-Napoleon elements in the country. The conspiracy was exposed and the leaders arrested and packed off to Mexico City to be treated with surprising leniency by Viceroy Lizana y Beaumont. The archbishop-viceroy sought to reconcile Creole autonomists or outright proindependence elements to the loyalists in the *audiencia*, the government, and the moneyed mercantile interests in order to forestall further erosion in colonial loyalties. Most prominent among the Valladolid conspirators was the native-born José Mariano Michelena (1772–1852), lawyer, military man, landowner, and scion of a prominent local family who would go on to an important political and diplomatic career in the young Mexican republic. Shorter-lived violent uprisings in New Spain, almost exclusively limited to single rural communities, were increasing in frequency in the preinsurgency decades, as I mentioned in the previous chapter. From just a handful every year before 1750 the total of rural riots and uprisings ascended to eight or ten annually to fifteen in the quinquennium from 1801 to 1805. And then, in the five years from 1805 to 1810, exclusive of the Hidalgo Rebellion itself, there were twenty such episodes. These outbreaks varied considerably in their details but often arose from economic pressures such as conflicts over taxes or the ownership of land or the interference of outside authorities (priests, local officials) in village politics. There seems to have been little direct relationship between such localized conflicts and the outbreak of the 1810 insurgency, but several villages, or clusters of them, were perennial hotspots before that date and came to be heavily involved in the broader violence of the independence struggle. Their increasing frequency points to a rising political temperature in the countryside paralleling the stress upon Creole property holders by the Consolidación de Vales Reales of the years 1804 to 1808, the royal measure to raise crown income for financing military expenditures during the Napoleonic wars in Europe.

FATHER MIGUEL HIDALGO Y COSTILLA

In this highly volatile political atmosphere in the last months of 1810 a salon conspiracy was organized in the important provincial city of Querétaro around the figure of don Miguel Gregorio Antonio Francisco Ignacio Hidalgo-Costilla y Gallaga Mandarte Villasenor (1753–1811). Hidalgo was the parish priest of the town of Dolores (now Dolores Hidalgo), a short distance to the northeast of the silver mining center of Guanajuato, in the Bajío region. The eighteen-year-old Lucas Alamán met Father Hidalgo at the home of some cousins in the city of Guanajuato during holiday celebrations in early January 1810. He later described the father of Mexican independence as of medium stature, somewhat hunched, with dark skin and vivacious green eyes. The fifty-seven-year-old priest was still vigorous in movement, partially bald and graying, his head somewhat drooping over his chest. This description corresponds quite closely to the clearly idealized representations of the insurgent priest, with his foamy wraith of white hair, so familiar from popular images in books, poster art, the works of Mexican muralists, and even comic books generated especially in the twentieth century as part of the mythology of nation building. Alamán found the curate of Dolores not particularly loquacious but animated in argument "in the style of the college" (Hidalgo had been a professor, after all). He dressed in the clothing common to village priests of the time, sporting a black cape, round hat, a large cane or walking stick, knee-length breeches, and a woolen jacket of a material imported from China. Lucas Alamán later evaluated Hidalgo as essentially an idealistic but incompetent dreamer, a dangerous egghead whose advanced, somewhat confused ideas far outran his capacity to bring them to reality, and who had no talent for controlling the forces he was to unleash.

Incompetent dreamer or not, Hidalgo was unquestionably an interesting man of considerable accomplishment and a broad education, formal and informal. A native of the Bajío region, he had completed his early studies at the Colegio de San Nicolás Obispo in Valladolid, then studied for a doctorate in theology at the Pontifical University in Mexico City, where he earned the sobriquet "El Zorro" (the Fox) owing to his mental agility in formal argument but failed to earn the degree. Ordained in 1778, he returned to the Colegio de San Nicolás as a professor in 1779, rising to the rectorship in 1790, but was ousted two years later when accused of improprieties in the management of colegio funds. Following his departure from the colegio Hidalgo served in a couple of smaller towns in the region and was then installed as parish priest in the prosperous town of Dolores in 1802–1803. Along the way he had liaisons with several women in serious breach of his priestly vows of celibacy, fathering a number of illegitimate children. Although not common, neither was this so very unusual among parish priests of the time, who in a nod to conventions of public propriety often called the long-term female sexual partners living in their households "nieces" (*sobrinas*). One of the unusual things about Hidalgo was not only his cosmopolitan knowledge of two or more Indian languages common to the region but also his command of European languages, French among them. This allowed him to indulge his taste for the reading of the *philosophes* to such an extent that his parish became known as "Little

Figure 5.3. Father Miguel Hidalgo y Costilla (1753–1811), priest, academic, and initiator of anticolonial insurgency in 1810. Wikimedia Commons/Public Domain.

France." Father Hidalgo was more egalitarian in his social attitudes than most similarly situated contemporaries, demonstrating an unusual degree of sympathy for the poor, especially his Indigenous parishioners. Along with ownership of his own hacienda and other entrepreneurial activities, he fostered a number of industries to encourage economic development and provide local employment opportunities.

Father Hidalgo's reasons for raising the standard of revolt on September 16, 1810, have never been entirely clear and remain the subject of controversy. He certainly had ample personal grievances against the Spanish colonial regime. He had lost his hacienda to debt under the Consolidación. He had been sacked by the episcopal authorities from the prestigious rectorship of the Colegio de San Nicolás, and as a result of being shunted off to some minor rural parishes on his way to Dolores, forfeited the pleasant urban lifestyle he had enjoyed in Valladolid. He had been hauled before the Inquisition for questioning some doctrines of the faith, although he had been absolved without penalty. Hidalgo had soaked himself intellectually in Enlightenment writings that interrogated hallowed theological doctrines and divine right monarchical political structures. But it is a long way from Father Hidalgo's personal grievances against the regime and his intellectual speculations to a massive, decade-long insurgency. Bridging that gap required ideas and means of transmission capable of mobilizing popular sentiment on a very wide basis, at least before the momentum of the movement itself drew common people into the vortex of political violence. The ostensible public justification of the rebellion in its earliest days was that the European Spaniards in New Spain were poised to hand the colony over to the usurping French government of Old Spain, and thus to Napoleon Bonaparte, whom some actually believed to be the Antichrist in the flesh. Principally feared from a French takeover of the country was the compromise of the Catholic religion, and just behind that the extinction of the Spanish Bourbon monarchy.

On a closer look these ideas become only slightly credible but were nonetheless widely regarded as established fact based on little more than rumor and a sort of collectively self-generated propaganda. The feared attack on religion grew from the representation of the French as rabidly anticlerical, priest-baiting Jacobins, an image dating from the early days of the French Convention and the Jacobin period (in which Napoleon played no role), by 1810 about twenty years out of date. The Civil Constitution of the Clergy enacted by the French revolutionary government in 1790 was a radical measure completely subordinating the Catholic Church to the authority of the French state, forcing priests to swear an oath acknowledging supreme state authority over the French Church and abjuring loyalty to the papacy. Accompanied by other anti-Church measures, the Civil Constitution was later abrogated and the Catholic Church restored to something of its former position in France by First Consul Napoleon's 1801 Concordat with the Pope. There was little popular sentiment for such policies in either European Spain or New Spain.

By contrast, the popular veneration of the Spanish king among the common people of New Spain fueled fears of his overthrow and derogation of the mystical pact widely believed to exist between king and subjects. This pact was believed to consist of beneficent protection from the king's side, loyalty (and the payment of taxes) on the side of the subjects, especially from Indian villagers. In placing his elder brother on the Spanish throne, it was Napoleon's plan to preserve the monarchical form while replacing the Bourbon dynasty with a Bonaparte dynasty. The ideas of sovereignty, divinely sanctified authority, royal absolutism, and a pact linking monarch and subjects forged a bond between popular groups and king that bred apprehensions over the long-term permanence of the usurpation. So it was mostly rumor and fear minimally based in political realities that fueled the initial uprising against the colonial regime led by Father Hidalgo and his lieutenants in the autumn of 1810. Also acting on popular beliefs and fears were other irritants, including hostility toward European Spaniards and resentments over the highly skewed distribution of wealth in the colony and the perception that European Spaniards were its beneficiaries. There was also widespread dissatisfaction with the sharp dealings of the itinerant rural merchants who roamed the Mexican countryside (many of them European Spaniards) and with the arrogance of colonial officials. Later on it would be the momentum of the insurgency itself that kept things going, the violence provoking violence in response, as well as a much more refined ideological platform, including the first attempts at a constitution for an independent Mexico. For the military men among the conspirators the overthrow of Viceroy Iturrigaray, himself a soldier with a distinguished military record, was a source of keen resentment.

Father Miguel Hidalgo had plausible personal motives for leading a rebellion while also publicizing the anxiety over French interference with religious practice in New Spain. But what he actually saw materializing from a successful insurgency has never been made clear, nor in all likelihood was it clear to him. We have only secondary accounts, and no written text, of his famous "Grito" ("Cry") of September 16, 1810. Now known as his call for Mexican independence from Spain, this theatrical episode is enacted annually by the Mexican president from the balcony of the National Palace on the patriotic holiday. The Grito was Hidalgo's exhortation to a crowd assembled around the door of the parish church in Dolores to rebel against the colonial authority structure in New Spain in defense of King Ferdinand VII and religion. It ran something like "Long live Fernando VII! Death to bad government! Long live religion!" The Grito may also have included a call for death to the European Spaniards in New Spain who had stolen Indigenous lands and usurped high office from the Creoles to whom it rightly belonged. The invocation of the traditional slogan "Death to bad government!" ("Muera el mal gobierno!") encapsulates a political program in which it was assumed that whatever faults there were in government were neither the responsibility of the king himself nor inherent to monarchy in general but assignable to the corruption and malign intentions of his ministers. If only the king knew what was going on, this doctrine proposed, he would correct it in the defense of his loyal and beloved subjects, a construction of monarchy sometimes labeled "naïve legitimism." Although the Grito as it has come down to us contained no explicit declaration of independence from Spain, my reading of Father Hidalgo's rebellion (September 1810–July 1811) is that he either harbored the idea of independence from Spain at the very start, masked by his acclamation of King Ferdinand VII, or came to it shortly thereafter. How this might have worked out concretely is a moot question because he did not survive long enough to articulate a plan.

THE MEXICAN INSURGENCY—FIRST PHASE

Father Hidalgo's "Grito de Dolores" launched an insurgency planned in a conspiracy denounced to the colonial authorities before the arrangements were fully in place.[6] The project for a rebellion in 1810 centered on the two cities of San Miguel (later San Miguel de Allende, after one of the principal conspirators) and Querétaro, in the central Mexican region of the Bajío. This was and still is a prosperous zone then dominated by the great silver mining economy of Guanajuato but also known as one of the most important bread baskets of the colony for its grain-producing rural estates. The regional population was somewhat less Indigenous in makeup than many other areas. But the Bajío was dotted with Indian villages among the mostly Creole-owned haciendas and ranches and the small cities and towns that would come to figure importantly as the sites of insurrectionary politics and battles. The conspirators believed that the people in the area, especially Indian villagers, rural laborers, small property owners, and even the wealthier Creoles of their own social stamp, would join the movement once it began. The insurrection did gain immediate traction among the humble people who flocked to the banner of the Virgin of Guadalupe elevated as the rebellion's standard by Father Hidalgo in the first days. The violence of the early weeks scared many Creoles away from what looked like a burgeoning caste war that might consume its white adherents in the course of time. The slaughter of whites on the French sugar island of Saint Domingue (today shared by Haiti and the Dominican Republic) nearly two decades earlier, and before that the ethnically tinged violence of the Andean uprisings of the early 1780s, also provided examples of the sort of hyperviolent race war that haunted Creole groups in Spanish America, always the minority among larger populations of color. One tough peninsular Spanish general commanding royalist forces remarked that had it not been for this alienation of the Creole population "Hidalgo's absurd insurrection" might well have succeeded within a short time.

Initially the major conspirators were the attorney Miguel Domínguez, *corregidor* (essentially chief magistrate) of the province of Querétaro, and two landowning sons of prosperous Basque merchants, both militia officers: Ignacio Allende (1769–1811) and Juan Aldama (1774–1811). Both were alumni of the 1809 Valladolid conspiracy who had been treated leniently by the viceregal authorities. Later other men were recruited to the conspiracy, planned to start on December 8, 1810, such as José Mariano Abasolo (1783–1816); the Creole nobleman, mine owner, and hacendado the Marqués de San Juan de Rayas (1761–1835); and Father Miguel Hidalgo himself. By August the plot had been betrayed to the Mexico City royal authorities by a collaborator in the project, but the capital's colonial officials did not at first take the denunciation very seriously and the royalist regime was slow to react. Warned of the plot's exposure and possible impending repressive measures in a message dispatched by Corregidor Domínguez's wife, doña María Josefa Ortíz de Domínguez (a national heroine now known simply as "La Corregidora"), the plotters resolved to act before they could be neutralized.[7] Early on the morning of Sunday, September 16, 1810, Hidalgo issued his Grito to an assembled crowd of several hundred men outside the parish church door in Dolores. The improvised force began moving through the central Mexican countryside, capturing European Spaniards where they did not flee its advance, garnering logistical support from local farmers, and quickly growing in numbers. Along the way Father Hidalgo seized from the parish church of the village of Atotonilco a banner with the image of the Virgin of Guadalupe, an icon of wide popular veneration that became the device of the rebellion. Later the royalist forces adopted on their standards an image of the Virgen de los Remedios, so that the two advocations of the Virgin Mary sometimes met each other across battlefields of the time. Soon capturing the important town of San Miguel in an orderly fashion, the rebels gained the adherence of an entire Spanish army regiment, and a few other regular military units would later follow. But discipline would break down when the insurgents moved on to other cities and towns. Not yet in evidence was the murder of large numbers of European Spaniards at rebel hands that came to mark the movement beginning with the capture of Guanajuato the following month, a practice that would spark sharp conflict between Father Hidalgo and his Creole lieutenants. This continued throughout the decade of the uprising, imparting to the movement aspects of a race war.

The tenor of the uprising began to change when the rebels took the major town of Celaya on September 19. Father Hidalgo threw down a chilling ultimatum to the town's defenders, many of who withdrew to the larger city of Querétaro. The irregular forces under his leadership sacked the homes of European Spaniards, a pattern later replicated many times. The insurgency's Creole military leaders abhorred the undisciplined actions of the mass of the irregular soldiery, disdaining from long-reinforced racial prejudices the Indian peasants and laborers who made up much of Hidalgo's following. Hidalgo himself would state several times that any attempt to suppress pillage by the common people or even try to prevent revenge killings for previous offenses would have alienated their loyalty. Because paying the rebels was highly problematic, looting was a form of material reward for the risks they were running. The insurgent priest then undertook the more formal organization of his forces, styling himself "Generalísimo of the American Armies," designating Allende a lieutenant general, and sending other men of his entourage as high-ranking commanders to recruit forces and undertake military actions in other areas of central New Spain, so that within a brief time his

Figure 5.4. Ignacio Allende (1769–1811), Creole landowner, militia officer, and leader of anticolonial insurgency. Wikimedia Commons/Public Domain.

forces were said to number 25,000 men or so and would grow at their height to about 80,000 by the beginning of 1811. This army dwarfed the available royalist forces but was largely untrained and vastly underequipped.

Figure 5.5. Father Miguel Hidalgo issuing the Grito de Dolores, town of Dolores, Guanajuato, on September 16, 1810. Wikimedia Commons/Jaontiveros.

Father Hidalgo's capture of the great silver city of Guanajuato on September 28, 1810, is the most famous single episode of the decade-long insurgency. It generated its iconic heroes: on the royalist side the principled, courageous, and stubborn civil and military commander of the province, the intendant, Colonel Juan Antonio de Riaño (1757–1810); and on the insurgent side the mythologized mine worker El Pípila. The city's historical and economic importance and its inherent beauty—winding, cobblestoned streets, a stock of lovely older buildings, the sites of its old silver mines, the mountain air and the light—have made of it a tourist destination and a UNESCO World Heritage Site. The object of a fierce siege by Hidalgo's forces and a frenzied slaughter of its defenders and civilian occupants when it fell, the Alhóndiga de Granaditas, the city's granary (now a museum), has become emblematic of the independence struggle as a whole.

As the rebel army approached Guanajuato in the waning days of September, Father Hidalgo issued at least one ultimatum for the city's surrender, rejected by Intendant Riaño. A former naval captain with a distinguished military record fighting for Spain in the New World, Riaño had been the chief Spanish official—civil, fiscal, military—of the province of Guanajuato since 1792. He was a man of enlightened intellectual tastes, a reformer cut

BOX 5.1. THE CAPTURE OF GUANAJUATO, 1810

Father Hidalgo's ultimatum to the city council and defenders of Celaya before his forces captured the town reflects the increasingly violent tone of the movement. The apparently deferential language ("God watch over Your Graces . . . ") is very much part of the formulaic courtesies of the time, even in communications between enemies:

Field of Battle, September 19, 1810

Gentlemen of the Ayuntamiento of Celaya:

We have reached this city with the intent of securing the persons of all the European Spaniards. If they surrender at their own discretion their persons will be treated with humanity. But if, on the contrary, there is resistance on their part and the order to fire against us is given, they will be treated with all the rigor that their resistance requires. We await your quick reply in order to proceed.

God watch over Your Graces many years.

Miguel Hidalgo and Ignacio Allende

P.S. The moment the order to fire against our people is given, the seventy-eight Europeans that we have at our disposition will be beheaded.[8]

Lucas Alamán, at one early moment an eyewitness to the insurrection, then absent in Europe during most of it, and many years later arguably its greatest historian, was himself manhandled by rebel soldiers in the family home in Guanajuato at the end of September. In his great *Historia de Méjico* he described the capture of the city of his birth in great detail, authoring a general impression of the insurgency. He wrote that by September 29, 1810, the day after Hidalgo captured the city,

Guanajuato presented the most lamentable picture of disorder, ruin, and desolation. The plaza [on which his family home fronted] and the streets were full of broken furniture, the remains of goods sacked from stores, liquor spilled out after the crowd had drunk its fill. [The mob] abandoned itself to every manner of excess, and Hidalgo's Indians presented the strangest figures, wearing over their own clothes items they had taken from the houses of the Europeans, among which were the [ceremonial] uniforms of city councilmen, and they strutted about barefoot with [fine] hats and embroidered coats in the most complete state of drunkenness.

In a more general analysis of the insurrection, Alamán wrote:

In a people in which, unfortunately, religion was almost reduced to merely exterior practice, in which many of its ministers, particularly in villages, were given over to the most licentious lives, [and] when the dominant vice of the mass of the population was the propensity to rob, it is not strange that there should be found so easily followers of a revolution whose first step was to set the criminals at liberty, abandon the properties of the richest part of the population to unlimited pillage, raise up the plebs against everything they had feared or respected until then, and given free rein to all the vices . . . . So it is that in all the villages the priest Hidalgo found such a strong predisposition, which only needed his presence to drag behind him all the masses. But the means he employed to win this popularity destroyed the foundations of the social edifice, suffocated every principle of morality and justice, and have been the origin of all the evils the nation laments, which all flow from that poisoned fountain.[9]

in the mold of the Bourbon Reforms, and a great improver of urban infrastructure and sponsor of cultural advancements. The elites of New Spain's provincial capitals and major cities were small and knew each other socially, so that Riaño and Father Hidalgo had been on cordial terms in the context of the town's cultivated literary culture. The teenaged Lucas Alamán, from one of the city's most prominent families, had known both the official and the priest and belonged to a circle of young elite men taken under the intendant's cultural mentorship. Riaño decided—perhaps ill advisedly, perhaps not—to concentrate what armed forces he commanded within the walled, fortress-like granary along with the town's wealthy inhabitants, arms, much silver and other treasure, and a substantial food supply, thus leaving the rest of the city undefended so that it fell easily. The rebels carried out extensive looting and destruction in the ensuing days, especially against the properties of those thought to be European Spaniards. But because it was difficult to distinguish a European from an American Spaniard, many Creole property and business owners either suffered directly or had European-born members of their families victimized. Royalist forces were concentrated in the relatively distant eastern uplands and Gulf coast of New Spain in anticipation of a French invasion that never materialized (at least not for another half century), so Intendant Riaño's urgent plea for reinforcements from other royalist

Figure 5.6. The Alhóndiga de Granaditas in the city of Guanajuato. Wikimedia Commons/Juan Carlos Fonseca Mata.

commanders went unanswered until he was dead and the city had fallen. In the Alhóndiga were reserves of maize stored under government aegis and released into the market progressively in times of dearth to smooth price fluctuations of the staple grain; the building therefore seemed to offer a defensible position in what turned out to be an indefensible situation. During the relatively short siege of the granary by overwhelming rebel forces a worker from the Mellado mine above the city, Juan José de los Reyes (1782–1863), known as El Pípila, was said to have tied a massive slab of stone to his back to fend off the bullets raining down on him from the ramparts of the building and, advancing tortoise-like upon the structure, set its wooden doors afire, an iconic act about which there is some controversy. In any case, the doors were burned and there is now a monumental statue of an idealized El Pípila at a site above the city. Intendant Riaño was killed instantly by an insurgent shot to the head in the first minutes of the siege.

Once the defenses of the Alhóndiga were breached, the rebels flowed in by the hundreds and a frenzied general massacre of the defenders and members of their families ensued. Hidalgo, Allende, and other rebel leaders could not control the violence, which probably also included the settlement of local grudges against the moneyed white population of the city and its environs. Historians have differed as to the number of occupants of the granary killed after the building was taken. Liberal, proinsurgency writers put it fairly low, while Alamán and other conservative, anti-Hidalgo historians suggest higher numbers. The heroic, nationalist, mythifying tradition has viewed the fall of the Alhóndiga as perhaps excessively bloody but necessary in setting the course of the rebellion firmly toward Mexican independence, much as the fall of the Bastille in Paris signified the violent start of the French Revolution. A contrary position has marked it as the frenzied unleashing of the insurgency's worst energies, a jacquerie embodying senseless violence that killed many innocents. The slaughter certainly ascended into the hundreds, and looting by individual rebels of the silver bars, coin, and other valuables gathered was extensive. A few people escaped, one of them Lucas Alamán's future father-in-law. Royalist forces arrived after a few days, too late to save the city's defenders and the people besieged in the Alhóndiga. They recaptured the city with relative ease and were able to hold it for the rest of the decade except for one brief interlude. Royalist retaliation was fierce against rebels unlucky enough to remain in town or those identified as supporters of the insurgency, initiating a pattern of regime counter-violence and repression that continued until 1821. For weeks following the "liberation" of Guanajuato, items of clothing and other goods looted from Spanish homes, businesses, and the Alhóndiga could be seen on the backs and in the pockets of common people and for sale in the city's bazaars, leading to some arrests and executions. But Creole sympathizers and collaborators with the rebels met the same fate. One young mining engineer, for example, who had tutored the adolescent Alamán in mathematics, was interrogated by royalist officers and was just at the point of being released as innocent when a note fell out of his coat sleeve indicating that he had helped to cast cannon for the rebel forces. He was promptly rearrested and executed a day or two later by firing squad in the Alhóndiga, where many such sentences were carried out.

THE INSURGENCY CONTINUES

The military struggle in Napoleonic Europe and the political ferment in New Spain formed the background of the insurgency launched by Father Miguel Hidalgo in September 1810. The highly complex story of the armed independence conflict in Mexico has been narrated by writers living during the period but also by historians of our own day. My strategy in this chapter is to sketch a very general picture of what happened rather than repeating those detailed narratives even in small measure.

The fortunes of the rebellion waxed and waned, reaching a low ebb around 1816 or so, but it was hardly snuffed out. The pitched battles between insurgent and regime forces of the rebellion's early years, moreover, had always been accompanied by intermittent but continued fighting in other theaters of action carried on by smaller contingents of rebels in the form of guerrilla warfare. This was met by counter-insurgency tactics involving locally based flying columns of cavalry, the concentration in strategic hamlets of rural populations deemed of questionable loyalty, and the selective application of retaliation and terror. The smaller-scale, more tactical military approach of the rebels tended to take over after the middle of the decade and was by definition harder to extinguish because it was a form of multipolar "popular" warfare. This tactical retrenchment was an effect of the highly localized, even "feudalized" nature of the rebel forces, which resisted centralized organization and even bred continual feuding and occasionally some mortal rivalries within the insurgent ranks. Tough line officers from Spain experienced in fighting against the French invasion of the peninsula fought the insurgents with everything they could muster. Occasional massacres of captured soldiers and undefended groups of people, and other acts of brutality, occurred on both sides, but so did acts of nobility and generosity. In the meantime, politics rolled forward on both sides of the Atlantic. Virtual military dictatorships were constructed in New Spain by the three Spanish military men who served successively as viceroy between 1810 and 1820. The rebellion itself produced its own heroes, among them Father José María Morelos, Guadalupe Victoria, Vicente Guerrero, Nicolás Bravo, and Anastasio Bustamante, the latter four of whom served as president of the republic at one time or another. On the royalist side Agustín de Iturbide and Antonio López de Santa Anna began as implacable military foes of the rebels only to switch loyalties later and dominate the national landscape, respectively, as short-lived emperor and perennial president of independent Mexico. Many men from both sides, insurgent and royalist, became prominent national figures in the life of the early republic. In the end independence came about through a combination of military exhaustion on both sides, crafty statesmanship by Iturbide and other military figures in New Spain, and the roil of political events in European Spain.

FATHER HIDALGO MOVES SOUTH

Turning his eyes toward the important provincial capital of Valladolid, lying about a hundred miles from Guanajuato in the Michoacán highlands, Hidalgo marched south in early October 1810. Valladolid was one of the more important cities of the realm despite its relatively small population of 15,000 or so. The city organized its defenses, but the European Spaniards fled as the insurgent forces approached, as would happen in other cities. Bishop-elect Father Manuel Abad y Queipo excommunicated the insurgent priest Hidalgo and his lieutenants Allende, Aldama, and Abasolo from the body of the Catholic faithful. One of the many ironies marking the independence movement is that Abad y Queipo was himself a man of the Enlightenment who had advocated certain peaceful reforms in New Spain, as mentioned in the previous chapter, and had fallen under the scrutiny of the Inquisition for his suspicious ideas and associations. The rebels entered the beautiful city on October 17, 1810, where some militiamen joined their forces. Here Father Hidalgo issued his own decree abolishing Indian tribute and African slavery, two measures in keeping with Enlightenment ideas but that might also have the secondary effect of winning those groups to the rebel cause.

Father Hidalgo's forces then advanced upon the viceregal capital, reaching its outskirts in the Toluca Valley in the last days of October. While some modern scholars have claimed that the priest's hope of recruiting Indian villagers to his cause as he traversed this densely populated territory met with disappointment, this is not exactly accurate. Inhabitants of some villages joined the force but in others local Indian officials arrested rebel stragglers. Pushing on over the range of low hills at the western edge of the Valley of Mexico, on October 30 the rebel army met a much smaller but better armed and trained royalist force at the pass of Las Cruces, which guarded the western approach to the great capital lying in its spacious valley below. After a battle lasting most of the day the badly mauled royalists retreated down into the city and the rebels advanced west as far as the village of Cuajimalpa, but Hidalgo did not press the immediate advantage by invading Mexico City. While he temporized over whether to attack the capital, he saw his army rapidly diminished by desertions. The rebel army left on November 3, backtracking north over its own path toward Querétaro. It has never been entirely clear why the insurgent commander did not lead his forces down into Mexico City. He may have feared the effects of unleashing his undisciplined army on the capital or anticipated strong resistance from royalist garrisons and irregulars there. The insurgency was never again to have the opportunity to capture the capital, with its population of over 100,000, until Agustín de Iturbide marched in with the Army of the Three Guarantees in September 1821. The fallback upon Querétaro, about a hundred miles to the northwest, was intercepted at the village of Aculco by a royalist force commanded by General Félix María Calleja del Rey, a tough peninsular Spanish soldier who would become viceroy of New Spain in 1813. The Battle of Aculco on November 7 further diminished Hidalgo's army less by casualties than by continuing desertions of Indians returning to their villages, farmers to their fields, and craftsmen to their work benches.

Now the insurgent forces split in two, Hidalgo retiring upon Valladolid, Allende to Guanajuato. European Spanish prisoners in Valladolid were executed, initiating a pattern that was soon to reach a sort of frenzy during the rebel occupation of Guadalajara. That important western city had been

captured on November 11 by a force led by José Antonio Torres Mendoza
(1760–1812), in his youth a muleteer. Torres became a major leader, surviving longer than many high insurgent officials only to be captured by the royalists and die on the gallows. While the rebels were driven from Guanajuato by
the royalists, Father Hidalgo entered Guadalajara triumphantly on November
26, 1810, there to establish a short-lived insurgent government and a newspaper, *El Despertador Americano* (*American Alarm-Clock*). Here Father
Hidalgo issued a number of decrees, among them one regarding Indian lands,
although none of this gained much traction because of the brevity of the
regime. The rebel occupation brought the unsparing execution of most of
the city's European Spaniards, carried out surreptitiously at night over the
course of a month at a barranca near the city where they were shot in groups
and unceremoniously dumped in the ravine. Estimates of the number of men
killed range from a few hundred to a thousand or so. There has also been
some debate as to Father Hidalgo's direct role in this slaughter. The massacre
certainly took place with his sanction, but much of the responsibility lay with
Agustín Marroquín (1774–1811), a former highwayman and escaped convict
who had been absorbed into the priest's entourage and into his confidence
as a bodyguard. Feeling that Father Hidalgo had lost control of his followers
and enraged by the atrocities being committed, Ignacio Allende considered
poisoning the Generalísimo, but never acted on the plan.

Father Miguel Hidalgo's downfall occurred over a two-month period
in early 1811. At the Puente de Calderón, a stone bridge to the east of
Guadalajara, Hidalgo's force numbering as many as 80,000 men faced a
much smaller but typically better-armed and organized royalist force on
January 17, 1811. The chance explosion on the battlefield of a cartload of
munitions on the rebel side created a panic among Hidalgo's men, who fled
the engagement, leaving the city to be retaken by the royalists. As he had
done earlier in Guanajuato, royalist commander Calleja carried out systematic reprisals against insurgents unlucky enough to fall into his hands after
the battle, as well as against sympathizers in the city. Brigadier José de la
Cruz (1786–1856) was now appointed commander of Guadalajara. Another
Spanish veteran who had interrupted his university education in Spain to fight
against the French, he had come to New Spain in the entourage of Viceroy
Francisco Javier Venegas in 1810. Cruz acted over the ensuing decade as the
chief civil and military authority in the province of Nueva Galicia, which
encompassed Guadalajara and much of western Mexico, becoming one of the
most effective and ruthless royalist commanders.

During the flight north of the insurgent chieftains after their defeat, possibly to attempt to secure aid in the United States, Hidalgo was stripped of
his authority by Allende, who assumed the title of Generalísimo. Traveling
with a relatively small armed force and hoping to reconstitute the rebel

army, the insurgent leaders (Father Hidalgo by this time a virtual prisoner of Allende and only a figurehead in the uprising) were captured by the royalists in the far north of New Spain, at Acatita de Baján in Chihuahua on March 21, 1811. After their trials and the curate's defrocking, all the leaders were executed, Hidalgo last, on July 30, 1811. The severed heads of the priest of Dolores, of Ignacio Allende, and Juan Aldama were all sent to Guanajuato to be displayed in iron cages at the corners of the Alhóndiga de Granaditas, where they moldered away for a decade. Some weeks before his death Father Hidalgo wrote a confession dated May 18, 1811, basically retracting his leadership of the rebellion. It is a highly articulate, dramatic document lamenting the destruction and bloodshed the uprising had brought, judged genuine by many modern scholars despite an enduring controversy over its authenticity. Independence achieved, the early 1820s saw the transport of the bones of these men to Mexico City to be venerated as patriotic relics. Today the remains rest, higgledy-piggledy, in a glass case inside the base of the monument to independence, a tall column topped by a golden angel in the middle of a roundabout in the capital's great east-west avenue, the Paseo de la Reforma. One takes one's life in one's hands crossing the legendarily fierce Mexico City traffic to the monument to view the heroic relics.

THE INSURGENCY CONTINUES—SECOND PHASE

By early 1811 the insurgency had already fragmented into many local movements headed by scores of chieftains (*cabecillas* in royalist parlance, from the Spanish *cabeza*, head) whose central coordination proved virtually impossible except for very brief periods, as for a time under Father José María Morelos up to 1815. Local clusters of rebels frequently operated independently and were often morbidly jealous of their autonomy. Actual pitched battles between opposing armies were relatively rare and the forces tiny, generally a few thousand men at most, in comparison with those deployed in European land warfare at the time. By comparison, at the Battle of Waterloo in 1815 there were 73,000 on Napoleon's side, 118,000 on Wellington's; when Napoleon had unwisely invaded Russia in 1812 his force initially numbered about 240,000 men. In Mexico relatively small irregular guerrilla bands on the insurgent side faced seasoned, better-armed, but equally small bodies of troops on the royalist side. Local defense forces were formed by both sides, the most striking being contingents of "loyal Indians" who fought for the royalist cause mostly within short distances of their villages. Weapons were hard to come by for the insurgents so that capturing them during armed engagements became a priority. The rebels managed to cast artillery pieces at some points, although experiments with wooden cannon in lieu of brass ones failed for obvious reasons. Sieges of rebel strongholds became more frequent in the later years. Among the most famous of these was the royalist siege of the fortified Island of Mezcala in Lake Chapala, south of Guadalajara. It was held for several years primarily by Indigenous people from the lakeshore villages, even against a royalist fleet of small armed naval vessels patrolling the lake waters. The island served as a base for raiding mainland settlements and military encampments in a conscious tactical maneuver to divert large numbers of royalist troops and keep them pinned down.

The disruption of economic arrangements during the rebellion was widespread. Farming and livestock raising were severely damaged as laborers fled to join the insurgency or to evade the violence, livestock and implements were stolen, and buildings were burned to deny their use to opposing forces or to exact vengeance on the owner. This of course created shortages and raised prices for articles of prime necessity. Transport networks were all but annihilated as muleteers decamped to join one side or another and the contending forces appropriated pack mules for military purposes. Funds to pay the royalist troops, silver, mail, and even food and other supplies had to be accompanied through the rebel-ridden countryside in large armed convoys that were fat, tempting, and slow-moving targets and might never arrive at their destinations intact. The mining economy was largely devastated as laborers fled, tools were turned into weapons, deep mine shafts were flooded, drainage and access tunnels collapsed, and production slowed to a trickle compared to the last years before the rebellion erupted.

Meanwhile, in Mexico City the viceroys—Venegas, Calleja, and Ruiz de Apodaca—all generals and all approximate contemporaries, succeeded one after the other in three-year stints following the short viceregal career of Archbishop Lizana y Beaumont. All three were ennobled for service to the Spanish crown in confronting the insurgency in New Spain, and all ironically for military advances against a mass uprising that in the end proved triumphant. A fair number of lesser-known peninsula-born Spanish officers also fought against the rebels for all or part of the decade with greater or lesser distinction, brutality, and effectiveness. Several high-ranking royalist officers, born either in Spain or New Spain, turned against the colonial regime in its last year or so and figured prominently in the political and military affairs of early republican Mexico, the most famous being Agustín de Iturbide, Antonio López de Santa Anna, and Anastasio Bustamante, all of whom became presidents. Nor was ardent interest in the liberation of New Spain from Spanish rule lacking outside the colony. Several US citizens fought for brief periods in the insurgent ranks, all of whom met their ends when captured by the royalists. There are no credible overall estimates of combined military and civilian casualties for the decade from 1810 to 1821, but given the length of time and the geographic scale involved, I would guess at a figure between

500,000 and a million, or approximately 8 to 15 percent of the total population. Brutality came to be a regular feature of the struggle, as it tends to do in a guerrilla conflict, with executions and beheadings carried out on both sides, but especially by the royalists. They applied such counter-insurgent policies as decimation: the execution of every tenth man in a village where culpability for some action could not exactly be ascribed to any single individual. Many thousands of rebels and suspected rebels were taken prisoner by the royalists and shipped to Mexico City and other sites for sentences at hard labor, some as distant as the Marianas Islands in the Pacific, or to Havana, Cuba.

Aside from its strictly military efforts to defeat the rebellion, the viceregal government put in place what security measures it could in the major cities of the realm to nip prorebellion conspiracies in the bud, suppress subversion and the "contagion" of antiroyalist sentiment, and control the movement of population and information. These were typical steps by an embattled regime in the face of a mass movement, even one as disjointed as the 1810 insurgency. Such efforts had only mixed results in the relatively vast Mexican countryside due to the distances involved, the difficult geography, the suspect loyalties of the rural population, and the limited human and fiscal resources of the colonial state. Although there was a good deal of subversive activity in urban areas—loose barroom talk, suspect sermons preached by parish priests, anonymous broadsides posted on walls, unguarded chats between neighbors—the cities of New Spain remained remarkably calm during the insurgent decade; they might be attacked or even captured from the outside but in general were not themselves breeding grounds for political violence. An exception to this, an important and much mythologized one, was the secret organization of Los Guadalupes active primarily in Mexico City and Puebla, which worked to support the insurgency with information and even funds. Members employed couriers, secret codes, pseudonyms, and even produced a secret newspaper. With Morelos's death the level of activity among Los Guadalupes declined notably but later revived in 1817. On the royalist side there was actually something like a committee of public security put together from officials in Mexico City, a passport system introduced, careful censorship of the press, and stepped-up policing within the city and at its entry points. Thousands of insurgent prisoners were remitted to Mexico City to labor on a defensive trench around it, the *zanja cuadrada*, but no concerted attacks materialized against the heavily defended capital. While tens of thousands of rebels were probably executed in the countryside, the colonial court system was almost totally overwhelmed in the capital and elsewhere in trying accusations of subversion and rebellion. Surprisingly, if accused rebels or subversives made it into the judiciary system as opposed to the more peremptory proceedings of military courts martial, summary execution, or death on the battlefield, many people tried in this manner were absolved. Pardons granted in the field by royalist officers and the viceroys were also applied widely. Although they could be effective in neutralizing active rebels, some of whom reversed their loyalties from the insurgency to the royalist regime, many such people repeatedly returned to the rebel ranks and were pardoned multiple times.

Following the deaths of Father Hidalgo and his lieutenants, the mantle of insurgent leadership passed to his former seminary student, Father José María Morelos y Pavón (1765–1815). Born in Valladolid (renamed for him as Morelia in 1828) of humble parents, Morelos was a mestizo with some African Black genetic mixture (see figure 5.7). He worked as an *arriero* (a mule driver) in his youth but later came to study for the priesthood at the Colegio de San Nicolás in Valladolid, where Father Hidalgo was one of his teachers. He was appointed priest of the Michoacán town of Carácuaro in 1798 and in the (clearly noncelibate) course of his ecclesiastical duties fathered three illegitimate children. (One of these was Juan N. Almonte [1803–1869], who in one of a number of ironies characteristic of the times died in Parisian exile after adhering to the usurping imperial regime of Maximilian von Habsburg in the 1860s.)

Morelos was commissioned by his former professor Hidalgo to raise insurgent forces in the south of Michoacán, drawing to himself the allegiance of several prominent southern rebels including Juan Álvarez (1790–1867) and Vicente Guerrero (1782–1831), both later presidents of the republic for about a year each. His forces twice besieged the Pacific port city of Acapulco, the second time successfully, while other notable military triumphs included the capture of the silver mining center of Taxco on January 1, 1812, and the city of Oaxaca toward the end of that year. Named commander-in-chief of all the insurgent forces by a national rebel junta, he later experienced sharp political and strategic differences with the rebel politicians who claimed civil leadership of the insurgency. His proclamation *Sentimientos de la Nación* marked the opening of the rebel Congress of Chilpancingo in September 1813, paraphrasing many of the ideas of the Constitution of Cádiz of the previous year—abolishing slavery, for example. In some ways a rather conservative document, its most salient feature was an open declaration of complete independence from Spain. There would be a declaration of independence in November and a bit later the first Mexican national charter, the Constitution of Apatzingán.

Written in the spring of 1814 but not published until October of that year, the Constitution of Apatzingán was composed of nearly 250 articles, much of it the brainchild of a liberal politician-insurgent from Yucatán, Andrés Quintana Roo (1787–1851), later several times minister in the central republican government under liberal regimes, congressional deputy, and implacable foe of the conservative Lucas Alamán. Quintana was an avid financial supporter of the insurgency, member of the Mexico City secret organization Los

Guadalupes, and republican-era journalist. This first constitution was never the functioning national charter but stands as an important avatar of Mexican constitutionalism. It established Catholicism as the exclusive religion of Mexicans, a republican political structure based upon popular sovereignty, a wide male suffrage including those of African blood, and mandated a three-branch government with legislative dominance. Quintana's contemporaries and modern scholars have debated whether the major influence on the charter was the Constitution of Cádiz of 1812, the French constitutions of 1793–1794, or the earlier US Constitution. The insurgent congress attempted unsuccessfully to secure aid for the rebel cause from the United States and moved around the country evading the royalist effort to suppress it. The body fizzled out amid internal squabbles and the pressures of the insurgency, Morelos all the while trying to defend it. During 1814–1815 Morelos turned increasingly to insurgent politics when his energies might better have been devoted to fighting the royalists. Captured by royalist forces at the end of November 1815 he was defrocked, declared heretic, and executed at the end of December. For all his ardent conservatism and condemnation of the insurgency for its violence, and for what he regarded as its political and strategic wrongheadedness, Lucas Alamán went out of his way in his great history of the independence movement to praise Morelos as first among all other insurgent leaders for his innate military talent, his integrity, and his generosity of spirit. With the priest's death what unity he managed to exert on the fractious independence movement dissipated to a large degree, giving way to smaller regionally or locally based factions led by veteran insurgents like Vicente Guerrero; these would only coalesce after some years under the unlikely leadership of a former royalist commander, Agustín de Iturbide.

NOTES

1. While the three chapters in this part of the book may be read independently, they really form installments of a single extended essay on the armed independence struggle. The conclusion of chapter 7, therefore, serves as a conclusion for the part as a whole.

2. Benedict O'C. Anderson, *Imagined Communities: Reflections on the Origin and Spread of Nationalism*, revised edition (London and New York: Verso, 2006).

3. Fray Servando Teresa de Mier, Mexico City, December 11, 1823, quoted in Jaime E. Rodríguez O., *"We Are Now the True Spaniards": Sovereignty, Revolution, Independence, and the Emergence of the Federal Republic of Mexico, 1808–1824* (Stanford: Stanford University Press, 2012), vii (Rodriguez's translation). Except where explicitly noted, all translations from the Spanish are my own.

4. Alamán, *Historia*, 5: 574.

5. The change in political regime was obviously less enduring in the French case because monarchy was reinstated with Napoleon's coronation as Emperor of the French in 1804 and the country continued as a monarchy, with a very brief interregnum, until Emperor Napoleon III was toppled in 1870.

6. There are many, many accounts by Mexican and non-Mexican scholars of the conspiracy and its exposure. One of the most balanced, detailed, and readily accessible remains the older work of Hugh M. Hamill, *The Hidalgo Revolt: Prelude to Mexican Independence* (Gainesville: University of Florida Press, 1966).

7. Ortíz de Domínguez (1768–1829) bore fourteen children. She influenced her husband to hold political meetings in their home in Querétaro that quickly turned subversive. She was imprisoned by the royalist regime in Mexico City until 1817, released, and due to her republican sympathies refused the honors conferred on her a few years later by Agustín de Iturbide. Her image, chiefly in profile, later graced Mexican coins and stamps.

8. Quoted in Rodriguez, *True Spaniards*, 123, taken from Alamán, *Historia*, I: Apéndice, Doc. no. 16, pp. 50–51.

9. Alamán, *Historia,* I: 281, 244 (my translation).

Chapter 6

Who Were the Rebels?

Following the capture and pillage of Guanajuato, Hidalgo's army contained perhaps 20,000 men, swelled to about 60,000 as it approached the capital, and counted some 80,000 at the climactic battle of the Puente de Calderón outside Guadalajara in January 1811. It embraced a heterogeneous collection of provincial militia soldiers and their commanders who had turned from the royalist cause, Indian villagers, and rural laborers and other working people of different ethnicities. The composition of the insurgent forces would change over the next decade but still remains in dispute. In the *tierra caliente* (the Pacific lowlands) of what later became the southern state of Guerrero, for example, local insurgent forces tended to have an African complexion, in the central valleys it was strongly Indigenous, while in the near north it was more mestizo. My own research findings for the decade from 1810 to 1821 have yielded the following overall breakdown, based on the arrest and other records of a sample of 1,066 captured insurgents, at a somewhat wild guess representing less than 1 percent of the total combatants on both sides. This is admittedly a tiny sample, but because of the episodic nature of the record-keeping it constitutes the best numbers we have so far.

The figures in table 6.1 show that the largest group among the insurgents was composed of village Indians. The share of Indigenous people among the rebels was very nearly equal to their weight in the overall population of New Spain, respectively 60 and 55 percent. People of mixed race made up about 22 percent of the insurgents as against 20 percent of the general population. On the other hand, Spaniards (that is, putatively "whites," whether natives of Old or New Spain) are overrepresented compared to their share of the colony's total population: 25 percent and nearly 18 percent, respectively.

Other characteristics of the insurgents together start to form a profile of the rebels. Given the overall life expectancy for men in New Spain—say, thirty-five to forty years—the thirty-year average age of rebels at capture is surprisingly high. This places in doubt the possibility that more suggestive, hormone-crazed very young men entered rebellion thoughtlessly as a sort of

Table 6.1. Ethnic breakdown of insurgents compared to that of New Spain as a whole, 1810–1821.

Source: Van Young, *The Other Rebellion*, 46.

Groups	New Spain, 1810		Insurgents, 1810–1821	
	Number	Percentage	Number	Percentage
Spaniards	1,108,000	18	265	24.8
(Europeans)	(15,000)	0.02	—	—
(Creoles)	(1,093,000)	17.8	—	—
Indians	3,676,000	60	588	55.2
Mixed Castes	1,338,000	22	213	20
(Mestizos/Castizos)	—	—	(165)	(15.5)
(Blacks)	—	—	(48)	(4.5)
Totals	6,122,000	100	1,066	100

lark, out of political naïveté, or in the spirit of adventure. In combination with a relatively high level of bachelorhood—nearly 40 percent of the sample—among the insurgents in a society in which working people generally married young, this hints at a blockage of the normal life course of family formation for many men, probably due to economic factors. Exactly what those factors were is hard to say with any precision, but falling real wages and a scarcity of farmable land relative to the rural population may explain frustration and resentment that might incline them to forms of political violence in the right combination of circumstances. Of members of the sample group whose occupations can be documented, nearly half were farmers or rural laborers, and mostly Indians. Another interesting correlation is that between the variables of ethnicity and distance between place of birth or permanent residence and place of capture by royalist forces. This is revealing because it suggests a relationship between the insurgents' spatial mobility (their propensity to move around the countryside) and their political horizon—that is, the geographical space whose security they felt invested in defending and in which they felt violence against the representatives of colonial authority to be justifiable. More than half the Indigenous people in the sample were captured within a relatively easy distance of their homes, a day or two by foot travel; Spaniards (again, whether native or European born) the furthest out; and mixed-race people somewhere in the middle. To summarize, then, the near-average insurgent was a man about thirty years old with a large chance of being unmarried and perhaps limited in his economic opportunities relative even to the modest expectations of country people. There was a good possibility of his being an Indian peasant or laborer and of his having been captured within a day or two's walking distance of his place of birth or permanent residence. I suggest here in more detail why such people might have taken up arms against the colonial state: to defend the integrity of their local communities and to keep the colonial state at arm's length, not to demolish it and still less to create an independent nation to replace it. In the meantime, let us follow Father Hidalgo's improvised army as it moved south from Guanajuato while taking a look at the local and intermediate leadership cadres of his rebellion.[1]

SOCIOLOGICAL DETOUR: THEME 1—INSURGENT *CABECILLAS* AND WARRIOR PRIESTS

Lest it seem that following Hidalgo's death Morelos's were the only armed actions occurring at any given moment, it should be remembered that fighting was virtually continuous for the entire decade, widely dispersed throughout the country, quite anarchic, and rarely stretching beyond regional limits. Father Morelos was for three years or so able to command relatively large bodies of men in a more formalized organization, to launch several "campaigns" in the sense of aspiring to planned military objectives, and to attempt the integration of the armed struggle with the burgeoning political structures of the rebel movement. Common people, including rank-and-file insurgents, experienced a much more chaotic situation. Especially important were the *cabecillas*, the local chieftains leading contingents of men in guerrilla-style combat that ebbed and flowed as military circumstances changed. I have described such men as "rough-edged . . . natural leaders in their military vocation, talented up to a point, mercurial, opportunistic, [often] lettered but substantially lacking in refinement or urban-style culture, with political views but little in the way of political philosophy or program."[2] Although as individuals they were very different from each other, most of them conformed to an "ideal type," that is, a sort of average with common characteristics and histories. They generally arose from humble rural origins and might in their prerebellion lives have been small property owners, managers of haciendas, mule skinners—in other words, a sort of rural *petit bourgeoisie*. Or they might simply have been tobacco smugglers (the processing and sale of tobacco products was a highly regulated royal monopoly that invited smuggling and fraud to evade it) or just plain bandits and highwaymen. A few survived into the republican period. Gordiano Guzmán (1789–1854), for example, was of substantially Indigenous antecedents, born in what later became the state of Jalisco. He campaigned as an insurgent in the hot lowlands of Jalisco and Michoacán, joining forces with Vicente Guerrero and eventually rising to the rank of general in the regular Mexican army after independence was won. An adherent of the liberal camp in politics, after independence he turned his home area into a personal sphere of influence; in other words, he evolved from a *cabecilla* into a *cacique* (the modern term for a political boss). He fought against the Americans in 1847 and opposed Santa Anna's last centralized dictatorship in

1854, provoking the perennial president to send forces against him, resulting in his capture and execution as a relatively elderly man in 1854. Another such figure was José Francisco Osorno (1769–1824), from the pulque-producing Apam region in the modern state of Hidalgo, a highwayman who had adhered to the rebellion. Of a tempestuous personality, ill disposed to follow orders from any superior authority, he murdered at least one other insurgent *cabecilla* out of rivalry but managed to die of natural causes on his rancho a few years after independence was won.

By all odds among the most colorful figures in the ranks of these secondary chieftains of the rebellion were José María "El Chito" Villagrán (ca. 1785–1813) and his father Julián (ca. 1760–1813). El Chito was described by a royalist official of the time as "a man most criminal; a delinquent by trade; a public, open, and famous thief; bold, disrespectful, resistant to justice; a rotten member of the body politic that should be cut off from it forever"—and that was just on his good days. Born about 1785 in the town of Huichápan in the modern state of Hidalgo, to the north of Mexico City, Villagrán was the son of Julián Villagrán, the patriarch of a moderately well-off family of mule drivers and small merchants related to a number of other extended clans. The relations among these extended rural clans were described by the Spanish soldier José de la Cruz as an "inextricable tangle of families" (*inextricable maraña familiar*). Self-styled "Julián I, Emperor of the Huasteca," the elder Villagrán mobilized a force composed of kinsmen, employees, other local men of similar social standing, and Indian villagers. He refused to accept orders from any of the political leaders of the insurgency, including Father Morelos, was known to have liquidated at least one insurgent rival, and worked closely with his son El Chito in actively engaging royalist forces in the region from their base in Huichápan. El Chito was basically a village bully and delinquent who was having an affair with a local married woman on the eve of Hidalgo's rebellion. When the cuckolded husband, a local hacendado and minor government official, caught the couple almost *in flagrante delicto* on September 20, 1810, El Chito stabbed him to death; the unfaithful wife and her children were dispatched by authorities to the capital for a period of detention in a female house of reclusion. Jailed while awaiting trial for his crime, El Chito was liberated by his father a few days after the insurgency erupted and the accumulated evidence for the prosecutorial case against him destroyed. Father and son fought side by side for nearly three years until El Chito was captured by the royalists in May 1813. When an officer proposed to Julián Villagrán that his son's life would be spared if he (Julián) gave himself up under a guarantee that he would receive a royal pardon, he refused the offer and El Chito was executed in May 1813, followed by the death of his father a month or so later. Among the ranks of the leadership and the common insurgents there were many men of principles, integrity, and a sort of nascent patriotism, but royalist bullets mostly tended to ignore the distinction between them and the shadier characters.

When Julián Villagrán was told that his son El Chito's life would be spared if he offered himself to royalist authorities for a pardon and laid down his arms, he is reputed to have replied, "I told those gentlemen that I am not so . . . naïve, nor such a child as to believe in the guarantee they propose, because I know only too well that when they capture me they will shoot me for the many injuries I have done them; and as far as my son is concerned, let them decapitate him; there are many women to bear sons, but I have only one fatherland."

The Catholic priest who probably authored the following letter to his ecclesiastical colleague in Chito Villagrán's name was by no means exceptional among the ranks of the insurgents. Father Hidalgo himself, of course, was a provincial parish priest, albeit of an elite background within the Church, cosmopolitan intellectual tastes, a very high educational level, and somewhat radical political sympathies. More typical of rebel priests was Father Morelos, but there were more such men of the cloth than one might think (and this is to say nothing of cloistered nuns). In New Spain in 1810 there were about 4,200 secular clergymen, as I noted in chapter 2—that is, parish priests for the most part, but also members of the upper Church hierarchy, members of cathedral chapters, etc. Hundreds more churchmen lived in monastic establishments of the various regular orders—Franciscans, Dominicans, Agustinians, etc. My own estimate is that at least 80 percent of these men remained loyal to the colonial regime during the insurgency, but that leaves many of ambivalent or outright insurgent loyalties. One experienced royalist officer, in characterizing the priests of Guadalajara early in the insurgency, described many as ostensibly loyal to the regime but as insurgent in their hearts (*insurgentes de corazón*). The royalist military commander of the important Bajío region in the center of the country put the problematics of clerical loyalty this way in a letter to Viceroy Apodaca early in 1817:

> The rebellion is a pernicious contagion which, in the manner of a pestilent epidemic, infects all those who continue much time in affected areas, although in the beginning they may have had the luck to remain loyal for some time. There are many examples of this truth among the secular and regular clergy who, having been either in favor of the King's cause, indifferent, or at least not openly rebels, continue to live in insurgent areas, where the extortions of the rebels, the liberty of social customs, a few worldly things gained, and above all the continual bad example [of the rebels] have inclined some to come out openly in favor of the rebellion, others previously neutral to join the rebel cause, and even those who were loyal to vary so in their political opinions that from true loyalists they become perjurers and rebels.

BOX 6.1. CHITO VILLAGRÁN
ON THE INSURGENCY

Some of the more important *cabecillas* traveled with entourages, often including a rebellious priest or two. On April 14, 1812, Field Marshal José María "El Chito" Villagrán sent a long letter to the priest of a village his forces had captured, demanding that if all the European Spaniards of the village did not immediately present themselves before him with their weapons he would raze the town. The long letter, only short passages of which can be presented here, sets out some of the ideological underpinnings of the rebellion against Spanish rule, including the idea that the French under Napoleon threatened Catholicism, that they had usurped Ferdinand VII's legitimate sovereignty, and even suggests elements of anti-Semitism. It is implausible that Villagrán authored the letter himself due to its elaborate counter-factual reasoning and its theological and historical references. More probably it was written by a priest in his entourage but almost certainly reflects his thinking and that of men who followed him and other insurgent chieftains:

I ask you . . . upon what basis rest the censures [that is, excommunication] fulminated against Señor Hidalgo and those who follow his party by the Holy Tribunal and the so-called Bishop of Valladolid [the unconfirmed Bishop Abad y Queipo]? If the Church does not hurl anathemas against the infamous Napoleon because, being a Corsican, he takes control of the Kingdom of France, nor against his brother Joseph who was crowned in Spain . . . why does it hurl anathemas against a nation that, to maintain pristine the Catholic Religion it professes, takes up arms to demand and acquire the rights usurped from it so long ago, to throw off a tyrannical government, and to take unto itself the sovereignty of its King, don Fernando, whom Napoleon and his emissaries (most of the Europeans in New Spain), after persecuting and almost decapitating, are trying to despoil of his rights? . . . [F]inally we should prepare to defend ourselves because all this threatened total ruin to our Religion. . . . Ah, Father Priest, how little you know of this matter of the Catholic, Christian American Nation of today! . . . Assume that not Saint Thomas the Apostle but the Europeans brought the faith to these regions, but seeing that they intend to destroy that which they have built, it is necessary to persecute them and drive them out. The Jews were the people beloved of God, those entrusted with the [true] Religion, and from whom the Messiah came, but not because of that do we forbear to burn them when we see them.

With few exceptions, priests in the upper reaches of the Church hierarchy remained loyal, so rebels were much more likely to be found among village clergy and less among those living in urban areas. Often, however, when their villages were under attack or menaced by the rebels, priests abandoned their flocks and fled to the relative security of cities. The sort of painful dilemma this situation might create—to stay or flee—is vividly demonstrated in a letter written from the priest of a small pueblo to the dean and chapter of the Mexico City cathedral in late December 1811: "The insurgents (according to general opinion) are approaching this pueblo [and will be here] within a few hours or days because there is no force to resist them. To oppose them is [the greatest] temerity; to surrender, disloyalty; and to abandon my sheep to the jaws of the wolf is out of keeping with my vocation. Therefore, Your Illustrious Lordships must tell me what I must do."

Both sides of the struggle saw their warrior priests—clergymen who actively took up arms, typically in command positions. The formidable rebellious young cleric Father José María Mercado (1781–1811), for example, after a stellar educational career in Guadalajara and having attracted much favor from the bishop of that city, took up the parish of Ahualulco, near Tequila. Of strong insurgent sympathies, he waited two months to join the rebellion but in mid-November gathered a force of like-minded men after the rebel capture of Guadalajara and undertook serious campaigning on the west coast. He captured the important coastal town of Tepic, then moved on to San Blas, a major Pacific port to the north, sending several dozen captured royalist cannons to Father Hidalgo's aid. When a counterforce of loyalists led by the local priest recaptured San Blas from the rebels in January, Father Mercado's brief but noteworthy insurgent career ended when he fell down a ravine while attempting to escape. In an act of gratuitous brutality showing how deep political enmities could run between insurgent and royalist clergymen, the priest who had spearheaded the ousting of rebel forces from San Blas had Mercado's corpse publicly whipped before interring him. On the opposing side of the conflict we have the fairly representative example of the priest José Francisco Alvarez, from the Zacatecas area, known simply as "el cura [the curate] Alvarez," noted both for his unusual height and his bellicosity. Beginning as the commander of an ad hoc smaller force he eventually rose to the rank of (salaried) captain in the royalist provincial militia in 1813. Arrogant, irascible, and disinclined to honor the authority of his military superiors, Alvarez was nonetheless an effective anti-insurgent commander. Spanish General José de la Cruz wrote to Viceroy Calleja of Alvarez that one "must swallow one's spit" in dealing with him, continuing, "He imposes taxes, appropriates livestock, allows the sack [of estates and villages] to please his troops, and without commending their souls to God or the Devil executes those [captured rebels] he should pardon, and pardons those who do not deserve it. Such are the reports I have of this Saint-Patriot-Priest."

SOCIOLOGICAL DETOUR: THEME 2— THE QUESTION OF MOTIVATION

The most difficult question to answer about the Mexican independence movement concerns the motivations of ordinary people to become involved in the insurgency. This is not a problem if one takes more or less at face value the traditionally accepted explanation for wide popular participation in the struggle. In this scenario humble people sought to throw off the yoke of Spanish colonial oppression and exploitation, the corollary being that they desired ardently to make a nation-state called Mexico, or something along that line. In this formulation the instrument to achieve these goals was the formation of a cross-ethnic, cross-class alliance joining individuals of the Creole elite with people of color—the vast majority of New Spain's population, made up of Indigenous people and varying mixtures of European, Indigenous, and African stocks. One may subsume somewhere here the yearning of some rebels and their supporters, primarily peasants and rural laborers, to appropriate productive resources from the wealthy and the desire of at least some Creoles to wrest back positions of political power from European Spanish overlords. Throw in the fear that the godless French would mortally attack Catholic belief and institutions and one has pretty well described the conventional view of the gamut of motives. But there are several problems with this structure of explanation. For one thing, only after the struggle resulted in the severing of ties with Spain in 1821 was that decade-long political and armed conflict seen to approximate the form of a "movement." While it was going on the struggle against the colonial regime was in fact so fragmented, uncoordinated, and even internally divided against itself that calling it a "movement" stretches the term to a breaking point. To understand events in New Spain this way imputes the motives to the outcome. This is, in essence, a technique of reverse social engineering upon which historians often rely absent other forms of evidence. While this may produce a "truth" because there were certainly *some* people striving toward independent nationhood, it may also just be a conveniently neat explanation that masks a much more complex, even contradictory reality. These critical comments are not meant to deny the presence, even the importance, of protonationalist or outright nationalist ideology among humble people, especially Indigenous insurgents, that some very good historians have emphasized.[3] But it is to insist that people can act out of multiple motives that jostle each other and may even be contradictory, and in which one idea may take precedence over another—in this case allegiance to place and the knotted associations of personal and community identity over aspirations to claim a national identity.

Second, some historians have suggested that an important component of the insurgency was an agrarian rebellion; that is, a violent uprising by peasants to redress age-old inequities in the distribution of land. It is true that during the insurgency some land was seized, rural estates were occasionally attacked, and other property was appropriated during the pillage of towns and villages captured by the rebels. Here we get into a very complicated issue, however, because the majority of large landowners were certainly not European-born Spaniards, but Creoles. Had there consistently been attacks against these rural estates, they therefore would have had little to do with independence and more to do with a civil conflict between haves and have-nots. There is very little direct evidence, however, that the insurgency was primarily a violent agrarian uprising by angry peasants and laborers in the way this would show up in the Mexican Revolution of a century later. While most of the rebels during the decade of the insurgency were peasants and other rural people, the rebellion itself was not principally an agrarian rebellion whose goal, however diffuse, was to restructure rural property relations in favor of the poor and dark-skinned even if economic want played a role in motivating rural dwellers.

Third, there is much merit in the argument that Creoles—that is, Mexican-born whites—sought to recoup the political power to determine the destinies of their *patria*. That control had been much reduced by the Bourbon monarchy's drive to rationalize—to "imperialize"—colonial structures of authority and to squeeze more fiscal resources out of New Spain to support Old Spain's European position. During the seventeenth century Spanish power had ebbed due to the decline of silver mining while the costs of empire had relatively increased due to the monarchy's political and military overextension in Europe. Much political power had devolved onto the American colonies through the crown's efforts to close gaps in its fiscal resources through such mechanisms as the auctioning of political posts to ambitious Creoles in New Spain and elsewhere. With the accession of the Bourbons to the Spanish throne after 1715 the political and bureaucratic pendulum swung in the other direction after 1750 or so as the monarchy sought to recover power that had gradually slipped from its hands by replacing Creole political, military, and ecclesiastical officials with European Spaniards. Such a policy naturally bred resentment among the Creole elite whose sons expected preferment in such offices. The problem with embracing this explanation for the rebellion is that it does not plausibly account for popular participation, especially that of the Indigenous villagers who made up the majority of rebels over time. For what would such people have gained from the rebranding of political office from Spanish colonial to Mexican national?

Let us descend briefly to the most granular level of people's experience to present a sampler of why and how individuals joined the insurgency, relying on the first-person testimony of those individuals themselves but reserving Indigenous villagers in general for discussion as a special case. Many individuals were drawn into the epic struggle in New Spain through friendship, kinship, and romantic attachment—for shorthand purposes, love. For example, there was the case of José Mariano de la Piedra, a married native of the Canary Islands captured by the royalists in September 1812 and executed by garroting (a form of mechanical strangulation) shortly thereafter. De la Piedra had joined the insurgency as a rebel tax collector mainly on the basis of a personal relationship with Father Morelos. Captured letters traced to him, written to Morelos in 1811 and 1812, demonstrated very little knowledge of insurgent ideology or concern with larger political objectives as opposed to the warmest and most intimate interpersonal relationship, so that his motives seem to have fallen into the affective category. Another instance among many is that of the fifty-eight-year-old Indian laborer Agustín Nasario, captured near the town of Cuautla in March 1812, who claimed that he had joined the rebel ranks to search for his son. Similarly, the friar José Mancilla, of the Franciscan monastery in the town of Toluca, captured after the Battle of las Cruces in November 1810, insisted that his only motive in joining the insurgency was to search for his thirteen-year-old brother. Or take the case of the young José María Canseco, a twenty-four-year-old unmarried blacksmith physically dragged into service by his father Joaquín Canseco, a *cabecilla* commissioned a colonel in the insurgent forces by Father Hidalgo himself. A number of credible witnesses testified that despite physical beatings and even imprisonment the younger Canseco had refused to participate actively in attacks on royalist forces but was nonetheless captured and accused of rebellion in 1811. Joaquín Canseco had offered in a letter to his son to come with a force to liberate him, but in an angry and emotional reply to his father the younger man refused:

> Your heart is not moved to compassion or charity either by my supplications or the imprisonment of me or my beloved brother. . . . You well know that I joined you only to be with my dear mother (. . . who if not dead, has not far to go . . .), and beloved sisters and you also know what it cost you to make me return when

I had fled to the Hacienda de Génguaro, when you gave the order that if I did not come back on my own they bring me back dead or alive, and with a bullet in me if necessary. . . . But in the end, beloved father, if being the cause of my ruin, and that of all my sisters and brothers and mother, does not convince you [to seek a pardon], perhaps you will be moved by considering that finally they will capture you as they did the priest Hidalgo, Allende, and many others who fell into their company.[4]

Documented in an unusually revealing way is the soap opera–like saga of the twenty-seven-year-old Creole law student and insurgent officer Joaquín Cárdenas of the town of Sayula in western New Spain, executed for high treason in mid-April 1811. He was swept into the rebellion by his love for the daughter of the major insurgent chieftain Rafael Iriarte (1772?–1811). Cárdenas had met the Iriarte family in 1809 while he was pursuing his law studies in Mexico City, falling almost instantly and passionately in love with one of the family's daughters, María Antonia. Lending support to the impoverished family, he followed them to the Bajío town of Acámbaro where he fell in as a sort of aide-de-camp to Rafael Iriarte, who joined the rebellion in its earliest weeks. Iriarte himself had an interesting history. There is some evidence of his involvement with the Querétaro conspirators, and thus being an early adherent of the rebellion. He became for a time the dominant rebel commander in the Zacatecas-San Luis Potosí area, considered going over to the royalist side, fell out with Ignacio Allende in the winter of 1810–1811, and may have attempted to kill him. His refusal to bring his forces to the support of Hidalgo at the climactic Battle of Calderón in January 1811 may well have contributed to the priest's disastrous defeat in that action and certainly earned Iriarte the fatal enmity of Allende. He was eventually executed by the insurgent leader Ignacio López Rayón (1773–1832) carrying out a direct posthumous order of Allende's, one of many fatalities within the fissiparous insurgent ranks. The young law student Cárdenas managed to evade active involvement with the rebels for several weeks while in the town of Acámbaro even though his own sympathies might well have been with the rebel movement. Eventually Iriarte named him a captain in the insurgent ranks, a position that several credible witnesses claimed the young swain had only reluctantly accepted to avoid the wrath of his beloved's father and to maintain his proximity to her. This cat and mouse game continued for a number of months until Joaquín Cárdenas's capture. The young man's letter to Iriarte was vacuumed up with some other documents in the possession of members of the *cabecilla*'s former band. Full of bitter recrimination, the letter detailed the physical beatings and other injuries suffered by Cárdenas at Iriarte's hand and the older man's harsh rejection of the younger's honorable intentions toward his daughter, including a threat to kill him if his attentions to María Antonia did not cease.

Other individual motives for becoming embroiled in the rebellion included simple suggestibility and peer pressure, curiosity, and want. Antonio Laureano Salazar, for example, a horse handler for a time under the command of the Father Mercado whom we have seen falling to his death down a gorge, insisted "that not only I, being a simple rustic, but many others who are not, were deluded by the partisans of insurrection." This statement suggests an almost agentless, guileless vulnerability of the man to the power of political seduction, peer pressure, and example—perhaps credible, perhaps not. Yet another captured insurgent, a twenty-seven-year-old Indian distillery worker from the town of Mescala, claimed that he became involved "to get the rebels off [my] back; and because [I] saw that [my] entire village had rebelled, [I] did the same thing." Curiosity drew some men, as it did the

BOX 6.2. A LOVELORN LAW STUDENT WRITES TO AN INSURGENT CABECILLA

Joaquín Cárdenas's letter to Rafael Iriarte was penned in March 1811, a month or so before the young man's execution. It is both ardent, restating this love for the rebel leader's daughter, and recriminatory, railing at the unjust treatment the young man had received from Iriarte. It read in part:

The services I did for you and the family for a year in Mexico City— how have they been repaid? My having abandoned my career for the family and you—how has that been compensated? With a thousand felonies . . . . What [did I gain] from having entered Guanajuato after your family while Calleja was furiously wading in blood [of the rebels]? What from having brought [the family] to you at Aguascalientes? What from having gone to spy on the enemy forces in Guadalajara? . . . What for having accompanied you to Saltillo with no other motive than love [for María Antonia], and for being resolved to accompany you to Hell itself? . . . My payment for all this has been . . . having you tell me that if I did not go along with you I would be shot . . . . Who has served you like me? No one. Who [except me] has not become rich at your hand? No one. And what [resources] have I to return to Mexico City and continue my interrupted career?

twenty-eight-year-old Indian carpenter José Juan de Dios Osorio, who had deserted with a number of other workers from the royal gunpowder works near the capital in mid-December 1811, ended up working for wages for the rebels, and was arrested by the royalists upon his return to his home in Mexico City. His lawyer argued that "as the Indian [Osorio] himself says, he is inclined toward novelty [for its own sake], and to do what others do, acting mechanically (*maquinalmente*)." Still other men joined the rebellion for economic reasons, hoping to bridge the hard times or even get a leg up economically in years during which the colony was experiencing harvest failures and the dislocation of workers. Illustrative is the case of José María López, a twenty-four-year-old married mine worker captured by the royalists in January 1811. Without work in his home district, in mid-1810 he had gone to search for employment in "the mines of Oaxaca" and finding himself in Puebla in August 1810 signed up as a royalist soldier. Eventually he had deserted and while returning to Mexico City was captured, condemned to hard labor in Havana while awaiting a general pardon, and before ever leaving for Cuba died while laboring with other condemned insurgents on the capital's fortifications in the fall of 1812. Such stories could be multiplied thousands of times, although they tended to fall into a few broad categories. Again, they do not necessarily suggest that humble people were without ideological motivation or knew nothing of politics but that many joined the insurgency out of purely personal and circumstantial reasons, while yet others had an amalgam of personal and political motives not easy to tease apart.

SOCIOLOGICAL DETOUR: THEME 3—INDIANS

I have set apart for separate treatment the question of participation of Indigenous people *as a group* in the decade-long insurgency. The documentary evidence does not tell their entire story or even the better part of it. Whole villages, while they seldom rose in rebellion as one person, were nonetheless repeatedly or almost continually wracked with antiregime violence. Some pueblos were trouble spots where collective violence spanned the late colonial and early national periods, displaying many of the same social characteristics across several decades and a history of collective violence that might dispose them to future violence. This suggests that similar forces were at work in and on them over long periods, casting doubt on the idea that a desire for independence as such motivated them to join their voices, bodies, and weapons to the insurgency of 1810–1821. Nor was it rare that villages might split down the middle, men of one part following the insurgents, those of the other remaining loyal to the Spanish crown and even taking up arms on the king's behalf as royalist militia. In such instances the division in village loyalties reflected some other tension within the community than whether independence from Spain was desirable or not. The splits might reflect conflicts among extended clans in villages substantially endogamous in marriage patterns or tensions over land ownership and the resulting differentiation in wealth between one group and another. Also figuring in such divisions were political battles internal to the village itself, sometimes overlaid with intergenerational struggles between a young generation of political aspirants and a gerontocracy of power holders. Or all of these might occur in combination.

It is a fact widely attested by historians and anthropologists that the bonds of community were, and are still, strong among village-dwelling Indigenous peasants in Mexico. This is by no means to say that such diminutive polities, "part-societies with part-cultures" as the anthropologist George Foster put it years ago, were as smooth as billiard balls, having no internal fissures or conflicts. Under normal circumstances, however, the agglutinative forces were stronger than the divisive ones, and social mechanisms evolved over time to contain stresses that might endanger internal solidarity. Collective action of some sort for common purposes was more likely to characterize Indigenous villages because of their strong (although not invulnerable) corporate structures even if they demonstrated splits along pro-and antiregime lines. There were a number of reasons for this. The strong identification of an individual with the community of birth was one. For example, the statistical tendency for Indian rebels to operate within a shorter distance of their birthplace or permanent community of residence differentiated them from other ethnically identifiable groups. Furthermore, a robust tradition of village celebratory life kept people close to their villages. This local religious culture might include church services, holidays, membership in confraternities, the festive observance of a village saint's day, etc., all of which reinforced intracommunity bonding and the attachment of individuals to their places of residence.

Anthropologists have hypothesized that the civil-religious hierarchy, or the "ladder system" as it has sometimes been known, was a "leveling" mechanism that by burning off accumulated material wealth in festive and celebratory events prevented the development of internal economic differentiation within peasant communities that might create unbridgeable gaps between rich and poor. On the other hand, the prestige attached to such practices was a type of human and spiritual capital acquired over years that tended precisely in the opposite direction, that of differentiation and therefore of the accumulation of power and prestige. The "leveling" and "hierarchizing" conceptions are not necessarily incompatible with each other, however, because their dual action would remove competition and accumulation from the economic to the nonmaterial sphere, a sort of conversion of energy in which an individual passed from the realm of Mammon to that of the (at least minimally) Divine. The civil-religious hierarchy itself was a very concrete manifestation of the intimate relationship between political and religious life in such communities—what I have referred to as the "double helix" of politics and religion forming the basis of village life. This makes all the clearer how the real or imagined threat of godless French domination of New Spain might be seen as menacing not only religious belief and practice but also the actual existence of small rural communities. This lent bite to the deadly brew of humble people's antagonism toward peninsular Spaniards and the wobbling structure of the colonial state itself. Finally, until the mid-nineteenth century most Indigenous communities owned property in common in addition to whatever private farming land individuals possessed. These property rights had been widely recognized by the Spanish crown from early on and in many cases were documented by ancient land titles, litigation records, and boundary maps and markers stretching back to the sixteenth century or even to preconquest times. Some of this might be repartitional farming land—that is, owned by the community as a whole but worked by individual families, technically inalienable and subject to periodic redistribution. Other parts of the land might be village commons dedicated to the pasturage of animals, wood collection, and the support of craft activities (clay digging for pottery, for instance) available to all householders in the community or rented out to produce village income.

Indian villages also enjoyed a great deal of political autonomy and control over their own affairs, and this autonomy was under threat by the Bourbon Reforms and by Mexico's internal economic and demographic situation in the late eighteenth century. Indian farming villages were fully integrated into the colonial state in many ways, it is true. These relationships included market linkages, in large part for the sale of their labor, but also small surpluses of farming production; their access to the colonial court system and embeddedness in administrative structures; and relation to the Catholic Church. There were non-Indian officials at various levels to administer colonial laws, adjudicate major crimes, collect the tribute payable by Indigenous adults, and oversee other activities where Indigenous people interacted with the colonial state. And such communities were notoriously litigious, especially when it came to asserting and defending land ownership either within the village, with neighboring settlements, or with non-Indian landowners. The platform of village autonomy, however, included a political life dominated by descendants (authentic or nominal) of local family dynasties considered a minor kind of nobility, people known as *caciques*, who functioned as chief magistrates or governors, although this habit of governance was somewhat diluted in many localities by the late colonial period. But even absent such authority figures the communities were certainly gerontocracies, that is, small polities in which political control over local affairs rested in the hands of senior men. These villages typically had their own form of town council (*cabildo*) and some electoral procedures that rotated office among eligible male household-ers. Except in the smallest hamlets, which as *sujetos* (subordinate settlements) would have been subject to the control of larger villages, there would have been a church, or at least a chapel, presided over by a resident priest or curate. Or they might be attended by a priest who rode circuit in an area and passed regularly through smaller settlements to perform weddings, baptisms, and other religious rites. The point of all this is to suggest that although there might be tensions or even open conflicts within Indigenous peasant commu-nities, the bonds that held such communities together were quite strong. The attachments to town or village of individuals, their identification as *vecinos* (householders), were likely to be among the strongest affective ties in their lives aside from the claims of the nuclear family unit—multistranded iden-tifications embracing place, extended kinship, subsistence, position in the political world, and religion.

The autonomy, the very integrity of Indigenous peasant communities was threatened during the late colonial period in New Spain, at least from the mid-eighteenth century. Ideologically, it was a defense of community rather than a desire for independent nationhood that drove most Indian villagers into the arms of the insurgency, even if for disparate personal motives in the case of individuals. Ironically, both the reforming efforts of the rationalizing Bourbon regime in the last century of colonial rule and those of the liberal nationalists of the early republican period in Mexico moved in much the same direction insofar as Indian villagers were concerned. A corporate community like the autonomous Indigenous village was seen as a distinctly unmodern, retrogressive form of social organization, as in many ways it still is by some scholars and policy makers. Both monarchical and republican regimes actively adopted policies to break it down or passively tolerated corrosive forces that exerted pressures in that direction. The goal here was to integrate its members into a larger polity under the terms of subjecthood in the univer-sal Spanish Empire or citizenship in republican Mexico. This is an extremely important strand of continuity bridging the colonial and republican eras, lend-ing meaning to the 1750–1850 periodization. Indigenous peasant grievance was actualized into massive violence when elite Creole political actors seized the initiative offered by the dynastic crisis in Spain to advance an ambition for greater autonomy for New Spain within the empire, an ambition whose auton-omist impulse was overtaken in relatively short order by the more radical idea of complete independence. *While not diametrically opposed to nation-state formation, the drive of Indigenous insurgents to protect the autonomy of the Indian peasant village was not the same as the drive of Creole rebels to stretch the autonomy of the colony into an independent polity. The two broad groups had different interests and different goals—imagined terminal points more at an angle to each other than incompatible.*

The policies implemented by the Bourbon Reforms, and the nonstate social forces concurrent with them, acted as severe stressors on village communities in the last colonial decades, accounting in general for the uptick in localized disturbances I have already noted after about 1780. At least two of these policies impinged upon the local religious and celebratory life so integral to the cohesion and identity of rural communities. In the first place, the enlightened Church (in the sense of the European Enlightenment) in the latter part of the eighteenth century sought to cleanse popular piety of the more florid elements of religious celebrations—processions of various kinds associated with liturgical events or the veneration of local icons, village patron saints, and spontaneous cults and chapels. Before about the last third of the century, manifestations of such popular piety had been tolerated or even encouraged in keeping with the exuberance of the baroque church and the tolerant doctrines of Catholicism as it evolved after the Council of Trent (held in Italy, 1545–1563), convoked chiefly to consolidate Catholic doctrine and practice in the face of the Protestant challenge. Popular forms of piety were now sanitized, restricted, or suppressed outright, provoking sometimes violent resistance on the part of Indigenous villagers, who did not like their *"usos y costumbres"* ("practices and customs") meddled with. Repeated viceregal decrees condemned "abuses" by Indians and others, including excess spending, gambling, drinking, and commercial activities carried on in connection with religious occasions such as Holy Week. Officials refused to grant licenses to Indians for the establishment of popular chapels in country villages. Several of the village riots or uprisings that erupted in connection with the Hidalgo rebellion in late 1810 were linked to popular frustrations with clerical attempts to suppress celebrations, especially those of All Saints (November 1).

Second, less a policy of the Bourbon Reforms than an indirect effect of efforts by the enlightened Church itself to discipline the undisciplined behavior of village Indians was the increase in the frequency of conflicts between villagers and their parish priests during the last decades of the colonial period. We have a romanticized image from all over the Catholic world in novels and films of the kindly old white-haired padre enduring with his village flock their tribulations and offering spiritual comfort along with the sacraments while possibly undergoing a spiritual crisis of his own or even martyrdom in the defense of community and religion. There was much of this, certainly, but the priest-parishioner relationship had always been a fraught one and was certainly not without its problems. For whatever reason, such tensions emerged more frequently in the late colonial decades. The colonial state's narrowing of religious customs gave a greater latitude for priestly abuses at the village parish level. There is substantial evidence of anticlerical sentiment among common people in the Mexican countryside in general becoming especially marked during times of open social conflict such as the independence struggle. In part this was inherent in the relationship because parishioners were people of color and their priests whites or mestizos. Especially irritating to parishioners was priestly interference in local political affairs, such as favoring one village political faction over another or invalidating elections. The same was true of secular officials, whose heavy-handed intervention in matters of community self-governance was always a sore point with villagers.

Other crown policies outside the sphere of religious practice and priestly authority also contributed to tension in the countryside, among them increasingly heavy fiscal exactions. An example was the viceregal regime's fattening of the fiscal stream from the colony to support war efforts in Europe and elsewhere by preying on community treasuries through forced "loans," appropriating funds intended for purposes like the upkeep of village buildings and the payment of schoolmasters. Royal monopolies such as that for tobacco—established in New Spain in 1764, it may be recalled, it was a vertical monopoly on the cultivation, processing, and sale of tobacco products—drained some resources from the domestic budgets of humble people. The reform of the tribute payments levied on Indians and some groups of color in the population tightened or eliminated exemptions that had existed until the late eighteenth century, imposing a considerable economic burden on Indigenous peasants. The abolition of the General Indian Court in 1791, which since the sixteenth century had been dedicated exclusively to settling legal disputes involving Indigenous people, eliminated a privileged legal venue that Indians might use. Although they might still take litigation to the royal courts, this state measure weakened the institutional protections afforded to Indians among the "impoverished classes" (*"los miserables"*). It is also the case that debts accumulated by rural workers under the system of labor peonage were enforceable by law with increasing frequency, limiting their freedom of movement. Considered individually these and other relatively small legal and extractive measures would not have created widespread resentment among the Indigenous population of New Spain, but taken as a whole they chipped away significantly at Indigenous incomes and protections.

Among nonstate social forces acting as stressors on Indigenous peasant villages two were of particular significance. One of these was population growth in the Mexican countryside. This did not occur at a breakneck pace, certainly, but it was perceptible during the last decades of the colonial era. The Indigenous population recovered from its nadir starting around the mid-seventeenth century. Population growth began to stutter around 1770 or so, but the regional picture was quite varied. Growing numbers of people in the Indian peasant sector of the economy pressed increasingly on finite resources of cultivable land so that Indigenous people continually complained of shortages of land and about new communities fissioning from larger ones to create villages hungry for farming land. This was relative to the retraction of Indian villages as their populations ebbed up to 1650 or so, when much land, whether for cropping or livestock, had been taken over by private landowners on the legal presumption that it was unoccupied. The increase of population left little room for the expansion of peasant agriculture on lands earlier abandoned as Indian population shrank or that was lost through other means to non-Indigenous sectors of the rural population. The appropriation of lands by nonvillagers was the second, complementary factor in the growing stress on pueblo economies. These scissoring trends—village population growth, expansion of commercial agriculture—would continue throughout the nineteenth century, giving rise to one of the major themes of conflict in the Revolution of 1910.

The various pressures on the religious identity and economic sustainability of Indigenous villages provoked collective action to defend the integrity of communities against the forces of dissolution menacing them externally rather than directed toward the formation of a new nation-state. This version of Indian participation in the insurgency may not square well with traditional or even some more recent interpretations of the independence struggle's makeup, but it does fit the facts well. To the degree it can be combed out of the rebellion in general, Indian rebellion was essentially coincidental. We have just reviewed the possible underlying *causes* of such collective behavior, long-term factors antecedent to the insurgency itself rather than the manifestations of them in action. These manifestations were quite fascinating, embracing forms of insurgent organization, the targets of violence, and the rare bits of evidence we have as to insurgent ideology at the village level. One example consists of the *absence* of a certain behavior rather than its presence: there was relatively little attack by Indigenous insurgents upon non-Indigenous landowners or their property, as I have suggested. Such attacks did occur where hacendado-peasant relations were particularly conflictive and had probably been so for some time, and they might also be carried out by insurgent forces to capture resources to sustain their armed actions. But the seizure of land for purposes of redistribution or armed action specifically to vindicate economic grievances were infrequent occurrences. Much of the insurgency during the rebellious decade was carried out by rural and farming people, but this was not an *agrarian* uprising as such. Much more at issue was the social and political integrity of the Indigenous pueblos with which people strongly identified in personal, familial, political, economic, and religious terms. While many of the stressors acting upon these communities were economic in nature, they were braided into political and religious factors. This absence of explicit agrarian grievance or expression of a yearning for the creation of a nation-state does not mean that rural people were apolitical. But their allegiances and ambitions, and therefore the typical horizon of their actions, were micro-political rather than patriotic in the larger traditional sense.

Another insight into the deep dynamics of Indigenous insurgency may be drawn from popular attitudes in the countryside of New Spain toward the Spanish king, Fernando VII. Known as "El Deseado" ("The Longed-for One" or "Loved One"—there are a number of plausible renderings into English of the Spanish verb *desear*), he was usurped and placed under house arrest by Napoleon Bonaparte in 1808 as part of the French takeover of the Iberian Peninsula. During the insurgency a representation of him showed up in New Spain (although he himself had never set foot in Spain's New World realms) as a widely venerated, even messianic figure. He was often sighted in connection with Father Miguel Hidalgo, whose uprising the king himself was believed to have instigated, reports that were particularly characteristic of Indian insurgents and sympathizers. This was a vivid paradox among rural people fighting against royalist soldiers sent into the field on the king's orders to suppress the rebellion. Among a group of young Indigenous insurgents captured in November 1810, for instance, several believed that in taking up the rebellion they were acting under the orders of the king of Spain, physically present in New Spain and riding about the countryside in a mysterious black coach. The king had ordered their village to kill the viceroy and all other European Spaniards. Another Indian rebel captured in 1811 asserted that "a person is coming in a veiled coach, and when people come to see him, they kneel down and go away very happy." A woman from a village near Cuautla, in the Cuernavaca area, offered to her neighbors the subversive idea that the king was wearing a silver mask, traveling in the company of Father Hidalgo, and supporting the priest's cause. Yet another rebel stated emphatically at his capture that King Fernando had appeared in New Spain by a particular and miraculous intercession of the Virgin of Guadalupe. The king was masked; he was invisible; he was traveling alone in a closed coach; he was with Hidalgo or Allende, not as a prisoner but a collaborator; he was working with the Virgin of Guadalupe to destroy the Spanish armies; he was spiking the guns of royalist forces. His person violated the unities of time and space. He was not only himself the beneficiary of unseen or divine forces but also their vessel. He could even endow his servants such as Father Morelos with the power to revive the dead, a whiff of divine powers that differentiates a messianic from a charismatic figure. Fernando VII was believed instantly capable of eliminating colonial oppression directed at his most humble and loyal subjects while retaining his role as monarch. So the agents of the king's government—from the ministers in Spain and the viceroy down to the colonial bureaucracy and the Spanish power holders in the colony—were the noxious actors in the colonial arrangement rather than the monarch himself, leaving him unblemished, the object of extreme veneration. This fit in well with the traditional motto of rebels against royal authority in the Hispanic world, "¡Viva el rey y muera el mal gobierno!"—"Long live the king, and death to bad government!"

The paradox of messianic expectation was focused on a monarch making every effort by the most unforgiving military means not to lose his grip on New Spain. If popular insurgents, of whom the majority were Indigenous people, were bent on breaking away from Spain one can hardly imagine that they would have elevated the king to a position of messianic expectation where he would actually remain in place as monarch in a sort of refurbished colonial arrangement. They could simply have denied the legitimacy of his rule and moved on to alternative forms of governance, but these were generally the recorded sentiments of the empire's humblest subjects. There were a number of reasons why this apparently self-contradictory situation came to exist. In the first place, this belief did not spring suddenly out of the conditions of the 1810 rebellion but had long historical antecedents in traditions of mystical kingship in Europe and the Iberian Peninsula. In New Spain (and also in the Andean region) there were movements of collective violence by humble, mostly Indigenous people featuring rebel leaders who claimed endorsement by the king of Spain in their efforts to overthrow the colonial order, of which the messianic expectation focused on King Fernando VII after 1810 was an echo. These earlier uprisings often embraced aspects of Aztec (or in the Andean case, Inca) revivalism, the reversal of the conquest of the Americas, and even a kind of vague world-turned-upside-down Utopianism in which Indigenous people would rule and whites would be killed, expelled, or relegated to a subject position. One such episode was the so-called Indio Mariano rebellion of 1801 in western Mexico in what is today the state of Nayarit, in which Indian conspirators aspired to create a Nahua (Aztec) monarchy revived at the behest of the Spanish king.[5] So the ground was already prepared in which messianic expectation could grow, focused on the figure of King Fernando VII and in a few instances on Ignacio Allende or Father Miguel Hidalgo.

Finally, there was also the fact that the monarchy had set itself up over three centuries as the protector of Indigenous people against the worst abuses of cruelty and rapacity perpetrated by the New Spain's conquerors and their heirs. This took root during the immediate postconquest period in the sixteenth century as a tactical measure on the part of the crown conceived as a counterweight to the dominance of *conquistador* and Creole elites in New Spain who might have challenged royal authority and set the colony in its first decades on a path toward early independence. Nor was such Creole patriotism (the phrase is historian David Brading's) simply a paranoid figment of the royal imagination. Virtually the first actions of Fernando Cortés were to establish his independence, first by political and then military means, from the government of Cuba, the Spanish Caribbean beachhead from which his expedition had set out in 1518, and not coincidentally from its governor, his cousin Diego Velázquez. In the 1560s a conspiracy to wrest New Spain from the control of Old Spain bubbled up among the second generation of *encomenderos* and conquerors in the form of a conspiracy to rebel planned by the brothers Ávila, which embroiled Martín Cortés, the illegitimate mestizo son of Fernando. The policy of making of Indians a protected underclass under the tutelage of the crown was less a humanitarian measure than a political one intended to dilute the power of colonial elite groups. Against this background of benign protective policies promulgated by the Spanish crown, especially in contrast to most private settlers' often harshly racialist and exploitative attitudes, the Spanish king naturally took on for native people a highly positive association that might over time, and under certain stresses, harden into the diamond of messianic veneration, as it did during the insurgency. Now let us return to the narrative of the rebellion.

NOTES

1. A good condensed account of the insurgency is to be found in Rodríguez, *Spaniards*, 195–267, which in keeping with the author's interests tends to concentrate on political rather than military events but is still very useful.

2. Van Young, *The Other Rebellion*, 100.

3. See, for example, Peter Guardino, *Peasants, Politics, and the Formation of Mexico's National State: Guerrero, 1800–1857* (Stanford: Stanford University Press, 1996); and Michael T. Ducey, *A Nation of Villages: Riot and Rebellion in the Mexican Huasteca, 1750–1850* (Tucson: University of Arizona Press, 2004).

4. Van Young, *The Other Rebellion*, 94.

5. For an account of this incident, see Van Young, "Millennium on the Northern Marches: The Mad Messiah of Durango and Popular Rebellion in Mexico, 1800–1815," *Comparative Studies in Society and History* 28 (1986): 385–413.

Chapter 7

The Consummation
of Independence

With the death of Father José María Morelos at the end of 1815 the plausibility of uniting all or most of the insurgency under one central authority and command to enable strategic coherence among the fractious elements of the rebellion all but vanished. In the end this may have proved the saving of the independence impulse because it made for many small targets rather than a few large ones and would eventually stretch royalist resources to the point of exhaustion; thus the label "Hydra-headed" rebellion invoked by some contemporaries and modern historians. Attempts to reconstitute an insurgent congress after the demise of the Congress of Chilpancingo proved unavailing despite Morelos's efforts. A sort of stalemate set in after the middle of the decade in which the insurgents found themselves unable to launch massive, coordinated attacks while the royalists were unable to stamp out the many foci of rebellion. The efficient causes of this feudalization, as I have called it, lie deep in the folds of Mexican history and culture. The tradition of stubborn localism in Mexico tended strongly against large-scale unification of violent protest groups. The structures of royal governance were laid atop the world of villages with somewhat limited downward penetration until modern times; this was a lumpy hegemony at best, thicker in some places than in others. The different ethnic makeup of various parts of the country discouraged the integration of insurgent factions into larger units, a tendency of like to cooperate with like. Another difficulty was that of communication, particularly between the central valleys of the country's uplands and the coastal areas, not to mention the vast, arid, and ever-receding north. Also in play was the personal opportunism of individual actors or dynasties at the local and regional levels, consolidated by the dominance of political bossism (*caciquismo*) throughout much of the country, almost as prevalent in the rebellion of 1810 as it came to be in that of 1910. Finally, the absence of a unifying ideology worked against the consolidation of smaller into larger units of action, even on a temporary basis. In fact the stubbornly localist and autonomist ambitions of Indigenous communities suggests that fragmentation *was an ideology in itself.*

THE INSURGENCY CONTINUES—THIRD PHASE

By 1816 the insurgency had receded but not guttered out. Defeats suffered by the rebels did not amount to defeat of the rebellion. The offer and widespread acceptance of royal amnesties weakened the leadership and somewhat depleted the ranks of common rebels. A general exhaustion from fighting, instability, and violent death seems to have set in on both sides. Royalist forces had done better in defending cities than in pacifying the countryside, even with the effective tactical application of antirebellion techniques such as flying cavalry columns stationed at key geographical points and the concentration of suspect populations in certain towns. There was banditry aplenty, but the remaining insurgents could not on the whole be characterized as bandits, as royalist authorities often did in order to delegitimate them. Rural brigandage was to emerge much more robustly after 1821, when a weak central state could not do much to suppress it and men mustered out on either side of the conflict, accustomed to bear arms and to live by violence and their wits, could not find work in the devastated economy.

Following the death of Morelos the insurgency struggled along for the next five years, mostly assuming the form of guerrilla warfare in the southern areas of the country. In this form it proved impossible to extinguish but lacked the resources to advance beyond an uneasy military stalemate until circumstances in European Spain converged with personal ambitions in New Spain to forge an alliance between royalist officers and major insurgent figures. After 1815 it fell to Vicente Guerrero to play the leading role in the rebellion. A southerner from a town near Acapulco in what would later be the state named for him, Guerrero was of mixed mestizo and Afro-mestizo background, dark complexioned and robust, a charismatic, imposing figure with a natural military talent. From a background of moderately successful rural merchants and landowners, in his youth he worked for his father as a muleteer, later took up gunsmithing, and joined the forces of Father José María Morelos in 1810 espousing proindependence sentiments. He rose quickly through the insurgent ranks and would enjoy an important political and military career during the first decade of the country's independent political life, always occupying a leftward ideological position until after a brief stint as president he was essentially assassinated judicially in 1831. During the latter years of the insurgent decade he sustained the rebellion primarily in the south of New Spain through guerrilla tactics, becoming by 1821 the most important surviving rebel leader. He would join forces with the turncoat royalist officer

Agustín de Iturbide in 1821, forming an unlikely alliance that brought down New Spain's colonial regime.

Some other insurgent leaders (to say nothing of the many royalist officers who collaborated with the Iturbide project), all of the generation of 1790 or a bit earlier but none as militarily effective as Guerrero, survived the reverses of the years following the death of Morelos to become prominent republican politicians and/or military figures. A few were from more economically comfortable backgrounds, but most were men of color from modest circumstances who with few exceptions had little or no formal education. Among the former group was Nicolás Bravo (1786–1854), from a landowning family in the south of the country, who fought under Morelos and was imprisoned by the royalist regime in 1817. He only gained his freedom in 1820, in time to embrace Iturbide's Plan of Iguala and go on to a distinguished political and military career in the young republic. Of a more elevated social background was José Miguel Fernández y Félix (1786–1843), who adopted the name Guadalupe Victoria and would serve as Mexico's first president (1824–1829), the only one to fill out a full constitutionally mandated term until mid-century. Victoria came from what is now the near-northern state of Durango, earned a law degree in 1811, and joined the insurgency under Morelos in 1812. After enjoying several years of success as an insurgent commander he refused a royalist pardon and went into hiding in 1817, emerging only to join with Iturbide in 1821 and enter national politics thereafter. Much more modestly situated in the preindependence social hierarchy was the mulatto farmer and *vaquero* Gordiano Guzmán (1789–1854), born in Tamazula, to the south of Lake Chapala in western Mexico, who joined the rebellion in late 1811 and whom we have already met. He fought under Morelos in the region of Jalisco and Michoacán, repeatedly refusing royal amnesty. Among the most intransigent of provincial chieftains, he rejected Iturbide's Plan de Iguala and survived to carve out a *cacicazgo* around Tamazula, his birthplace, fighting in every major civil imbroglio and against the Americans in the late 1840s only to fall victim to his enemies in 1854. Longer lived and a bit better educated was Juan Álvarez (1790–1867), born to a peninsular Spanish father and Afro-Mexican mother in the future state of Guerrero, of which he would be the first governor. He too worked as a farmer and cowboy but had some primary education. Álvarez identified strongly in his politics with humble Mexicans of color, ardently embraced federalism in the young republic as a more populist option than aristocratic centralism, and fought against the short-lived Iturbide monarchy in the first days after independence. He constructed a regional sphere of political power in his native zone and died in his bed of old age after struggling to expel the French usurping regime in 1867. Most of these men fought to sustain the insurgency in the years between Morelos and Iturbide and shaped national politics in the early republican era.

SPANISH POLITICS, ITURBIDE, AND THE
CONSUMMATION OF INDEPENDENCE

Mexican independence originated in the medium term in the Napoleonic invasion and occupation of the Iberian Peninsula in 1808 and the Hidalgo rebellion in New Spain that followed two years later. In the short term, however, we must look again to political events in Spain in 1820 for the immediate circumstances that triggered the severing of ties with the metropolis. By early 1814 the Spanish partisans and regular army forces were operating with British expeditionary forces under Wellington. Fortuitously aided by the famous defeat of Napoleon's Grande Armée by the harsh Russian winter of 1812, they had retaken Spain from the French and restored King Ferdinand VII to the throne. But neither by personal ability nor political beliefs was the restored monarch really up to the task of reconciling the conflicts within the Spanish Empire. By May 1814 he had surrounded himself with a cabal of ultraconservatives and abolished the 1812 constitution and the Cortes. He reduced the powers of his ministers to concentrate absolutist authority once more in himself and block any potential center of reforms, undertaking a ferocious persecution of the Spanish liberals of 1808–1814. The king slow walked or buried reform proposals, revived the Spanish Inquisition, restored the Jesuits to the Spanish realms (expelled in 1767, it will be remembered), and squashed the critical press. Along with the weakening domestic economy, these measures sapped the legitimacy of his regime in Spain. At the beginning of 1820 a rebellion broke out among Spanish military officers, many of whom were members of Masonic orders, slated to be sent to fight the Spanish American insurgents. They forced King Ferdinand in March to swear allegiance once more to the 1812 Constitution, reviving along with it the empire-wide Cortes during what came to be known as the *trienio liberal* (liberal triennium), 1820–1823. The leaders assumed not only that this would (again) usher in a new dawn for Spain but would also win back the loyalty of the monarchy's American subjects, but it was to prove too little too late.

During this pendulum swing back toward a more liberal regime in Spain the political opening in the absolutist clouds let in the sunshine of a general proconstitutional hubbub encouraging the flowering of pamphletry that electrified the political atmosphere even more. The Cortes deputies who had supported King Ferdinand during the preceding five years of absolutist rule were in turn persecuted by the liberal elements of the temporarily restored constitutional government. Elections to the newly reconstituted imperial parliament were held starting in June 1820. The number of American deputies would grow to nearly eighty after elections were held in the Spanish overseas realms. The contingent of deputies from New Spain included Lucas

Alamán, representing his native Guanajuato. Although a larger group than in 1810–1812, the Spanish American deputies were still far outnumbered by their peninsular cousins. The summer of 1820 saw the proliferation of elective *ayuntamientos* (city councils) in Mexican cities mandated by the revived constitution and the revival or establishment of several provincial deputations, entities that would mutate into state legislatures after independence. This wider dispersion of political power in Mexico within the next eighteen months made for a much broader base in favor of absolute independence as Agustín de Iturbide was forming his plans. In Madrid the new more liberal Cortes suppressed monastic orders, reexpelled the Jesuits, and abolished ecclesiastical and military *füeros*, the special corporate exemptions enjoyed by members of these groups in regard to taxes and civil judicial jurisdiction. These measures raised alarms within the Church and the army in New Spain, both of which felt threatened by the elimination of their privileges and the weakening of the absolutist system. The American deputies did accomplish certain things in the Cortes, among them the enactment of legislation freeing up the silver mining industry in New Spain from some onerous regulations, aimed at the sector's revival. They also achieved the recall of several royalist commanders in the Spanish American realms considered unsympathetic to the reinstatement of the 1812 constitution, including Viceroy Ruiz de Apodaca and Field Marshal José de la Cruz in New Spain, old comrades-in-arms who had become tense rivals. Various plans were discussed in the Cortes to create a sort of commonwealth structure within the Spanish Empire granting the overseas realms much greater political autonomy within the framework of a constitutional monarchy, but these came to nothing. By this time the overseas realms were well on their way to being lost to Spain, and the reinstatement of the 1812 constitution failed to satisfy the Spanish Americans. The European majority in the parliament continued virtually to ignore the situation as events boiled over across the Atlantic.

Events in New Spain were moving rapidly, meanwhile, the lack of synchronization between the two Spains greatly aggravated by the several months required under the best conditions to communicate back and forth across the Atlantic. In January 1821 the Spanish government dispatched fifty-nine-year-old Juan O'Donojú (1762–1821), a liberal, Mason, and distinguished military officer in the peninsular war against the French as captain general and superior military chief of New Spain, hoping that the reinstatement of the constitution and the replacement of Viceroy Apodaca would calm the situation in the country. O'Donojú got to New Spain at the end of July 1821 under the misapprehension that he had been authorized to install a regency in the country along the lines of the commonwealth proposal under discussion in the Cortes but in fact never enacted. He arrived to find a military plot in full swing aimed at overthrowing Viceroy Ruiz de Apodaca.

This conspiracy was led by Colonel Agustín de Iturbide (1783–1824), one of the more controversial figures in Mexican history, seen as a hero by some Mexicans or as an ambitious opportunist by others. In fairness one could say that he demonstrated moments of political brilliance clouded over in the long term by bad judgment and that in the end he was an opportunist with heroic flashes. Born in Valladolid (later Morelia), Iturbide came of a prominent landed family of Basque origins, studied at the Colegio de San Nicolás in his native city (in which Father Miguel Hidalgo, a distant relation, had been professor and rector some years before Iturbide's time), joined the army in his teens, and married into another socially prominent landed family. In social origin and personal profile he resembled Ignacio Allende, Juan Aldama, and other youngish Creole military men who led the insurgency. Offered a commission by Hidalgo he opted instead to support the royalist cause and became an enthusiastic pursuer of rebels. Personally brave, with considerable military ability, he was relentless and brutal in his treatment of insurgents who fell within his grasp. He was suspended from the service in 1816 on the basis of well-founded charges of war profiteering and other irregularities. Although he was absolved of the corrupt and brutal practices alleged against him, his reputation had suffered and he was not restored to his command. Without a military position, shadowed by disgrace, and thwarted in his ambitions for advancement he shifted his loyalties to the insurgency, although when exactly this occurred is not clear. In November 1820 Iturbide was recalled to the royalist service by Viceroy Apodaca, who sought an experienced, efficient, and none too punctilious military commander to extirpate the stubborn rebellion in the south of the country led chiefly by Vicente Guerrero. It is unclear whether the two men were negotiating an alliance to gain independence from Spain from early in Iturbide's reinstatement or if this arose from a sort of military stalemate in which the royalist forces were unable to achieve consistent advances against the rebels. In any case, it appears that Iturbide was contemplating a conspiracy to overthrow the viceregal regime even as he was offered his command in late 1820.

With considerable conspiratorial aptitude Iturbide set about recruiting high military officers, both Creole and European, and local and regional political authorities to the support of his cause. The coalition Iturbide built through the spring and summer of 1821 embraced a number of high Church officials and royalist military officers, several of whom would become prominent military politicians in the new republic following the fall of Iturbide's Mexican Empire in 1823. The nature of Iturbide's motives at this point has to my eye never been clear—whether simply naked personal ambition or adherence to broader currents of elite political opinion he tapped into, including a fear of the liberal tendencies of the revived Spanish constitution and liberal Madrid Cortes, or a (quite justified) doubt that the Spanish regime would

DON AUGUSTINO ITURBIDE.

Figure 7.1. Agustín de Iturbide (1783–1824), royalist officer, late convert to the cause of independence, and Emperor of Mexico (1822–1823). Fayette Robinson, Mexico and Her Military Chieftains, from the Revolution of Hidalgo to the Present Time. Comprising Sketches of the Lives of Hidalgo [and Others], 1847.

ever grant autonomy to New Spain within the imperial arrangement. The plan that coalesced was originally aimed only at forestalling the application of the revived 1812 Constitution in New Spain, but its tenor changed with the rapidly developing circumstances. It was felt that the best way to protect the Mexican church and the army against the liberal measures being enacted in Spain, which extended considerably beyond the provisions of the constitution, and to satisfy the aspirations of those men advocating independence, was to establish an autonomous monarchy in New Spain in the name of King Ferdinand VII. The programmatic basis of this rather odd program was the Plan of Iguala, officially titled the "Plan de Independencia de la América Septentrional" (that is, "Northern America," meaning the extensive territories of New Spain) promulgated and signed by Iturbide and Guerrero at the town of Iguala, in what is today the state of Guerrero, on February 24, 1821. The plan spoke of an established Church, absolute independence from Spain, and the legal and political equality of all inhabitants of the country within the framework of citizenship (N.B.: *not* in the status of monarchical subjects) including those of African, Asian, and Indigenous descent. These were known as the "Three Guarantees" and the combined military force of Iturbide and Vicente Guerrero as the Trigarantine Army (Ejército Trigarante), composed by the early spring of about 1,800 men, a large force for the time and place. Other provisions included the guarantee of existing property rights, meaning that there would be no expropriation of European Spaniards' properties and no land redistribution in a downward direction. Another clause preserved ecclesiastical and military *fueros*. A Mexican throne would be offered to King Ferdinand VII (who would, of course, insist that he could not be offered what he already possessed legitimately by God-given right) and failing his acceptance to a Bourbon prince or another candidate. An interim junta would be established to govern the country while the pieces of the new political order fell into place. An offer to head the interim junta went to Viceroy Ruiz de Apodaca, who unsurprisingly rejected it. Several important figures in the regime steadfastly resisted adherence to Iturbide's Plan, among them the recently arrived archbishop of New Spain and the Spanish general José de la Cruz, the military commander and political chief of the enormous area of western and northern Mexico who had been recalled by the liberal Spanish Cortes. As royalist officers continued to join Iturbide, however, strategically and materially important areas of the country fell into his hands through the spring and summer. Alleging Viceroy Apodaca's incompetence to deal with the rapidly changing situation, in early July 1821 elements of the royalist army in the capital forced his resignation and replaced him with Field Marshal Francisco Novella (1769–1822), who ruled as viceroy for just two weeks or so, unconfirmed by the metropolitan authorities. Apodaca sailed back to Spain in the same ship that had brought Juan O'Donojú to New Spain.

The Spanish general and newly designated political chief of New Spain O'Donojú was thus left holding the imperial bag, so to speak, in circumstances foreseen neither by him nor the Spanish ministry that had dispatched him. He succeeded the irregularly elevated Novella officially in late July with virtually no resources at his disposal in the face of the Iturbide-led military mutiny that had rapidly gained momentum and by now controlled almost the entire country. There was little he could do but negotiate with Iturbide for the least damaging cession of authority possible. The two met on August 23, 1821, at the town of Córdoba, about fifty miles or so west of the Gulf port city of Veracruz. The following day saw the signing of the Treaty of Córdoba, which essentially ceded New Spain's independence on the terms set out in the Plan de Iguala. Independent Mexico was thus brought into being as a moderate constitutional monarchy under the rule of King Ferdinand VII or another prince to be determined, a provisional junta, and a regency established to govern the country until the new monarch arrived. In the capital, meanwhile, Novella refused to accept the arrangement but was repudiated by the civil and ecclesiastical authorities, to which he yielded on September 14, 1821. General O'Donojú entered Mexico City on September 27, 1821, much celebrated for his statesmanship, the same day as the triumphal Army of the Three Guarantees, headed by Iturbide (whose thirty-eighth birthday it was) and Guerrero, old enemies now pressed by circumstance and ambition into uneasy alliance. O'Donojú had little time to ease the transition, however, dying of pleurisy on October 8, 1821; his widow survived him and lived on in Mexico City for many years.

As his richest colonial holding slipped away and traitorous liberals dominated the domestic politics of Spain under a restored constitution that he had reviled, King Ferdinand VII appealed for aid on the home front to the other European monarchs who had been parties to the post-Napoleonic settlement of restored absolutist rule embodied in the Congress of Vienna (1815). The penultimate French Bourbon monarch, the hugely corpulent King Louis XVIII (1755–1824, r. 1815–1824), under pressure from ultraconservative politicians in France to go to the aid of his Bourbon cousin, dispatched an army across the Pyrenees in the spring of 1823, the Hundred Thousand Sons of Saint Louis (who really numbered only about 60,000). By the late fall Cádiz had fallen to the French, the Cortes had dissolved itself, and King Ferdinand VII was restored to an absolutist throne. Breaking his promise to Spanish liberals to respect the 1812 Constitution in return for their adherence to his regime, he abrogated the charter once again, restrained in his retaliation against the liberal traitors only by wiser French counsel. By this time New Spain had forever gone its way to become for a few months the Mexican Empire and then the Republic of Mexico. King Ferdinand would not let things rest so easily, however. Spanish military forces retained control of a fortified island slightly off the coast of Veracruz in the Gulf of Mexico whence they meddled with incoming oceanic shipping and occasionally shelled the mainland, only to be dislodged in 1825. In 1829 an ill-planned Spanish invasion force attempted to recapture the errant colony, but its hopes drained away in the sands of the northern Gulf coast. Diplomatic recognition of independent Mexico was not accorded by Spain until the 1830s.

CONCLUSION

The period of the Mexican independence struggle was both a bridge and a chasm, simultaneously a passage of both change and continuity. At the beginning of chapter 5, I cited both changes and continuities in the political, social, economic, and cultural spheres during the passage from colony to nation. Of these spheres the quickest to change was the political in the transition from a monarchical form of governance within an imperial framework to a nation-state ruled by a federal, and at times a centralized, republic, with a brief hiccup of national monarchy under Agustín de Iturbide in 1822–1823 (dealt with in the following chapter). Under the surface of republican politics there was always the steady thrum of a socially widespread desire for a monarchy. The slowest changes were in the cultural realm, where longstanding and deeply engrained habits of life such as religious belief, gender relations, child-rearing practices, patterns of social deference, beliefs about the nature of nature, and a multitude of others underwent alteration more as a function of Mexico's advancing modernization than of political change as such. What took much longer to change than institutions of governance was *political culture*, not so much the written and unwritten rules of the political game—how elections were held, what the powers of the executive branch were as opposed to the legislative, definitions of active versus passive citizenship, and so forth—but at the deeper layer of what was to be *expected* of political life, of what politics was *about*. Who were its major beneficiaries, and what were its covering myths? Where was the locus of power, and was it to be broadened out or kept within strict limits? What were believed to be its boundaries, and where did politics blend into private life? What was the nature of citizenship in the new nation, how was it related to people's socioethnic and economic condition, and what was the individual's relationship to the state? And hanging over all these questions was the issue of political legitimacy, of the willingness of political actors, whether elite or popular, to abide by rule-based political outcomes because they were produced by processes agreed acceptable to all parties, winners and losers alike. These questions were to emerge fully only in the post-1821 era, when the nature of political life and its reigning institutions were in constant dispute within the field of liberal-conservative contention. These tensions are not to be understood without reference to the colonial era (neocolonialism aside for the moment) and thus the theme of this book.

Insofar as the insurgency of 1810 itself was concerned it only became more or less clear after the passage of several years marked by much violence that it aimed at total severance of the ties with Spain. I have suggested that rather than independence the integrity and autonomy of the local rural community were really the issues for the multitude of country people, especially Indigenous villagers, who at all times made up the bulk of insurgent combatants. This is not to say that sectors of the popular insurgency and individuals among the rebels did not embrace the creation of a new nation-state as a goal, or even that it did not jostle other ideas of a political nature in people's consciousness. But independence was largely a Creole project, even if many of the men who helped bring it into being were not Creoles. Independence as such was thus largely at a right angle to the aims of the popular insurgency. The strands of personal and communal identity—religious, political, kin-based, geographic, economic, affective—were for ordinary people knotted at the village level, not in a real or imagined state attached to a national persona.

One great continuity across the divide of independence was the drive of the colonial and national states, successively, to forge some sort of supralocal loyalties among common people, most particularly Indians: to make them into *novohispanos* or Mexicans. The colonial order was of course substantially built upon the theory and practice of *dos repúblicas* (two republics), one embracing Indian people, the other everyone else. An ethnically marked underclass was set apart from the rest of society by a number of factors. The imperial regime was also schizophrenic, however, in encouraging the integration of Indigenous groups into colonial society through such institutions as access to the courts and broader legal systems, the use of notaries and official documentation of all kinds, the (albeit somewhat haphazard) enforcement of a pro-Spanish language policy and the encouragement of literacy, and incorporation into the community of the Catholic faithful. Spanish crown policy was to make Indians into good subjects, if of diminished subjecthood. The same ambivalence marked the national period, where the goal of many political actors was to make compliant citizens of Indigenous people. Some factors worked against this, such as overt race prejudice directed at Indians. Yet others worked in its favor, among them wide male enfranchisement at times, the obligation to perform military service and the socialization this entailed, and the official removal of bars to public office. Another apparently benign, prointegration policy that took hold in the immediate wake of independence and wound its way into the twentieth century was the breakup of village communal lands under liberal free market doctrines, then their reconstitution as *ejidos* (collective holdings) after 1910, and more recently a swing back to breakup policies under neoliberal regimes. In the long run the putative benefit of thus creating a class of small independent farming landowners seems to have been overshadowed by actual reduction to the status of landless laborers and poverty. The question of how to make Indians into good subjects or citizens resonated throughout the country's history and still does today.

One enduring legacy of the insurgency arose from the serial overthrow of the highest governing authorities by political pressure or force several times between 1808 and 1821. The effects of this would become immediately obvious in the early republican period. This chain of illegitimacy, as it were, contributed to the endemic political instability for which Mexico was to become famous during the nineteenth century as a land of revolutions, coups, and uprisings. It was brought to a halt by the Porfirian regime between 1876 and 1911, followed by one last, spectacular spasm of massive political violence in the revolution (1910–1921) and several aftershocks during the 1920s and 1930s. Then something like a permanent settlement was reached by the institution of a one-party hegemony, the *dictablanda* only recently challenged and apparently overturned not by collective violence but by electoral processes. But if Viceroy Iturrigaray could be overthrown in 1808 by a group of Spanish merchants then why not subsequent chief magistrates? The current government regime's foundations once shaken and its legitimacy questioned, why should succession to the highest offices in the political structure be determined by royal appointment, established by custom, precedent, and divine right sanctification or by elections mandated by republican ethos rather than by force of arms covered by the fig leaves of "public opinion" or the "general will"?

Finally, was the independence struggle a "movement," much less a revolution? Can the insurgency be called a "movement" in the sense that people and groups joined together to achieve a common cause through collective action? It is hard to make the case for this. The deep fault lines within the insurgency were both vertical and horizontal, corresponding roughly to socioethnic and spatial divisions, respectively. The vertical ones, as I have suggested, made the rebellion assume two co-occurring but fairly distinct forms, related in some ways but really moving more in parallel than unity. One of these was essentially a Creole project, first for autonomy within the Spanish imperial scheme of things, then over time, in the face of developing internal dynamics and stubborn Spanish metropolitan resistance, evolving into a drive for independence from Spain. The other tendency within the rebellion took the direction of the defense of village communities on the part of Indigenous people rather than any strong push for the creation of a national state. The horizontal divisions were just as profound, manifested in the fragmentation of the insurgent groups over the space of New Spain and the absence, except for brief periods, of centralized coordination of insurgent violence directed at the colonial regime, or of a unifying ideology of protonationalism that might have bridged the gaps. One has, then, a confluence of tendencies rather than a "movement" producing independence from Spain. For purposes of postinsurgency national cohesion there developed, both spontaneously from below and as an artifact of state action, a prevailing narrative of cross-class and cross-ethnic alliance, and unity of purpose grounded in a teleology of liberty, equality, and purposive action toward a common goal of nation-state formation. As to revolution, the forces unleashed were certainly violent, touched every social sector and corner of the country, and over a decade severely disrupted Mexican society. But did they produce a "revolution" in any but the most limited political sense? By 1821 there had been no significant redistribution of accumulated wealth or the means of production except to make the society as a whole poorer from the destructive effects of the decade of fighting, while most social norms and expectations remained in place. The social hierarchy remained essentially little altered except that men of color now found some space in the arena of politics and military life. This was not a trivial realignment, but while some men of mixed blood rose to positions of power and influence the lives of most ordinary people were hardly touched by the insurgency.

PART III

Inventing Independent Mexico

Chapter 8

From Transient Empire to Fragile Republic, 1821–1832

New Spain's transition from colony to independent Mexican nation-state, and thence to a nominally democratic republic via the eye blink of the Iturbide monarchy, took place over about a dozen years. The question of where the human capital to support that change came from is interesting, but let us concede that a Mexican political class developed quickly during and immediately after the independence struggle. Where political ideas were concerned, the general concepts about how to construct, govern, and maintain an independent nation were not that hard to come by; the devil was in the details. History was full of examples, and many of the men (especially the civilians) who assumed leadership roles in the young nation were well read in history and politics even though most of them, unless they were priests or physicians, had no university education in the modern sense. They were for the most part not well traveled (Lucas Alamán and Lorenzo de Zavala were conspicuous exceptions here) until exiled for one political sin or another. Their access to the work of mostly European writers on history and politics may have been crimped by the efforts of the Inquisition to enforce the proscriptions of the Index Librorum Prohibitorum (the index of prohibited books), but it was by no means totally cut off. As a smarty-pants late adolescent intellectual, for example, Alamán briefly fell under the baleful gaze of the Inquisition authorities for reading the prohibited *History of America* (1777) by the Scottish minister, historian, and University of Edinburgh professor William Robertson (1721–1793). This multivolume work offered a notoriously unfavorable account of the Spanish conquest of the Americas and the Spanish Empire and was therefore proscribed by the Church, one of whose bulwarks was the Spanish monarchy. Many other examples could be cited of political, scientific, and historical works that slipped the weave of Inquisition censors and got into the hands of Mexican readers. So a quarry of ideas and controversies about state and nation building certainly lay to hand. Nationhood as such was hardly an alien concept by the early nineteenth century, although the ancient and modern models drawn from the Western history that Mexican literary and political intellectuals knew best were often blurred by the concurrence of empire in the most familiar polities—France, England, Spain herself. Nor was experience of political processes absent entirely because strong local traditions of municipal and even Church governance in conciliar structures were deeply rooted in the Hispanic world.

MONARCHY OR REPUBLIC?

The question of what form the governance of the country would assume absorbed the full attention of these political gentlemen from the advent of the independence struggle in 1808 if not earlier, particularly after the issue of autonomy within a refurbished Spanish Empire had tilted in favor of absolute independence. It was easier to tear down, or at least opt out of, what already existed, however, than to build a viable replacement. For at least a few years the continuities in political institutions surveyed at the beginning of chapter 5 provided a bridge during the unpredictable passage from colony to nation. Historian Jaime E. Rodríguez O., who has written extensively and with acute judgement on the period, puts this well:

> The new country of Mexico that emerged from the breakup of the Spanish Monarchy retained many of the shared institutions, traditions, and practices of the past. Although political ideas, structures, and practices evolved rapidly after 1808, *antiguo régimen* social, economic, and institutional relationships changed slowly. Throughout this period of transformation, new political processes and liberal institutions merged with established traditions and practices.[1]

Until the adoption of the Mexican federalist Constitution of 1824 the Cádiz charter of 1812 was the regnant framework, and the influence of the earlier charter on the later was profound, some passages even passing intact from the one to the other. This was not only a matter of expedience but also of conviction about the merits of the 1812 document, in which the executive power was assigned to a constitutional monarch but the legislative power was given a dominant role. Despite the provisions of the Plan of Iguala, however, ratified in the Treaty of Córdoba signed by Agustín de Iturbide and Juan O'Donojú in August 1821, the political path ahead of the newly independent Mexico was anything but clear. Iturbide's plan assumed without discussion that the newly independent state's form of governance would be monarchical. Failing King Ferdinand VII's or his brothers' acceptance of the crown, the designation of a candidate who might actually occupy the throne of "Mexican America" remained purposely open. It does seem possible that the Plan of Iguala and the Treaty of Córdoba that codified it were well considered tactical moves to assure in the end a complete and definitive separation from Spain rather than the somewhat ambiguous solution of the colony's continuation under the same monarch in a different location. Iturbide and other military leaders of the moment were amply aware of King Ferdinand's deep conservatism and his stubborn vindictiveness. While acknowledging that his situation in Spain was extremely difficult during the *trienio liberal* and that decamping to New Spain as the Portuguese Prince Regent João had done in fleeing with his court to Brazil in 1807 might offer him a way out, it was scarcely plausible that he would accept the crown of New Spain on the terms offered by the Plan of Iguala. Or were the plan and the treaty actually intended to set an impossible condition, anticipating that it would be acceptable neither to Ferdinand, his brothers, nor his ministry and using the pretext of rejection to strike for absolute independence rather than pseudo-independence or autonomy within a shambling commonwealth arrangement? Even if this were the case, however, the question of who would assume the monarchical throne of a newly independent Mexico remained open.

It is important to keep in mind that in the early nineteenth century the idea of republicanism was already tightly woven into Euro-Atlantic political thought. The "classical republicanism" embodied in the Greek and Roman republics was a staple reference point both rhetorically and theoretically. Although never enacted, the insurgent Constitution of Apatzingán of 1814 was an important signpost in Mexican constitutional thought. Operationalizing republicanism, however, was another matter at a historical moment when monarchy was the default position. The Swiss Confederation was an outlier and the French First Republic (1792–1804) influential but short lived. One of the two chief reference points for Mexican political thinkers was Europe, exclusively monarchical in 1821 as some of it still is, at least nominally.[2] Brazil was a monarchy and remained so until 1889, the rest of Ibero-America republican. Certainly there was a tendency toward strong, king-like executives in most of the newly liberated former colonies and endemic struggles between the legislative and executive powers, as occurred in Mexico. The other major reference point was the young United States, the chief exemplar of a republic for Mexican political men, some of whom extolled it while others reviled it. There has long been a debate among constitutional and historical scholars as to the major influence on early Mexican constitution making, the triangle of influences being the American Constitution of 1789, the French charters of 1791 and 1793, and the Spanish of 1812, the American and French documents republican, the Spanish monarchical. In Mexico the default position in politics with few exceptions seems always to have been monarch-ish, executive-dominated regimes, and only during two brief moments (1822–1823, 1864–1867)

actual monarchy. In 1840 the outcry over prominent politician-diplomat
José María Gutiérrez de Estrada's (1800–1867) public manifesto openly
advocating a return to monarchy for Mexico would force him into exile but
only gave voice to a strong undercurrent already existing in political thought
and public opinion. Just before the Mexican-American War there blossomed
momentarily a monarchist "conspiracy" involving the Spanish ambassador
to Mexico, a sitting Mexican president, Lucas Alamán, and some ancillary
actors, but it collapsed within a few months. Gutiérrez de Estrada would later
lead the successful efforts of Mexican conservatives to recruit the Austrian
Archduke Maximilian von Habsburg (1832–1867) to occupy the throne of
a short-lived Second Mexican Empire (1863–1867) alongside his empress,
Princess Charlotte ("Mama Carlota" in Mexican popular song) of Belgium
(1840–1927). This episode ultimately produced the triumph of republicanism, the definitive end of monarchical projects in Mexico, and a romantically
tragic end for Maximilian (an event pictured in a famous painting by the
French artist Édouard Manet), survived by Carlota in her mad widowhood
for sixty years. Later republican regimes leaned strongly toward executive
dominance, especially under Porfirio Díaz from 1876 to 1911, but even after
him in the presidentialist governments of the last hundred years. While this
was not exactly monarchism, it certainly was monarch-ish.

It is therefore hardly surprising that newly independent Mexico should
have been constituted briefly as a monarchy under Emperor Agustín I during 1822–1823. Iturbide's personal ambitions played no small role here,
although beyond that his motives have always remained somewhat ambiguous. Viceroy Ruiz de Apodaca, who gave him his big opportunity in 1820 by
reviving his military career and dispatching him to fight Vicente Guerrero,
thought him power hungry. Like Julius Caesar, Iturbide claimed that the
weight of circumstances had forced the imperial diadem onto his brow
against his personal inclinations ("but, for all that, to my thinking, he would
fain have had it"; Casca, Shakespeare's *Julius Caesar*, Act I, scene 2), making
his own acclamation as monarch by a Mexico City crowd in May 1822 something of a burlesque. Many of the men who supported him politically were
high-level European Spanish military officers whose allegiance he had won
away from the crumbling Spanish colonial regime during 1820–1821 but not
necessarily from the institution of monarchy itself, under whose sheltering
wings they had made their careers. Others were Creole former insurgent officers, among them Antonio López de Santa Anna, one of whose many political
changes of heart and resulting opposition to Iturbide would play a large part
in bringing down the infant imperial government in the spring of 1823. On
the other hand, like Julius Caesar, Napoleon Bonaparte, and others before
and after him, Iturbide was a military chieftain justifiably viewed as heroic
by large segments of the Mexican public. Had a more disinterested man of

great stature and republican sympathies—Father José María Morelos, for example—seized the moment to shape the political future of the new nation the outcome might well have been very different and monarchy relegated to a marginal position among political options. But of Iturbide's possible competitors Morelos was long dead and other prominent men such as Vicente Guerrero, Guadalupe Victoria, or Nicolás Bravo, later all major figures in Mexican political life, lacked the public cachet, the political astuteness, and the military muscle of Iturbide in late 1821. Nor were external factors unfavorable to New Spain's absolute independence under whatever form of state the Mexicans might choose for themselves. The United States extended formal diplomatic recognition to Chile, the Rio de la Plata, Gran Colombia, Peru, and New Spain in March 1822, and President James Monroe issued his doctrine on December 2, 1822, about six months after Iturbide had assumed the crown of Mexico for himself and his heirs.

IMPERIAL ITURBIDE

Readers may puzzle at the relatively detailed attention devoted in the following pages to the Iturbide regime while longish periods of the following three decades are treated only synthetically. The rise and fall of Agustín de Iturbide in its entirety took up scarcely two years, and he enjoyed the apogee of his power during only six months or so before the earth began to give way beneath him. This early phase of Mexico's nationhood saw the unequivocal emergence of four major overlapping themes that came to dominate the political life of the nineteenth century and extended their reach in somewhat different forms into the twentieth. First, the question of monarchism versus republicanism emerged during this brief period, the monarchical experiment failing and republicanism emerging triumphant if chaotic. Second, the struggle between the executive and legislative powers in government saw its first dramatic trial during Iturbide's reign and in subsequent regimes would account for pendulum swings now in one direction, now in the other, but the outcome over the long term favored the executive power. Third, the rough division of political men into conservative and liberal factions emerged quickly before Iturbide's election as emperor in the spring of 1822 and ever more clearly as the first national congress took shape during its abbreviated life in 1822–1823. Finally, the question of the spatial distribution of power within a national polity took the form of centralism versus federalism, respectively the claims of the national government and its capital city versus "la provincia," a derogatory term sometimes still heard in Mexico for everything outside the capital. (This attitude is encapsulated in the adage "Fuera de México, todo es Cuauhtitlán"—"Everything outside Mexico City is Cuauhtitlán"—metaphorically, "the sticks."[3]) Some of these tensions were already latent in the colonial regime but emerged explicitly during 1821–1823, setting much of the pattern in Mexican politics for the early republican era. What all four of these pairings have in common in one way or another is the question of concentration of power, whether it should be closely held or dispersed to some degree. So the brief Iturbide period is an origin story worth telling for what it reveals of processes that unfolded in the following decades and that have left their imprint on Mexican public life ever since.

Control of the capital was quickly assured in September 1821 by Iturbide's Army of the Three Guarantees with the fig leaf of sanction by Juan O'Donojú, who had no other option because he lacked independent resources of any kind. Transitional organs of government were then created under Iturbide's tutelage. "When I entered Mexico [City]," Iturbide later wrote, "my will was the law; I commanded the public force; the tribunals had no power other than that which emanated from my authority. Could I have been more absolute?"[4] He handpicked a provisional governing junta (the Soberana Junta Provisional Gubernativa) through a process as yet undocumented. Made up of thirty-eight prominent military men, ecclesiastics, landowners, and officials, the junta claimed for itself exclusive national sovereignty and the legislative function until a Mexican congress could be elected. The junta generated an act of independence and appointed Agustín de Iturbide president of a five-man regency (including Juan O'Donojú), the government's executive and military arm. The regency, in turn, established administrative departments with their corresponding bureaucracies: treasury, war, justice and ecclesiastical affairs, and interior and exterior relations, a structure that would endure with occasional alterations up to mid-century. Despite the junta's overall elite status and sympathy with Iturbide, discussions within it arose as to how much power should be delegated to him. This foreshadowed tensions between the legislative and executive powers that were to endure for the rest of our period and end with the presidentialist regimes of Benito Juárez and Porfirio Díaz. Control of the army rested almost exclusively with former royalist commanders, all friends and collaborators of Iturbide's with monarchist sympathies, the sole exception among this military elite being the old independence chieftain Vicente Guerrero, whose alliance with Iturbide was one of pragmatic politics on both sides and was always tense. Despite the presence in the junta of those who favored some sort of absolutist regime headed by Iturbide, the call (*convocatoria*) for elections issued by the body envisioned a legislature of a single house and a virtually universal male suffrage. Iturbide's much more conservative proposal favored a bicameral legislature with an upper house of corporative structure (military, Church, etc.—a plan eventually dropped), a lower house of deputies elected on the basis of population (one deputy per 50,000 inhabitants), and a narrower franchise. Iturbide was able to intimidate the junta through public displays of his military power and by obtruding himself menacingly into its assemblies. Without legal authority to do so he appointed a second commission that endorsed his plans for congressional elections, thus hijacking the *convocatoria*. Carried out in December 1821 and January 1822, voting was based on a sort of compromise embracing a nominally wide franchise and a complicated system of indirect balloting. By the end of November 1821, meanwhile, Iturbide had begun jailing alleged plotters and political opponents, establishing a pattern in Mexican political life for the rest of the century. At this very moment, in November 1821, the Council of State in Madrid was drafting a plan for the pacification of the American colonies, insisting that there would be no dismemberment of the empire on any terms. The newly elected deputies of the Mexican national congress were sworn in on February 24, 1822. In March news arrived that the Spanish government had repudiated the Treaty of Córdoba, refused to recognize the independence of New Spain, and planned to send commissioners to negotiate the continued adherence of the colony to the Spanish monarchy.

In this chaotic situation relations between regency president Iturbide and the Mexican congress (called a *Cortes* after its Spanish model) deteriorated quickly. Adding to his authority for the moment was a cultish adoration of him as the savior of the fatherland, which extended itself to his family. For his services to the nation he received from the national government a huge sum in cash and an enormous grant of land in Texas as rewards. Between his regency and the congress there arose an issue over army salaries, Iturbide favoring maintaining or even increasing them, the congress attempting to reduce them to relieve intense fiscal stress on the national treasury. Furthermore, Iturbide was demanding an increase in the size of the regular Mexican army and of state militias, raising fears in congress of a military dictatorship propped up by the army and the Church. The regency's somewhat more sympathetic attitude toward the remaining Spanish forces in the island fortress of San Juan de Ulúa, across the harbor from the port city of Veracruz, also clashed with congress's demand for their immediate evacuation to Spain. In early April Iturbide pressed congress to widen his powers to deal with conspiracies to revive Spanish rule and to repel an invasion of reconquest, a move that raised arguments within the congress and between it and Iturbide to a fever pitch. (A similar issue—civil political resistance to expanded military and taxation powers in anticipation of what turned out to be a botched Spanish invasion of reconquest in 1829—played a major part in the fall of President Vicente Guerrero in 1829–1830.) Although the ostensible questions in Iturbide's clashes with the congress concerned the military, beneath them lay what would become the perennial problem of legislative versus executive power. By May a serious debate had arisen in the congress about reconstituting Mexico as a republic. This arose from considerable intellectual sympathy for that form of polity, but also from legislators' fears of a military dictatorship and of Iturbide's obviously growing ambitions to assume executive dominance, albeit within a constitutional framework.

By mid-May 1822 crowds in Mexico City were acclaiming Iturbide as emperor, supported and encouraged (and possibly bribed) by his allies among the high military officers. Several officers issued a manifesto to the Mexican Cortes demanding the election of Iturbide as constitutional emperor by "the will of the people" under the still reigning 1812 Constitution. On May 19 army units commanded by *iturbidista* officers surrounded the congress, from which many of the would-be emperor's political opponents had already fled, forcing Iturbide's election in what amounted to a military coup. A formal proposal mandating his election as emperor within a constitutional framework, with ultimate sovereignty still residing in the congress, was offered by the Guadalajara-born medical doctor and ardent liberal Valentín Gómez Farías (1781–1858), a leading *puro* (radical) liberal of his day. Gómez Farías would be president of the country briefly several times, enacting radical reform measures aimed at reducing the influence of the Church. He attached his political cart to flawed but charismatic figures, first to Iturbide, then for many years to Antonio López de Santa Anna. The proposal was approved by the remaining deputies (of whom there appears to have been a quorum), Iturbide taking the oath of office on May 21, 1822, as "Agustín, by Divine Providence and by the Congress of the Nation, the First Constitutional Emperor of Mexico"; his official coronation took place only in July.

In the heated political atmosphere of the capital anti-Iturbide conspiracies blossomed among men of liberal political thought, several on their way to public prominence and long careers, such as Carlos María de Bustamante, Juan Pablo Anaya, and the liberal gadfly Fray Servando Teresa de Mier. By the end of October Iturbide moved to consolidate his power by arresting opponents and disbanding what remained of the congress. He claimed that the elections had been flawed (ever the resort of would-be dictators) and created in its place the Junta Nacional Instituyente from a block of the elected deputies supporting him.[6] This body eventually included forty-five deputies from the suppressed congress and was therefore claimed by itself and the emperor to represent the nation. Although its members were selected by the emperor himself it was by no means a rubber stamp. Meeting for the first time on November 2, 1822, the junta was charged with writing a preliminary outline for a new constitution heavily weighted toward the executive, write a new *convocatoria* for congressional elections, and reform the national treasury. The constitutional project it produced followed the lines of the Plan of Iguala, but its critics and the emperor's opponents saw it as expanding the powers of the executive inordinately. Proposals emerged to reform the national treasury, primarily by imposing new taxes, reviving old ones, and

BOX 8.1. ITURBIDE AND THE
THEATER OF RELUCTANCE

Iturbide's written and public pronouncements about his popular acclamation as emperor, the ratification of his elevation through election
by the Mexican congress, and his struggles with that body make for
interesting reading. In his memoirs he wrote, "At my entry into Mexico
[City] on the 27th of September, and at the time of giving the oath for
Independence on the 27th of October they wanted me even then to be
emperor; I was not proclaimed only because I would not be, and I had
great difficulty to make those who had raised their voices desist from
the project." Wrote one political figure to him at the time, "If the common view of the people, that is, not of some individuals in particular
but of the people in general, fulfilling their duty of gratitude, proclaims
Your Excellency as emperor . . . how can Your Excellency resist the
vote of the nation?"

   Of the Mexico City crowd's (made up largely of soldiers) proclamation of him as emperor on the night of May 18, 1822, Iturbide wrote
in his memoirs:

   My first impulse was to go forth and make known to the people my reluctance to accept a crown whose weight already oppressed me excessively.
   If I restrained myself from appearing before them for that purpose, it was
   in compliance with the advice of a friend who happened at that moment
   to be at my side. "They will consider it to be an insult," he scarcely had
   time to say, "and believing themselves treated with contempt, an irritated
   people can become a monster. You must make this fresh sacrifice for the
   public good. The country is in danger; remain a moment longer unde-
   cided, and you will hear the death shouts." I felt it necessary to submit to
   this misfortune which was the greatest I had yet suffered.

He continued:

   I was the depository of the will of the Mexicans; in the first place because
   what I signed in their name [that is, the Treaty of Córdoba] is what they
   ought to have wished for; in the second place because they had already
   given me many strong proofs of their real approbation to it, joining to
   me those amongst them capable of bearing arms, others assisting me by

all the means that were in their power, and receiving me in all the towns through which I passed with acclamations and praise. . . . As no-one was compelled by force to make these demonstrations, it is evident that they approved my design, and that their will was similar to mine.

At the end of May the newly elected Mexican emperor wrote to Simón Bolívar, the president of Gran Colombia, "I am far from considering as a benefit as act which lays upon my shoulders a burden that oppresses me! I lack the strength needed to sustain the scepter. I abhorred it, but in the end I agreed to accept it in order to prevent evils to the country that was about to succumb anew, if not to the former slavery, at least to the horrors of anarchy."

And in his memoirs he defended himself against charges of despotism by blaming the congress for disputing power and authority with him out of base motives:

I have already said and never shall cease to repeat, that I accepted the Crown to serve my country and save it from anarchy. I was fully aware that my lot would grow worse by it; that envy would persecute me; that it was impossible to please everyone; that many would have been displeased with the measures that were unavoidable to adopt; that I was going to oppose a body of men [that is, the constituent congress] actuated by pride and ambition, which while it inveighed against despotism was endeavoring to collect in itself all power, reducing the monarch to the condition of a phantom. . . . A tyranny [is] still more unsupportable when exercised by many than when such an abuse of power is in the hands of a single man. If the Congress had succeeded in its project the Mexicans would have been less free than the people of Algiers.[5]

decreeing forced loans on wealthy merchants and other property holders to meet the lopsided budgetary deficits of the government and imperial household; these were never enacted because the regime fell early in 1823. In view of this grab for dictatorial power, when the first viable Mexican constitution of the post-Iturbide era actually was written and promulgated in 1824 it was federal rather than centralist in structure, tilting heavily toward legislative dominance.

Agustín de Iturbide's dominance of the national political scene unfolded quickly, his fall as rapid as his rise. While he play-acted as supreme imperial highness on the great stage of the capital (Lucas Alamán wrote that the regime resembled more "a dream or a theatrical representation than an empire"), resistance to his rule was developing among always-restive military chieftains and regional civil authorities in the Mexican provinces. Some of these men were prompted to action by jealousy and ambition, others by genuine conviction that a republican form of government suited Mexico better than the rule of Emperor Agustín I. Iturbide's behavior as monarch very soon antagonized both major political actors and general populace, undermining support for him in a remarkably short time. The extravagant display of the imperial household was a major factor here. Iturbide developed an elaborate court ritual, swelling the number of titled nobility, members of nobiliary orders, and attendees at his court, distributing grandiloquent titles among his own family members and making their birthdays into national holidays. He expended large sums on a number of imperial residences and on the support of the imperial household. He was unable to address the critical issues facing the new nation: its fiscal problems (which his extravagance aggravated), the withdrawal of Spanish troops from the national territory, the rise in banditry by men demobilized from insurgent bands who had few prospects in the shattered economy, and the generation of a national charter to replace the Spanish Constitution of 1812. As early as the summer of 1822 a subversive pamphletry had begun to characterize Iturbide as a tyrannical despot.

The movement that toppled the First Mexican Empire was initiated by the remarkably long-lived Antonio López de Santa Anna (1794–1876), a political survivor who would rise to the position of political arbiter and perennial president of the country through the 1820s and 1830s. Born of a moderately prominent family in the Veracruz region, his father a royalist army officer, he was always to make of the Gulf coast area the base of his personal wealth and military power. He came to own vast rural estates in the region, where he planted colonies of old soldiers upon whom he could draw in political and military crises. The most famous of these properties was his Hacienda Manga de Clavo, to which he frequently retired from the presidency. The estate was burned by invading American forces during the Mexican-American War, never to recover.

Santa Anna had more schooling than many young Creoles of his generation but chose to pursue a military career rather than the commercial one favored by his parents. Joining the royalist forces as a youngster of sixteen he fought against the insurgency and rose quickly through the ranks until trading sides and joining with Iturbide, who later promoted him to brigadier general. Early marked by the emperor as talented and ambitious but potentially threatening to his rule, Santa Anna was removed from command of the port of Veracruz and posted to Mexico City where Iturbide thought him more closely under his control. But he returned to his native Veracruz and on December 2, 1822, pronounced (thus the term *pronunciamiento* for the multitude of military

Figure 8.1. Antonio López de Santa Anna (1794–1876), royalist officer, late convert to the cause of independence, military man, and several times president of Mexico. DeGolyer Library, Southern Methodist University.

uprisings plaguing Mexico in the nineteenth century) an uprising against the imperial regime. In two separate declarations, however, his justifications for the rebellion were somewhat at odds with each other. One of these favored a republic on the basis that the congress had been illegally disbanded by the emperor and that Iturbide's election was invalid because effected under duress, which was true enough.[7] The other declaration said nothing of a republic but only that Santa Anna rose to defend the rights of the army, compromised by the despotic emperor. A few days later he was joined by the former insurgent chieftain Guadalupe Victoria in the Plan de Veracruz, which more formally repudiated Iturbide's actions but not monarchy as such. This plan declared that the nation through its duly elected representatives had the solemn right and duty to determine its own form of governance. The alliance of ex-royalist officer and ex-insurgent leader soon attracted the adherence of Guerrero and of Nicolás Bravo (1786–1854), another major insurgent chieftain and future president. Defeated by the government's army and their men dispersed, Santa Anna and his collaborators were soon joined by another disaffected military man, the Spanish-born commander of Iturbide's own forces, General José Antonio Echávarri (variant spelling Echáverri). On February 1, 1823, the collaborators issued the Plan de Casa Mata, named for the Veracruz town where it was proclaimed, ramping down Santa Anna's initial demands to the election of a new national congress with the continuation of formerly elected deputies who might meet with the approval of their home constituencies. The plan also advocated an increased degree of home rule for the provincial deputations originally mandated by the Madrid Cortes, numbering some twenty-three by 1822. What the plan did not demand was a change of government to a republican form or the overthrow of Iturbide, whom the rebels assumed would still occupy a prominent role in the state apparatus, but whether as monarch was not clear.

After some weeks of a hazy political situation, Iturbide's fall was quite sudden. He initially dismissed the uprising as unimportant, especially after his forces inflicted military defeats upon the rebels and confined Santa Anna's armed elements to the city of Veracruz. But by the end of February 1823 military units in the capital and elsewhere began falling away from the emperor until by March he was virtually isolated. Failing to endorse the call for new congressional elections and confronted with increasing resistance to his rule from the Mexican provinces as well as the Casa Mata plotters, Iturbide recalled what remained of the old congress hoping thus to arrest developments, but the rebels were not appeased. A standoff ensued for several days, Iturbide weakened by political and military defections but unwilling to start a civil war to defend his throne. In the absence of a quorum the recalled congress debated what the limits of its authority were, while the Casa Mata rebels waited to see what would happen. His situation untenable, the emperor submitted his abdication to congress on March 19. On May 11, 1823, a British ship bore him away into Italian exile at the Tuscan city of Livorno with a substantial party of family and servants, supported by whatever he could carry with him of personal wealth and a substantial but by no means munificent annual pension guaranteed by the new executive authorities.

At the end of 1823 the exiled former emperor relocated to London. In Mexico a number of plots had been hatched to bring him back to the throne but were squelched by timely arrests. By the spring of 1824 Iturbide determined to return to Mexico in response, he insisted, to the anguished pleadings of people who felt anarchy and national dissolution imminent; he believed he was the indispensable man who could forestall this catastrophe. Leaving aside the question of whether his presence would have calmed the situation or not, this was an accurate reading of political conditions in Mexico because the period from 1823 to 1824 saw an upsurge of federalist movements in the former provinces, now states, that threatened to tear the country apart. Iturbide and a small party sailed from Southampton on May 11. Unknown to him, the newly elected congress had declared his election to the imperial throne invalid because achieved by force and intimidation. Alarmed by the prospect of his return the congress first suspended his pension, then declared in a law of April 28, 1824, that should Iturbide return to Mexico he would be subject peremptorily to the death penalty without further judicial proceedings. He never received this news before setting out, nor is it clear that such a threat would have dissuaded him from returning. Landing on the northern Gulf coast in what is today the state of Tamaulipas, Iturbide and a companion immediately fell into the hands of local military authorities and the ex-emperor was executed by a firing squad on July 19, 1824. Whether this was a martyrdom or the just desserts of an overweening and seriously miscalculated ambition, Iturbide's reputation has been highly mixed in the two centuries since his death. Even many of his political foes at the time conceded that he had played a key role in consummating independence from Spain, although some of the outliers, among them the politicians Carlos María de Bustamante and Father Servando Teresa de Mier (whom we shall both meet soon), openly advocated sending him to the gibbet. The hegemony of republicanism in Mexican political life after his time has tended to turn his brief monarchical rule into a freakish experiment that many Mexicans would prefer to disavow even while ignoring how logical it was at the moment and what a long genealogy monarchy had had in the country.[8]

THE INFANT REPUBLIC, 1823–1827

The fall of the imperial regime left behind it a political vacuum that over the next eighteen months or so sucked into itself heated debates and even armed conflict about the locus of sovereignty in the newly independent Mexico, the balance of power between the central government and the provinces/states, and about whether the executive or legislative branch of government should be dominant. It became immediately clear that monarchy had been discredited and that a republic should be installed. The reasons for this disillusionment with monarchy were many, among which three figured centrally. First, while monarchy seemed the natural default position when considering how the country should be governed there was sympathy for republican forms and a successful exemplar in the United States. This did not involve any slavish emulation of American political models but an awareness of possibilities. Second, although a presidential-republican system might well lend itself to authoritarian rule, as would become clear in the case of Santa Anna, the federalist republic that quickly emerged in 1823–1824 addressed the fears of many political men regarding the concentration of power in the hands of one person. This was the major motive in congress for the construction in 1823 of the Supreme Executive Power (see discussion shortly) as a triumvirate rather than a single executive with wide powers. Finally, a republic offered the possibility of a wider, more open political field than an aristocratic court orbiting around a monarch. In this way the ambitions of upwardly mobile men of color, professionals of some education, and other men of the small but growing Mexican middle class might have more space for political participation than would be offered in a monarchical-aristocratic regime.

It is very difficult to determine the opinion of the mass of the Mexican population regarding the supposed virtues of a republican versus a monarchical form of governance. Elections for public office were nearly all indirect, interposing slippery layers of indeterminacy between voter and aspirant to political post. While electoral outcomes provide some gross index of political trends, they are not reliable guides to the direction of public opinion more concretely. There is also a good deal of doubt about how informed voters were and whether they were bribed by one political faction or another to vote a certain way. Furthermore, one of the chief differences between the colonial arrangement and the early republican period was the dispersion of power and authority outward from the viceregal capital to the major cities of the realm. The dispute over the geographic distribution of power was virtually unceasing over the next several decades, but most of the major political action took place in Mexico City. Early discussions in the congress about moving the national capital to Puebla or Querétaro were abandoned quickly in the face of the economic, political, cultural, demographic, and historic weight of the capital, whose dominance was ratified by the creation of the Federal District in 1824. The capital is where "public opinion" manifested itself most loudly and clearly even though its inhabitants made up at most about 3 percent of the national population. But what ordinary people actually thought about politics is hard to tell. The newspapers that rapidly proliferated with independence especially in the capital—there were about thirty in Mexico City in the 1820s—but also in other cities were most often the mouthpieces of powerful individuals or cliques, and all claimed to represent "the people." Because large sectors of the capital's people were barely or not at all literate, how much the combat journalism of the day actually formed opinion or represented it, as opposed to broadcasting the ideas of the journalists and their sponsors, is open to question. This is not to say that the broader public was entirely inert politically or disconnected from public life but only that the infant republic came close to being oligarchic. This organization of political consciousness and engagement corresponds to the idea of a "political nation" embracing a few thousand men scattered around the country and concentrated in the cities, above all Mexico City. These individuals occupied the upper reaches of the state bureaucracy, the Church, the army, the legislative bodies in Mexico City and "the provinces," the small educated professional class, and the more important miners, merchants, and landowners.

The reconvened congress initially failed to summon a quorum but by late March was able to declare itself in session with 103 deputies. They created a political tabula rasa by formally annulling the Plan of Iguala and the Treaty of Córdoba and repudiating Iturbide's election as emperor while retaining at least temporarily the Spanish Constitution of 1812 as an operating charter. In reaction to the high-handed tactics of the former emperor the congress appointed a three-man executive. When a new constitution came to be drafted later on there was some sentiment for retaining such an arrangement as opposed to vesting undivided executive powers in a single individual, but it dissipated quickly. The Supremo Poder Ejecutivo (Supreme Executive Power) was made up during the spring and summer of 1823 by the independence *caudillos* Nicolás Bravo and Guadalupe Victoria, along with Pedro Celestino Negrete (1777–1846), one of the top peninsular-born generals who had fought the insurgency vigorously but at the eleventh hour joined Iturbide. All these men have been called Bourbonist-centralists. The "Bourbonist" label did not necessarily indicate a literal predilection for a monarch of the Bourbon dynasty but for a highly powerful centralized executive with king-like attributes. The Supreme Power's makeup changed later on but with one exception remained composed of prominent military men. During these months the debate over the form of government continued to rage in Mexico City, the provincial legislative bodies, and the political press. Within and outside the reconvened congress some political men felt that national sovereignty should reside exclusively in that body and that it should undertake to draft a constitution, while others thought congress' legitimate function strictly limited to the calling of new elections.

Meanwhile, the provinces whose political opposition to centralist rule under Iturbide had been a major factor in his fall were now on the way to declaring themselves sovereign states, espousing different degrees of autonomy from a central government still trying to find its way. Oaxaca and Yucatán (the latter of which would enjoy a highly conflictual relationship with the central government, some years later even attempting to break away from Mexico to form an independent nation) envisioned an extreme form of federalism similar in some ways to the government of the Anglo-American colonies under the Articles of Confederation (1777–1789). This political option was even more vividly exemplified by the province of Guadalajara, shortly to become the capital of the "free, independent, and sovereign" State of Jalisco, the political center of the once-vast Kingdom of New Galicia, a subordinate but semiautonomous unit within the colonial Kingdom of New Spain. Regional officials there disavowed the authorities of Mexico City entirely, both Supreme Executive Power and congress, on the grounds that they were illegitimate and that with the fall of the empire political power had devolved to the provinces/states. Under the leadership of former royalist officer turned *iturbidista* Luis Quintanar (1772–1837), the political/military chief of Guadalajara and then the first governor of the State of Jalisco, the spring and summer months of 1823 saw a real possibility that the Mexican west might secede from the rest of the country to form an independent nation; some feared that Yucatán might follow the same path. During May the provincial deputation of Guadalajara, in the words of historian Stanley Green, "in effect declared independence from the national government," and by June eleven of the eighteen deputations had declared no confidence in the central government.[9] Whether secession was a realistic project or not is questionable, but the possibility hung in the air at the time.

The Supreme Executive Power could hardly run the apparatus of government by itself, so a ministry was soon appointed with portfolios of war, treasury, justice and ecclesiastical affairs, and internal and external relations. *Relaciones* (Relations) was the most important post, going to the thirty-one-year-old Lucas Alamán, recently returned from long years of study and travel in Europe and a prominent role as a Mexican deputy in the Spanish imperial parliament in Madrid. With the federalist impulse rampant among politicians of the newly forming states, his main job was to oversee relations between them and what was left of the central government. Primarily through an intense correspondence with the more prominent and obstreperous provincial chieftains, during these months Alamán struggled to keep the country together with his bare hands. Combined with changing political circumstances, the intervention of other political actors, and a sense of reality settling on the more ardent federalist firebrands, his efforts were successful in keeping Mexico in one piece, although the national constitution of 1824 would amply embody the federalist impulse.

During the summer and fall of 1823 political complications (of which I can provide only the barest summary here) proliferated quickly. Fishing in troubled waters, as he was to do for the next three decades, Santa Anna proclaimed a "plan" espousing the creation of a federal republic—effectively already happening on the ground—and appointing himself "protector" of federalism. His movement failed to flourish, however, and the twenty-nine-year-old burgeoning *caudillo* returned to Mexico City to face a military court of inquiry. A well-led and well-equipped army was sent from the capital to bring the recalcitrant western provinces to heel, but a compromise was reached by which a military confrontation and a possible civil war were avoided when conditional recognition of the central government and its taxing authority were recognized by the states of Jalisco (Guadalajara) and Zacatecas. In mid-June a new electoral law was issued by the rump congress over the signature of interior minister Alamán convoking (thus the term *convocatoria*) congressional

BOX 8.2. LUCAS ALAMÁN ON FEDERALISM

As several provinces of New Spain, now becoming the states of the Mexican nation, contested the authority of the central government in 1823, the newly appointed secretary of interior and exterior relations in the central government Lucas Alamán authored a dense, even impassioned correspondence with provincial chieftains. The language of eighteenth- and nineteenth-century political theory echoed in many respects arguments aired decades before in the fledgling United States in the Federalist Papers of Alexander Hamilton, James Madison, and John Jay. The essays concerned national and state sovereignty, the right to impose taxation, the nature of factional political competition, and other matters vital to the life of a republic. Reading Alamán's words gives a sense of the stakes involved and of the tone of political discourse at the dawn of the Mexican nation. To General (and later Governor) Luis Quintanar, the leader of provincial autonomists and ardent federalist spirits in the vast western province centered on the city of Guadalajara, the minister of the interior wrote in June 1823:

Lacking the unifying center that should exist in any government, whatever its form—a center that cannot be maintained if the segregation of the provinces were to proceed without previously establishing the bases for their federation—this disunion would open the door to cruel despotism, a necessary and inevitable consequence of anarchy. . . . It is incontestable that Sovereignty resides in the Nation. But from this principle it does not follow that each section of it may have the faculty of altering the constitutive laws recognized by the whole, and to disobey the orders of the legitimately constituted government. . . . How can it not be recognized that in whatever the form of government ultimately adopted, there must be demands common to the entire Nation, as there are common obligations to undertake? . . . Will we not precipitate ourselves into anarchy, and into the most frightening disorder, [if we] attempt to separate from the government at [such] critical moments? It is not to be thought that the provinces [will] attempt to govern themselves in isolation [from each other] and with no center of union until they unite again under the arrangements of federation.

When in the spring of 1823 Antonio López de Santa Anna declared himself the "protector" of federalism, minister Alamán responded on behalf of the government in a printed circular of June 3, 1823:

There can be only one power in the nation, and only the supreme [that is, central] government can wield it. To create another, separate [power] to guarantee rights that this congress has [already] known how to respect and sustain, to form an army independent of the power to which it owes obedience . . . to entrust to that army the faculty of activating a call for elections that is already decreed and nearly published, to offer forces to the provinces to carry forward a system [that is, a republic] that the representatives of the Nation have yet to reject, to divide [the Nation] at precisely the moment when union is most essential . . . to appropriate without any legal authorization an alarming title [that is, Protector de la libertad Mexicana] that tends openly toward the violation of the [as yet unwritten] constitution, to division, and to anarchy—these are things that amid such delicate circumstances can be the origin of infinite troubles, [that may] take us to the most horrible disorder, and because of it to the despotism that disguised [though it may be] under any name would produce in the nation that sad influence we have [recently] experienced.

To Quintanar in Guadalajara, an acknowledged supporter of the return of Agustín de Iturbide, Alamán wrote in late July 1823 of the ex-emperor's rumored return (which would not actually occur until the following year, and then with fatal results for Iturbide):

The falsity of that news is almost palpable and no man gifted with common sense would dare to give it any credence. . . . The supposed arrival of D. Agustín de Iturbide at a port of some neighbor state of course is a means to fragment [public] opinion into factions, alarm the population, and tear it apart and [thus] introduce the most disastrous anarchy, afterward gathering the fruit of such a brutal misfortune. And the situation may even become more delicate: it is not a remote prospect that the political affairs of Europe may become more and more delicate. The League of sovereigns [arrayed] against the liberties of the [Iberian] Peninsula perhaps has as its object not only the [maintenance] of royal absolutism on the European continent; our [own] independence and liberty, secured by the most prodigious effort, may be endangered if we find ourselves divided. If the provinces, repudiating the very federation they proclaim, appropriate to themselves at their whim the faculties of the Government, impeding its policies, what could then be done in the possible case of an exterior attack? . . . [Internal] separation will always

> damage general interests, but in the present circumstances no better
> means could have been invented to make our independence and liberty
> illusory. To avoid the approaching storm we see coming upon us, the
> Supreme Executive Power sees no other remedy that can save us from
> shipwreck than union.[10]

elections for later in the year. The newly forming states recognized only that part of the *convocatoria* mandating elections for a national congress but not elections for the provincial deputations that for the most part had converted themselves into state legislatures, thus effectively repudiating the authority of the national government to intervene in any way in provincial/state affairs. Completing the swing to an unambiguously nationalist-republican political system, the still sitting reconvened congress declared Father Hidalgo, Father Morelos, and other insurgent heroes "beneméritos de la patria" (something like "distinguished [men] of the Fatherland"). A grand procession conveyed their remains to the capital's cathedral for ceremonial reburial. Writing with typical irony many years later, Lucas Alamán commented that the same people now paying their respects to the heroic insurgents were the very ones who had ordered the martyrs shot. Elections for a new national congress were held throughout the country in August and September 1823. The political tendencies of the deputies ranged across a wide gamut, although the body tilted in the direction of federalism; relatively few of the 144 deputies had served in the first congress. The most radical federalists basically favored a confederal model of very loose national integration with the central government reduced almost to a dimensionless point, while ardent centralists espoused a heavy concentration of power in the national government. Reflecting the federalist tendency of the congress a preliminary draft of a constitution, the Acta Constitutiva, was enacted in November 1823, promulgated officially the following January pending the ratification of a permanent charter the next year. This declared Mexico to be a "popular, federal, representative republic" and still exclusively a Roman Catholic one. In the months that followed a committee of political luminaries in the congress drafted the final document, although the major issues were never resolved definitively, as the history of the following decades would demonstrate.

The unquiet political life of the young republic, meanwhile, hurtled along during 1824. The continued occupation of the island fortress of San Juan de Ulúa by Spanish forces, the occasional bombardment of the city of Veracruz by its artillery, and the stubborn ambition of King Fernando VII for the reconquest of the breakaway colony provoked apprehensions of an invasion most likely launched from Cuba and caused an upsurge in anti-Spanish feeling in the country. Lynchings of European Spaniards were known to occur, and in 1824 a brief military rebellion demanded the expulsion of European-born Spaniards from Mexico. In July Agustín de Iturbide reentered Mexico only to suffer the fate already described. The Anglo colonization of the vast province of Texas continued under contracts made earlier with entrepreneur Moses Austin (1761–1821) and continued with his son Stephen (1793–1836). Americans poured into the region, many bringing with them their black slaves, their Protestantism, and their distinct political culture. This tide of settlement would lead directly to the Mexican-American War two decades later and the loss of half the national territory to Mexico's northern sister republic. But for the moment such colonization seemed a good idea to hold and populate the empty territory—empty, that is, but for its native inhabitants—if the tempestuous settlers could be controlled and Mexicanized, which was to prove impossible. Another territorial adjustment occurred when the United Provinces of Central America, part of newly independent Mexico, went their way in the summer of 1824, the province of Chiapas opting after some wavering to stay with Mexico.

The most important thing to happen during this eventful year was the adoption of the new federal constitution (Mexico's first, if one discounts the never-enacted 1814 Constitution of Apatzingán) by the recently elected congress and its ratification in early October 1824. In a highly polarized political environment the new national charter could hardly be all things to all people. One prominent deputy, the picaresque political priest Fray Servando Teresa de Mier (1765–1827), signed it dressed in black, as for a funeral. The document was set aside and succeeded by two others (1836 and 1843)—not strictly called constitutions but functioning as such de facto—before the enactment of the "liberal" constitution of 1857. That document prevailed until the present charter was adopted in 1917, during the Mexican Revolution, although it has often been amended since. The 1824 constitution definitively established Mexico as a popular, federal, representative (and exclusively Catholic) republic. As with the Constitution of Apatzingán scholars have argued over whether the major influence in the charter's formation was the revolutionary constitution of the French Republic, the US document of 1789, or the Spanish Constitution of Cádiz of 1812. The general consensus is that elements of the 1812 Spanish constitution prevailed, in some passages literally, with the key difference that Mexico was to be a republic rather than a constitutional monarchy. A three-branch model was laid out with a single chief executive accompanied by a ministry, a Supreme Court, and a bicameral legislature made up of a chamber of deputies and a senate. The president was to be popularly elected for a single term of four years (although there was a complex system of electors based on the states of the federation, and thus indirect election); the runner-up in the election would serve as vice president and take over the presidency in the event of the chief executive's incapacity or absence on military campaign. During his many stints as chief executive Santa Anna's vice presidents took over in his place a number of times when he either retired for reasons of "health" (aversions to the work of decision making, one suspects) or was off leading Mexican armies in campaigns that almost all ended disastrously. Freedom of the press and the right to private property were guaranteed, the determination of the extent of the franchise (exclusively male) was reserved to the states as in the United States constitution, and the major fiscal support of the central government consisted of customs duties and subsidies due from the states. Under the weak federal system (in contrast to the United States) the entities of the union retained great authority to manage their own affairs including the maintenance of armed militias. The balance of power in the national government leaned strongly in favor of the legislature. Still, the 1824 constitution was something of a compromise, assigning considerable power to the central government, located primarily in the congress, but retaining numerous spheres of action to the states.

In the presidential election of 1824 independence heroes Guadalupe Victoria (the *nom de guerre* of José Fernández y Félix, 1786–1843) and Nicolás Bravo (1786–1854) faced each other, both centralists. Victoria carried the election in the chamber of deputies by eleven states to six for Bravo, who therefore assumed the vice presidency. Victoria was the last president for many decades to serve out his entire term in office (1824–1829). Although the executive branch was at first politically centralist and relatively conservative, congress elected to its own presidency the radical democrat, federalist, and physician Lorenzo de Zavala (1788–1836), one of the more interesting figures of the period. Born in Yucatán, Zavala was from his youth a Freemason of the more liberal York Rite of the organization introduced into Mexico in 1826; served as a Mexican deputy in the Spanish imperial parliament in the early 1820s; and was at various points governor of the State of Mexico, a senator in the national government, and minister of finance, while continually a combat journalist. He traveled widely in the United States and wrote about it, married an American woman after the death of his first wife, owned land in Texas, and became vice president of the Republic of Texas, where he died in 1836. Victoria proved a relatively weak president because in the face of congressional dominance his maneuvering room was limited. He at least tried to act in a nonpartisan fashion while struggles among the still nascent political tendencies, not yet parties as we might recognize them, were growing fiercer. He drifted further and further toward federalism and away from the moderate centralism he brought with him into office. This provoked some considerable turnover among his cabinet ministers, including Alamán, who resigned in the fall of 1825. While liberalism and conservatism mapped moderately well onto federalism and centralism, respectively (although there were interesting crossovers), rather than formal party structures these were ideological tendencies manifested in factional loyalties, political discourse, the combative and totally nonobjective journalism of the day, and struggles over policy.

In lieu of formal political parties these tendencies crystallized more and more in the 1820s in the membership of many political men in one of two orders of Freemasonry. In our own time Masonry (technically, Freemasonry) looks to most people like an anachronistic, somewhat silly, ostensibly exclusive secret society peopled by elderly men who wear funny ceremonial gear and pronounce mumbo-jumbo rituals in dark halls, basically play-acting at being conspiratorial. But in the eighteenth and nineteenth centuries Masonry was a powerful, recondite international brotherhood of enlightened men seeking to make the world a better place through self-improvement and political sympathy. Conspiracy theories, mostly apocryphal, have abounded over the centuries about the Freemasons' presumed secret power to control governments, foment revolutions, and direct the fate of humanity. Freemasons espoused Enlightenment ideas, were most often antimonarchical in their politics in a world still ruled by monarchs, and constituted a sort of shadow state of far-reaching influence if not actual control. The basic tenets of Masonic belief were freedom, independence, liberty, and equality. There were several different orders of Masons in the Atlantic world, each with its own rituals, symbols, and hierarchy of positions. There were a number of Freemasons in the generation of the American Founding Fathers, including George Washington, Benjamin Franklin, John Hancock, Aaron Burr, John Marshall, Paul Revere, Samuel Adams, and Thomas Paine; the Marquis de Lafayette was a Mason; Thomas Jefferson was long suspected of being one but probably was not, while James Madison probably was a member, and James Monroe certainly was; Benedict Arnold was also a Mason. Among European Enlightenment figures there were many Masons, including Voltaire, Rousseau, Diderot, and their amorous contemporary Giacomo (Jacques) Casanova; the French revolutionary figure Comte de Mirabeau was one. Beethoven was a Mason, and so was Mozart, whose opera *The Magic Flute* is riddled with Masonic symbolism. Among major figures more directly involved in our period were Iturbide, the South American Creole patriots Simón Bolívar and José de San Martín, and usurper of the Spanish throne Joseph Bonaparte.

York Rite Masonry penetrated Mexico starting in 1825, introduced by an early United States envoy, Joel R. Poinsett (1779–1851), while the Scottish Rite of Freemasonry had existed in Mexico since at least the beginning of the nineteenth century. Born in South Carolina, Poinsett was educated in part at the University of Edinburgh and owned a slave-worked plantation, as many prominent Southern politicians of the pre–Civil War period did, including most presidents. He served in the US House of Representatives for several years, as secretary of war under US president Martin Van Buren (1837–1841), and as envoy to Mexico between 1825 and 1829 during the Victoria administration. As a younger man he had traveled widely in Europe and South America, had some role in the independence of Chile, and was fluent in Spanish. Something of an amateur horticulturalist, he popularized in the United States the plant *euphorbia pulcherimma*, a species native to Central America, lending the poinsettia his name. As a member of the York Rite Masonic lodge himself he introduced the organization into Mexico and secured recognition for the Mexican lodges in the United States. In the Mexican context the York Rite (its adherents known as *Yorquinos*) tended to be more liberal in political conviction, more democratic in admitting men, and more inclined toward federalism (although this was not always the case), while members of the Scottish Rite (known as *Escoseses*) leaned toward more conservative ideas and politics. Military man and twice future president Anastasio Bustamante (1780–1853) belonged to the York Rite introduced by Poinsett, as did Lorenzo de Zavala and other prominent political figures, while Santa Anna and Victoria may have belonged. Through the latter part of the 1820s membership in one or the other of the Masonic sects served as the organizing principle in political life.

Poinsett was reviled by contemporary conservatives and subsequent generations of historians for violating the customary limits of Western diplomatic practice by which the envoys of foreign states were to remain resolutely neutral in the domestic politics of the capitals to which they were accredited. In addition to introducing the York Rite he connived to advance the fortunes of federalism (as a good Southerner favoring states' rights) and made public statements in favor of liberalism. Although Poinsett's residence in Mexico overlapped by only a few months in 1825 with Lucas Alamán's tenure as the chief minister in the Guadalupe Victoria cabinet, the two men grew to dislike each other intensely. The undiplomatic American diplomat saw the powerful, relatively conservative, centralist Mexican minister as a sinister Metternichean figure leaning strongly toward British interests in Mexico (as opposed to those of the United States), while Alamán viewed the American as a blustering political busybody exercising an unwelcome influence over domestic affairs in Mexico; there was a large grain of truth in both views. To be fair, Poinsett was not the only US emissary to Mexico to mix in domestic politics, especially because Washington has at various times viewed Mexico as an uneasy ally, a client state, a volatile little sister republic, or all three simultaneously, but always as a major economic market and resource.

THE LATER 1820s

With these tensions already roiling the country's public life, a weak presidential administration drifting slowly leftward toward federalism, and continued anxieties about a possible expedition of reconquest by Spain, the year 1827 saw political polarization grow ever more clamorous. A key event in this drift toward violence was the brief eruption in January 1827 of a conspiracy in Mexico City led by a Spanish-born Franciscan friar, Joaquín Arenas (ca. 1777–1827), whose ostensible goal was the restoration of Spanish rule in the country. Several high-ranking Spanish-born military officials were involved in the plot. In short order the plan was discovered and Arenas along with about a dozen other men were tried for treason and executed. Although anti-Spanish sentiment was already very much present at all levels of Mexican society the Arenas Conspiracy escalated it into virulent hostility. The major newspapers in the capital aggravated the situation with their heated rhetoric. All the states of the federation ended up undertaking anti-Spanish measures of variable severity. The national congress decreed the peremptory exclusion of all European-born Spaniards from public office, followed by a second broader decree in 1829 mandating the expulsion from Mexico of all European Spaniards. Although numerous exemptions were managed through political influence and enforcement across the country was uneven, some families were torn apart and the loss of human and financial capital was substantial. Conservatives were more and more alienated from the national government, Alamán invoking his favorite bogeyman, the French Revolution, in excoriating the Victoria regime and the liberal congress as "Jacobins."

In the meantime the promise of relative public calm and potential prosperity introduced by the Guadalupe Victoria presidency withered in the last two years of his term as the country careened toward the endemic political instability that would endure for the next five decades. One index of this is the yearly number of the military uprisings that came to be a continual feature of public life until 1875 or so. These *pronunciamientos* were for the most part limited uprisings staged by army officers to extract some sort of political concessions from the central government according to a list of grievances called a "plan" but rarely intended to topple the regime in place or kick off a true revolution. From an average of perhaps four or five per year up to 1829 they rose to a dozen in that year, then to nearly a hundred in 1832, topping out at 260 in 1834. This gave Mexico the reputation of being a super-sized "banana republic" until President Benito Juárez began to impose some sort of stability after the defeat of the French-backed usurper Emperor Maximilian in 1867. Making himself the indispensable man, Juárez's one-time political protégé Porfirio Díaz consolidated that stability in the last quarter of the nineteenth century through a policy of continual reelection over nearly thirty-five years, economic development, significant foreign investment, suppression of political dissent, and skill at balancing important political interests against one another. Coupled with the chronic instability of the early republican decades except for very short periods, the weakness of the national tax base severely limited the ability of any given regime to make public investments in infrastructure, education, public health, or other public goods. (An income tax was enacted in mid-1823 but failed, and even now Mexicans' evasion of their income tax obligations is notorious.) This debility was due largely to the retention of much revenue by the states and the generally shaky condition of the economy during the entire period. The major source of revenue for the central government was customs duties and the major expenditure by far the support of the army, leaving few resources for anything else. Some years produced reasonable revenues, as for example 1823–1827 and the early 1830s, but generally the national accounts ran well into the red. The fiscal inadequacy gave rise to the practice of government borrowing from private domestic financiers known as *agiotistas*, to whom the central state was always beholden; the policy of levying forced "loans" on the population, chiefly on wealthy merchants and landowners; and the manipulation of tariffs on foreign imports as a fiscal measure. Beginning with Iturbide a series of sovereign loans (loans extended to the central government for public purposes) were contracted at ruinous rates of interest chiefly from British bond holders. One end thus served was the formation of a small fleet of ships that besieged the fortress of San Juan de Ulúa, helping to expel the Spanish forces concentrated there. This was an extremely tangled skein of arrangements involving the personal ambitions and competition among Mexican politicians, the bankruptcy of various English firms, and an enormous national debt overhang for the struggling young republic. Mexico defaulted on the interest payments very quickly, ruining its international credit standing and saddling the country with a huge "British debt" only liquidated in the 1880s.

The natural successor to Guadalupe Victoria was presumed to be Vicente Guerrero, unlettered and intellectually undistinguished but a hero of the insurgency and Iturbide's partner in consummating independence under the Plan of Iguala. In the face of the Yorquino (York Rite Masonry) radicalism associated with Guerrero, however, a more moderate Yorquino group was able to promote the candidacy of Manuel Gómez Pedraza (1789–1851), one of the many political generals who dominated the politics of the period. Having fought the insurgents when a young royalist army officer, he joined Iturbide and made his career in politics as minister of war during the Guadalupe Victoria administration. With the election campaign of summer 1828 Gómez Pedraza emerged narrowly triumphant over Guerrero, with the votes of eleven states against Guerrero's nine. Before he could take office, however,

Santa Anna launched an anti–Gómez Pedraza coup. This failed, but a second rebellion, one of whose guiding spirits was the radical Lorenzo de Zavala, sent the president-elect into foreign exile in the closing days of 1828 and brought Guerrero into the presidential palace instead. Gómez Pedraza would return from exile later, carry on a relatively distinguished political career in and out of the national legislature and government ministry, and in another turn of the political wheel actually serve out some of his aborted presidency for the first three months of 1833. With little alternative in 1829, congress confirmed Guerrero in early January with another political general, Anastasio Bustamante (1780–1853), as his vice president. Bustamante was yet another royalist officer who had joined Iturbide in 1821 and would himself serve twice in the presidency, in 1830–1832 and 1837–1841. In historical perspective the one-year presidency of Vicente Guerrero was clearly illegitimate, terminating with his ouster from office and then his judicial assassination in early 1831. Guerrero was himself of mixed race; identified strongly with common people, especially those of color; and was a heroic, rather sympathetic, but ultimately tragic figure. The rebellion and coup that brought him to power was the first move in the pendulum swings of coups, counter-coups, "revolutions," and usurpations that would wrack the country for more than thirty years.

DETOUR: ON POLITICAL LEGITIMACY AND INSTABILITY

Before we continue Guerrero's story let us pause to ask why political violence was so pervasive up until the last quarter of the century, and why even greatly talented public men failed collectively to establish an enduring stability in Mexican political life. The pages that follow propose an inventory of the factors accounting for instability in the early Mexican republic. The most important of these was in my view certainly the last discussed—the legitimacy vacuum that ensued after the sweeping away of the Spanish monarchical regime, followed by the hiccup of the Iturbide monarchy. The weakness or outright illegitimacy of any given government of the moment was essentially a habit of mind in Mexican political culture, a failure of all parties to the political game to attain consensus of what was *right* and *fair*. But all the factors in combination frequently worked to induce political actors to resort to armed violence and the seizure of power to resolve disputes. One reason for the turbulence of the political waters was institutional weakness along axes I have already mentioned—the relations between the executive and legislative powers and between the central government and the states, both conflicts that often proved proxy battles between liberals and conservatives. This may be seen as a continual process of overcorrection from one government regime to another—on occasion from one to its immediate successor, sometimes over a period of years—with few if any mechanisms to dampen the oscillations. The Supreme Court, for example, might have acted to contain the arc of the swings through insistence in legal findings that basic constitutional and statutory laws be observed. If not an absolute nullity the court was at least gelded for the most part and played a relatively weak and reduced role in political life. As for the 1824 Constitution, it imposed severe restrictions on executive authority in reaction to royal absolutism during the colonial era, and against Emperor Agustín de Iturbide's shutting down of congress and increasingly authoritarian rule. The presidential powers surged again with the government of Vicente Guerrero, one of the chief accusations leveled against him during his overthrow at the end of 1829. The surge continued with the Anastasio Bustamante regime after him but oscillated back in the direction of congressional dominance at various points in the 1830s and 1840s. The 1824 charter saw the apotheosis of federalism with the reservation to the Mexican states of a great degree of both fiscal and military power. Pendulum swings back in the other direction occurred with centralist regimes under constitutions of 1836 and 1843 when the "free, sovereign, autonomous" states were reduced to "departments," as in the French model.[11]

A second reason for instability turns on the material interests of political elites; that is, the fear of men in contending factions that they would be ruined if they lost power, or conversely that they might reap economic advantages if they attained it. There were cases in which losers in the political contest had their property expropriated by the winners. If not seized outright property might be left behind and the economic interests of the "outs" permanently damaged as they went into exile or retreated from political life and lost the leverage that access to forms of public power afforded them for the accumulation of wealth. The sacrosanct nature of private property became axiomatic in both liberal and conservative thinking not only as a basic principle of natural law but also as a discursive line in the sand concerning the proper limits of state action. It was no accident, for example, that Lucas Alamán, in the very first number of one of the newspapers he established to back conservative ideas after the Mexican-American War, published in translation a famous French thesis on the inviolability of private property as the bedrock of an orderly and prosperous society. This principle of the absolute right to private property tended to be honored more in the breach than in the observance by ruling regimes that exacted forced loans from the civilian population to bolster weak state finances, a form of predatory state action that transcended party or ideology.

A third factor in the endemic instability was the play of interpersonal enmity and rivalry within the political world. These forces may not have been any more disruptive in Mexico, admittedly, than in any other political system of the time. If one reads about the English House of Commons or the US Congress in these decades, for example, the presence of clashing personal ambitions and just plain dislike is palpable. For example, the British politicians Benjamin Disraeli, a conservative, and William Gladstone, a liberal, disliked each other very much, which affected their political actions, and interpersonal violence was known to break out in the American Congress fueled by a volatile mixture of personal dislike and political difference, especially over issues related to slavery. To take but one instance in Mexico, while there was an enormous political chasm separating the conservative Lucas Alamán from the radical liberal Lorenzo de Zavala, they also seem personally to have disliked each other quite strongly. In this as in other cases it is extremely difficult to untangle personal animosity from ideological incompatibility, but whatever the proportions of the mix the strong antagonism was there. On the other hand, in informal social situations these and other men of opposing political loyalties and convictions were able to interact civilly and in some cases even maintain fairly cordial relations with each other.

It also seems that the vagueness of factional affiliations until later in the century—that is, the absence of clear party structures as opposed to ideological tendencies as an organizing principle in politics allowing one clearly to distinguish friend from foe—threw men back on notions of personal honor to establish boundaries and loyalties, thus personalizing politics in ways that made rivalry and interpersonal conflict points of great touchiness. The historian Joanne Freeman has suggested as much for the first decade or so of the US Congress under the Constitution, when the Federalists prevailed.[12] That there appear to have been few if any duels between politicians of opposing camps during the early decades of the Mexican republic is surprising, especially when one considers that many prominent political men arose from military backgrounds in which hypermasculinity within a context of real or potential violence was such a fact of life. In the United States dueling between politicians was quite common, by all accounts. Alexander Hamilton was killed in 1804 by Aaron Burr at virtually the same spot in Weehawken, New Jersey, where his eldest son Philip Hamilton had been mortally wounded in a duel in 1801. And Andrew Jackson, of course, a contemporary of the events in Mexico being narrated here, was famous for fighting duels, over a hundred of them over points of honor personal and political. By themselves such interpersonal conflicts, even absent the tradition of dueling and a code duello, cannot account for the instability of Mexican politics in the period, but combined with other factors they added at least something to the mix.

A fifth element making for instability must not be discounted—ideological differences among major political actors. These differences basically boiled down to the split between liberals and conservatives, which became ever sharper only to fade into a convergence under the general umbrella of "liberalism" by the end of the century under the Porfirio Díaz regime. This was one of the major elements enabling the impressive economic development of the Díaz period along with a more or less stabilized national mythology. The meanings of these ideologies were in many respects the reverse of what they are in today's world. Conservatives favored centralized government, state action in the economy, elite domination of political life, and prominent roles for Church and army. On the other hand, the liberals advocated a contracted sphere of state action, decentralization of power, broad popular participation in political life, an expansive civil society, perhaps a greater degree of church-state separation, etc. In the early republic there were numerous shadings of political ideology even among those who might have shared the labels of "liberal" or "conservative," and many public men changed their spots over time. The most notorious case of this was Santa Anna, who switched back and forth a number of times between federalism and centralism, associated respectively with liberalism and conservatism. Always tending toward authoritarianism in style no matter what ideology (or label, because some historians have insisted that he had no ideological convictions) he embraced, over his career he did move discernably from federalism toward centralism. The other of the most prominent politicians of the period, Alamán, began as a moderately liberal republican able at least for a time to work under the federalist regime of Guadalupe Victoria. His later years saw him shift to the position of a highly conservative centralist and even a monarchist for a time, although never the reactionary that some believed him then and since.

Finally, looming over these destabilizing factors was the more diffuse political malaise I mentioned earlier, the failure of an overall principle of legitimacy to take hold among political actors. The idea here should have been that no matter what the turn of the political wheel established institutions, rules of procedure, and habits of civility were accepted as *right* and *fair*. Or that such rules were at least necessary for a viable political system and should be adhered to, and that stakeholders should implicitly agree to this no matter what the formal, explicit commitment might be, such as an oath of loyalty. One's interests might be addressed, if not at any given moment, then through compromise with opposing parties or possibly in other circumstances later on. An ethical, moral, or even religious sanctification was useful here along with what one might call political empathy, but not strictly essential. An acknowledgment of the practical necessity of mutual respect between political opponents was required, or at least the performance of forbearance even if one were in violent disagreement with their opinions or actions. This entailed a basic belief that change might be accommodated through peaceful institutional means and that violent differences of opinion need not translate themselves into violent physical confrontation. Such a belief in the fundamental legitimacy of regnant institutions would certainly require the occasional sacrifice of one's particular interests for the sake of a larger interest in the peaceful transaction of political business. The corollary was the calculation that violence to achieve one's ends would incur higher costs than acquiescence to the rules and working within them. Such interactions needed to be embedded in a larger structure of regulations and practices, in the institutional framework that would guarantee generally agreed rules of play, fairness in collective decision making, the continuity of agreements—that is, that a resolution reached today would not be arbitrarily abrogated tomorrow—and that violation of rules would face sanction.

A case can be made that the initial implantation stage of any new governing regime might be characterized more by violence than comity among political actors to achieve their ends, including gaining the upper hand over antagonists. Force might therefore be required to stabilize such a situation by instilling habits of subordination, respect, and forbearance, although typically force, even if it becomes terror, cannot maintain such a system for long. Something like this situation had existed in the first decades of the Spanish conquest of the Americas until royal authority was established and over time came to be recognized by the colonists as legitimate. There was by no means a perfect correspondence between legitimate monarchical authority and the compliance of subjects, but the basic legitimacy of royal authority was seldom if ever contested. The discourse of colonial political life demonstrated this, particularly at points of stress or resistance to royal decrees or of their circumstantial inapplicability. The formula invoked by officials when resisting the application of misguided or inappropriate royal directives, for example—"Obedezco pero no cumplo," "I obey but do not comply [or fulfill]"—acknowledges the legitimate authority of the monarch to dispose but suspends compliance for compelling local reasons. Another formula often heard on the lips of colonial rioters or rebels—"¡Viva el rey y muera el mal gobierno!," "Long live the king and death to bad government!"—achieved a similar sleight of hand in recognizing that while the instruments of the royal will, typically its ministers and/or local officials, might be corrupt or fallible, the legitimacy of monarchical rule remained intact. While force might be employed as an initiating condition to contain political actors within the system, it was not sufficient to maintain the rules indefinitely; the *habit* of compliance, if not consent, must be developed based upon a belief in the fundamental justice of the ruling structures.

The administration of justice was an attribute of a judge and especially under the Habsburgs the Spanish king exercised this function, if not directly then through his agents, a basic feature of the first two centuries of Spanish rule in the Americas that has often been recognized. The Habsburg monarchy was not only conciliar and consultative in structure, but the kings were judges arbitrating among competing groups rather than absolutists asserting their authority under the principles of "enlightened despotism," as the Bourbon dynasty strove to do in the last century of colonial rule. Nonetheless, the essential property of the monarch as ultimate arbiter or judge was not so easily erased from colonial political culture. The authority of this supreme arbiter rested upon the long history of European and Iberian kingship; that is to say, it was perceived as *natural*. But it was also reinforced by public ceremony, by religious practice and belief—it was a *divine right* monarchy, after all— and by sanctification at every turn: in public ritual, in legal proceedings, in political activities, in the very stamped paper upon which people wrote legal documents. Moreover, the Iberian tradition of pactation between monarch and subjects persisted for three centuries, embodying the idea that should the king violate his end of the bargain, benign rule in return for the payment of taxes and his subjects' acquiescence within certain limits, the subjects might accuse him of tyranny and reclaim sovereignty for themselves. This concept actually strengthened the legitimacy of the monarchy because it provided a theoretical exit and therefore implied volition on the part of subjects. It was a *willing* compliance rather than a forced one, although the rule of law was ultimately backed up by the potential of sanction or violent enforcement, the state having a monopoly of such powers.

When this royal authority was swept away with independence in 1821 it left behind it a legitimacy vacuum only temporarily filled by a frail monarchical regime under Agustín de Iturbide. This was immediately followed by the construction of a republic in 1823. The rules of the political game were hardly at issue under the colonial regime because there had been no politics such as extralocal elections, parties, or political actors in a parliamentary system exercising sovereignty in a public arena to decide policies previously determined by the monarch and his ministers. There were bureaucratic politics, of course, under the colonial regime, and they could be fierce; and there were local politics in the village, town, and city governments. The revived imperial diet, first in the Spanish Cortes of Cádiz of 1810, then in the once more revived Madrid parliaments of 1820–1822, also provided laboratories in which American deputies, many of who became leaders in the new Spanish American republics, developed their political skills. But who was now to guarantee justice and fairness in public life in the new republics of Spanish America in place of the Spanish monarch; or more exactly, what *idea* was to be the guarantor? The European Spaniards still had their king, albeit at least temporarily reduced to the condition of a constitutional monarch.

But what did the Mexicans have? If the Spanish monarch had embodied legitimate sovereignty under the empire, with independence that sovereignty migrated to the nation, residing in the Republic of Mexico, that *corpus mysticum* of the Mexican people whose guardian and agent was the national state.

But a state does not necessarily make a cohesive nation. A "national" sensibility took time to develop; it could not just be ginned up on the spot. In the perception that a nation is an "imagined community," not simply a territory with a government but an *affective* neighborhood, the political scientist Benedict Anderson was right even if he got the timing wrong by a century or so.[13] Lucas Alamán had his political prejudices, but he was also an extremely acute observer of Mexican society. At the end of our period (1852) he remarked in his great *Historia de Méjico* that "in Mexico there are no Mexicans." By this he meant that in the wake of the Mexican-American War in the late 1840s there was very little identification by Mexicans with each other *as* Mexicans, little national unity, little national sensibility. More than the description of a short-term problem brought on by defeat in war, he meant this aphorism to describe the history of the country since its birth as an independent nation in 1821. While the "sovereign nation," or the *idea* of it, might have served as the repository of legitimacy in place of the Spanish monarchy and as guarantor that the political rules of the game were fair, it failed to do so because the allegiance to that idea, which might have contained the play of competing individuals and groups, was weak. In a sense the remedy of this weakness was what conservatives, among them Alamán, sought in their attempts to centralize government. In the pendulum swings in their favor they tried to impose what might be called (after Emile Durkheim) a mechanical solidarity on the national territory in the face of the centrifugal forces of federalism that sought to disperse sovereignty and drain the legitimacy out of the center. The centralizing efforts were excessively alloyed with the individual interests of economic and political elites, unfortunately, making them appear as nothing more than power grabs. The project did not really succeed until about the last third of the century after a prolonged civil war and the defeat of a foreign usurper backed by an imperialist European power, when most Mexicans began to take seriously the idea of a nation, the sovereignty inhering in it, and the legitimacy emanating from it.

THE WAR OF THE SOUTH

Let us return here to the sad tale of Vicente Guerrero's brief presidency. His predecessor Guadalupe Victoria having left office in "a blaze of passivity" in the words of one historian, Guerrero assumed the presidency on April 1, 1829. The moving spirit in the new president's Yorquino cabinet, as Alamán was to be in the conservative centralist regime that followed Guerrero's, was treasury secretary Lorenzo de Zavala. But the new government hardly had time to work out any of its populist agenda about the redistribution of wealth and other measures because it had barely nine months in office, all the while plagued with a dozen *pronunciamientos*, especially clustered toward the end of the year, and more importantly a Spanish expedition of reconquest in the late summer. This was led by the Spanish General Isidro Barradas, by all accounts a singularly unlikable character who commanded an invasion force of several thousand men organized in Cuba. After considerable difficulty with the weather in the Gulf of Mexico this army landed near Tampico, on the northern Gulf coast on July 5, 1829. Believing that the Mexican population would welcome the expedition with open arms, his forces were ill-supplied for a long engagement. They were besieged and quickly defeated by a smaller Mexican army led by none other than Santa Anna, acting on behalf of the central government, who thereafter bore the label "Hero of Tampico," trading on it (as why should he not?) to forge his political career. Santa Anna was supported by another political general, Manuel Mier y Terán (1789–1832), a moderate considered at one point a strong presidential possibility. In depression over the state of the country and his personal affairs a few years later, Mier would take his own life by running on his sword, Roman fashion, at the spot where Agustín de Iturbide had been executed eight years before.

In the meantime, in anticipation of a second possible invasion attempt a reserve army of some 3,000 men had been assembled near Jalapa, in Veracruz, under the command of Vice President Anastasio Bustamante. This provident military measure was to be Guerrero's undoing because the army and its commanders soon turned on the president and ousted him. The chief grievances against Guerrero were the abuse of the emergency powers he had extracted from congress to face the invasion and the taxes imposed to support it by treasury secretary Zavala. According to the 1824 federalist constitution these measures had violated the prerogative of the states to control most fiscal revenue. Added to this source of tension was a falling out between the victorious Santa Anna, now a popular hero as savior of the nation, and Zavala over a matter of political patronage as well as the brewing anti-Yorquino sentiment among prominent military commanders of the Reserve Army. A more general underlying reason for resistance to the regime was simply that many powerful politicians regarded it as too "left wing" in modern terms—too populist, too inclined to favor common people of color (the majority of Mexicans, after all) over the interests of the light-skinned, powerful, and ambitious. Moreover, Guerrero himself was a man of color of mixed Indigenous and African blood, which provoked the racialist prejudices of a political elite still predominantly of European descent.

Things escalated quickly. The president's order to disband the Reserve Army after the defeat of the Spanish invasion was ignored by the force's commanders, while Bustamante and Santa Anna remained aloof if sympathetic to the developing anti-Guerrero movement. As early as mid-October Zavala was thrown under the bus, resigning from the cabinet under pressure. After some abortive negotiations between Guerrero and Lucas Alamán acting on behalf of the *pronunciamiento*, the Chamber of Deputies hastily designated an interim chief executive because Vice President Bustamante could not assume office while commanding an armed force in the field. This was all done under the auspices of the Plan of Jalapa, one of the hundreds of "plans" declared in the uprisings of these decades. There is strong evidence that Alamán was a key figure in this uprising, the *eminence grise* behind the rebellion even though not in any official capacity, coordinating the actions of the major military commanders. Around Christmas a government council met and appointed a second provisional executive, this time a triumvirate composed of General Luis Quintanar, Alamán's old federalist adversary from Guadalajara; Lucas Alamán himself, his thorny relations with Quintanar at least temporarily repaired; and a third man. This was the only occasion on which Alamán, the most brilliant statesman of the era, was to occupy the presidency of the republic, and then only for a few days. As Bustamante advanced on the capital Guerrero's forces deserted him. After switching sides to the government and back again Santa Anna withdrew his support from the Guerrero regime and Vicente Guerrero was forced from the office he had himself assumed in a coup some months before. Vice President Anastasio Bustamante, for the two and a half years in which he would head the national government, was always referred to as the vice president. By the end of December 1829 Bustamante had taken over the chief executive spot as the constitutional successor of an unconstitutionally seated president. His forces entered the capital on January 1, 1830. Alamán was the first ministerial appointment, taking over the dominant post of interior and exterior relations. Guerrero had withdrawn to his hacienda near the west coast to await further events. Early in 1830 the congress invoked a rather vague article of the 1824 Constitution (similar in some ways to the Twenty-fifth Amendment of the US Constitution) allowing for the removal of the president from office should he be in some way incapacitated, applying it to Guerrero on the grounds that he was "disqualified" from holding office. Arguments adduced in the debate leading to this action invoked Guerrero's lack of formal education, his diminished physical capacity from his old war wounds, and so forth, but the underlying rationale was really that many in congress and out thought him insufficiently intelligent to discharge the presidential duties and resisted the elevation of a man of color to the first magistracy of the nation. The original draft of the legislation described him as "morally disqualified," although upon passage this was modified simply to "disqualified."

Predictably neither Vicente Guerrero nor his supporters among the more radical political and military men, some of them veterans of the 1810 insurgency, were willing to accept this situation and so took up arms against what they regarded as an illegitimate government. During the rest of 1830 and into the early weeks of the following year the country was wracked with a violent civil conflict known as the Guerra del Sur (the War of the South) because most of the action took place in the southern part of the country, especially in the southwest. Guerrero's base of military strength lay primarily along the torrid lands (the *tierra caliente*) of the Pacific coast and its hinterland, in the area known as the Costa Grande, centering on the important coastal port city of Acapulco, the modern tourist mecca. Heavily Afro-Indian in its ethnic makeup, Guerrero's uprising was moved by his desire to reclaim the presidency of which he felt he had been robbed and to further prosecute the political struggle of the Yorquino faction against the more conservative Scottish Rite Freemasonry by force of arms. It also embraced elements of agrarian rebellion by peasants against landlords, a racial conflict pitting humble people of color against white power holders, and of Indigenous villagers' struggle to maintain a tradition of autonomous political life against the demands of a centralizing government in Mexico City. Alamán, the government's chief minister, characterized the War of the South as a "race war" and his fellow cabinet member, war minister José Antonio Facio (1790–1836), saw the conflict as moved by "barbarous, inhuman, and ferocious hatreds." Among centralist politicians and journalists there was luridly racist talk of "savage Haitian hordes" (a reference to the Haitian Revolution of forty years earlier) descending on the capital from the steamy Pacific lands. The central government won a major victory against Guerrero's forces early in 1831, throwing the rebellion onto its back foot. Guerrero himself was captured in January in an infamous act of treachery involving an Italian ship captain named Francisco Picaluga posing as his friend. The ousted president was taken to Oaxaca and tried in a military court martial marked by numerous legal irregularities. There were trumped-up charges, many evidentiary weaknesses, an inadequate defense, and quite concrete although never explicit directives from the Bustamante cabinet in Mexico City to dispose of him while honoring the theatrical performance of a judicial proceeding. After a brief trial Vicente Guerrero was executed on February 14, 1831. Although ultimate responsibility for this judicial assassination lay with Vice President Bustamante as head of the government (think of John Adams tried and executed by directive of President Thomas Jefferson), its actual plotting and execution were traceable to the ministerial cabinet. Viewed by many then and since as the arch-reactionary enemy of an uppity man of color, Lucas Alamán was long blamed as principal author of the crime. The ignominy followed him for the rest of his life, to his grave, and beyond. While the minister of relations definitely had some role in the killing of Guerrero, both by supplying some financial support from a secret slush fund his ministry controlled and by failing actively to oppose the plan in cabinet deliberations, the real author of Guerrero's death was war minister José Antonio Facio with the assent of Vice President Bustamante. Alamán remarked in a letter to a friend that the government had sent "some important people to the scaffold" but that the "rod of iron" was necessary to counteract the anarchy of the preceding years.

THE CENTRALISTS IN POWER

The next twenty-eight months or so saw the centralists firmly in power. Through his intelligence, the force of his personality, and his political acuity, but also because Vice President Bustamante tended to abdicate to him not only policy formulation but also other tasks like the writing of his speeches, Alamán, with the portfolio of interior and exterior relations, became so dominant in the government that it has sometimes been called the "administración alamánica." Historian Stanley Green has summarized the minister's influence this way:

> Alamán's great gift was that he had not only a clear image of a desirable Mexican state, but also the will and energy to force public policy in that direction. The Alamán program under Bustamante was the first attempt to proceed toward a comprehensive, coherent set of goals. Up to this point independence governments had essentially reacted, dealing with problems on an ad hoc basis while drawing in desultory fashion from Spanish and North American precedents.[14]

Alamán's influence rested upon a political alliance between Creole reformers, some of them Freemasons of the Scottish Rite, with supporters of Iturbide, Bustamante among them. While congress was not always compliant, the Bustamante administration tended to get its way much of the time. Minister Alamán's annual reports to congress embracing policy recommendations were models of data-driven synthesis and analysis written from a conservative point of view.

Although much of Alamán's effort during this and his other stints in office was directed toward establishing political stability in Mexico, his primary objective—the thing that politics was *about* rather than the gaining and exercise of power for its own sake—was always the economic development of the country, which could hardly be expected to advance when unpredictability, chaos, and violence were the norm. A German scholar of Spanish and Mexican history, Walter Bernecker, has put this well in discussing the protectionist tariff policy advocated by Alaman with the object of protecting and encouraging domestic industry:

Alamán's protectionist concept represented the attempt to find a path of nationalist and self-sufficient [economic] development directed toward autonomous
industrialization. A condition for the functioning of this idea was not only a
stable political system with a State with the capacity for action, but also an efficient administration and a functioning system of tax collection.[15]

Economic development, in Alamán's view, chiefly in the form of industrialization along the lines of the most important North Atlantic nations—Britain,
France, the young United States—would create the conditions for political
stability because it would expand the size of the economic pie and thus eliminate a struggle over resources as a cause for contention in society. There was
admittedly a certain circularity in this thinking: that economic development
could only occur with the establishment of political stability and that political
stability would be encouraged by economic development. Economic development would generate employment for the Mexican population, raise domestic
living standards, reduce poverty, develop markets for agricultural production
to fuel industry and supply the wants of a growing industrial proletariat,
encourage foreign investment, and link the protection of that investment
by non-Mexican stakeholders to foreign governments' interest in ensuring
Mexican stability and independence. Industrialization, of which the entering
wedge was large-scale textile production, would further national integration
as a countrywide market developed, turning Mexico from a society of strong
regional identities and a weak class structure to one of weak regional identities and a strong class structure. That these goals could not be realized quickly
was not entirely clear during the second quarter of the nineteenth century.
After a stuttering beginning in the 1830s and 1840s they would begin to be
realized in earnest beginning in about the 1880s. The frequent recurrence
of Lucas Alamán's name in my account of the life of the young Mexican
republic is not primarily due to the fact that I have recently published a biography of the man but rather to his actual prominence in political life during
the period, whether in or out of government. The most perceptive American
historian of early Mexican liberalism, the late Charles Hale, saw Alamán as
the most important political figure of the age, bar none.[16]

The government Lucas Alamán built with the backing of Vice President
Bustamante, his fellow ministers, and much of the congress was a comparatively repressive one but hardly a dictatorship or an authoritarian regime,
even assuming that he and his boss aspired to one, for which there is little
evidence apart from the denunciations of his political foes. There were limits
to the repressive capabilities of the centralist regimes that wobbled in and out
of the capital over the next decades. All governments of the period, including
the most centralist in aspirations, simply lacked the fiscal resources and the
technologies of power to enforce their visions of what Mexico should be like.

Neither the railroad nor the telegraph existed, it must be remembered, making communication and the movement of armed forces slow and difficult. The resources of the state were limited, the national budget running into the red many years chiefly due to support of the army. This forced a reliance upon occasional "forced loans" exacted from the citizenry and upon expensive borrowed funds from domestic private lenders, as I have mentioned, because loans from foreign bond markets were effectively debarred by the debt over-hang and resultant bad credit from the British loans of the 1820s.

By the standards of the day the Bustamante government could nonetheless make life difficult for its political opposition in a variety of ways. One of the first acts of the *jalapista* regime was to issue an election law with a more restricted franchise than under the Guerrero government, so the fall congressional elections brought in a chamber of deputies more in line with the style of a conservative centralist administration. The initiative in February 1830 to remove Vicente Guerrero from office faced some resistance in congress, but some of the old *caudillo*'s defenders, or deputies who simply felt the proceedings to declare him "unqualified for office" to be impolitic as well as unconstitutional, were intimidated into silence, jailed for sedition, forced out of the country, and in some cases even physically assaulted by government troops or police. An extremely draconian law authored by Alamán under the Supreme Executive Authority in 1823, passed by congress and now widely applied, suspended the civil rights of bandits and requirements for judicial due process when trying them. "Banditry" was loosely enough defined that the law could be made to embrace Vicente Guerrero in 1831 as well as the brother of former president Guadalupe Victoria and others and was used as a tool of political repression. This law was also one piece of a generalized effort to suppress rural brigandage and urban crime not just for political reasons but to promote the security of property and persons in an "ordered republic." Control of information and opinion proved just as much an object of centralist government as the corralling of crime. Like the political class the newsprint culture grew up rapidly, so especially in the capital the press received a great deal of attention from the regime. Some of the scores of newspapers in the capital city in the 1820s were short lived and all of them fell on one side or the other of the liberal/conservative political divide. Aside from street corner and barroom gossip the newspapers were a major medium for the diffusion of political opinion and propaganda among common people. Some opposition newspapers were fined out of existence on the basis of sedition laws, some editors and press patrons were simply arrested, printers were intimidated, and censorship was exercised with a heavy hand. Proregime periodicals were subsidized by the government and the official newspaper, the *Periódico Oficial*, was substantially edited by the minister of relations himself. The government had political informants and outright spies in many parts of the country.

Alamán did what he could to weaken the militia forces supported independently by the states, thus undermining the ability of provincial politicians to
resist centralist authority.

But there was more to the regime as Lucas Alamán guided it than political repression and the effort to stay in power; the constructive side reflected
Lucas Alamán's own predilections. The national archive, today's Archivo
General de la Nación, was established, one of the greatest repositories of
historical documentation in Latin America; the national museum was put
on a sound footing; the government encouraged archaeological exploration
and preservation; and the importation of European high cultural production,
including the theater and Italian opera, were encouraged and even subsidized
with the object of making the country more "civilized." The curriculum of
the capital's university was the object of a "modernizing" reform. Whether
for good or ill the Catholic Church was strengthened, but there was more
to this particular aspect of the government's policy than political expedi-
ency. Toward the end of his life, in the wake of the Mexican-American War
(1846–1848), Alamán wrote that in the absence of a strong national identity
on the part of Mexicans the force of Catholic religious belief and practice was
among the few elements acting as a sort of social glue holding the society
together. So reinforcing the institutional foundations of the Catholic Church,
still by law the exclusively tolerated religious cult during this period, made
sense both as a political and cultural project. Much or all of this was accomplished while the Bustamante administration was pitted in a civil war against
ousted president Vicente Guerrero and his supporters.

But even the Guerra del Sur would pale beside the rapidly unspooling consequences of a problem developing for the Mexican state during the 1820s
and which the Bustamante government, its foreign affairs in the hands of
Lucas Alamán, could only hold at bay for a few years. This was the issue of
the colonization of Texas by the Anglo-American settlers who poured into
the region from the southwestern zone of the United States—areas such as
Tennessee, Kentucky, Arkansas, Louisiana, and elsewhere—and even from
the Northeast. Many of the Southerners were slave owners who saw Texas
as prime cotton country and brought their enslaved Black labor force with
them to work it, while others were family farmers and still others ranchers.
Neither Spain nor independent Mexico had done much more than set up a thin
military and missionary presence in the area, having neither the population
nor financial resources to truly colonize and hold it. So inviting land-hungry
Americans into the area, provided they swore allegiance to the Spanish/
Mexican government and observed certain other conditions, seemed a good
tactical move to consolidate control over the immense northern territories
of New Spain nominally stretching up to what is now Oregon. The area had
been neglected during the 1820s, and colonists had come in under contracts

made by the late colonial government with a less than successful Connecticut businessman, Moses Austin (1761–1821), and carried on with the Mexican Republic by Austin's son Stephen (1793–1836). By 1830 the Mexican government became alarmed at the growing American presence and the colonists' tendency to look toward the United States for models of local government, religion, and trade. African slavery was outlawed in Mexico by Vicente Guerrero in 1829, causing yet another point of friction with the Americans, although the colonists were allowed to keep the Black slaves they already owned. Mexican efforts to bring in Northern European colonists, Mexican families, or even Cherokee Indians all failed, and the region proved beyond the reach of Mexican military forces otherwise occupied domestically. A law was finally passed in the spring of 1830 cutting off further colonization by Americans but proved unenforceable. Negotiations over the status of Texas and halting attempts to arrive at a treaty of friendship, trade, and navigation (as such treaties were known at the time) between the United States and Mexico continued during the two and a half years of the Bustamante government, but even their ratification did little to stop the colonists continuing to flood in from the United States. Eventually Texas broke away from Mexico (for which see the discussion shortly), established itself for nearly a decade as an independent republic, and then joined the United States as a slave state in 1845, provoking the Mexican-American War. Mexico did manage to sign a treaty with the United States in the spring of 1832 recognizing Mexican sovereignty over Texas, but it proved too little too late. If in the realm of foreign relations the Bustamante regime achieved only a brief delay in forestalling the disaster of Texas, it saw more success in obtaining diplomatic recognition from major powers such as the United States and Great Britain and in beginning to lay the groundwork for the recognition of the country's independence by Spain (finally achieved only in 1836), carried on chiefly through British intervention.

In the column of positive achievements of the centralist government must be placed one of the most ambitious and forward-looking projects of the era, traceable directly to Alamán's thinking about political economy, his observations of the industrializing economies of Europe during his youthful travels there during the late 1810s and early 1820s, and his own experience as an economic actor. This assumed the form of a government-sponsored development bank dedicated to spurring industrialization in the textile industry. Given his background and the history of New Spain as a cornucopia of mineral wealth his efforts had first turned to a revival of the mining industry. Alamán had been raised in the great silver mining city of Guanajuato and was himself trained as a mining engineer. He came from a background of prodigious wealth generated by the late colonial boom in silver mining, although by the time he reached young manhood that wealth had been dissipated. In the 1820s, first as a private citizen, then as a government minister, then again in the private sector he had forged a relationship with British investors aimed at reviving the Mexican silver mining industry, which had languished during the insurgency of 1810–1821; the condition of the silver mining economy and Alamán's efforts to revive it through the massive investment of British capital are discussed in chapter 10. Chastened by his experience with the substantial failure of these efforts by 1830 or so, minister Alamán's thinking about political economy turned increasingly toward manufactures rather than extractive activities as the road to economic modernization for Mexico. Although his thinking had already long assumed this direction, an 1844 letter to a friend was a clear statement of what he and a few other Mexican modernizers believed about refocusing Mexico away from her centuries-long dependence on silver as the linchpin of the economy:

> To be rich and happy, the republic must have manufacturing, for without it her agriculture will remain reduced to a state of languor and poverty, and the treasures torn from the bowels of the earth, passing immediately from the mines . . . to the ports from which they are embarked, will only serve to demonstrate with this rapid and unproductive passage, that the wealth does not belong to the peoples to whom nature conceded it . . . but rather to those who know how to utilize our precious metals and increase their value.

The project he brought to reality by sponsoring enabling legislation in the fall of 1830, the Banco de Avío para Fomento de la Industria Nacional (Bank for the Development of National Industry, or more simply Development Bank), has been much written about by historians and is also discussed in chapter 10.[17]

THE FALL OF THE CENTRALIST REGIME

There had been a steady thrum of acrimonious criticism by liberal opponents from the very inception of the Bustamante government, but this grew into a roaring cacophony by early 1832 or so. One major grievance involved the death at the government's hands of independence hero Vicente Guerrero under dishonorable circumstances of betrayal and highly irregular legal proceedings. Another was the Bustamante government's attack upon the principles of federalism enshrined in the 1824 Constitution. There were numerous specific complaints raised against the government such as the jailing of its political opponents, the suppression of unfriendly newspapers in direct contravention of the press freedom guarantees of the constitution, the meddling with state legislatures to ensure majorities in sympathy with the regime, efforts to geld the powerful militias in some states, and the restriction of the voting franchise in congressional elections. Many of these actions were real, some exaggerated, a few fabricated, but on the whole they made up a damning bill of particulars. Lucas Alamán and his conservative allies were often the explicit targets of these attacks as he had been during the Guadalupe Victoria administration a few years earlier. By late 1831, nearly two years into the Bustamante regime, a conspiracy had formed among antigovernment actors to bring back to the presidency Manuel Gómez Pedraza, legally elected in 1828 but ousted by Vicente Guerrero. The conspirators were backed by an alliance of the ever-rebellious states of Jalisco, Zacatecas, Guanajuato, and San Luis Potosí. When a protégé of his was removed from command of Veracruz port Santa Anna got into the act with a *pronunciamiento* at the beginning of 1832 demanding of Vice President Bustamante the removal of the entire ministerial cabinet including Alamán and his colleagues at the port-folios of war, treasury, and justice. The movement widened, military engagements followed, and the government's position grew increasingly untenable over the rest of the year despite some military victories led by Bustamante. Through the spring and summer the ministers resigned one after another, but it was increasingly obvious to all observers that the rebels' demands would not stop with the removal of the ministry. By July the governor of Zacatecas state had joined his powerful militia to Santa Anna's forces behind a demand for the return of Gómez Pedraza, living in exile in New Orleans. Also in July the Zacatecas state legislature formally recognized Gómez Pedraza as president, other states followed suit, and Santa Anna's forces began an advance on the capital. The last days of December 1832 saw a pact signed by Bustamante and Santa Anna in which Gómez Pedraza was named interim president with new elections scheduled for March 1833. On January 3 Santa Anna entered Mexico City to a riotous reception accompanied by the temporarily reinstated Gómez Pedraza. In the elections that followed some weeks later Santa Anna was elevated to the presidency for the first time, a post he would occupy inter-mittently for much of the next two decades. His vice president was the liberal Jalisco physician/politician Valentín Gómez Farías, who acceded temporarily to the presidency when Santa Anna retired to his Veracruz hacienda immedi-ately upon his election, claiming he was too ill to take office. This arrange-ment—Santa Anna's occupation of the presidency, his temporary withdrawal due to illness or battlefield command, and Gómez Farías's interim succession to the office—recurred several times over the coming years, four times during 1833–1834 alone. The playing out of this new array of political forces awaits us in the following chapter, in which Antonio López de Santa Anna becomes the dominant figure in the Mexican public landscape.

Although on the surface these two or three chaotic years just exemplify another of the many tedious pendulum swings in the political history of the early Mexican republic, we can still discern a revealing pattern in them. There were several cyclical recurrences of conservative or liberal accession to power through violence, followed by a period of apparent short-term stability, an increasing tension among the political "outs," criticism of the regime and opposition, and then a new cycle of armed violence leading to an overthrow of the sitting government and the installation of a new one. My extended meditation on political legitimacy some pages back may have some relevance here. Had Vicente Guerrero and his radical political allies like Lorenzo de Zavala recognized the legitimacy of the 1828 presidential election, Manuel Gómez Pedraza might have served out his term possibly succeeded by Guerrero through election; but this did not happen. Certainly the 1828 election was close—eleven states in favor of Gómez Pedraza, nine for Guerrero; there was a great deal of politicking surrounding the polling, including an armed rebellion in the capital. Personal ambition played its part—as on many other occasions, Santa Anna took a central role, but there were other actors as well. But discrediting the electoral institutions essential to republican practice itself appeared to the major players not too great a cost for the assertion of personal ambition, factional hegemony, and ideological triumph. Some political observers at the time even identified the problem but were quick to ascribe it to the corruption and anarchic impulses of their opponents, thereby confirming out of their own mouths their complicity in the very problem they lamented. In an 1831 letter to a friend in Guadalajara, for example, Lucas Alamán, minister of interior and exterior relations at the time and perhaps the most perspicacious political analyst of the age, wrote:

> I have seen with great sorrow that some individuals are [questioning] . . . the legitimacy with which the Vice President is exercising the executive power. . . . [T] he low interests that provoked the war in the south . . . appeared to have no other object than murder, robbery, arson, and the finishing off of whatever morality remained to us. . . . [T]he agitators who have now shone themselves openly . . . will in the end push us into the pit from which we had [only just] miraculously escaped. It is therefore our duty to offer Resistance . . . saving once more the national honor, the federal laws, and the public tranquility.

In formal terms the legitimacy of the Bustamante regime that so deeply concerned Alamán rested upon the frail reed of an 1830 congressional declaration based upon a highly ambiguous provision in the 1824 constitution of President Vicente Guerrero's incapacity to carry out his executive duties. But this was a fig leaf, not a solution.

CONCLUSION

It has been said that Agustín de Iturbide sought to construct a humane tyranny, not quite the oxymoron it sounds. A monarchical form of governance within a constitutional framework (at that moment the Spanish Constitution of Cádiz) was certainly a plausible default position given the history of New Spain within the Spanish Empire and the relative rarity of republican governments in the world of 1821. But a number of factors combined to bring the first Mexican Empire low. There was Iturbide's own ineptitude as a monarch in contrast to the political skill with which he had built a coalition in 1820–1821 to consummate the overthrow of the colonial order in New Spain. Other contributing factors included the rising ambitions of Santa Anna, and not only his, but that of other military and civilian politicians as well; the impecuniousness of the national treasury and therefore the weakness of the state; and the fractiousness of the congress. In the aftermath of Iturbide's fall the eruption of federalist sentiment and the federalist chieftains' game of chicken with the central government created a major crisis of national unity revealing a double absence in the public life of the country: that of a national sensibility and that of a generally accepted principle of legitimacy among the political elite. The republic seemed to breathe a sigh of relief and things smoothed out a bit with the advent of the Constitution of 1824 and the election to the presidency of Guadalupe Victoria, who completed his term in office, led an active postpresidential political life in service to the republic, and died of complications from epilepsy in 1843. In the later 1820s there was even a glimmer of economic possibility as British capital poured into the mining industry and more British capital underwrote loans to the Mexican government, albeit loans deeply discounted against their face value to compensate for the risk to investors and to guarantee payment of the high interest rates. On the downside British textiles and other imports into Mexico undermined traditional artisanal production, compounding the economic stress created by the decade of insurgency. The repulsion of the Spanish invasion in 1829 was a triumph, as was the withdrawal earlier of the last occupying Spanish troops from San Juan de Ulúa, but these were largely overshadowed by the tragic episodes of Vicente Guerrero's coup, the Guerra del Sur, and the *caudillo*'s death. These events foreshadowed the violent power struggles that would cloud much of the next three decades, highlighting the legitimacy vacuum at the center of political life. The competing Masonic orders of York Rite and Scottish Rite represented a sort of legitimacy *manqué* honored closely *within each faction* but scarcely applied to the political arena as a whole.

Of the centralist regime of Anastasio Bustamante of 1830–1832 there are possible at least two different views. Lucas Alamán was effectively at the helm of the government, at the high-water mark of his political influence (he was just short of forty years old when forced from office). One may choose to see the government of these years as an attempt by enlightened politicians (conservatives, to be sure) to impose a top-down solution to the chaotic politics of the Guerrero period at the very end of the 1820s or as a program to implant an authoritarian system to benefit the rich, white, and powerful while squashing popular aspirations. One may suggest that it laid a certain foundation for cultural and economic institutions that flowered in later years or that it set a pattern for political repression, the hollowing out of civil rights, and state violence that cost the country more than the policies of the regime benefited it. In the end the regime embodied elements of all these things. It was simultaneously an earnest and opportunistic attempt to deliver on the promise of what many felt Mexico could be—a stable, republican, relatively democratic, burgeoningly prosperous society. The fate of the country would be guided by a small group of public men, the *hombres de bien* as they were sometimes known—the closest translation in English being good men, gentlemen, honest men, or perhaps honorable men; in other words, an untitled aristocratic republic. These were stakeholders in Mexican society who frankly thought they knew better than either their opponents or the common people what was best for the country. Yet how "modern" was this regime? Stability as such was not modern, nor was prosperity, nor was political centralization because older monarchical states had achieved these goals at various times. The modernization hinged on doing all this within a republican and at least nominally democratic framework and in the halting steps that were taken to diversify the economic basis of the country from extractive to industrial activities, both of which projects showed only mixed results. One would have to say that the chief manifestation of "modernization" in the centralist government was aspirational. The treacherous elimination of Guerrero, the corrosive effects of the civil war, and the harshly repressive tactics of the regime under the effective leadership of Lucas Alamán were intended to construct an era of stability but provoked just the opposite situation. A violent backlash broke out against the Bustamante regime, of which the prime mover and great political beneficiary was Antonio López de Santa Anna. It is to the two decades of his fragmented but nearly always dominant political power that we now turn.

NOTES

1. Rodríguez, *True Spaniards*, 335.
2. In the modern world of nearly 200 sovereign states, there are almost 30 monarchies remaining, about 15 percent of the total.

3. Cuauhtitlán is a smallish, formerly independent city (population about 100,000), once a village, on the northern edge of Mexico City.

4. Cited in Rodríguez, *True Spaniards*, 272; Rodríguez provides an excellent, detailed narrative of this period in his chapters 8 and 9.

5. The quotations are from Timothy Anna, *The Mexican Empire of Iturbide* (Lincoln: University of Nebraska Press, 1990), 34, 74–75, 81, 117–18, his translations.

6. *Instituyente* is virtually untranslatable into English but implies that the function of the body was to create fundamental institutions of governance, including a new constitution.

7. One biographer of Santa Anna, José Fuentes Mares, *Santa Anna, aurora y ocaso de un comediante* (Mexico City: Editorial Jus, 1967), 35, wrote that Santa Anna was never a republican, "since to be a republican, as to be a Communist or anarchist, it is necessary to have certain ideas, and [Santa Anna] never had any." The compelling recent biography of the famous *caudillo* is Will Fowler, *Santa Anna of Mexico* (Lincoln: University of Nebraska Press, 2007). Fowler makes the case that although Santa Anna was an opportunist of flexible political convictions, he did have political ideas, evolving in his views from liberal republicanism to authoritarian conservatism during the period from 1821 to 1855.

8. The controversy over Iturbide's role in Mexican history lingers even today, as exemplified in a brief discussion over who "consummated" independence: Hidalgo and Morelos or Iturbide, in the political scientist-historian Roberto Breña's review of the definitive modern biography of Father Morelos by Carlos Herrejón Peredo, *Morelos*, 2 vols. (Zamora, Michoacán, Mexico: El Colegio de Michoacán, 2015), "Morelos: La gran biografía," *Nexos*, December 1, 2019.

9. Green, *Mexican Republic*, 38.

10. The "league" of European monarchies to which Alamán referred was the Holy Alliance of Russia, Austria, and Prussia formed in the wake of Napoleon's defeat in 1815 and managed by Prince Klemens von Metternich, the Austrian state chancellor. This mutated into a broader alliance in the years that followed but was effectively defunct by 1825. The alliance endorsed the French King Louis XVIII's invasion of Spain early in 1823 to quash the resurgent Spanish liberal government and restore the absolutist regime of his Bourbon cousin, King Ferdinand VII.

All translations are my own, from documents in the historical archive of the Mexican foreign ministry.

11. Peter Gourevitch made helpful comments as I was thinking through this section of the chapter.

12. Joanne B. Freeman, *Affairs of Honor: National Politics in the New Republic* (New Haven, CT: Yale University Press, 2001).

13. Anderson, *Imagined Communities*.

14. Green, *Mexican Republic*, 191.

15. Walter L. Bernecker, "Industria versus comercio," in *La industria textil en México*, ed. Aurora Gómez-Galvarriato (Mexico City: Instituto de Investigaciones Dr. José María Luis Mora, 1999), 114–41, at p. 119.

16. Charles A. Hale, *Mexican Liberalism in the Age of Mora, 1821–1853* (New Haven, CT: Yale University Press, 1968).

17. *Avío* is a virtually untranslatable word whose literal English meaning can be "loan" or even "provision" in the sense of providing the means to do something. I have chosen to render Banco de Avío as Development Bank because that is what the institution was intended to do.

Chapter 9

The Age of Santa Anna

There were a great many other political actors bustling on and off the great stage of Mexican public life between the fall of Agustín de Iturbide in 1823 and the advent of Santa Anna's last presidency in 1853.[1] But Antonio de Padua María Severino López de Santa Anna y Pérez de Lebrón threw himself into almost every corner of political life even during the long periods of his absences from it, or appropriated events to his own credit and legend, disavowing the failures or shifting the blame for them onto someone else (as modern politicians have been known to do). His shadow looms over the history of the Mexican Republic for a quarter century. He lived his final years in poverty and relative obscurity in Mexico City, dying there in 1876 at the advanced age (for the time) of eighty-two. As to the comparison with Napoleon Bonaparte or even Julius Caesar sometimes invoked during his lifetime, Santa Anna had neither the prodigious military nor the political talents of these men. He was a charismatic *fanfarrón*—not in the sense of a loudmouth, because he certainly knew the tactical value of silence and of a theatrical self-presentation, but of a self-mythologized hero, martyr, and indispensable man. The accounts of contemporaries show him often affecting the weary resignation to the call of patriotic service of a Cincinnatus (c. 519–430 BC), the even longer-lived Roman military man and statesman who when the political storm had passed renounced the absolute power of a dictator in the Roman Republic to return to the life of a humble farmer. Santa Anna retired from the presidency to his rural estate in Veracruz on several occasions ostensibly to restore his health, sacrificed on the altar of the nation; was frequently absent commanding armed forces in the field; and spent long stretches in exile out of the country.

The historical resonance with the Roman statesman was not lost on Fanny Calderón de la Barca (see figure 9.1), whose letters left brilliant accounts of the country's people, places, and customs well worth reading today. She penned an oft-quoted description of Santa Anna, whom she met near the end of 1839 when he was in his mid-forties:

Figure 9.1. Fanny Calderón de la Barca (1804–1882), wife of the first Spanish envoy to Mexico and author of *Life in Mexico*. MS Eng 1763 (57). Houghton Library, Harvard University.

In a little while entered the General Santa Anna himself, a gentlemanly, good-looking, quietly-dressed, rather melancholy-looking person, with one leg, apparently a good deal of an invalid, and to us decidedly the best looking and most interesting figure in the group. He has a sallow complexion, fine dark eyes, soft and penetrating, and an interesting expression of face. Knowing nothing of his past history, one would have said a philosopher, living in dignified retirement—one who had tried the world and found that all was vanity, one who had suffered ingratitude and who, if he were ever persuaded to emerge from his retreat, would only do so, Cincinnatus-like, to benefit his country. It is strange, and a fact worthy of notice in natural history, how frequently this expression of philosophic resignation, of placid sadness, is to be remarked on the countenances of the most cunning, the deepest, most ambitious, most designing and most dangerous statesmen I have seen. [They have] a something that would persuade the multitude that they are above the world, and engage in its toils only to benefit others—so that one can hardly persuade oneself that these men are not saints. Witness Van Buren—but, above all, witness the melancholy and philosophic Santa Anna.[2]

He was not lacking in astuteness. For example, he consolidated a lifelong basis of power in his native region of Veracruz by settling on his lands in military colonies followers who owed allegiance to him alone. A great gambler and aficionado of cockfighting, he owned several extensive rural properties to which he retired periodically, his favorite the Hacienda Manga de Clavo. He married twice to wealthy women, sired four legitimate children, acknowledged in his will four others born out of wedlock, is believed to have fathered yet three others, and lived for long periods in exile from Mexico in tropical climes such as Colombia and St. Thomas, in the Virgin Islands, awaiting the chance to return to power.

PRESIDENTIAL/MINISTERIAL INSTABILITY

My strategy in this chapter will be to discuss major events and trends rather than rendering in detail all the political comings and goings of a very chaotic three decades in Mexican national life. Changes at the top of the political structure, played out against violent contention for power between factions (not yet parties in the strict sense of the term), and actual or threatened foreign predation upon the country, made Mexico especially unstable. Spain attempted to reestablish the colonial relationship through armed invasion, France to exact tribute through a naval blockade (the 1860s would see a much larger-scale though ultimately only temporary French occupation of the country), and near the end of the period the United States tore off half the national territory in a cynically opportunistic war of expansion. Ministries in the national government turned over with remarkable speed, making consistency in the execution of policy exceedingly difficult for the bureaucracies under them even had the fiscal resources been available to support active policy agendas. Between the spring of 1837 and the spring of 1839, for example, a dozen men moved through the ministry of the interior and a dozen more through the ministry of foreign relations when the two departments were temporarily split from each other. A similar turnover in office marked the ministry of the treasury between the summer of 1848 and the summer of 1850. The average ministerial tenure during these periods was about two months, notwithstanding that some of the same men served more than once. These are extreme cases but convey a general idea of the political volatility that prevailed. The cabinet-level ministers were all presidential appointees whose tenure in office, like the movement of weather vanes or the column of mercury in a barometer, was exquisitely sensitive to changes in the political atmosphere of the moment. It is possible, of course, to view this "noise" as an epiphenomenon of limited effect upon the everyday political and economic life flowing on beneath it. But the volatility itself took on great importance because it created a permanent environment of insecurity, increased Mexico's vulnerability to foreign predation, and undermined investor confidence in the country's prospects.

To help clear a path through the political underbrush for the discussion of broader trends and significant events during these three decades, the summary of turnover in the presidency given in table 9.1 may prove useful.

There are some important things to note about this remarkable list of turnovers. First, only three of the eighteen distinct individuals who occupied the president's chair during these decades were civilians (that is, men not of military backgrounds or on active military service) and all the military politicians had had some role in the insurgency of 1810–1821. This is a telling illustration of praetorianism (from the Roman *praetor*, high military officers who made and unmade emperors at certain junctures), the tendency for the military to dominate domestic political life. Of the three civilians—José Justo Corro, Manuel de la Peña y Peña, and Valentín Gómez Farías—the first two were lawyers, the last a physician. While Peña y Peña served for less than two months, Corro was in office for nearly fifteen months; neither man's name is widely known. But the radical liberal Gómez Farías was a major political figure for a long time, associated with Santa Anna, serving in his place for short periods several times in the early 1830s, and the sponsor of many important reform measures, many of which Santa Anna would repudiate on returning to office. Second, most of this movement through the presidency was not due to violent overthrows of the government, conventional wisdom notwithstanding. Constitutionally mandated to relinquish the first magistracy to a vice president or other high official while engaged militarily, the sitting president, a military man, would take leave to command forces in the field to fight against a domestic rebellion or a foreign aggressor and then return to the active exercise of office. So in fact the presidency *appears* more unstable than it actually *was*, at least in terms of how the individuals who occupied the office came into it. Finally, the extreme volatility in the late 1840s was due to the special circumstances created by the war with the United States. Santa Anna's name dominates the list because he occupied the presidency a dozen times, alternating periods of rule (the longest were about twenty

Table 9.1. Presidents of Mexico, 1832–1855 (c = civilian).

Dates of Office	Name	Comment
August 7–December 24, 1832	Melchor Múzquiz	Interim president
December 24, 1832–April 1, 1833	Manuel Gómez Pedraza	Elected 1828
March 30, 1833	Antonio López de Santa Anna	Elected
April 1–May 16, 1833	Valentín Gómez Farías (c)	Vice president
May 16–June 3, 1833	Santa Anna	
June 3–June 18, 1833	Gómez Farías	
June 18–July 5, 1833	Santa Anna	
July 5–October 27, 1833	Gómez Farías	
October 27–December 15, 1833	Santa Anna	
December 16, 1833–April 24, 1834	Gómez Farías	
April 24, 1834–January 27, 1835	Santa Anna	
January 28, 1835–February 27, 1836	Miguel Barragán	Resigned due to health
February 27, 1836–April 19, 1837	José Justo Corro (c)	
April 19, 1837–March 20, 1839	Anastasio Bustamante	Left to command army
March 20–July 10, 1839	Santa Anna	Resigned
July 10–July 19, 1839	Nicolás Bravo	
July 19, 1839–September 22, 1841	Bustamante	Left to command army
September 22–October 10, 1841	Francisco Javier Echeverría	Overthrown by Santa Anna
October 10, 1841–October 26, 1842	Santa Anna	
October 26, 1842–March 4, 1843	Bravo	
March 4–October 4, 1843	Santa Anna	Provisional president
October 4, 1843–June 4, 1844	Valentín Canalizo	Interim president
June 4–September 12, 1844	Santa Anna	
September 12–21, 1844	José Joaquín de Herrera	Interim for Canalizo
September 21–December 6, 1844	Canalizo	
December 7, 1844–December 30, 1845	Herrera	Interim president overthrown
January 4–July 28, 1846	Mariano Paredes y Arrillaga	
July 28–August 4, 1846	Bravo	
August 5–December 23, 1846	José Mariano Salas	
December 23, 1846–March 21, 1847	Gómez Farías	In lieu of Santa Anna
March 21–April 2, 1847	Santa Anna	
April 2–May 20, 1847	Pedro María Anaya	Substitute president

May 20–September 16, 1847	Santa Anna	
September 26,–November 13, 1847	Manuel de la Peña y Peña (c)	
November 13, 1847–January 8, 1848	Anaya	Interim president
January 8–June 3, 1848	Peña y Peña	
June 3, 1848–January 15, 1851	Herrera	
January 15, 1851–January 6, 1853	Mariano Arista	Resigned
January 6–February 8, 1853	Juan Bautista Ceballos	
February 8–April 20, 1853	Manuel María Lombardini	
April 20, 1853–August 12, 1855	Santa Anna	Resigned

and twenty-seven months, respectively, in 1833–1835 and 1853–1855) with leaves either to recover his health or take command of the army. By that criterion alone the label "Age of Santa Anna" seems justified.

SANTA ANNA IN POWER

The first task of those who replaced the *jalapista* government was to exact revenge upon the former ministry, a pattern that would become familiar over the next years. This was initiated under Manuel Gómez Pedraza's brief government early in 1833 and was focused principally upon the chief architect of the Bustamante regime, Lucas Alamán, and his fellow cabinet member, war minister José Antonio Facio. The effort continued in earnest during the brief interim presidencies of the liberal Gómez Farías, whom Alamán in his private correspondence occasionally referred to as "Gómez Furias," essentially "Raging [or even Mad] Gómez." After receding into private life for a number of months after his resignation from the ministry in May 1832, Alamán was brought up on various charges before a grand jury seated in the Chamber of Deputies in February 1833. The allegations were raised by Juan Álvarez (1790–1867), another major insurgent *caudillo*, primarily related to the killing of Guerrero but also including other putative crimes. The charges were supported by petitions from several state legislatures that had not fared well at the ex-minister's hands. The effective author of the treachery, former war minister Facio, fled to Paris, published a spirited defense of his behavior, and died in 1836 before he ever came to trial.

In the face of a war department order for his detention along with the other former ministers, Alamán justifiably feared that Guerrero's vengeful partisans might do him in, so he went into hiding in Mexico City for the next fifteen months. Out of touch with his wife and large family except through occasional brief messages delivered in secret by friends, the ex-minister apparently hid himself for at least some of the time in the home of the American emissary who had succeeded the meddlesome Poinsett. This was Anthony Butler (1787–1849), a South Carolina and Kentucky politician and Andrew Jackson crony with whom the fugitive Alamán developed an improbably cordial relationship given his distrust of the United States. His business affairs in free fall, with a cholera epidemic raging in the city for several months killing many of his friends and intimates, Alamán at one point compared himself to the young cavaliers and gentlewomen who closed themselves up in a villa near Florence to escape the ravages of the Black Plague in Boccaccio's *Decameron* (1353), waiting out the epidemic by telling tales of love. With no library at hand and with little else to keep him occupied, Alamán authored a brilliant short book defending himself against all the accusations that had driven him into internal exile. The upside of this period of hiding was that he also began an autobiographical memoir that in his final years would mutate into his five-volume *Historia de Méjico* (1849–1852), perhaps the greatest work of nineteenth-century Mexican historical writing and the greatest single history of the Mexican independence struggle. When Santa Anna returned to the presidential throne after an extended absence he sought to reverse the radical reform measures initiated by Vice President Gómez Farías and quashed the government's pursuit of Alamán, allowing the former minister to emerge from his self-imposed exile in mid-1834. The case eventually ended up in the Supreme Court. Here one of his defenders before the court, a certified attorney (which Alamán was not), trotted out the racist trope about Guerrero's forces in the War of the South: "Ah! What masses of horror we would have seen if General Guerrero had penetrated as far as this capital leading those hordes of coastal barbarians, that barely have the form of men and all the ferocity of tigers!" The court absolved Alamán in 1836, but history has failed to do so; the charge of his central complicity in the death of Vicente Guerrero followed him to his grave and beyond.

There is some question about whether Antonio López de Santa Anna actually wanted to be president at this point in his career. Historians less sympathetic to him have maintained that while he gloried in the public attention and the opportunity for personal enrichment that the office conferred, he shunned the responsibilities. His most recent biographer, Will Fowler, suggests that at least he felt some ambivalence about it and had maneuvered himself into the position of having his potential vice president, the political liberal Gómez Farías, take over the office to perform its functions and make policy. Most probably there was a bit of both, behavior typical of a man who was always attentive to the performative aspects of his public life and his own advantage but did wish good to the nation if it could be accomplished without damaging his own interests. He wrote to Gómez Farías: "You, my good friend, can take charge, supposing you are elected Vice President, and the election [of president] falls upon me. Then the Mexican people will have nothing more they could wish for, or anything to fear with regards [to] their liberties." He added in a later letter that it was better that "the reins of government not be in the hands of a poor soldier like me, but in those of a citizen like you, known for his virtues and enlightenment." Santa Anna did not actually attend his own inauguration, showed up in the capital six weeks or so later, and spent only a few months of his 1833–1836 presidential term in immediate control of the government.

Valentín Gómez Farías (1781–1858) was a major politician, as I have pointed out, and an interesting figure in his own right (see figure 9.2). One has the impression that he was a bit of a prig—upright, principled, serious, rather humorless, and very much a self-conscious modernizer. Throughout his political career he sought to make Mexico over more into the image of France, Britain, or the United States; to break the economic power of the (in his view) benighted Catholic Church; to loosen the Church's hold over Mexicans' minds; and to distance the army from political life. From a middle-class background in Guadalajara, the largest city in western Mexico, he was trained as a physician, entering politics in 1820. He initially supported Iturbide until he closed congress, then along with Lorenzo de Zavala and a few other political intellectuals became one of the leaders of the more radical liberals, called *puros*, and represented his native state of Jalisco in congress (1824–1830). As Santa Anna's vice president for short periods during 1833–1834 while the president was on leave, Gómez Farías remained temporarily in charge of the government, proposing and carrying through the liberal congress of the period various radical reforms that Santa Anna repudiated and rescinded upon his reoccupation of the presidency. Among these measures was the abolition of the privileged judicial status (*fuero*) of the army and Church entitling members of these supremely powerful corporations to be tried for crimes only by their own judicial organs rather than before the civil courts. He reduced the size of the regular army, always the major drag on state fiscal resources and Santa Anna's great base of power. He pushed measures to secularize the educational establishment, among them closing and reorganizing the University of Mexico along nonreligious lines. He sought further to undermine Church influence by making the ecclesiastical tithe, an obligatory 10 percent tax on agricultural produce, into a purely voluntary contribution, as well as seizing land and other resources held by ecclesiastical corporations, thereby reducing Church economic power. The conservative reaction to these modernization measures led Santa Anna to drive Gómez Farías from office, but much the same scenario would be repeated in 1846–1847 when Santa Anna, commanding Mexican forces against the American invaders, left the presidency in the hands of Gómez Farías, again his vice president. Santa

Figure 9.2. Valentín Gómez Farías (1781–1858), physician, ardent liberal politician, and several times vice president under Santa Anna. Historic Images/Alamy Stock Photo.

Anna's return to office in 1834 was to usher in what one modern historian of the period has called the "conservative ascendancy" of the next dozen years, until the Mexican-American War in 1846.

THE LOSS OF TEXAS

While all the politics of the first Santa Anna presidency were stumbling forward in central Mexico, on the country's northern fringe the province of Texas (Tejas) was fast slipping from the government's grasp. Several factors had served to loosen Mexico's hold on this far-flung territory. These included the fiscal incapacity, institutional weakness, and political volatility of the national government; Indian incursions from the north that discouraged permanent settlement; and slow population growth within the rest of the country, relieving any potential incentive for serious colonization toward the north. On the other hand, the explosive demographic energies of the young American republic, the booming cotton economy of the US South under the slavocratic regime, and the Louisiana Purchase (1803), which put Mexico and the United States directly up against each other geographically, made American territorial expansion toward the west and southwest virtually inevitable on the way to realizing its ambitions to be a continental power. Under the colonization contracts with the Austins, American settlers, ranchers, and planters poured into Texas with their African slaves, their Protestantism, and their distinct political culture. Of the nearly 30,000 people living in Texas (including Indigenous groups) by 1830 less than 5,000 were native Mexicans, and a report on the area by a central government boundary commission stressed the tenuousness of Mexico's hold on the region. Despite the specific exemption of Texas from the measure, President Vicente Guerrero's abolition of African slavery in 1829 nonetheless raised American colonists' fears of central government infringement on their lives and livelihoods; the imposition of new taxes and tariffs added fuel to the fire of their resentments. A law of 1830 aimed to choke off Anglo colonization, but to no avail. Santa Anna's turn toward centralism after his resumption of the presidency threatened to curtail the degree of provincial autonomy enjoyed by the Anglo settlers. Three tendencies were quickly established among them: a vehemently proindependence sentiment; an equally vehement feeling in favor of annexation to the United States, led by Jackson crony and latecomer Sam Houston (1793–1863); and a more conciliatory stance toward Mexico championed by Stephen F. Austin (1793–1836). But the more ardent spirits prevailed and when in June 1835 some Anglo settlers staged an attack on a Mexican customs house and formed a settler "army," Santa Anna undertook an expedition late in the year to suppress what was now seen from Mexico City as an open rebellion.

The expedition's disastrous outcome was foreshadowed by the weak logistical planning and the harsh conditions of a winter march through the Mexican north, when illness and the scarcity of food and clothing took a heavy toll on the ill-equipped national force. Anglo victories at Goliad and

San Antonio initially bred overconfidence in their leadership and led to the dispersal of their forces while declaring independence from Mexico on March 2, 1836. A few days later Santa Anna fought a return engagement with the Americans, famously wiping out the numerically overwhelmed defenders of the Alamo mission fortress in San Antonio (among the dead were Davy Crockett and James Bowie) and shooting the few captured prisoners in violation of the accepted international norms of warfare. This action was followed by another massacre at Goliad. The situation was definitively reversed again by the Americans at the Battle of San Jacinto in April 1836. Santa Anna's army escaped destruction, but its commander was less fortunate and was captured by his foes, prompting wide speculation in Mexico that he had been killed by the Texas settlers. To secure his own freedom and return home Santa Anna signed two treaties. The public one ended the war, pledged the evacuation of Mexican forces, and agreed that Mexican military elements would remain south of the Rio Bravo (the Rio Grande to the Americans). In a second, secret treaty the disgraced Santa Anna promised to urge the recognition of Texas independence in the Mexican congress and acknowledged the Rio Bravo as the border. Previously the Rio Nueces, further north, had been recognized as the boundary of Texas, an adjustment that furnished the *casus belli* for the larger war a decade later. Spared the hanging that many American rebels urged as punishment for his perfidy, Santa Anna was sent to Washington, DC, to offer further assurances to President Jackson of Mexican peaceful intentions and was then returned to Veracruz on an American ship in February 1837, immediately retiring to his Hacienda Manga de Clavo. Texas was now an independent republic and despite its annexation to the United States in 1845 would, as the Lone Star State, remain stubbornly distinct in political culture and mythology up to our own day. In the meantime Anastasio Bustamante had been recalled from his exile in France by President José Justo Corro to aid in the reconquest of Texas but was elected to the presidency for the second time in his own right by the Mexican congress in April 1837. He repudiated Santa Anna's agreements with the Americans, insisting on the Rio Nueces as the southern limit of Texas and thus setting the table for the Mexican-American War a decade later. Some political men believed that a Texas whose independence was guaranteed by Britain would serve as a buffer between weak Mexico and her avaricious northern neighbor, but in the end this proved illusory.

THE CENTRALIST CONSTITUTION
OF 1836 AND OTHER REFORMS

Since independence Mexico's history has been marked by pendulum swings
between greater and lesser national integration. Over time the trend has been
toward the growing concentration of power in the central state, fostered by
material and intellectual technologies invented or adapted for the purpose.
Periods of central state weakness and devolution of power to the regions or
states have occurred at times of nationwide political violence—for example,
the Reforma era in the third quarter of the nineteenth century, the Mexican
Revolution of 1910–1921—but the Leviathan on the Zócalo (the Mexican
state) has increased its strength and reach ineluctably. One of the first explicit
signposts of this process in the postcolonial age was the centralist constitution of 1836.

Political conservatives thought that the difficulties facing Mexico as
Texas slipped away, including virulent political factionalism and instability,
regional uprisings, fiscal debility, economic stagnation, territorial loss, and
national humiliation, might be attenuated if not outright cured by the imposition of a strongly centralist regime to replace the federalist arrangement of
1824. Men of the "aristocratic party," Lucas Alamán most prominent among
them, now had their day under the second Bustamante administration, authoring a new constitution known as the Siete Leyes that supplanted the 1824
charter. The breadth of the electoral franchise was much reduced through
income and other qualifications, and the balance of power was altered among
the three branches of government in favor of the executive. Key aspects of
the changes were the downgrading of the states to "departments" under a
more unitary conception of the national territory, as in the French model; the
demotion of the state legislatures to small, elite-dominated "juntas departa-
mentales" whose members were designated by congress; and the transition
from elected state governors to ones appointed by the president. The term of
the presidency was extended to eight years and the president's election made
the product of an elaborate, indirect Rube Goldberg–like machinery involving the participation of the congress, the Supreme Court, and the executive
branch. A great innovation adopted from the writings of the French politician/
political theorist Benjamin Constant (1767–1830) was the creation by the
Siete Leyes of essentially a fourth branch of government, the Supremo Poder
Conservador (Supreme Conservative Power, SPC). This organ was intended
to dampen the enthusiasms of republicanism by making government less
immediately responsive to popular influences and to prevent the drift toward
dictatorship of the executive in a republican government. A body of five
men of moral and civic virtue, the Poder could depose presidents, suspend

congress, annul laws, etc.; it was a sort of executive branch superego, in other words. That the balance of the first SPC favored political conservatives was hardly surprising in view of the fact that the Siete Leyes had been cooked up by leaders of that tendency. On the whole the charter was elitist, discouraged broad popular participation in politics, and aimed at placing the fate of the nation in the hands of the *hombres de bien*, mostly white men of property, education, gentlemanly status, civic virtue, and conservative ideas. Mexico remained for the time being representative and republican but less popular and no longer federal. The centralist charter immediately came under constant attack by the federalist press. In the late 1830s a score or more of *pronunciamientos* took place around the country in any given year, but this still looked like relative stability bracketed by the 260 such uprisings in 1834 and more than a hundred in 1842.

In keeping with the centralizing impulse of the government under the Siete Leyes, a series of activist measures were undertaken to strengthen the economy and the state administration. Among these was a commission appointed to look into the problem of copper money and to issue a series of recommendations to remedy the inflation that accompanied the proliferation of small denomination copper coins. The emission of these coins was linked in complex ways to the continuing outflow of silver (diminishing in absolute terms due to the deterioration of the mining industry) and the resulting domestic scarcity of ready money. Supported by most liberals and arrogated from the states to the central government by Vicente Guerrero in 1829, the object of copper mintage had been to democratize the domestic economy, obviously at odds with the newly oligarchical style of government under the Siete Leyes. Moreover, rampant falsification of the small denomination coins had unloosed inflation. One recommendation of the commission (headed by Lucas Alamán) was to establish an amortization bank to retire much of the copper, the gradual diminution of which triggered a number of serious urban riots. President Bustamante established yet another commission to overhaul the system of public administration, all of whose recommendations tended to strengthen the centralization established by the Siete Leyes but most of which were never undertaken due to the fiscal stress of the years after the Texas debacle. Chief among the targets of this proposed reform was the treasury, where in the words of the commission's report "the disarray [is] even greater than the scarcity." One reform implemented, in the name of efficiency and a manageable workload, was the separation during several years of the ministry of relations into interior and exterior departments, although by 1841 they had been merged again. Another among many recommendations in keeping with centralist aspirations but not enacted was the establishment of a national constabulary whose chief object was the suppression of endemic banditry but which only came into being later in the century under President Benito Juárez as the famous Rurales.

THE PASTRY WAR

Virtually on the heels of the loss of Texas followed what was by all odds one of the strangest episodes of foreign aggression toward Mexico, inscribed on a scroll of shameless predatory incursions featuring the United States, the French, the English (in a passive role for a time in the 1860s), the Spanish, and various filibustering expeditions by foreigners. The diplomatic and military imbroglio of the so-called Pastry War with France in 1838–1839 arose from Mexican unwillingness to satisfy financial claims by France, accumulating since the late 1820s on behalf of her private citizens, of whom by this time there were about 4,000 living in Mexico. Receiving almost immediate French diplomatic recognition of its independence, the Mexican government had looked with favor upon the July Revolution that brought the "bourgeois king" Louis-Philippe to the French throne in 1830, but relations had begun to sour by the mid-1830s. In the end the war was basically a mistake born of irreversible prickliness about national honor on both sides, aggravated by a racialized contempt for the Mexicans that induced the French to underestimate the resistance they would face if they sent military forces against the country. It was also one of the early attempts by France to assert herself internationally in the post-Napoleonic period, leading to the imperialist scramble for colonies to compensate for the loss of Canada, the Louisiana Territory, and exclusion from India by the English. The immediate trigger of the conflict with Mexico, which gave the war its comic opera name, was the damage caused in 1832 by Mexican soldiers to the shop of a French pastry chef in Tacubaya, at that time a small town lying to the west of Mexico City but today incorporated into that vast metropolis. The owner's claim of damages was highly exaggerated given the actual value of his shop and goods but was rolled into the overall sum of 600,000 pesos (three million Francs) demanded as an indemnity by the French government that the Mexicans refused to pay. The French envoy to Mexico encouraged his government's aggressive stance, writing to the French foreign minister in mid-1837 that "what these people [the Mexicans] need is a lesson, a severe lesson, to knock a little reason and justice into their heads."

In the face of adamant Mexican refusal to pay this indemnity along with resistance to other demands of a commercial nature, the French government determined in 1838 to launch a naval blockade of the Gulf port of Veracruz, thus holding hostage the customs revenues that generated the lion's share of the Mexican government's fiscal resources. A small French naval squadron was reinforced; King Louis-Philippe's son, the Prince de Joinville, joined the expedition; and following a brief bombardment the fortress of San Juan de Ulúa fell to the French at the end of November 1838. The Anastasio Bustamante government in Mexico City refused further negotiations, declared war on France, expelled all French citizens from the country, and appointed Santa Anna commander of Mexican forces. Santa Anna's men offered a spirited defense against the invasion of Veracruz by a large French contingent, but in the fighting the commander was severely wounded in the left leg, which had to be amputated below the knee the following day. In short order the threatened arrival of a British naval flotilla from Canada and a diplomatic intervention by the British envoy to Mexico brought the parties back to negotiations. The Mexican government agreed to render the indemnity of 600,000 pesos to be delivered in installments beginning in March 1839. Although diplomatic relations between the two combatants were restored this sum was never paid, providing in part the pretext for the altogether more serious French invasion of the early 1860s. Aside from an embarrassment for France and a cause for nationalist pride among the Mexicans, the incident provided Santa Anna with another sacrifice on the altar of the fatherland and thus a potent element in the construction of his personality cult. Initially buried on his Manga de Clavo estate, his amputated lower leg was later exhumed and reinterred in a state funeral in Mexico City, only to be disinterred from its mausoleum by an angry mob in 1844 and dragged around the city on a rope.

THE RUN-UP TO WAR WITH THE UNITED STATES AND A MONARCHIST PLOT

Between late 1841 and the summer of 1845 there were nine presidencies of the country with five individuals in them, four of them political generals, including Santa Anna three times. In the eight years that followed, between 1845 and 1853, there were fifteen presidencies, temporary or constitutional, with eleven men, Santa Anna again in office three times and most of the occupants of the presidential chair military men. The portfolios in the ministerial cabinet turned over even faster, as we have seen. This instability at the top levels of the government was a product in large measure not just of momentary circumstances, including the war with the United States, but also of the fundamental vacuum in political legitimacy discussed in a previous chapter. And because republican institutions were thrown so much into doubt it is hardly surprising that a return to monarchy was briefly envisioned by several major political actors, in the lead-up to the war, among them Lucas Alamán. There must have been substantial popular support for such a proposal, although it is difficult to say how deep it went. But the disruptive movements at the level of high politics did not tell the entire story of instability in the country. From 1842 to 1845 there was a large-scale peasant rebellion in the southwestern region centered chiefly in the state of Guerrero, and another in the Sierra Gorda region in the near northeast a short time later. The even more famous Caste War of Yucatán, in the southeast of Mexico (briefly discussed shortly), which began in the late 1840s, waxed and waned in violence until the twentieth century.

The few years before the war with the United States were especially chaotic in Mexican political life, which is saying a lot, but I will try to convey only the gist of the period here. Back from exile and radically liberal as ever, Valentín Gómez Farías attempted an armed coup against the Anastasio Bustamante government, the forerunner of a successful effort led from Guadalajara in the summer of 1841 by General Mariano Paredes y Arrillaga (1797–1849) quickly adhered to by Santa Anna and other military politicians with the armed forces at their disposal, generally quite small in numbers. After a certain amount of to-ing and fro-ing the Bustamante government collapsed, forcing Bustamante into European exile yet again and clearing the way for the provisional takeover of the presidency by the Napoleon of the West. Bustamante would return to Mexico in 1845 to lead a distinguished political and military career until his death in 1853, but never again as president. Santa Anna was once more elected president late in 1843, confirmed by congress in early 1844, and on the basis of yet another even more authoritarian constitution, the Bases Orgánicas (Organic Bases), built a military dictatorship in all but name. To replenish the nearly empty treasury President Santa Anna went on a taxing rampage, imposing forced loans on the Church and especially heavy extraordinary imposts on the wealthy and merchants. During 1844 the number of *pronunciamientos* around the country spiked up to nearly one hundred while the Southwest Peasants' War roiled the southern part of Mexico. In November of that year, for example, there were some 25 *actas levantadas* (essentially petitions or manifestos associated with these uprisings, stating their goals and demands), chiefly by groups of military officials in Jalisco, Aguascalientes, San Luis Potosí, Guanajuato, Querétaro, Michoacán, Tamaulipas, Coahuila, Sonora, Oaxaca, and Chiapas.

Leading up to the war with the United States in 1846 the pace of uprisings and coups really gained speed, although we will not tramp far into those particular weeds. The war with the United States was a major episode to which I devote some pages here because it is of relevance not only to Mexico, which was victimized by it, but also to American readers of this volume. What was once part of Mexico, after all, and now embraces the US Southwest (including Texas—the eastern part of the state as much southern as southwestern), large swaths of the Rocky Mountain region, and California contains roughly 100,000,000 people, or almost a third of the national population of the United States. In May 1844 news reached Mexico City that US president John Tyler had submitted a treaty for congressional approval to annex the Republic of Texas as a state. This set off a chain of events whose outcome was Mexico's disastrous defeat in war and the loss of half the national territory. Santa Anna instituted a conscription system to build up the armed forces for the now inevitable conflict with the United States, as Paredes y Arrillaga led yet another revolt against the government. At the very end of 1844, however, José Joaquín de Herrera (1792–1854), another political general and at the time president of the regime's Governing Council, managed to overthrow the Santa Anna government, occasioning the Mexico City riot that disinterred the much-revered leg of the hero of Veracruz, now viewed with popular scorn as the symbol of a military tyrant; the rest of Santa Anna was sent into exile for life at a general's half-pay. Herrera is a noteworthy character among the military politicians who dominated public life during these decades, seldom getting his due as a man of integrity and politically moderate centralism. After fighting against the insurgency on the royalist side during the independence struggle he adhered to Iturbide's program in 1820–1821. Entering congress in 1822–1823, he then turned against the emperor as his brief regime became more and more arbitrary. Subsequently he served in the presidential cabinet as minister of war and three times as president of the republic: for about ten days in 1844, for most of 1845, and from mid-1848 to the very beginning of 1851. In a period when many politicians themselves expected, and were expected by most Mexicans, to become enriched from office, when he left the presidency in 1851 to return to private life Herrera was a poor man. While liberals urged war over Texas, Herrera favored negotiations rather than armed confrontation with the United States, acutely aware that a military contest would be extremely uneven. Accused of being insufficiently bellicose toward the United States, Herrera in turn fell to a coup by Paredes y Arrillaga, whom he had sent north with a force to face the Americans but who had headed south instead and turned those very forces against the government. Paredes assumed the presidency in January 1846. Between then and early 1847 the first magistracy passed successively from Paredes's hands through those of General Mariano Salas and Valentín Gómez Farías to end up with Santa Anna once again. He had returned from exile in Cuba a convinced liberal and was named president by congress early in 1847 under the auspices of that Lazarus of constitutions, the federalist charter of 1824. I do not mean to suggest by this schematic treatment that these changes at the top of the Mexican government were at all trivial or in themselves inexplicable but simply that the complicated circumstances of each were quite specific to the moment when they occurred and would require a great deal of space to relate in detail.

The monarchist leanings of which Alamán and some of his political allies were continually accused by liberal politicians and press from the 1820s onward blossomed into a menacing but abortive conspiracy in late 1845 and early 1846 during the brief presidency of Paredes y Arrillaga. It was carried forward both in secret correspondence among the plotters and more openly in the capital's conservative press. The incident is of interest chiefly for what it suggests of the strong monarchist sentiment among a sector of the political elite, initially subterranean but later voiced quite publicly; of the robust way in which republicanism had nonetheless rooted itself among ever larger groups; and of the political debates in the country in the wake of the disastrous war with the United States. By the 1848–1850 period monarchist discourse would recede to a more traditional conservatism and even the establishment of a formal conservative party, but it still came to serve as a sort of foil for a heated national conversation about the viability of republican institutions, the virtues and vices of wide popular participation in politics, and the form and legitimate reach of the central state.

The idea of installing a foreign prince on a Mexican throne was already on the table as a major provision of Iturbide's Plan of Iguala and of the debates in the empire-wide Cortes in Madrid in 1820–1822. Some idea of the headwinds faced by the monarchical project after Iturbide is conveyed in a letter of late 1840 from a prominent Mexican politician to the liberal priest, politician, and historian Father José María Luis Mora (1794–1850) in Paris; the reference to Gutiérrez Estrada is to the open letter the politician from Yucatán published that year advocating a return to monarchy in Mexico, mentioned earlier:

> Your good friend Gutiérrez Estrada finds himself at this moment in a very difficult position. . . . This week he published [a letter] proposing the establishment in Mexico of a monarchy with a European prince. You cannot imagine the hornet's nest he has stirred up with this. In public everyone speaks the language of the most exalted republicanism: some from personal resentments, many out of calculation and ulterior motives, and very few because they truly believe in it. They have pronounced an anathema against the poor author, who has had to hide himself, leaving the printer to face the consequences. Everyone is in [a state of] alarm, and fearing the future, which today seems darker than ever.

We may reasonably discount the note of cynicism about the genuineness of prorepublican feeling among the public. Most people espousing republican ideas almost certainly believed that a republican form of government, even if not a robust popular democracy, was best for the country.

There is a great deal of fascinating detail and a deep backstory in the conspiracy but the gist of it can be conveyed in a paragraph or two. The chief conspirator was the Spanish envoy to Mexico, the lawyer, diplomat, and literary figure Salvador Bermúdez de Castro y Díez (1817–1883). He was charged by the government of his queen, Isabel II, to do everything possible to create conditions for the enthronement of a Spanish Bourbon prince in

Mexico, a revival (or survival) of the stubborn irredentism of King Ferdinand VII more than twenty years earlier. Bermúdez had funds secretly provided by the Spanish government, primarily to bribe Mexican officials and pay sympathetic journalists to argue for the cause. President Herrera chose to pursue secret negotiations over Texas with an American representative of President James K. Polk (1795–1849), the southern Democrat politician John Slidell (1793–1871), who arrived in Mexico at the end of 1845 even as American forces gathered menacingly along the country's northern border. Yielding to political and public pressure Herrera then refused to see Slidell and ordered Mariano Paredes y Arrillaga to march on the northern frontier. Arrillaga refused the order, eventually staging his own *pronunciamiento* essentially accusing Herrera of betraying Mexico in favor of a settlement with the Americans. Supported by a rash of sympathetic uprisings around the country Paredes managed to topple Herrera and assume the presidency. One of his backers among conservative politicians was Alamán, who cofounded a highly conservative newspaper in the capital a scant few weeks after Paredes's ascent to power. The stage was now set for the unfolding of a plot to enthrone a Spanish or other foreign prince as monarch of Mexico.

The Spanish envoy Bermúdez de Castro and Lucas Alamán were the main plotters, the Spaniard the senior partner. As a foreign national and diplomat he enjoyed protected status even while interfering in Mexican domestic politics and illegally applying secret funds to influence the course of government action. Alamán's promonarchist position was made clear by his editorials in the newspaper he had cofounded, *El Tiempo*, supported financially by the Spanish envoy, so in that sense his monarchism was hardly "conspiratorial." But it did reflect an evolution in his political thinking over the two preceding decades from his position as a moderate centralist republican during the Guadalupe Victoria presidency. He now acted as a conservative monarchist desperate to calm the endemic political chaos of the country, which he saw as an absolute prerequisite condition to further economic development and modernization. In an editorial of February 1846, he wrote that "the republic has created nothing; it has destroyed everything." Republican democracy, he continued, was not just unsuited to Mexico but absolutely pernicious. The idea here was that a constitutional monarch, modeled along British lines but without the accompanying aristocracy, would be rich enough to avoid corruption or the furthering of factional interest and would be above political struggles. For his part President Paredes y Arrillaga had expressed sympathy for at least the past decade for the installation of a monarchy but tended to equivocate about whether it could viably replace republican institutions and was in any event opposed to the candidacy of a Spanish prince. He corresponded with Bermúdez de Castro and Alamán over a number of months, tending to support republicanism in public and monarchism in private. Whether Paredes y

Arrillaga would actually have stepped aside in favor of a foreign prince is something of an open question but seems to me highly doubtful. After sending out a good many mixed signals about his attitude toward the monarchist project, in March 1846 he finally declared publicly an unequivocal commitment to uphold republican institutions until the new congress should decide the fate of the country's governance, thus double-crossing the conspirators. The entire "conspiracy" was by this time on its back foot, overtaken by the outbreak of war with the United States in April 1846; the US Congress approved President Polk's declaration of war in May. Bermúdez de Castro confessed to his government that the window of opportunity for a return to monarchy in Mexico had slammed shut. Alamán's promonarchist newspaper *El Tiempo*, the mouthpiece for the movement, folded after only four months. Early April saw the advent of an antigovernment *pronunciamiento* led by the southern *caudillo* Juan Alvarez, whose central demand was the return of Santa Anna, then in Cuba, to the presidency as the only man who could save the country. Santa Anna had secretly colluded with President Polk to return to Mexico with American help on the understanding that he would end the Mexican armed response to US forces and cede certain territories, an agreement he had little trouble reneging on once he returned from exile. By August he was back in the country, the 1824 Constitution had been reinstated, new congressional elections had been decreed, all of Paredes y Arrillaga's measures had been voided, and Paredes himself was gone, exiled to France. He would return briefly, participate in another armed revolt, and die in obscurity in 1849.

THE WAR WITH THE UNITED STATES

The American invasion and brief occupation of Mexico in 1846–1848 was certainly the single most important event between the winning of independence in 1821 and the fall of Santa Anna's last government and the definitive ascent of liberalism and the Liberal Reform of the years after 1855, which marks the close of our period. In the Carthaginian peace imposed by the victors Mexico was shorn of half its national territory. With about 23 million people in 1850, the US population was three times the size of Mexico's, with a much larger and more advanced economy and concomitantly superior war-making powers. These differences in favor of the United States would have resulted in an extremely asymmetrical military contest even had Mexico been internally united politically, which it was not. A critical loss to Mexico as a result of the war were the California gold fields, first discovered in 1848, the very year the conflict ended with the Treaty of Guadalupe Hidalgo. There was also the loss of more than 500,000 square miles of territory to the United

States and beyond that a huge damage to national confidence. Moreover, the pressure on native peoples from the renewed influx of American settlers in the newly won territories pushed Indian incursions against cattle ranches and rural estates further south into Mexico, even as far as Zacatecas. The losses in human life in the war were considerable even by the standards of European warfare in the age. The United States lost nearly 15,000 men, mostly to disease and nonbattle conditions, and the Mexicans, apart from uncountable civilian deaths, some 25,000 dead and wounded. By comparison, at the Battle of Waterloo three decades earlier, of the French casualties of over 40,000 about 10,000 died in battle, and of the allied forces' (primarily those of the United Kingdom, the Netherlands, and Prussia) 24,000 casualties the Duke of Wellington's army suffered 3,500 deaths and the Prussians only about 1,200. While the terms of the treaty ending the war committed the United States to an indemnity of fifteen million dollars to compensate Mexico for the loss of territory, and the assumption by the US government of up to five million dollars in claims of US citizens against the Mexican government, the money was a pittance compared to the territorial, human, and psychological losses Mexico incurred and was quickly frittered away.

Although by 1844 Mexico had finally come to see the reconquest of its errant province as quixotic, tacitly recognizing the independence of the Texas Republic. It was clearly understood by both Mexico and the United States that the annexation of Texas to the American Union would be a cause for war. Early that year President John Tyler (1790–1862) began the process of annexation with a submission to the US Congress. His successor, southern Democrat James K. Polk (1795–1849), pledging a one-term presidency devoted to settling the Oregon Territory controversy with Britain and annexing Texas, narrowly won election over antiannexationist Whig Henry Clay (1777–1852). The annexation bill was pushed through Congress in 1845 and Texas formally admitted to the Union on December 29, 1845. In American domestic affairs this was a superheated issue because it was understood by all parties that Texas would enter the Union as a slave state. Whigs, abolitionists, and northerners feared this would destroy the fragile equilibrium between slave and free states, really the central question in US politics since the framing of the Constitution nearly six decades earlier. Now clearly intent on triggering a war with Mexico, President Polk ostensibly claimed the boundary question as the major issue: whether the southern limit of the State of Texas was the Río Nueces or the Río Grande (known to the Mexicans as the Río Bravo), about 150 miles to the south. In reality he was aiming to appropriate New Mexico and California, making the United States a truly continental power. In July 1845 he sent General Zachary Taylor (1784–1850) to the Río Grande with a force of American soldiers and in late April 1846 managed to provoke an armed confrontation with Mexican forces. This prompted

Polk to his famously indignant claim that the Mexicans had "shed American blood on American soil," a statement characterized by the freshman Whig congressman from Illinois, Abraham Lincoln, as "a bold falsification of history." In his memoirs (1885) President Ulysses S. Grant, who had served as a lieutenant under General Taylor, wrote of this opportunistic provocation by President Polk:

> The presence of United States troops on the edge of the disputed territory farthest from the Mexican settlements, was not sufficient to provoke hostilities. We were sent to provoke a fight, but it was essential that Mexico should commence it. It was very doubtful whether Congress would declare war; but if Mexico should attack our troops, the Executive could announce, "Whereas, war exists by the acts of, etc.," and prosecute the contest with vigor. Once initiated there were but few public men who would have the courage to oppose it. . . . Mexico showing no willingness to come to the Nueces to drive the invaders from her soil, it became necessary for the "invaders" to approach to within a convenient distance to be struck. Accordingly, preparations were begun for moving the army to the Rio Grande.

Polk's assertion led to a declaration of war on May 13, 1846, but even in advance of that Taylor's forces had pushed south, winning two quick victories over the Mexicans. Outnumbered from the start of the conflict the Americans nonetheless enjoyed an edge in terms of the economy supporting them, financing, weaponry, military techniques, and generalship. One advantage, for example, was the use of what was called "flying artillery," light cannonry pulled into battle by mounted artillerymen who thus enjoyed tactical superiority over the heavy, much less mobile Mexican artillery. Despite the Americans' advantages the Mexicans gave an excellent account of themselves but were unable to stop their enemy's progress.

Cynical as the American intervention in Mexico was, the fighting provided the military apprenticeship for a number of men later prominent in US politics, among them future presidents Zachary Taylor, Franklin Pierce, and U. S. Grant, future commander of Civil War Union forces George McClellan, and Confederate generals Stonewall Jackson and his chief, Robert E. Lee. The most acclaimed military leader among the Americans was General Winfield Scott (1786–1866), although Taylor was the immediate beneficiary of his war reputation, parlaying it into election to the presidency in 1848. A Virginian trained as a lawyer, and despite his southern birth and plantation background a solid Union loyalist, Scott took up a military career at the beginning of the nineteenth century. He compiled what is still to this day the longest career as senior commander in the US army. Known as "Old Fuss and Feathers" because of his strict insistence on professionalism and punctilious military etiquette in the armed forces, he grew so corpulent in his late years that he had to be helped on and off his horse. But his notable strategic and organizational abilities, diplomatic skills off the battlefield, care for his subordinates, and determination to follow orders from his civilian chiefs even when he disagreed with them distinguished him as one of the outstanding American military men of the nineteenth century. After his capture of Mexico City in late 1847 the Duke of Wellington, in a position to judge because he had been a central military figure in the liberation of Spain from the French in 1814 and defeated Napoleon at the Battle of Waterloo in 1815, proclaimed Scott the greatest military figure then active in the world. Scott commanded an American force in the Canada theater in the War of 1812 and fought in the Indian campaigns of later years. Then, to his discredit in the eyes of history, under orders from President Martin Van Buren in 1838 he oversaw the removal of the Cherokee Indians from their ancestral home in the US southeast along the Trail of Tears to what is now Oklahoma, continuing a policy initiated by Van Buren's patron and predecessor Andrew Jackson. Promoted to the rank of brigadier general at the age of twenty-eight, Winfield Scott sought the Whig nomination for the presidency in 1840 and 1844, losing the contest in 1848 to Zachary Taylor (1784–1850), another Mexican War veteran. The old soldier finally attained the Whig nomination in 1852 but lost the election to Franklin Pierce (1804–1869). Scott was chief commander of the Union forces in the Civil War up to November 1861, when Lincoln replaced him with the tactically immobile George B. McClellan, known as "Little Mac" and much loved by his men. Scott's strategic plan to surround and strangle the Confederacy (the "Anaconda Plan") by dominating the Mississippi River was discounted early on by the civil authorities in Washington but substantially carried through later in the war by Grant, who in 1864 received the old general's memoirs inscribed "From the oldest general to the youngest."

While Zachary Taylor's forces were fighting in Texas and northern Mexico, Stephen Kearny (1794–1848) and John C. Fremont (1813–1890) were making their way to California overland and Commodore John Sloat (1781–1867) by sea. Weakened by a shift of troops to Winfield Scott's command, Taylor's army refused to retreat from Saltillo, in the northern state of Coahuila. Having intercepted a letter between the two American commanders discussing the decrease in Taylor's forces, Santa Anna reasonably believed this to indicate great vulnerability in the Americans' position and headed north with an army of 20,000 men determined to destroy Taylor's force before pivoting to engage Scott. But when the two met in the field at the Battle of Buena Vista near Saltillo in February 1847 Taylor's outnumbered force emerged victorious and Santa Anna retreated to the south. Meanwhile, on March 9, 1847, Winfield Scott staged a daring amphibious landing at Veracruz with 12,000 American soldiers, besieged the city, and began fighting his way inland against determined Mexican army and guerrilla resistance. Bold as it was this strategy was not unprecedented because it duplicated almost exactly what Fernando Cortés had done more than three centuries earlier in confronting the Aztecs in 1519–1521. In fact, many of the officers under Scott's command carried with them on their expedition copies of *The History of the Conquest of Mexico* (1843) by the American historian William H. Prescott (1796–1859), which gave a romanticized but well documented account of Cortés's achievements and had enjoyed a great popular success with the American public. Unaccustomed as they were to the climate many in the American army fell victim to disease, the supply lines back to New Orleans grew more and more attenuated, and Mexican guerrilla forces exacted considerable casualties on the invaders.

By August 1847 Winfield Scott's invading army had arrived in the Valley of Mexico. His forces and those of his subordinate commanders were encamped on the southern and southwestern margins of Mexico City, which although dense in its central districts was less than 1 percent as large in population and many times smaller and more compact in area than it is today. A number of fierce battles took place between the opposing armies during which the Mexicans, with few exceptions numerically superior but badly outgunned, stood up remarkably well even while ending up on the losing side. One of these late critical confrontations took place at Churubusco on August 20. Now absorbed into the monstrous urban sprawl that is Mexico City, Churubusco was then a village with a convent lying some miles from the capital to the south of a river. In the twentieth century the area became the site of a huge complex of motion picture sound stages and other production facilities, and it remains to this day the center of the Mexican film industry. The Battle of Churubusco was one climactic engagement in which the force strength was reversed, the Americans outnumbering the Mexicans by about two to one (8,500 to 3,800), the former under the command of generals Scott and Twiggs, the overall command of the latter by Santa Anna but with General Pedro María de Anaya one of the immediate commanding officers. When the battle was over and General Twiggs demanded that the defeated Anaya surrender his ammunition, the Mexican general replied with classic bravado, "If I had any ammunition, you would not be here." Following this engagement brief armistice negotiations between the parties broke down and active combat resumed in early September. On September 13 Scott captured Chapultepec Castle, a large colonial construction on a hill to the west of the capital, later the residence of Emperor Maximilian and Empress Carlota and today a magnificent historical museum located in a much frequented urban park. In 1847 it was the site of the Mexican military academy, due to its elevation commanding an important approach to the city. After a long assault by the Americans the defending military cadets under the command of Nicolás Bravo retreated except for a few very young men, six of whom famously opted to die fighting the Americans and have been incorporated into the national mythology as the Niños Heroes, the "Boy Heroes." As legend has it, one of them leaped to his death from a parapet of the castle wrapped in a Mexican flag so that it would not be captured and thus dishonored by the invaders.

In the wake of these and other engagements and Santa Anna's retreat to the north with the bulk of the remaining Mexican forces, Mexico City was left defenseless to the advance of the American army. Santa Anna divided the army, taking part of it with him in the vain hope (as it turned out) of recovering Puebla and organizing further armed resistance to the invasion and leaving part under the command of General José Joaquín de Herrera, who would shortly be elected to the presidency after Santa Anna resigned in order to escort the provisional government to Querétaro. On September 14 the Americans, numbering some 8,000 men (later to be reinforced considerably), entered the city and by September 16, the anniversary of the country's independence, the US flag was flying over the National Palace. Many of the capital's wealthy and elite citizens had fled the American advance, among them Lucas Alamán and his family. There was considerable looting by the Americans at first, but quite soon a more orderly occupation and billeting was imposed by Scott with harsh measures applied against Mexican civilian resisters. Furious but largely unarmed, the common people of Mexico City put up an unorganized but strong resistance to the invaders, exacting several hundred casualties within a few days. American stragglers making their way in less frequented parts of the city were at great risk, occasionally murdered by Mexicans while seeking female companionship or easy pickings in abandoned homes. More generally, the Mexican political elite feared that the effective emasculation of the central government might produce a caste war by humble people of color not only against the invaders but also their Mexican overlords, an anxiety fueled by memories of the racial undertones in the Guerra del sur of 1830–1831, born out by the outbreak of a massive Indian peasant uprising in Yucatán in July 1847. This episode, known as the Caste War of Yucatán (briefly discussed shortly), would continue for the next fifty years, provoking leaders in that state to contemplate for a time seeking annexation to the United States or even Spain. The weakened condition of the national government, meanwhile, provided an opening for the states to reassert themselves in fiscal, defense, and other matters while major Mexican ports on the Gulf and Pacific coasts remained under blockade by American naval forces until mid-1848. After his attempts to retake Puebla or mount an organized rump resistance to the invasion fizzled, Santa Anna resigned the presidency in late September 1847 and fled into exile in Colombia, returning to Mexico only in 1853.

Amid the chaotic conditions following the end of the fighting negotiations moved toward a peace settlement highly advantageous to the United States.

BOX 9.1. LUCAS ALAMÁN ON THE AMERICAN INVASION

An interesting guide to the events of the war and the political volatility in Mexico in these years, although a highly opinionated one, is Lucas Alamán, whose activities and ideas have popped up repeatedly so far in this book. He wrote very little about the American incursion into the country in the closing chapter of his magisterial history of the independence movement (published 1849–1852), in which he meant to bring the history of the country up from 1821 to 1850 or so. But by way of compensation, his decades-long correspondence with the Neapolitan nobleman the Duke of Terranova and Monteleone, the descendant and heir to the extensive Mexican properties of Fernando Cortés, contains much information on the war and Mexican politics as they were unfolding after 1845 or so. Alamán provided quite a detailed account of the fall of the Gómez Farías government and the designation by the Mexican congress of Santa Anna as president in March 1847: "Since that day [March 21, 1847] everything has been revolution . . . and thus we have passed the entire month of March only hearing cannon fire and knowing of deaths and misfortunes, without being able to walk in the streets, or do anything . . . [and] all the houses are shut up." Following Scott's capture of Jalapa he added, "If some bomb has not finished me off, I think I will write [my next letter to you] under the dominion of the United States."

Alamán tended to set the threshold quite low for describing a political situation as "anarchy," but as a man of large experience and a keen eye his observations are nonetheless worth considering. When Pedro María Anaya had assumed the presidency in place of the campaigning Santa Anna, the statesman-historian wrote to Terranova with a splash of caustic wit in May 1847:

> The city is in the most complete anarchy that can be imagined: everything is in disorder, [there are] robberies, and clashes among the governing authorities, whom no-one obeys. It is impossible that a nation can remain so for any time without being entirely annihilated. Revolutions here are so frequent that you write congratulating one of our presidents on his election, and [by the time] the letter arrives he has fallen. This is what happened with the letter you sent to me for [José Joaquín de] Herrera and the same thing has happened with the one you sent for Santa Anna. Defeated everywhere, insulted and mocked in the newspapers, he lost all

prestige and has been dragging along in a sad existence in the presidency [May–September 1847]. . . . We will see if in these continuous vicissitudes he rises again, which would not be at all strange, so I will save your letter until then.

In a later letter to the duke he expanded on this comment, writing that the nobleman's formulaic

letters of congratulation to presidents Santa Anna or Herrera "serve for nothing now, and with the rapidity with which revolutions overthrow those who rise, it would be necessary to have an assortment of letters of all the imaginable people [who might occupy the presidency], or a blank one [that is, a form letter] to apply to whomever might be in charge at the moment."

As Winfield Scott's army advanced toward the Mexican capital Alamán wrote in June: "Notwithstanding this [riskiness of his route of march] it appears to me certain that he will take the city, because all the troops [defending it] are forcible recruits, commanded by generals whose speed in retreat is well-known, and the mass of the population does not move for anything, since they are looking at this as though it were occurring in a foreign country, so fatigued are they from the many uprisings."

Alamán advised the duke to place little trust in some reassurances Santa Anna had offered in his letters regarding the security of the nobleman's properties in Mexico,

since he is a man to whom falling into the most jarring contradictions between conduct and words matters nothing. . . . Thus we here live without security of any kind in anything, looking with the greatest mistrust on anything coming from the government, not knowing those in authority except to judge who is the worst, and allowing ourselves to be robbed unconscionably. And it is this that explains why an army of 10,000 Anglo-Americans has arrived at the center of the Republic and is at the point of capturing the capital without anyone taking an interest in whether or not it is captured.

By the spring of 1848, while the Treaty of Guadalupe Hidalgo was awaiting ratification by both the US and Mexican congresses, Alamán wrote of conditions in the American-occupied capital:

The city is an encampment of bandits, and there is almost no night on which there is not a robbery or violent assault. Four or five nights ago there was an attack on the house of Muriel, one of the principal merchants, on a very central and much-frequented street. The attackers were a dozen North Americans who fled when shots were fired, one of which killed the principal employee of the business. One of the invaders, having been caught within, by his declarations revealed that in the gang were three officers of the American army, and the rest [of them] soldiers and servants [of the officers], who have been arrested and will be tried. Yesterday, Sunday, people returning from a walk alongside a canal, were attacked at the embarcadero by a party of bandits in the service of the North American army . . . posted there to rob the returning people. [In the ensuing battle] there were fourteen killed on one side or another.

Against the background of the Caste War of Yucatán some time later, Alamán wrote that the departure of the American occupiers,

which in other circumstances would be a joy, is to be feared as the beginning of new disasters, since at that moment will begin an interior war that will assume the character of a caste war among the various groups that form this society. And the least numerous among them being the white race, it and all its properties will perish.

By May 1848 Santa Anna had decamped for Colombia and both Manuel de la Peña y Peña (1789–1850), the president of the Supreme Court, and Pedro María de Anaya (1795–1854), a military politician, had served brief stints in the presidency, to which the congress, meeting in Querétaro, elected General Herrera in June 1848. Under Peña y Peña's government the Treaty of Guadalupe Hidalgo was negotiated and ratified by both combatants, ending the war and sealing the cession of half of Mexico's national territory to the United States. The American negotiator was Nicholas P. Trist (1800–1874), chief clerk of the US Department of State, who had been sent to Mexico by President Polk to undertake negotiations. Trist was a Virginia-born lawyer and politician married to Thomas Jefferson's granddaughter. Recalled by Polk for discussions in Washington in the face of Mexican resistance to the terms being offered, Trist ignored the recall order and remained to continue talks, generating the Treaty of Guadalupe Hidalgo, named for the town to the north of Mexico City where it was signed by Trist and the Mexican commissioners on February 2, 1848, and ratified by both the US Senate and the Mexican congress some months later. The territory acquired included fixing the southern

Texas border at the Río Grande and all of the states of California, Nevada, and Utah, most of Arizona, New Mexico, and Colorado, and bits of Oklahoma, Wyoming, and Kansas. The Gadsden Purchase of 1853, under Santa Anna's last government, would complete the acquisition of Arizona and New Mexico. Trist had been instructed to acquire the Baja California peninsula, if possible, but it remained with Mexico. The United States agreed to pay an indemnity of $15,000,000 (about $440,000,000 today) and to assume over $3,000,000 in private American property claims against Mexico. Mexicans in the newly conquered lands had the option of assuming full American citizenship within a year or being repatriated to Mexico; an estimated 90 percent chose to remain and adopt US citizenship. Two provisions that went largely unfulfilled assured the property rights of Mexicans within the ceded territories and obligated the United States to punish Indian raids into Mexico originating in American territory.

The American acquisition of this enormous territory by violent armed theft (for there is really no other realistic description of it) had tremendous economic, political, social, and cultural consequences for both sides in the conflict. Not the least has been a continual wave of immigration of Mexicans over the past 170 years to the side of the border once part of Mexico, which remained heavily Mexican in many of its aspects and was therefore more welcoming than other areas of the United States. The population of these areas will become majority Mexican-origin in the near future. On the Mexican side there was a sense of national humiliation and grievance, an emotional irredentism that persists in some measure to this day. And this is not to mention the loss of the California gold fields, the Colorado and Nevada silver mines, the Pacific coast anchorages and fisheries, and the vast plains that came to be devoted to farming and cattle raising. What lies beyond the scope of this book are the middle-term political results of Mexico's near failure as a state due to the excision of half the national territory. Chief among these was the Reforma that began with the overthrow of Santa Anna's last government in 1855, the ascent of liberalism embodied in the figure of Benito Juárez (1806–1872) and his ideological heirs, and the civil struggles of the late 1850s and early 1860s that far transcended in scope and violence the *pronunciamientos* so characteristic of the young Mexican republic up to that time. While these trends and events would most probably have occurred anyway, the Mexican-American War was a major accelerant. And although many Mexicans have crossed northward anyway, the descendants, both biological and spiritual, of those who remained in the formerly Mexican lands rather than move south often say, "We did not cross the border; the border crossed us."

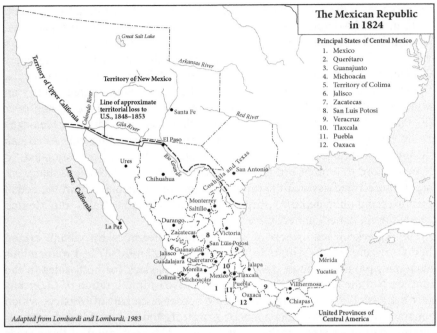

The Mexican Republic
in 1824

Principal States of Central Mexico
1. Mexico
2. Querétaro
3. Guanajuato
4. Michoacán
5. Territory of Colima
6. Jalisco
7. Zacatecas
8. San Luis Potosi
9. Veracruz
10. Tlaxcala
11. Puebla
12. Oaxaca

Adapted from Lombardi and Lombardi, 1983

United Provinces of
Central America

Map 9.1. The Mexican republic in 1824. Lombardi and Lombardi, *Latin American History*, 50.

THE CASTE WAR OF YUCATÁN

Whether the Mexican countryside has historically been more violent than that of other nations is an open question. Certainly, Mexico has a long history of rural violence ranging from relatively infrequent large-scale rebellions, to uprisings more limited in scope, down to local riots and politically tinted banditry. In most of that history the protagonists, or at least the mass of the participants, have been Indigenous peasants, even if the leaders have often been townsmen or members of social categories somewhat raised from the peasantry. This makes sense when one considers that for much of its history the large majority of Mexico's population has been devoted to small-scale farming for its livelihood; to peasant forms of production, in other words. Where nonpeasant leadership is concerned it often goes unacknowledged, for example, that the heavily peasant villager southern wing of the Mexican Revolution of 1910 was for much of its life led by Emiliano Zapata, a man on the rise from a peasant background but who himself could be characterized neither as a peasant nor an Indian. Exactly a century earlier the independence movement in New Spain was for much of its ten-year life heavily peasant and Indigenous in its makeup. My own research has indicated that at least up to

1815 and beyond about 50 to 60 percent of the combatants on the insurgent side were humble rural people, mostly laborers and family farmers. There were peasants among the insurgent leadership, and more of them as one descended to localities and micro-localities, but most of the top echelon was not drawn from the peasantry.

While not all Mexican peasants have been Indigenous people, particularly as the percentage of Indigenous people in the general population declined to the 10 to 14 percent or so where it now stands, the overlap is so great that episodes of rural political violence, ipso facto, have often been Indian in their makeup. Because "peasant" is basically an economic category pertaining to a specific sort of small-scale rural cultivator and "Indian" is a sociocultural designator attached to an ethnically and linguistically marked underclass, the question naturally arises as to whether such violent outbreaks can be ascribed to class or ethnic stressors or antagonisms. The fact that both identities may impel people forward into political violence makes rather difficult the application to Mexican history of traditional models of political violence, many of which are class-based. In these movements the classic peasant grievance of asymmetrical struggles with more commercially oriented rural estates over access to land is often entwined with other issues, such as the political autonomy of rural communities or the liberty to exercise traditional forms of religious observance, or it may be muted or missing entirely. It is difficult to see Indian peasant participation in 1810–1821 as a massive agrarian revolt, as I have tried to show in chapters 5 through 7, although agrarian elements did sometimes emerge. In many instances of riots, uprisings, or larger-scale rebellions in Mexican history it makes sense to take both parameters into account. For Indigenous rural cultivators, access to land underwrote community existence and therefore the ethnic identity so intimately tied to community, while the double helix of ethnic identity and the existence of a political community made access to land beyond individual family holdings essential to the maintenance of villages.

One of the most thoroughly "Indian" of rural rebellions in Mexico carried forward by peasant farmers and estate laborers almost entirely undiluted by the presence of non-Indigenous leadership was the Caste War of Yucatán. This long-sustained conflict broke out in July 1847 as the American army was fighting its way toward the country's capital against determined Mexican resistance and was only brought at least nominally to an end by central government armed action in 1901. The fiscal, technological, and political resources of the Porfirian regime were at their height at that point, although violence even lingered episodically beyond that time, into the early 1930s. The most important modern Anglophone historian of the Caste War, Terry Rugeley, has referred to it as the "largest and most successful rural rebellion in nineteenth-century Mexico."[3] This all depends upon what one means by "successful." Certainly, the Maya peasants were able to sustain the war for a remarkably long time as they carved out a virtually independent state in the eastern part of the peninsula. But by the time the conflict was finally suppressed in the twentieth century most Maya people in the peninsula lived in a state of dependency and virtual slavery in much of the northern and western areas, subjected to the brutal labor regime of the henequen industry. This was at its height on large haciendas around 1900, producing hard fiber for cordage from a variety of agave cactus. Its chief market was the wheat farmers of the United States who used it as binding twine and the chief commercial intermediary the International Harvester Company. While a full account of this major episode lies outside the scope of this book its start does fall just within the 1850 boundary, and like Santa Anna's last presidency (1853–1855), which lies just over that line, it is a meaningful bookend for the long century examined here.

Beyond the inherent interest of its more arresting aspects—its "Indianness," the religious cult of the Speaking Cross that sustained the rebels spiritually and emotionally, or the fact that it lasted for fifty years—the Caste War is significant in at least two ways. First, it embodies the endemic conflict over land between the peasant and commercial agricultural sectors that was to characterize the following seventy-five years or so, up through and somewhat beyond the Mexican Revolution of 1910. Such struggles were long familiar in the Mexican countryside but grew in frequency and magnitude during the eighteenth century. During the latter half of the century, in particular, the Indigenous population rebounded from its nadir around 1650 and pressed more heavily upon available farming land, which in the hands of the estate sector was increasingly devoted to feeding the urban population and mining centers. But the latter part of the nineteenth century was even more conflictual in this respect, peasant resistance to landlord hegemony growing in tandem with the repressive capacity of the central state as the Porfirian regime consolidated itself. There is some controversy over the actual power exercised by the Díaz government. A widely accepted position among historians now is that the regime, in the words of historian Thomas Passananti, was something of a "paper tiger," more a ritualized performance than the real thing, a sort of Kabuki theater of power. The advent of the railroad and other modern forms of communication and weaponry did extend the reach of the state considerably in support of "order and progress," the regime's motto, and with it the further ascendancy of large-scale agriculture and stock raising. The political and social bill for this expansion of commercial agriculture, state violence, and dispossession of the peasantry came due with the revolution of 1910. Second, the Yucatán Peninsula in the 1840s was isolated from the rest of Mexico, which meant that enforcement of the central government's writ was difficult. Aggravated and facilitated by the federalist ideology dominant among sectors of the Yucatecan political elite, the weakness of the national state meant that the peninsula's centrifugal tendencies and its retraction for a time into actual political independence as the Republic of Yucatán (1842–1848) lay beyond the power of the central government to neutralize. At length internal squabbles within the peninsular elite and the need for assistance in putting down the Caste War drove Yucatán back into the Mexican union. So both the Caste War and the impulse toward secession largely grew out of the debility of the Mexican central government to control the situation even if, paradoxically, the two movements were fatally opposed to one another. In this sense the Caste War of Yucatán is a good illustration of the effects of the central state political incapacity that prevailed for much of the period up to mid-century.

The Caste War erupted in the early morning of July 30, 1847. There was a long backstory, including a history of intraelite struggles and growing ethnic and economic antagonism between haves and have-nots. The Yucatán Peninsula had been a backwater during the colonial period, the large estates dedicated chiefly to nonintensive stock raising built on the labor of the Indians. Primarily dedicated to rural labor and subsistence agriculture, the Maya population outnumbered the non-Indians by about three to one. Yet the Maya peasantry had been linked into the regional money economy through their labor and petty entrepreneurship, and with the prevailing Yucatecan power structures through the prosecution of lawsuits over land and mobilization in intraelite disputes. The Maya of the eastern peninsula were connected through commercial exchanges with the colony of British Honduras to the south, now the independent nation of Belize. Despite its relative isolation the peninsula was not immune to the same forces of excessive tax burdens, military conscription, conflicts over land, and official government and church interference in local political affairs that provoked Indian peasant resentment and occasional violence elsewhere in the colony. It was simply too distant and too isolated to participate much in the market economy of central New Spain. In 1839 a revolt formally separated the Yucatán Peninsula from Mexico, leading to the declaration of a completely separate Republic of Yucatán between 1842 and 1848. The 1847 revolt was sparked by Creole (that is, white) efforts to squelch a rumored Maya uprising led by Maya local elites, the *batabs*, and early on featured the public execution of several Maya leaders and later on massacres and counter-massacres of an especially bloody nature. The leaders' goals were vague but tended to focus on the traditional grievances related to land, burdensome taxes (imposed by the central government to finance the war against the American invaders), and official interference in village political affairs. Absent overall leadership the revolt was highly diffused, so by the spring of 1848, after capturing much of the peninsula, the Maya rebels were pushed back to the eastern forests that were to remain their strongholds for decades. Creole elites dominated the north and west of the peninsula with the henequen industry that flourished until the Revolution of 1910. This activity created some great family fortunes, a regional white planter plutocracy of wealth, privilege, and political power called (with some sarcasm) the "Casta Divina" (Divine Caste) who projected themselves into national politics in an important way.

Pressed militarily into the forested eastern extremity of the peninsula, by 1853 the Maya carved out a virtually independent state with its capital in the village of Chan Santa Cruz, while the rest of Yucatán had rejoined the Mexican Republic as a major political player based on the wealth of the hard fiber export industry. The religious cult of the Speaking Cross had developed around an icon whose priests conveyed the cross' orders to its Maya followers, known as *cruzob*, the people of the cross. The beliefs associated with the cross were a mix of supposedly long-suppressed Maya practices and Christian elements along with prophetic pronouncements, insistence on God's love for his Maya children, and commands for continued resistance to campaigns of military repression in particular and Creole society more generally. In the 1850s Britain extended tacit diplomatic recognition to the Maya enclave state because of its importance to the British foothold colony in the Atlantic lowlands of Honduras to the south. By the early 1850s the internal schisms and power struggles among the white elite of the peninsula had resurfaced and in the breathing space thus provided new *cruzob* leaders emerged who led the Maya rebels in a military resurgence that delivered to them control of almost the entire east coast of Yucatán, imposing more or less stability on the Indian shadow state of Chan Santa Cruz. The economic devastation caused by the rebellion was only reversed with the full flowering of the henequen industry from the 1870s, while the peninsula population had declined by 1850 perhaps by half, to some 300,000, less from the effects of combat than from widespread scarcity and disease. The most intense period of the Caste War was between its outbreak in 1847 and 1853, but continued violence, with episodic *cruzob* raids on villages in the pacified zone of the peninsula and a constant low level of armed conflict, continued for the rest of the century. In 1901 Mexican central government forces managed to capture Chan Santa Cruz and end the capacity of the *cruzob* to carry out any but the smallest-scale violence, although there was residual resistance to state and central government authority until the early 1930s. In considering the history of the Caste War of Yucatán, however, it is a misnomer to transpose the concept of a "caste system" intact from South Asia to Mexico. Although an elaborate ethnic classification scheme and some legal distinctions between groups existed during the colonial period, as I have discussed in chapter 2, they never achieved the detailed elaboration, functional specificity, or religious sanctions of the system in India; such official categories were abolished with independence from Spain and the first Mexican constitutions. Nonetheless, important informal distinctions and some quite virulent prejudices and social practices continued, and traces of these attitudes still can be found, chiefly distinguishing Indigenous from non-Indigenous people. In Yucatán the term "caste war" was meant to convey the rigidities of socioethnic structures and the fierce racial antagonisms that could prevail between people of color and dominant white elites.

SANTA ANNA'S LAST STAND

During his long public career Santa Anna was apparently more interested in attaining power than in exercising it and in pursuing personal glory rather than advancing the development of his country. He took constitutionally mandated leave from the presidency to lead the army several times (mostly to lose battles), but apart from those occasions he withdrew to his Veracruz estates in 1832–1834, 1835–1836, 1837, 1842, and 1843–1844. His long periods in exile—1845, 1848–1853, 1855–1864, and 1867–1874—embraced almost two-thirds of his active political life and more than a quarter of his eighty-two years. His last exile out of the country, which brought him back to Mexico City in 1874, just two years before Porfirio Díaz's coup d'état (he was not formally elected president until the following year), was spent mostly in Charlotte Amalie, now the capital of the US Virgin Islands in the Caribbean, then under Danish sovereignty. In his various exiles he had his family with him, accumulated a good deal of property, and kept in touch with friends and political allies in Mexico. During 1854, the second year advertised by Santa Anna's backers as a temporary military dictatorship, Karl Marx wrote in a letter to Friedrich Engels that although he held the Mexican people as a whole in low regard, "the Spaniards had produced no talent comparable to that of Santa Anna."[4] The last presidential administration of the Mexican *caudillo*, stretching to 1855, marks a point of inflection in the country's political history ushering in a period of unusually protracted and widespread violent national civil conflict in a land that had already been wracked by three decades of nearly constant political upheaval. It also forms the prelude to a period known as La Reforma in which a new national constitution (1857) took shape and liberal politicians and ideas gained at least nominal ascendancy in national life. The 1850s also saw the rise of a generation of relatively new political actors, among whom Benito Juárez was preeminent, who took over from men like Santa Anna, Gómez Farías, and Alamán. None of the new generation had fought on either side in the independence struggle. Santa Anna outlived every one of his generation of political generals: Anastasio Bustamante and José María Tornel (1795–1853—general, politician, ardent santanista, and historian) both died in 1853, Herrera, Bravo, and Arista between 1854 and 1855.

In January 1851 the first peaceful transition in the presidency took place since Guadalupe Victoria had assumed the prime magistracy from the Supreme Executive Power more than a quarter-century before, President Herrera yielding the office to the politically moderate, newly elected Mariano Arista (1802–1855), who managed to achieve very little during his two years in office. But considerable change occurred in national political life nonetheless, with the consolidation of more clearly identified parties: Alamán established the conservatives, a Santanista party took more defined shape under the leadership of General José María Tornel, and liberals jelled into moderate and Puro (radical) tendencies. In the summer of 1852 a rash of *pronunciamientos* beginning in ever-tumultuous Guadalajara quickly engulfed the rest of the country, demanding the removal of Arista, the restoration of the federalist system, the seating of a new constituent congress, and the construction of a temporary dictatorship to keep the lid on. Failing to receive the backing of the sitting congress to quell the uprisings, Arista resigned at the beginning of 1853, thus postponing at least temporarily a bloody civil war and sailing away into exile, where he would die two years later on the way from Portugal to France. A group of generals agreed to sanction a one-year temporary dictatorship, invited Santa Anna back from exile to assume the presidency, and planned to write a new constitution—republican, representative, and popular. Yet another general stepped in as a proxy for Santa Anna, occupying the presidency from February to April 1853. On March 17, 1853, Santa Anna's improbable political comeback was sealed by a vote of the states. Returning from his Colombian exile to Veracruz on April 1, he was met by a large delegation of supporters, notables, and office seekers, among them a number of prominent conservatives. One of these delivered a letter to Santa Anna from Lucas Alamán dated March 23 and sometimes referred to as the statesman-historian's "political testament."

Alamán's letter summarized the political agenda of Mexican conservatives and addressed the returning *caudillo* in a remarkably schoolmarmish tone, something to which the great statesman was prone if he did not self-censor. The letter is worth parsing at least briefly because it synthesizes in very general terms the conservative thought of the era. He did not go quite as far as suggesting that Santa Anna be a placeholder for a European prince as Mexican monarch, but there are definitely elements of monarchical thought in the document. He hazarded the prophecy that Santa Anna's government was likely to be a disaster should he lend his ear to flatterers and place seekers, pursue personal vendettas through the power of his office, neglect his duties, and indulge his ego, which is in fact what occurred after the death of Alamán a few weeks into the administration and of Tornel four months after that:

In truth, we fear . . . that whatever your convictions may be, that constantly surrounded by men who have nothing else to do but adulate you, you may give in to their blandishments, since we [the conservatives] will not [always] be present, nor will we fight with that kind of weapon. We also fear that some affairs may be undertaken by which you are perhaps impressed because you have not examined them sufficiently . . . and which may discredit you. No less are we fearful that arrived here, you will shut yourself away in Tacubaya, making it difficult to see you . . . and that in the end you will retire to Manga de Clavo, leaving the government in hands that will place [executive] authority in a ridiculous light and cause you to act precipitously, as happened before.

The letter looms large in the history of Mexican conservatism more as a statement of conservative principles than as an important factor in Santa Anna's return to power because when he received it he was already on Mexican soil, and absent the letter he would certainly have attempted a comeback anyway. Many of the ideas were embodied in the decree promulgated from the national palace on April 22, 1853, in the "Bases para la administración de la República hasta la promulgación de la Constitución," generally ascribed to Alamán's pen, although most of it remained in limbo during Santa Anna's brief time in power. The use of the term "administration" indicates, by the way, that the basic form of governance—nominally republican, presidential, highly centralized—was not at issue, but only the management of enabling structures.

The Alamán letter proposes only a few policy recommendations, none of them in concrete detail. It lays the blame for the uprising that had brought Santa Anna back to the country on backlash against the anticlerical policies of liberals like Gómez Farías and Melchor Ocampo (1814–1861), one-time governor of the State of Michoacán and a prominent political ally of the liberal Benito Juárez. The letter argued that the first principle among conservatives was an unflagging government support of the Catholic Church and the social utility of its belief system and ritual practices: "The first [principle] is to preserve the Catholic religion, because we believe in it, and because even if we did not accept it as divinely [inspired], we consider it the only common bond that links all Mexicans [to each other], when all the rest have been broken, and the only one capable of sustaining the Hispanoamerican race, and that can liberate it from the great dangers to which it is exposed." The counter-factual assertion in this passage about the essentiality of the Catholic faith and practice to Mexican society—"even if we did not accept it as divinely [inspired]"—is interesting because it implies a sociological appreciation for the function of a common religious tradition as a sort of social glue among Mexicans when all other bonds and common identifications were weak or nonexistent. Alamán had suggested much the same thing in the final volume of his history of the independence struggle, published just a year earlier, when he wrote that "in Mexico there are no Mexicans," referring to what he perceived as the lack of national sensibility in a society strongly divided by geographic, ethnic, class, and political distances, a perception shared by many liberals. This is one reason why conservatives viewed ultra-liberal attacks upon the Church as traitorous political experimentation made up of dangerously corrosive ideas. Other props he held to be essential to an ordered society were the army, the power of the landed families whose political loyalty underwrote the conservative cause, and the inviolability of private property, the bedrock of any rational social arrangement. The erasure of the federal system in practice and of federalism as an ideology were other key elements in the conservative program. Alamán went so far as to recommend reducing the states once more to the status of departments; the construction of some smaller, select advisory and legislative councils to replace the congress; and the abolition of popular elections ("We [conservatives] are opposed to the representative system through the practice of elections"). These were all very radical solutions to the problems of stability and development. The mass of the population, including the Indigenous people who made up the largest element of it, were left aside in favor of elite rule and an all-powerful executive, a republic without republican institutions, clearly antifederalist, antipopular, and, paradoxically, arguably antirepublican.

Santa Anna's final time in power lasted less than thirty months and within a year its foundations started to wash away as the rising tide erodes a sand castle on the beach. Some of this was due to changing political circumstances over which the aging dictator had little control, but much of it was due to his ineptitude and his growing inability to face reality. By mid-April 1853 he had named a cabinet with a decidedly conservative-centralist tilt despite countervailing pressures, most obviously with the appointment of Alamán as minister of foreign relations (interior affairs was split off into another ministry). But two of his most capable advisers, Alamán and José María Tornel at war and navy, died in the early months of the regime. Their deaths removed two figures from Santa Anna's orbit who might have functioned as counterweights to his bad decisions and increasingly florid megalomania (he came to be addressed as "Most Serene Highness"). His despotic ruling style allowed the adulation from his followers and his desire to eliminate any opposition to his impulses or policies to dictate his actions. He exiled and imprisoned critics (Juárez went to New Orleans for a time), turned against his allies, alienated his one-time friends, raised taxes, and countenanced rampant corruption. Among the most discreditable of his actions during the first year of his administration was the signing of the Treaty of Mesilla, also known as the Gadsden Purchase, negotiated under the Franklin Pierce administration by American ambassador James Gadsden at the end of 1853 and ratified by the US Senate in mid-1854. This agreement transferred by sale to the United States about 30,000 square miles encompassing much of southern Arizona and the southwestern corner of New Mexico for $10 million (about $230 million in today's values). The money basically drained away in a mysterious manner into the pockets of Santa Anna administration officials, leaving the Mexican treasury as depleted as ever.

After only a year of Santa Anna's presidency, in March 1854 liberals rose to throw him out of office, launching the Revolution of Ayutla (a town in the state of Guerrero where they published their plan), which would later mark the apotheosis of liberalism in the Constitution of 1857. The Plan de Ayutla demanded the removal of Santa Anna from office and the convening of a constituent congress to write a new constitution. The Ayutla movement was led by the independence fighter and *caudillo* of Guerrero state Juan Álvarez and Ignacio Comonfort (1812–1863), a moderate liberal (*Moderado*) and military politician of French parentage, a man of the new political generation that came to maturity after 1821. Comonfort would eventually serve as governor of Tamaulipas and Jalisco, as secretary of war and navy in the presidential cabinet, and as president during 1856 and 1857. During his administration the liberal, markedly anticlerical Constitution of 1857 was adopted, which would remain the reigning charter of the country until a new constitution was framed in 1917 during the Mexican Revolution. Comonfort fought against the French invasion of Mexico in 1862 but was to die the following year at the hands of bandits in the Bajío. The military action in Santa Anna's overthrow was fought primarily in the south of the country in two unsuccessful campaigns led by the president himself. With the two most talented men in his cabinet gone, the military reverses mounting up, and public support for him ebbing, Santa Anna resigned in August 1855 and sailed into his last exile, ironically enough aboard the ship *Iturbide*.

CONCLUSION

It is impossible even to begin to understand the first three decades of Mexican national political life without reference to Antonio López de Santa Anna. On the other hand, to explain the major events and trends of that period with reference solely or chiefly to his part in them is to trivialize the complex cross-currents of the era. For all that has been written about him by historians, the process whereby he came to dominate Mexican public life seems to me somewhat mysterious. His return as supreme military commander and/ or president was virtually the default position in national politics for several decades. He fell under a cloud or outright into disgrace a number of times—as a royalist officer during the insurgency due to his brutality and corruption, as the "Protector of Federalism" in 1823, after the loss of Texas in 1836, and following the Mexican-American War—but always returned to scale new heights. The exception to this pattern, of course, was his ouster into his final exile at the hands of the Revolution of Ayutla in 1855, although he harbored hopes of a political comeback even then.

Although the whole of his career added up to more than the sum of its parts, one key element was the quality of charisma: an unusual attractiveness in the eyes of other people, an ineffable charm, a force of personality, and even an air of mystery at odds with a certain histrionic aspect in his character much attested by those who encountered him. But charismatic leadership lies as much in the eyes of the followers and admirers as in the inherent qualities of the charismatic person, a gift of power and authority contingent for the choice of its recipient upon political circumstances and cultural predispositions. This suggests that any charisma Santa Anna enjoyed was very much the product of a desire among his idealizers for a great man to believe in, of whom the model in this and later eras of history was Napoleon Bonaparte, dubbed the "world-spirit on horseback" by the German philosopher Georg Wilhelm Friedrich Hegel (1770–1831). It must be acknowledged in this regard that Santa Anna was hardly alone among the Spanish American military politicians cut in the "*caudillo*" mold. Other examples among many were Simón Bolívar and José de San Martín in South America and Mexico's own Agustín de Iturbide, dubbed "heroes on horseback" by historian John Chasteen.[5] Here Santa Anna's construction of his own personality cult, in which other people were complicit and for whom he was a screen for their longings and a proxy for their ambitions, played some role in his political longevity. There was the fetishization of his amputated leg, for example, as a selfless sacrifice on the altar of the fatherland, which in an almost literal sense it was.

There were several astute tactical ingredients in his enduring position in the popular regard. One was his construction of a political, military, and economic power base in his home state of Veracruz with the vast properties he owned there, his gift of employment to thousands of people on those estates, and his creation of what were essentially military colonies of former insurgents and mustered out soldiers in a number of villages. Another element was his devotion to the interests of the regular Mexican army, which he always favored above other public institutions and which reciprocated with its loyalty to him, at least most of the time. The other side of the coin of this astuteness was his willingness to take risks, both political and military, a boldness shared by few other figures of the time even among the military politicians who dominated much of the public stage in these decades. As a political opportunist, moreover, he was less anchored to a single ideological position than most other prominent public men and therefore flexible enough to adapt to changing political circumstances. On the conservative end of the spectrum we find Alamán, for example (although his ideas did change over time from moderately liberal to ultraconservative), and on the radical liberal end figures like Lorenzo de Zavala and Valentín Gómez Farías. Santa Anna did drift toward the centralist, authoritarian end of the spectrum over a number of years, particularly after the loss of Texas in 1836, although early on he appears to have been a more or less sincere liberal. The war with the Americans a decade later was an ideological turning point for many people. He had few political ideas of his own but rather labile sympathies whose movement is epitomized in a response to an ungenerous comment by Joel R. Poinsett that as a prisoner of the American rebels in Texas in 1836 Santa Anna got much of what he deserved for his political inconstancy:

> Say to Mr. Poinsett that it is very true that I threw up my cap for liberty [that is, liberal federalism] with great ardor, and perfect sincerity, but very soon found the folly of it. [For] a hundred years to come my people will not be fit for liberty. They do not know what it is, unenlightened as they are, and under the influence of Catholic clergy. A despotism is a proper government for them, but there is no reason why it should not be a wise and virtuous one.

The resonance with Iturbide's "humane tyranny" is hard to miss, as also with the political weariness expressed by Simón Bolívar in his comment that implanting democratic practices among the people of South America was like plowing the sea. So while he may not have been all things to all men, he was enough things to enough people to make him an indispensable leader, or at least a plausible one, at many critical turns in the history of the young republic. And while Santa Anna was by no means gifted with the commander's tactical genius of a Napoleon or a Robert E. Lee, and he lost many important battles, he did win some key engagements, as against the Spanish expedition of reconquest in 1829 (fortunately for him the invasion had been badly planned logistically).

Although he may have presented the extreme form of the military politician, Santa Anna was not alone in his style of self-presentation or of governance while in power, while few if any of his contemporaries enjoyed the degree of charisma that he did. Five civilian politicians became president during these decades, all briefly, four of whom (Corro, Echeverría, Peña y Peña, and Ceballos) were quite forgettable, although the fifth, Gómez Farías, was remarkably long-lived and exercised a major influence in Mexican politics among the more radical liberals. There were a number of other important civilian politicians, of course, including Alamán, Zavala, Father Mora, Ramos Arizpe, and so forth, but none reached the presidency. So what we have here are three decades of Bonapartism with short breaks: strong man rule by more or less charismatic political generals, authoritarian in style when not officially dictators, relying upon army support, antielitist in tone with a sprinkling of populist rhetoric, and quite deeply conservative.

Under the flux of military uprisings (there were 1,243 pronunciamientos between 1821 and 1855), "revolutions," personal politics, vendettas, and foreign predation, however, profound struggles were at play involving fundamental ideas about political life. Among the principal oppositions were military versus civilian rule, federalism versus centralism, the legislative versus the executive power, ardent support for the Catholic Church versus critiques of it or outright anticlericalism, and republicanism versus monarchy. Although there were many shades of opinion among partisans of each dyad, underlying all these binaries at a still deeper level was the opposition between liberalism and conservatism. This had to do less with ultimate goals for the country, which overlapped considerably between the two groups because both aspired to create a stable, prosperous, externally secure nation, than with the means to achieve that condition. But the attempts to codify the framework within which the game of politics was played and to direct the destinies of the nation in a predictable and rational manner were plagued by the failure of political actors to arrive at consensus about legitimacy in the operations of the state. Despite the constitution making, the presidential decrees, and the legislation coming out of the Mexican national congress, what prevailed for most of the time was the rule of men, not of laws. An example of this is the construction of the Supreme Conservative Power (SCP) of the centralist constitution of 1836, the Siete Leyes. This was meant to function as a fourth branch of government whose function was to oversee the other three, to exercise a moderating influence against the arbitrary exercise of power by any one branch, and to dampen the enthusiasms of popular republicanism. Apart from their having served creditably in high office, one of the major criteria for the five members making up the SCP was personal virtue. But by what normative standard was virtue to be determined? This considerable space for judgment signified that the occupants of these offices must be *hombres de bien*. Therefore a body of virtuous citizens whose corporate function was to interpose themselves between the general citizenry and the exercise of arbitrary power was itself the product of somewhat arbitrary criteria.

Hovering in the background of the entire period was the issue of what to do about Texas and its northerly and westerly extensions, the vast territory I have called "Greater Texas." This came to have a transcendent importance for Mexico. At first there was a significant but resolvable question involving the United States, thought to have been settled by the Adams-Onís Treaty of 1819 between the United States and Spain. By this agreement Mexico ceded Florida to the United States, the latter assumed certain financial responsibilities, and the border between the two powers was settled all the way from the Gulf of Mexico to the Pacific Ocean. As Anglo-Americans began filtering in from the east of the territory a series of colonization contracts were made with the Austins, father and son. In 1830 the Mexican government tried without success to shut off the flow as the trickle of Americans reached flood proportions, relatively speaking. The Anglo settlers became restive and in 1836 managed to break away from Mexico, throwing a major stain on the escutcheon of Santa Anna less because of his military defeat there than because of his double dealing with the American government in the wake of the defeat.

After the Treaty of Guadalupe Hidalgo ended the war in 1848, wresting away from Mexico half the national territory, the Mexican political class, as historian Charles A. Hale demonstrated in a number of works, went through several years of probing self-examination and self-recrimination provoked by the defeat itself and what it might portend about the country's vulnerability to foreign adventurism. As Hale put it, "The very independence of Mexico was now threatened. Such an easy victory by a powerful neighbor would mean that Mexico might at any moment be absorbed by the United States, especially when there was a movement for that purpose already afoot north of the Rio Grande."[6] Liberals and conservatives carried on a sharp debate, much of it in the newspapers of the capital and often despairing in tone, about how Mexico could have arrived at this state of national humiliation and danger of dissolution. In the liberal paper *El Siglo XIX* of June 1, 1848, for example, an anonymous author (almost all the articles in these newspapers went unsigned) wrote in words that echoed Lucas Alamán's aphorism that "in Mexico there are no Mexicans," "The elements of disintegration which have accumulated in the country, previously [in the form of] internal discord and recently as foreign war, now have such force and are so numerous . . . that at first glance one could doubt if our republic is really a society or only a simple collection of men without the bonds, the rights, or the duties which constitute a society." The politician-journalists writing in the *capitalino* newspapers frequently pointed to the contrast between the stubborn, heroic resistance offered by the Spanish people to the invasion of the French during the years 1808–1814 with what they viewed as the relative passivity of Mexicans in the face of American military aggression after 1846. As a solution to the country's critical situation liberals proposed a root-and-branch political reform, reshaping the state from the bottom up, eliminating corruption and the corporate privileges that undermined the promise of modern citizenship, and recapturing the potential of the representative, popular, federal republic. On the other hand many conservatives, although not all, argued that republicanism had failed its greatest test, that of forging a nation, that as a system for organizing public power it was bankrupt, and that now was the time to reinstitute a monarchy, but this time a constitutional one, of which the model was surely the British. The two positions advocated more republic and less republic, respectively. The conservatives carried the day for about two years with the last Santa

Anna regime, but eventually the liberals triumphed with the Revolution of Ayutla in 1855. Without the Texas debacle and the subsequent war this would in all likelihood have occurred anyway but along a much more protracted timeline, and perhaps with less violence.

NOTES

1. An excellent modern biography, on the whole kinder to Santa Anna than I, is Fowler's *Santa Anna of Mexico*.

2. Fanny Calderón de la Barca, *Life in Mexico: The Letters of Fanny Calderón de la Barca, with New Material from the Author's Private Journals*, ed. Howard T. Fisher and Marion Hall Fisher (New York: Anchor Books, 1970), 65. The reference is to Martin Van Buren (1782–1862), a New York State politician, protégé, and vice president of Andrew Jackson and himself president of the United States from 1837 to 1841.

3. On the Caste War, see especially among the works of Terry Rugeley, *Yucatán's Maya Peasantry and the Origins of the Caste War* (Austin: University of Texas Press, 1996), and *Rebellion Now and Forever: Mayas, Hispanics, and Caste War Violence in Yucatán, 1800–1880* (Stanford, CA: Stanford University Press, 2009).

4. Fowler, *Santa Anna*, 308.

5. John C. Chasteen, *Heroes on Horseback: A Life and Times of the Last Gaucho Caudillos* (Albuquerque: University of New Mexico Press, 1995).

6. Charles A. Hale, "The War with the United States and the Crisis in Mexican Political Thought, *The Americas* 14 , no. 2 (1957): 153–73.

Chapter 10

Elusive Prosperity

ECONOMY AND SOCIETY, 1821–1855

The instability in Mexican public life in the middle two quarters of the nineteenth century paralleled the situation of the nation's economic sphere. Perceptible but by no means universal, changing over time spatially as well as by sector, the sluggishness and in some cases the backward movement of the Mexican economy was certainly influenced strongly by political forces. Instability contributed to the stagnation but was not the sole determining factor. The role of instability in the country's economic woes would have been clear even absent the endemic political violence of the years 1821–1855. Under the clangorous politics there was a larger argument about Mexico's future going on at a deeper level of ideological ferment, experimentation, and debate. I have suggested that while some political actors struggled for power as an end in itself or for the personal benefits its exercise might confer, some, among them Valentín Gómez Farías and Lucas Alamán, strove to put Mexico on a path toward modernization, prosperity, and viable political arrangements. The modernizers' prescriptions did not always achieve the coherence of a program, and their ideas differed in significant ways. Some advocates of modernization linked it to industrialization in the fashion of the North Atlantic nations. Others, following the ideas of Adam Smith, believed that Mexico's comparative advantage lay in doing what it had done for the past three centuries, only more of it, more intelligently, and without any outside claim on its resources: exporting primary products requiring little or no processing, chief among them silver and other minerals, and importing manufactured goods. Lucas Alamán, the principal moving spirit behind industrialization in the early republican period, modified his thinking by 1830 or so from an emphasis on silver extraction to manufacturing. The hopes of the industrializers, however, embodied a fundamental contradiction: they

271

sought to develop the industrial sector of the economy while leaving certain social and economic conditions unchanged. Historian Walter Bernecker has put this well in highlighting Alamán's key role but also in noting certain blind spots in his vision:

> The conservative politicians who surrounded Lucas Alamán comported themselves as progressives from the economic point of view in setting in motion processes of industrialization and awakening the spirit of investment in some Mexican entrepreneurs; but at the same time they showed themselves incapable, and lacking the will, to carry out the necessary social changes, leaving agrarian structures intact. The necessary constitution of an internal market with strong demand was not brought to reality. These difficulties characterized the internal contradictions of the conservative government[s] and of the social class that supported it. They wanted to conserve the *statu[s] quo* and at the same time industrialize, consume foreign goods and simultaneously produce them domestically. . . . Any effort [to industrialize] had to fail in the face of these mutually exclusive objectives.[1]

The result was that Mexico had a sort of dual economy up to 1850 and beyond. A large subsistence sector was populated principally by peasants and farmers more generally; and a modernizing sector, after a precocious beginning and what some historians have even called a "false boom" in the 1830s and early 1840s, failed to produce an industrial revolution.

THE CONSTRAINTS TO DEVELOPMENT

Even the most intelligent and capable of public men did not have infinite degrees of freedom with which to act but worked within severe constraints imposed by externalities; that is, factors not within the political sphere and therefore not subject to their control. Among these were the country's difficult geography, which meant highly expensive and time consuming transport of people, goods, and capital equipment, a problem not overcome until the railroads took hold after 1875 or so. This condition affected economic possibilities but also limited the reach of the national state. Another externality limiting economic development was Mexico's vulnerability to predation by foreign powers and the insecurity that came with it. Where industrialization was concerned—the spearpoint of the modernization some Mexican statesmen, entrepreneurs, and thinkers strove to advance—the country started off in a disadvantaged position ascribable in large degree to its colonial condition. The essence of colonial subordination was to maintain an asymmetrical system of exchange over time, with a net outflow of wealth toward Spain, although more developed European economies than Spain's were primarily the ultimate beneficiaries of this. While more capital than is commonly supposed remained within New Spain during certain periods, the colonial arrangement constantly drained potentially productive resources, mostly in the form of silver. A particularly vivid example of this was the 1804–1808 *Consolidación de vales reales* mentioned previously. In this policy, the financing of Spain's government and warfare activities during the Napoleonic period were supported by the calling in of ecclesiastical mortgages by the Spanish crown. This amounted basically to a very sudden and massive credit contraction, primarily in New Spain, that caused cascades of bankruptcies and widespread economic hardship among the propertied groups. Father Miguel Hidalgo was affected by this decapitalization of the Mexican economy. The *Consolidación* was a planned, institutionalized policy form of this asymmetrical relationship, but the year-by-year drip, drip, drip of silver exports on a less formal basis contributed even more toward decapitalizing the economy of New Spain over most of three hundred years. And the country was basically poor, its wealth quite concentrated and the mass of the population poor, even if not living in grinding poverty. This was the reality despite the public relations script of Mexico's infinite economic potential that originated at least with Alexander von Humboldt's 1803 book *Political Essay on the Kingdom of New Spain* based on his travels, observations, and research there. Because industrialization gained a foothold and progressed most rapidly in those North Atlantic economies that had already attained relatively high levels of per capita wealth, this situation put newly independent Mexico at a historical disadvantage.

While there is a fair amount of controversy among historians of this period as to what the causes of the economic stagnation were that gripped Mexico for three or four generations and as to how generalized it actually was, there is some evidence to suggest that the country's economy was softening even before the destructive effects of the independence war took hold. I have already pointed to a fall in real wages of something like 25 percent for a large part of the population from at least 1775, and therefore a drop in popular living standards. This was not favorable to economic development in general or industrialization in particular because while it potentially reduced labor costs to entrepreneurs, it also undermined the ability of working people to consume. Estimates of per capita income based on admittedly imprecise calculations of gross domestic product (GDP) in New Spain/Mexico parallel this trend and after declining did not surpass late colonial levels until well into the last third of the nineteenth century. Economic historian John Coatsworth estimated that around 1800 per capita income in Mexico was about one-third that in Britain and one-half that of the United States, but that by 1877 Mexico's per capita income had shrunk to some 10 percent of that in the industrialized North Atlantic nations.[2] The rate of population increase in New Spain seems to have flagged in the latter half of the eighteenth century. While the productivity of agriculture—the marginal capacity of a given quantity of labor or land to produce calories, essentially—is difficult to calculate, there is little evidence that it improved in the late colonial decades. Production did seem to increase in certain regions, on the other hand, principally through vegetative expansion, the putting of more labor or land to use but with little or no improvement in the ratio of output to input. And although in absolute terms silver production reached new heights after 1800, propped up by subsidies offered to miners by the colonial government in the form of tax breaks and reduced prices for some production inputs (most obviously mercury) under state control, its rate of growth had begun to falter. So while there is no question that the slowness of Mexico's economic development during the middle two quarters of the nineteenth century was due principally to the destruction wrought by the insurgency of 1810 and the endemic instability of the early republican decades, these deficits were superimposed on an economy that was already displaying signs of vulnerability. Not only was economic development during the early republican decades constrained by the externalities I have mentioned, but what we can know about it suffers from constraints imposed by a spotty documentary record. Despite the increasing interest of historical researchers in recent decades in the Mexican economy between 1821 and 1875 or so, our knowledge is episodic and much stronger about the periods on either side of this stretch, the long eighteenth century (up to about 1820), and the Porfiriato (1875–1911).

The overall size and the direction and rate of change in the national population were major limiting conditions of whatever economic recovery might take place in Mexico in the wake of the highly disruptive insurgency of 1810–1821. The sluggish pace of population growth was both a cause and a symptom of the halting economic development of the early republican decades. As we know from the problems of some developing nations in the contemporary world, population increase can run well ahead of economic development, overwhelming the availability of essential services such as education, medical care, and the social safety net. It can also oversaturate the labor market, forcing down wages, undermining domestic consumer capacity and thus effective demand, and making a national economy into an exporter of cheap labor either in the form of people themselves or in attracting foreign investment that feeds off the differential cost of labor in the international market. Mexico's problem was somewhat different. During the eighteenth century, population growth ran at between 0.5 and 1 percent annually, with the faster rate during a few decades following 1750 or so. Except for the roughly decennial harvest failures, widespread hunger as such seems not particularly to have been a problem. But declining real wages for a large part of the population did create difficulties for many people and strains on family budgets. At the same time increasing pressure upon farming land by rural population increase, modest though it may have been, was aggravated by a shift of this resource from the peasant sector to the estate sector as commercial agriculture expanded to feed the mines and cities and as the landlord class was none too fastidious about its methods of gaining access to additional farming land. Putting aside the loss in population caused by the armed conflict of 1810–1821, when it is estimated that as many as 600,000 people died, by the mid-nineteenth century overall growth had slipped back to less than 1 percent annually. The population of Mexico City, for example, fluctuated between 120,000 and 200,000 from 1820 to 1890. The national population was just over 6,000,000 in 1810 and had increased to just under 8,000,000 people nearly fifty years later. During the nineteenth century recurrent episodes of epidemic disease, such as cholera morbus, took their toll. By way of comparison, in 1820 Mexico's population was only one-third less than that of the United States. Between 1820 and 1870 the country's population increased by 40 percent, while that of the United States (partly through immigration, a negligible factor in Mexico) grew by 315 percent, and Brazil's 117 percent. In the period we are looking at labor scarcity was less a problem for economic development than a weak domestic market for manufactured goods, a demand easily met and then oversaturated even by artisanal and domestic fabrication, let alone by the country's limited industrial capacity.

"EVERYTHING SEEMS OBSTRUCTED": DESTRUCTION AND RECOVERY IN RURAL MEXICO

Let us begin in the countryside.[3] The insurgency that wracked New Spain was not chiefly an agrarian rebellion as such; that is, a violent political uprising by poor rural people to reclaim land, redistribute sources of wealth more equitably, or avenge themselves on their oppressive overlords. But rural people were major protagonists in the conflict, and because almost all the fighting took place outside the cities, rural Mexico suffered the brunt of economic and population loss. There is much testimony about this from the entire decade of the rebellion. In 1816, for example, the Count of Pérez Gálvez, one of the colony's great landed magnates, wrote to the government in a secret report about the Zacatecas-Durango region that "many hacendados, although they are lords of valuable properties, have no cash, nor any means of getting any . . . . Everything, everything seems obstructed, without roads to get their crops to market; the tenants losing their few livestock, the fruit of a whole life-time of labor; the laborers naked, because they have no money to clothe themselves." Bishop-elect Manuel Abad y Queipo of Michoacán commented that the population of the once bustling city of Valladolid had declined from about 25,000 to 3,000 inhabitants by 1815 due to the insurgency. As historian Margaret Chowning has observed in an important book, the agriculture of the surrounding zone for many miles in all directions had been devastated—standing crops ruined, buildings destroyed, livestock carried off or consumed in place by insurgent or royalist forces. Haciendas thereabouts lost almost half their market value during the insurgency.[4] By 1818 the region around the once prosperous town of Apatzingán, in Michoacán's "tierra caliente" along the Pacific coast, which lent its name to Mexico's first constitution, the insurgent charter of 1814, was described as "completely destroyed," the surrounding farms stripped as if by locusts. Pénjamo, one of the richest farming areas of the wealthy Bajío region, was described in 1818 as "ruined"—stripped of food and horses, not a lamb, sheep, or goat to be found, and incapable of supporting royalist forces. Many districts in Oaxaca were in the same condition, with indigo, cochineal, and cotton textile production severely damaged. The entire area between the towns of Lagos and León, to the north of Mexico City, was called by one observer a "desert." Many other formerly prosperous regions, and some less prosperous, could be added to this sorry inventory. Foreign travelers to Mexico in the early 1820s told the same story, commenting on the ruined state of farms and haciendas over wide swathes of the countryside. While this was not true of all regions of the country, it was of many in the central, most densely populated zones where much of the previous decade's fighting had taken place.

With certain exceptions depredations of the estate sector of the rural economy were due less to anger aimed directly at the sector of large landowners by humble rural people than the natural collateral damage typical of continuing large-scale violence in rural areas. The devastation stemmed overwhelmingly from the requirements of armies and smaller bands of armed combatants (and after 1821, bandit gangs) for food and other matériel to prosecute the conflict. Yet where they did occur such incidents could be bloody and highly destructive, bringing to a climax extended histories of friction and resentment between haves and have-nots. For instance, late on November 1, 1810, the evening of All Saints Day, near the very beginning of the Hidalgo uprising a riot took place in the pueblo of Atlacomulco, to the northwest of Toluca. Four Spanish citizens of the little town, at least one of them a European-born Spaniard, were lynched by large mixed crowds of Indians and mestizos. The European Spaniard, a local merchant and landowner, had been attacked in his home and brutally murdered, his American-born son gravely wounded and then finished off by men he knew personally, and another family member and an employee of the family business killed in the violence. The women of the family escaped the violence but were reduced from a condition of economic comfort to a state of penury. The following day a predominantly Indigenous crowd sacked the murdered family patriarch's hacienda just to the west of the town, pillaging the estate not only of its grain crops but also its livestock and equipment, down to the locks on the storehouses. A day later still, in a second sacking of the estate local rioters made off with everything remaining from the previous night, including the nails in the doors and the wrought iron work on the windows.

Some larger farmers, hacendados, and estate managers fled the intermittent fighting of the insurgency seeking safe haven in the cities and larger towns. Peasants, who made up the large majority of the rural population, had nowhere to go and no resources to support them and so remained in place as the tides of war swept back and forth over them. Both adversaries in the armed conflict expropriated grain, livestock, cattle, transport animals, and tools as they moved over the countryside living off the land. Some military commanders actually left receipts promising to make good the losses to property owners when the fighting should conclude and their side emerge victorious. Others simply took what they needed to support their forces or to deny food and other resources to the enemy and moved on. Some of the locusts wore royalist uniforms as commanders, using their power to corner markets in grain and other commodities and make money for themselves, among the most egregious offenders Agustín de Iturbide.

Dark as the situation was, however, agriculture seems to have recovered relatively quickly in certain areas once the generalized violence of the insurgency ebbed. This is hardly surprising; large estates suffered much more substantial damage than small farms or peasant holdings because there was more to be gained from pillaging them, so that the smaller holdings might recover more quickly. The most capital intensive of the large agrosocial units were the sugar plantations located primarily to the south of Mexico City in the Cuernavaca area, although they were scattered around the country wherever environmental conditions proved welcoming. But even most large estates were in fact technologically primitive and could be brought back into production relatively quickly, as occurred in the Orizaba, Puebla, Aguascalientes, and Michoacán regions and even in the Bajío, perhaps the hardest hit by the decade of intermittent violence. Capital for the reconstruction of buildings, replenishment of livestock, and the mobilization of a reliable labor force might be problematic, but these tasks seem nonetheless to have been accomplished in many places. Peasant farming might suffer more from the farmers being recruited for either side in the conflict than from material destruction because in normal times peasants retained little in the way of surpluses, large herds of livestock, or tools and therefore little to pillage. But such activity could easily be reestablished and might even have enjoyed an advantage for a time following 1821, filling the gap created by the damage to larger, more intensely commercial farms because it could supply some small surpluses to urban markets while at the same time supporting the families that relied upon it.

As some of the more recent research is bringing to light, where haciendas specifically and the pace of economic life more generally are concerned, there were regions of the country that recovered from the destructive effects of the 1810 insurgency earlier than was thought. For example, Margaret Chowning, whose work I have already cited, focuses much of her study of elite families, wealth, landholding, and politics in the State of Michoacán on the fortunes of the Huarte family. The patriarch of this major elite clan in Valladolid, Isidro Huarte, saw his third daughter married in 1805 to the son of a moderately prosperous elite family, the future Mexican emperor Agustín de Iturbide. As happened to other elite landowning families the Huartes were basically ruined by the 1810 insurgency. A modest resurgence in the estate sector of the region's farming economy came in the latter 1820s and a more robust recovery in the late 1830s and 1840s followed by another depression. The recovery of commercial farming on haciendas, especially the second resurgence, was in the hands of a group of new proprietors whose capital and entrepreneurial energies replaced those of many of the older landowning families, thus illustrating one form of the limited but visible social mobility for which independence cleared a path. The main point here, however, is that although the Michoacán region did experience waves of economic resurgence and recession, the hacienda sector was not mired in a continual depression between 1821 and 1880 or so but could and did recover relatively quickly despite the destruction wrought by the independence struggle.

Another example of remarkably rapid economic recovery in the wake of the insurgency's devastation was the San Luis Potosí region, across Mexico from Michoacán on the country's eastern flank. Historian Sergio Cañedo Gamboa has found that the regional economy showed signs of recovery as early as 1825 and kept to that trajectory for many decades.[5] Like Chowning's, his study focuses on the fortunes of an elite family, the Gordoas. The occupation of the San Juan de Ulúa island fortress off Veracruz opened an opportunity for an alternative port of entry on the Gulf, northward up the coast at Tampico. Geographically this favored the city of San Luis Potosí as the port's commercial center in the hinterland, and prosperity spread from there. Signs of demographic and economic expansion date from 1825 or so, although in this case the driver was primarily commercial activity linked to the ocean-born commerce that came through Tampico. Beginning in the mid-1820s the regional silver mining economy exhibited increasing dynamism, commerce flourished over a wide area, and the property market became much more active. Although the commercial sector led the economy, relative prosperity quickly spread to the estate sector as well, which here as elsewhere provided a safe investment, stable if relatively modest returns on capital (at something like 5 percent annually), growth in value over time, and a mixed business portfolio that helped to buffer the risks of mining and commerce. Local taxes on the sale of real property increased substantially from early on, and rural estates could gain greatly in value over a relatively brief time. The family's Hacienda de Malpaso was valued at just under a whopping half million pesos in 1832, for example, but increased in value by 15 percent over the following four years.

The ripple effects of the widespread damage to the rural economy from the insurgency can easily be inferred, although our information is episodic. Tax income of all sorts declined greatly, both because collection itself was more difficult in such conditions and because the economic base had shrunk. Government revenue between the last years of the colonial regime and the initial years of independent Mexico shrunk nearly 85 percent, from 39,000,000 pesos in 1806 to 5,400,000 pesos in 1823, so that the new republic began its life in an extremely precarious financial position. This prompted it to take on the disastrous loans from British lenders that would plague the Mexican state until near the end of the century, forcing it to rely upon financing by domestic capitalists. The drop in fiscal resources occurred not only on a national scale but locally as well. Sales tax collection and thus municipal income in the town of Tula, for example, the ancient pre-Spanish Toltec capital to the northwest of Mexico City, saw severe declines between 1804 and 1815. The Church's mandatory agricultural tithe of 10 percent on non-Indian-produced agricultural goods (made voluntary in radical legislation of 1833) plummeted in value everywhere because of the damage inflicted by the rebellion, affecting everything the Catholic Church did from celebratory to welfare activities. The trade in livestock and agricultural products was badly disrupted on both the farming and consumption ends, and the propensity of people to consume many products that could be taxed dried up a good deal. For instance, the great annual trade fair at San Juan de los Lagos, in the area known as the Altos de Jalisco in the northeastern part of the state, which had thrived for centuries, was described in 1811 as completely ruined and really never regained its preinsurgency vigor, negatively affecting an entire region.

MINING

We know a good deal more about the effects of the insurgency on the silver mining industry, and the situation was not pretty. We also know a good deal about the major efforts to revive the industry in the three decades following 1821, chiefly on the basis of a tremendous influx of British capital in the late 1820s. Mining was already softening in the last several decades of the colonial era. Agriculture by its very nature was highly dispersed in discrete units;

very difficult to track statistically, tax, and regulate; and unimaginable to subsidize. Mining was much more concentrated geographically and therefore by contrast with farming more easily subject to state intervention of various kinds. It was also the object of much more intense concern by both government officials and private economic actors because it was seen as the single most important sector in the economy of New Spain, the key to the country's prosperity past, present, and future. The income it produced was central to the fiscal health of the Spanish Empire despite the fact that it only represented about 10 percent (a rough estimate) of New Spain's total economic activity by value. By the end of the colonial period other sources of income from the colony proved important and lucrative for Old Spain's tottering colonial enterprise. These included the income from tribute (a head tax) paid by Indigenous subjects of the crown and from the royal monopoly on tobacco products. But for more than a century it had been mineral wealth, overwhelmingly in the form of silver, that had made the Mexican colony the jewel in the imperial diadem. This was especially the case as the mineral wealth of the Peruvian viceroyalty declined from its earlier leading position in the production of New World wealth. It is estimated that on the eve of the independence struggle Mexican silver accounted for about two-thirds of the world's silver production from some 3,000 mines employing nearly 50,000 workers. Much of this outpouring of wealth actually stayed in the Western Hemisphere, paying the costs of imperial defense in the Caribbean region. Silver production became increasingly fragile, however, despite the vast wealth it was still pumping out. Actual physical production of silver, as measured by the index number of 100 for the quinquennium from 1755 to 1759, reached its highest point in the five years preceding the outbreak of the insurgency, at 186; but having reached an annual growth rate of 3.3 percent around 1795, its *rate* of increase (not physical production itself) declined considerably by 1810. Late Bourbon-era subsidies to the industry in the form of tax remission and the pricing of mercury, a factor essential to the patio refining process, and gunpowder (for the blasting of rock) helped to keep the sector afloat. There was also a good deal of new investment as capital fled from the once highly restricted trans-Atlantic commerce, thus reducing profit margins for large merchants and a search for alternatives as trade was freed up among Spain and her overseas dominions after 1789. Mining costs increased as older mines faced diminishing yields, upping production costs for the extension of shafts in pursuit of the mineral and thus relatively decreasing returns on investment.

And then came the insurgency of 1810. In describing in an earlier work of my own one of the country's great mining complexes, at Guanajuato, in the early years of the rebellion, I noted that the abandoned mines had been "left to flood, their timbers rotting and the empty, echoing tunnels collapsing; their refinery and other outbuildings burned or severely damaged; their workers scattered or recruited to the insurgent ranks, their managers and supervisory personnel killed or fled to the cities." The mines in this region, which along with Zacatecas to the northwest and Pachuca to the southeast made of it one of the great silver-producing areas of the world, were under repeated attack because the zone was a major theater of fighting at the heart of the insurgency kicked off by Father Miguel Hidalgo in the nearby town of Dolores. Many mines continued to be worked during the rebellion, although at much reduced levels, making their output an irresistible target for both sides in the struggle. The American Joel Poinsett, whom we have met in his role as an early US emissary to the young Mexican Republic and a controversial political figure, passed through Guanajuato in 1822 and noted the "melancholy effects of the late civil wars." He described the great Valenciana mine there as ruined, its previous work force of some 22,000 men reduced to 4,000. Of the Guanajuato mines in general he wrote, "The state of these mines is deplorable. The expenses of working them have already been prodigiously augmented by the depths of the shafts and prolongation of the galleries [lateral tunnels], and it will require a large capital to establish . . . pumps to extract the water. In many instances it will be impossible to employ steam as the moving power, from the great scarcity of fuel [that is, wood]." The neighboring Cata mine from which Lucas Alamán's ancestors had taken an enormous fortune and a title of nobility several generations back, and in which the family still held shares that the statesman-historian consistently described after 1830 or so as worthless, was described by Poinsett as "now [1822] nearly filled with water, and but partially worked." These descriptions were fairly representative of those offered by foreign travelers and by Mexican observers themselves in the years after 1810. In quantitative terms silver coin minted in Mexico fell from nearly 25 million pesos in 1809 to six or eight million in 1813–1817, recovering to eleven million by 1819 as the fighting ebbed. Although the situation had improved somewhat by 1840 or so silver production had still only attained about 50 percent of its preinsurgency level.

The taxes on silver formed a major stream of fiscal resources for the Spanish crown during the colonial period, while remissions of refined mineral and minted coin by private parties in commercial transactions added considerably to the outflow of wealth from New Spain. The linkage between silver production and the fiscal health of the new republic warrants a few words here about the Mexican state's fiscal situation during the decades from 1821 to 1850. Of royal income for most of the period the share furnished by taxes on silver mining declined during the last few decades from about 40 percent to about 20 percent even as the absolute value of silver production continued to rise (if at a slower pace than earlier in the century) at the end of the colonial era. Under the rationalizing schemes of the Bourbon Reforms items such as the royal tobacco monopoly accounted for an increasing percentage of fiscal income, as I have suggested. With independence Iturbide immediately reduced taxes of all sorts to levels that produced government insolvency, at the same time spending lavishly from state coffers on the trappings of the new imperial regime. By early 1823 the fiscal collections of the new nation amounted to less than 150,000 pesos. Aside from growing the economy to expand the tax base, a long-term project, there were basically three ways the gap in fiscal intake could be made up: increasing taxes immediately, borrowing from domestic or foreign sources, or realizing substantial income from customs receipts. Except for ad hoc forced loans imposed on the public, increasing taxes was extremely difficult to do in any systematic fashion because of limited state capacity. An even bigger problem here was that the federalist arrangement put in place by the 1824 constitution was extremely decentralized, empowering the states to collect taxes and keep a large share of the revenue back from the central government—or all of it, should they opt to violate the federalist pact and defy the Mexico City authorities. In the early 1820s the fiscal crisis was solved temporarily by contracting sovereign loans from British investors, as we have seen. But Mexico gained little breathing room with these high-risk, high-interest loans, quickly defaulted on them, lost its international creditworthiness, and ended up settling the "London debt" only late in the century. Beginning in the 1830s domestic lenders, the *agiotistas*, lent the government large sums at very high rates of interest; by mid-century the internal debt reached nearly 100 million pesos. The colonial-era tribute levied on Indigenous people was no longer viable when dealing with citizens of a republic, even poor disenfranchised ones, and the wealthy classes simply refused the imposition of regular direct taxes on income.

Customs receipts therefore loomed large over several decades in government budgets whose major expenditure was for the military. As a percentage of national fiscal income they reached 63 percent in 1852, just at the end of our period. In the latter half of the 1820s, through 1832, of the total fiscal intake customs receipts amounted to about 45 percent, declining to around 20 percent from the mid-1830s, then rising somewhat in the late 1840s. Tariffs imposed on the import of foreign products, mostly manufactured items, also served the purpose of protecting Mexican domestic industry and financed the development bank Alamán established in 1830 to jump-start the domestic textile industry. The manipulation of customs policies as a revenue measure and to foster domestic industry was common to a number of the new Latin American republics. At almost exactly the same time and for similar reasons—to protect the development of northern domestic industry against less expensive foreign imports—the United States during the John Quincy Adams presidency enacted the so-called Tariff of Abominations on foreign (chiefly British) imports in 1828. This measure played a major role in provoking the

Nullification Crisis of 1832–1833 during the Andrew Jackson administration and was a prelude to the US Civil War thirty years later. But tariff policy was tricky. If customs rates rose too high they would exclude foreign-made products completely, thus sparking resentment among economically well-situated consumers and high-end merchants while encouraging contraband to evade the import duties. If too low they would cut the government revenue stream and lead to the flooding of domestic markets with less expensive foreign-made goods, especially textiles from the British mills. There were some very high tariffs and outright exclusions during these three decades, and on the whole customs duties remained a major issue in congressional debates and government policy.

Most of early republican Mexico's GDP was submerged in the form of subsistence and lightly commercialized agriculture and therefore largely unquantifiable, but the country's mineral wealth was highly visible. The silver gouged from the earth in the colonial period that had made New Spain so valuable a colony was felt by many to be the potential motor of the national economy if only the industry could be pulled out of the doldrums into which it had fallen during the insurgency. The destruction of "sunk" capital during the insurgency (that is, the fixed physical facilities of the mines) was enormous and the Mexican economy of the 1820s not even close to the capacity to repair, replace, or improve it. Imports from abroad still needed to be paid for; in the 1820s nearly two-thirds of Mexico's imports were still cotton textiles. There was continual export of dye products, but even the debilitated silver mining sector far outstripped these in value. Because silver offered the possibility of substantial export earnings, the revival of the industry seemed the only feasible path forward. The logic of Mexico's situation in the 1820s was therefore to mobilize capital in Europe to revive the mining sector, and the dominant European economy in the post-Napoleonic era was Great Britain's. The 1820s proved to be a period of short-lived but frantic investment by Britons, and to some extent Frenchmen, all over Latin America but particularly in the mining of precious metals, above all silver and gold, and most especially in Mexico, a trend referred to at the time and since as "Mexicomania." A significant contributor to this fashion was the wide familiarity in Europe of the savant-traveler Alexander von Humboldt's famous *Political Essay on the Kingdom of New Spain* (available in English from 1811), which extolled the possibilities of Mexican natural resources. Other authors based their work substantially on his, among them English diplomat Henry George Ward's widely read *Mexico in 1827*. Humboldt's work was republished a number of times in French, Spanish, and German, and when the investment frenzy had ebbed in later years disillusioned British investors blamed Humboldt for having led them on.

The key Mexican figure in getting British capital into the Mexican mines, as in so many economic initiatives of the period, was Lucas Alamán. As one of the elected Mexican deputies to the Cortes of Madrid during 1821–1822, essentially an empire-wide parliament under the auspices of the briefly revived Spanish constitution of 1812, he proposed and was able to see enacted legislation for New Spain reforming the tax structure of the languishing silver mining industry. This measure was later adopted by the newly independent Mexican national government forming even as he and other Mexicans were proposing ideas to restructure the Spanish Empire and then returning to Mexico with their task uncompleted. As the minister of exterior and interior relations during the years 1823–1825 in the early national governments in Mexico he took special care to foster the revival of the industry, partly out of conviction that it could lead the country into prosperity and stability, partly out of more self-interested motives because his family still owned substantial mine holdings in his native Guanajuato. Having traveled and studied in Europe between 1814 and 1820 Alamán made a number of influential contacts among scientists, scholars, statesmen, and business leaders, the most famous being the much older Humboldt, with whom in later years Alamán maintained a correspondence. Through these contacts, his personal qualities, and his interests in science the young Mexican gained something of a Europe-wide reputation that reassured British investors of the soundness of putting money into the Mexican mining industry in the later 1820s. With Britain enjoying a tremendous prosperity in the wake of the Napoleonic Wars and swimming in ready cash, investors there were willing to put money into a variety of foreign ventures, most especially in mining but also in government bonds issued by the newly independent Latin American countries, among them Gran Colombia, Peru, and Chile. Mining investments by Britons went into concerns whose shares were sold by London investment bankers and handled by merchant concerns. Among those companies formed for ventures in Mexico, many of them short lived, were the Catorce Company, which went bust as early as 1826 with the bankruptcy of the merchant banking house B. A. Goldschmidt (which had participated in the loans of this period to the Mexican government); the Tlalpujahua Company (d. 1828); and the smaller Mexican Company, which lasted only a very short time. The Anglo-Mexican Mining Association (or the Anglo-Mejicana as it was known in Mexico) survived until 1838, and the Bolaños and Real del Monte companies until 1849. With such large quantities of capital at stake there were sure to be bankruptcies but also scams. One famous fraud perpetrated on British investors in the early 1820s, not immediately related to mining but representative of the overheated investment environment of the time, was that of the totally apocryphal Land of Poyais. This was the invention of a Scottish military man and soldier of fortune named Gregor MacGregor, who bilked hundreds of people into paying him to colonize a paradisiacal "kingdom" on the Gulf coast of modern-day Honduras.[6]

Founded with British investors by Lucas Alamán, by far the most important figure in the attempted revival of Mexican silver mining in the 1820s and the company's managing director, the United Mexican Mining Association was incorporated in London in February 1824 and was one of the biggest concerns of the era. It lasted only for a decade or so before being liquidated. One way in which enthusiasm for the investments in this and other mining companies all over Latin America was drummed up was for the English managers to commission pamphlets or articles in the London newspapers and journals, among them highly respected venues such as the *London Times* and *Quarterly Review*, extolling the prospects of the mines, ranches, or other enterprises and the virtues of the Latin American managers and technical personnel running them. Thus it was, for example, that the director of a venture capital firm contracted with the young Benjamin Disraeli (1804–1881)—novelist, conservative politician, and future British prime minister, barely in his twenties at the time and scratching out a living as a writer while he studied law—for the composition of a number of pamphlets to publicize the potential of the Mexican mines.

Aside from the wealth and thus the capital for other enterprises that the regeneration of the mining sector might produce in the country, Mexican leaders saw other good reasons to encourage such foreign investment. There were the taxes that might come to the national treasury, of course. But by creating foreign, especially British, stakeholders in the Mexican economy, and therefore in the country's sovereignty and political integrity, they hoped naturally to invite recognition by European sovereign states of the country's independence, thus warding off the threat of Spanish reconquest. And they saw British diplomatic recognition, which came in 1824. as a possible counterweight to the pretension of the United States to hemispheric hegemony, enunciated in President James Monroe's Doctrine of 1823 warning European powers away from the Americas. After legislation from the Mexican congress cleared the way for foreigners to form partnerships with Mexican mine owners to exploit their properties, competition became stiff among British companies to form contracts in Guanajuato, San Luis Potosí, Real del Monte, and other mining zones. The cutthroat rivalry between Alamán's company, the Unida, and the Anglo-Mexican Company to harvest contracts for the mines of Guanajuato created much bad blood between the two firms and their directors. Several of the companies brought in technical personnel from Germany, which had a number of famous mining districts in the Harz Mountains, or from Wales, in Britain. Expensive and extremely heavy equipment of various sorts was imported and experiments (largely unsuccessful) were made to drain the mines with steam power. In the end it turned out that

BOX 10.1. BENJAMIN DISRAELI
PROMOTES MEXICAN MINING

The best known of Disraeli's pamphlets, at 135 pages really a short book published in 1825, began with the portentous note: "Among the undertakings of the present age, paramount in importance for the magnitude of the interests, which are involved in their management, may be ranked the [Latin] American Mining Companies." Never having set foot in the New World, Disraeli wrote authoritatively about "the brilliant expectations [that] we should almost be tempted to believe . . . Eldorado [*sic*] was no longer an idle dream."

The young English scribbler wrote of the backwardness of the Mexican mines not to discourage investors but to induce the belief that European capital and expertise had the potential to bring forth great wealth if applied strategically. He devoted particular and favorable attention to the United Mexican Mining Association and to

> Don Lucas Alamán . . . appointed President of the Mexican Board of Management . . . one of the most influential men in Mexico . . . now a leading member of the Mexican administration. . . . [T]he present state of the Mexican mines arises only from the revolution of 1810, which to borrow the words of Alamán "began in the districts in which the richest mines are situated, and their proprietors were the first victims." The mines [Alamán] observes "are the fountain of the true riches of this nation; and whatever some speculative economists have said against this maxim has been victoriously refuted by experience."

In a passage of truly Disraelian literary flair the future British prime minister, favorite of Queen Victoria, and novelist described the way in which Mexicomania had spread in Britain:

> Then began the game. We heard of Lord Knows-Who lounging upon [Ex]Change, of Sir Frederick Fashion's Colombian curricle [a light two-wheeled carriage], and of the Honourable Mr _____ condescending to become a Director of "the New Company." The mines were *la chose* [the fashionable thing]; they were the *sujet* at concerts, conversaziones [*sic*], and clubs . . . and the hebdomadal *assemble* of the Athenaeum [an exclusive London men's club] diversified their usual topics of

conversation, strictures on modern literature, and their own execrable wines, by an occasional inquiry "after the state of the market." . . . A mining story was as regularly expected [among those dining out] with the second glass of Johannisberg [wine], as a dissertation on the operatic legalities, or the latest piece of scandal served up with the sauce piquante . . . of modern exaggeration, and jeweled beauty listened, if not to tales of "Africa," at least "to golden joys."

at the time many of the traditional technologies for draining and working the mines were the most appropriate given conditions in Mexico. Lucas Alamán explained this in an early report concerning the rehabilitation of the Cata mine in Guanajuato, alluding to some of the factors I have already mentioned:

The draining of Cata is to me the clearest demonstration, that in this country, until we have better roads, iron foundries, and many other material resources, the machines commonly employed, although very imperfect, are notwithstanding preferable, except in some particular cases, to those which might be substituted for them from Europe. . . . You know the time that has been employed in draining, and consequently are in possession of the data necessary to compare the system that has been followed, [and] with the consequences that would have resulted if a steam engine had been employed. Consider the cost [of a steam engine] of a power equal to four whims [these were capstans similar to anchor-raising mechanisms attached to chains and buckets] briskly worked; the expenses and enormous difficulties of conveyance from Vera Cruz to Guanajuato [and other difficulties]; and the conclusion appears to be, that if this method had been adopted in Cata, much more money would have been expended, and perhaps not a drop of water would at this time have been extracted. . . . It appears to me that, unless in some very rare cases, no other machines should be used in this country, than those which are easily constructed on the spot where they are required.

The share prices of the English mining companies in Mexico were quite volatile, responding not only to the actual health and profitability of the enterprises themselves but to all sorts of external circumstances. The execution of Agustín de Iturbide in July 1824, for example, was believed to improve the political situation in Mexico by promising greater political stability, causing share prices to rise. Shortly thereafter the news that the British government was about to sign commercial treaties (usually seen as a preliminary to diplomatic recognition) with Mexico, Colombia, and Buenos Aires pushed share values even higher. The continuing frenzy of incautious investment underwrote some seriously undercapitalized concerns and the bad faith of some speculators gave rise to disputes within those already established. The Real del Monte company, for instance, founded to rehabilitate the legendarily rich mines in Pachuca, fell into an internal dispute that ended up in the English courts. As early as the spring of 1825, after only about a year, the overall prospects of mining investments in Mexico had begun to soften a bit, stock sales of all sorts were slowing, and the Mexican companies began to feel the effects. The value of the recently contracted Mexican government bonds had fallen, not a direct cause or result of the mining situation but part of the same malaise of a shaky confidence level. Alamán's company was not immune to these forces, surviving where other companies failed most probably by association with his name, but the overall trend line pointed gently downward surrounded by up and down fluctuations. In general, the unhappy fate of British investment in the Mexican mines had grown out of two miscalculations on the part of almost everyone involved: an overestimate of the richness of the silver ores remaining to be exploited and an underestimate of the costs involved in rehabilitating the older mines. As early as the fall of 1825 formerly abundant capital was scarce due to the previous rush into investment in Latin America because stock and currency manipulations in France had attracted great amounts of liquidity to Paris and because the British capital market underwent the periodic flutterings and recessions characteristic of capitalist systems. Over the next six months or so there was a shakeout among the weaker concerns, and many a fortune must have been lost in the process, bringing "total ruin to thousands of English families" in the words of one investment banker.

As for what was actually happening in the mining operations, let us take three of the major Guanajuato mines as examples. Over the eighteen months or so between mid-1824 and the end of 1826 the value of the silver produced relative to the investment poured in was about 20 percent, with one of the three garnering an enormous profit of nearly 75 percent by dint of an unanticipated bonanza, a new strike of rich ore in an old mine. But there were losses elsewhere so that overall things balanced out to much more modest earnings levels than expected. One example of the less favorable expense/income ratios that forced many British investors out of mining was the Real del Monte Company, which between its establishment in 1824 and its dissolution a quarter-century later saw a total investment of about £3,250,000 and earnings of about £2,230,000, for an overall loss of about £1,000,000.[7] By early 1827 an economic recession in Britain had ebbed but news of the increasingly difficult political situation in Mexico began to make British investors more nervous than usual. Still heavily involved with the Unida, Alamán wrote to his English correspondent with characteristic pessimism that "the state of this country is truly distressing in every sense, and everyone is fearful of greater calamities to follow." There were some exceptions to the disturbing picture for the mining concerns, but most of the mining companies appeared to be in some degree of trouble.

Most modern scholars have suggested that even though British investors enjoyed some small successes, the fall in silver production in the second quarter of the nineteenth century was catastrophic and the overall picture for the industry quite grim until the Porfiriato. The annual share of silver as a percentage of Mexico's GDP dropped from about 10 to 5 percent during this period. The reasons for this we have reviewed earlier but can be boiled down principally to a rise in the price of mercury (essential for refining) by the early 1850s to three times that of its late colonial levels; the exhaustion of ores—that is, diminishing returns—in many mines; the political instability of the era, which proved a disincentive to investment for most of the period; and vacillating, unpredictable, and often predatory government fiscal policies. The value of shares in the surviving British mining companies in general, including Lucas Alamán's United Mexican Mining Association, dropped precipitously and would continue to decline into the future. Shares in the Real del Monte Company, for example, which had reached a price of £1,479 at the beginning of 1824 (against a nominal face value of £400 when they were issued), had fallen to £21 by 1836 and to £.63 by 1848, virtually nil. The tentative steps toward recovery in some of the Mexican mines resulted from their draining and rehabilitation; the constant inflow of British capital during a boom that took off, peaked, and began to fade in no more than about three years; and the conditions of relative peace that prevailed in the country during the presidential term of Guadalupe Victoria from 1824 to 1828. When the sudden spurt of silver production ebbed and British investment slowed to a trickle, then to nothing, then to reverse itself, the fragile equilibrium was ruptured and the potential profits did not warrant the amounts of money invested or the risks undertaken. As for Alamán, the prime mover in the mining investment boom of the latter 1820s, he never came near realizing the personal wealth to which he aspired. By 1830, just as he was assuming the central role in the government of the years 1830–1832, he had withdrawn from the company almost certainly out of disappointment in the industry's progress. But he also fell out with the English management both in London and with those Englishmen sent to Mexico to help run the company, whom he felt cramped his style as the experienced in-country decision maker. His public pronouncements regarding the central place of silver in the nation's economy changed from enormous optimism to an almost dismissive attitude during these years, so that as early as the beginning of the 1830s he was advocating the diversification of the national economy away from a dependence on silver toward domestic factory-based manufacturing; in other words, not primary resource extraction but industrialization, a strategy to which we now turn.

OBSTACLES TO INDUSTRIALIZATION
IN THE EARLY REPUBLICAN ERA

At the dawn of the Republic, Mexico's problems included the collapse, stumbling, and only partial recovery of silver mining; the dependence on the import from abroad for luxuries and even many basic necessities of life, as well as the instruments of modern technology; the regionally uneven and generally feeble recovery of agriculture; the reliance of the government for its operation on expensive borrowed funds, foreign or domestic; and the excess of idle hands, especially in rural Mexico. In the thinking of people like Lucas Alamán, the Puebla industrialist Esteban de Antuñano (1792–1847), and a few other men the path out of this mess, and toward the country's advance to prosperity and stability, lay in industrialization and a move away from economic dependence on the export of primary products and therefore upon the whims of foreign markets, investors, and exchange rates. Although his thinking had been trending in this direction for at least a decade, in a report to President Santa Anna in 1843 Alamán wrote:

> If, then, our nation cannot pay for the goods it receives from abroad with the products of its agriculture; if it cannot count on any consumption for those [agricultural] products within any market [other] than the domestic one; and if this [market] depends upon the physical constitution of [the nation's] territory and upon the distribution of population on its surface, factors that do not lie within the power of men to change; if the products of mining cannot enrich the country by themselves—it is [then] necessary to recur to the development of industry as the sole source of a general prosperity. In effect, Sir, due to the peculiar circumstances of our nation, only [industry] can give an impulse to agriculture, providing the market for its products and multiplying their use; only [industry] can increase the wealth of the property owners, giving a value to their estates that they hardly possess at the moment, except in this or that point somewhat richer and more populous; only [industry] can make the population grow [by] providing means for its subsistence, and with this improving the state of its inhabitants, and [industry] alone can stimulate more than any other alternative all social advancement. With industry will come peace, abundance, morality and liberty established upon the bases of order, property, and enlightenment, and without [industry] there will be nothing but poverty, disorder, and servitude.

The models for industrialization since the eighteenth century had been Britain, to some extent France and other pockets in Europe, and then the fledgling United States, the leading sector the textile industry because it produced consumer nondurable goods in wide demand. An opening for such development in what we can call "traditional" economies might be provided by the faltering of external sources of supply to less industrialized nations from already industrialized economies under stress. Such was the so-called import substitution industrialization that occurred in some countries, for example, during World War I and especially with the Great Depression of the 1930s. This had taken place in New Spain to some degree during the 1790s with diversification in textile production and the development of milling, soap, glass, ceramics, and even some steel production as trans-Atlantic shipping was interrupted during the French revolutionary wars, a development that failed to maintain its momentum. In the case of early nineteenth-century Mexico external sources of supply of manufactured goods were if anything excessive. Those from Britain could be shipped across the Atlantic, sustaining transportation costs, insurance, and moderate tariff impositions and still undercutting domestically manufactured goods to dominate the Mexican market and drive smaller manufacturers and artisans out of business.

I have mentioned in the opening pages of this chapter the difficulties Mexico faced in establishing factory-style industrial production between 1821 and about 1850 and want to expand on them a bit here. If taken singly these difficulties were formidable but not insuperable, but combined with a political environment of almost continual armed civil conflict and episodes of foreign predation they created a situation in which industrialization was able to get a promising start in the period from 1830 to 1845 or so, but then stumbled and faltered. Of the world's "late industrializers"—that is, nations other than in Europe or the United States—Mexico established its first factories earlier than anywhere else other than Egypt, did well until mid-century, then fell behind as countries like Brazil and Japan forged ahead. So the share of manufactures in the GDP remained stable at about 20 percent from 1820 until past mid-century; by 1870 Mexico was still overwhelmingly rural and preindustrial, even if not precapitalist.

One of the major elements in the catalog of obstacles to industrialization in Mexico seems almost trivial, although it was anything but trivial: the inadequacy of the transportation system to meet the requirements of developing industry. The country's transportation infrastructure was frankly primitive, limited to small-scale coastal shipping (cabotage), wheeled carts, and the backs of animals. One modern researcher has referred to a "technological involution" (regression from a more to a less developed state) in transport between the colonial and republican eras. While this may be true in a strict mathematical sense, the colonial transportation system was basically made up of the same elements as the early national one. The quality of the roads may have been slightly better at the end of the colonial era because local merchants' guilds in the major cities undertook to improve them, maintain them, build bridges, and so forth, and of course the Spanish crown also took a hand. But after independence the state's always nearly empty coffers could ill afford this infrastructural investment and it became more profitable for capitalists to lend to the government than build toll roads. Only high-unit-value goods repaid the costs of moving them over long distances, and except in terrible emergencies this did not apply to grain or other common commodities, although items like refined sugar might just manage it. The English diplomat Henry G. Ward noted in 1827 that it was much cheaper to buy flour in Veracruz that had been imported by sea from Kentucky or Ohio than to buy that produced in Puebla's Atlixco Valley, distant about 150 miles. Around the same time, moving very heavy minting machinery from the Gulf port of Veracruz to Guanajuato in carts and on mule back took nearly a year. Where roads were concerned, by mid-century Mexico had about five kilometers of cart roads per 10,000 inhabitants, the United States about ten times as many, a canal system, and a burgeoning railroad network to boot. By 1877, admittedly well beyond the further limit of our period, Mexico's 600 kilometers or so of rail lines amounted to only about 25 percent of those in Argentina or Brazil, and even Peru had far outstripped Mexico. Under such conditions, the difficulty and expense of moving industrial inputs or finished products across the map inhibited the development from a highly segmented market to an integrated national one, discouraging industrialization.

Another problem slowing Mexican industrialization was the lack of trained, experienced personnel to operate new forms of technology. This expensive work force had largely to be imported from Europe or the United States on a contract basis to install, adapt, and oversee modern equipment in textile factories or mines. Such men were known to become disenchanted with Mexico or with their working conditions and were often left kicking their heels on full salary and expenses when they arrived in the country ahead of the machinery they were meant to install, operate, and maintain. Some enterprises in Puebla dedicated to the manufacture of glass and porcelain, for example, failed because of the high costs and salaries involved in bringing such expert personnel to Mexico. In the early republican era state efforts to spur technical education to meet this problem were not widely successful. Another issue was the lack of economical sources of power in a geography not well endowed with rivers adequate to the purpose and where steam power mostly proved impractical for lack of wood as fuel in many areas where industry was located. Furthermore, the unpredictable supply of primary material inputs in the cotton textile industry and other activities could raise prices considerably for finished products, or even idle a factory or reduce its production to a point at which installed capacity far exceeded what was in use. An inhibitor of widening and deepening the market for textiles and other factory-made items was the low levels of per capita income in Mexico, which for many popular groups seem actually to have moved backward during the period compared with what was happening in the United States. Once manufactured items or the money to pay for them got on the roads banditry became a factor in interfering with the market and inflicting losses on all parties involved. Furthermore, the internal tariffs and taxes (*alcabalas*) on the movement of goods from one state or department to another that underwrote provincial autonomy also took their toll on commercial movement in general and the market for manufactured goods more particularly. Finally, the institutional setting of these decades discouraged industrialization. There was no banking system as such, although the Catholic Church partially served this function in deploying its financial resources in the form of loans, and private parties made loans to other private parties. These mechanisms responded to market signals hardly at all, however, and were mobilized by interpersonal and social network contacts, making them inefficient as a method of allotting capital, much of which was soaked up in any case by the central government from the *agiotistas.* No laws existed for the formation of limited liability companies or for the protection of long-term investment, there was no modern patent system, and judicial litigants faced a corrupt and unpredictable judicial system. Where the weakness of the national market is concerned, economic historian Guy Thomson has summarized the situation well:

> Essentially, these restrictions were a reflection of the polarized, dual social structure of Mexico. Many Mexicans—[particularly] indigenous people— practically did not consume manufactures either Mexican or foreign. And the Mexicans who did—workers in the mines and haciendas—consumed very little (one estimate indicates their consumption was five meters of cotton cloth per capita annually). . . . In no part of Mexico could significant signs be found that in rural zones the taste and demand for [manufactured goods] was broadening, as for example in Pennsylvania, where they sustained the first phase of the industrial revolution in the same period.[8]

THE INDUSTRIALIZATION OF TEXTILES

Against these headwinds the industrialization of textile production, chiefly that of cottons for the everyday clothing of common people, offered the best possibility for the development of a domestic factory system that could take advantage of a national market. It met many of the criteria believed to be the benefits of industrialization: the absorption of labor power, the raising of living standards among a significant portion of the population, a market for industrial inputs (domestically produced raw cotton), and so forth. Moreover, New Spain had had a textile industry since the sixteenth century in the form of *obrajes*, unmechanized woolen cloth manufactories employing essentially artisanal production methods on a relatively large scale. Until later colonial times these proto-factories sometimes used Black slaves as their work force. Scholars estimate that by 1800 the textile workshops and independent artisanal weavers employed perhaps 90,000 people, 50,000 of whom were concentrated in the major textile centers of Puebla, Querétaro, and Guadalajara. Cotton cloth was manufactured with a more or less modern technology in Guadalajara, where the industry had grown considerably during the eighteenth century, but with independence it was deeply affected by cloth imports through the Pacific ports of entry. Although such enterprises provided Mexican entrepreneurs and artisan weavers experience in the production of textiles, they were never efficient enough to be converted into modern factories, and in any event this industry was largely destroyed during the 1810 insurgency by the same forces that virtually gutted the silver mining sector. Large-scale, typically water-powered cloth production had been the entering wedge of industrialization in the North Atlantic economies, churning out consumer nondurable goods with a short half-life satisfying what amounted to an inelastic permanent demand. The initial problem in getting a mechanized, large-scale cotton cloth industry started, one that could compete with cheap British imports, was mobilizing sufficient capital to build the factories and productive capacity.

To remedy this absence an industrial development bank was established in 1830. In Mexico at this time there was no banking system, as I have pointed out, and loans for industrial startups from private investors, even assuming they could be obtained, would have proven prohibitively expensive because the national government was essentially competing for the money from private financiers, the *agiotistas*, to fund its operations in the face of perennially inadequate fiscal collections. While chief minister in the government from 1830 to 1832 Lucas Alamán was able to get legislation passed establishing the famous Banco de Avío, an institution prepared to some extent to assume some losses for the sake of jump-starting domestic industry. Intended to be self-sustaining after hitting a certain capital threshold, the Banco was funded from selective tariffs on imported textiles, especially from Britain. A management board was set up staffed largely from among Alamán's cronies with the minister at its head while he was in the government. In 1830 the Banco started making loans to entrepreneurs with promising projects to set up yarn and cloth factories with modern, mechanized equipment, although a few other industries such as iron foundries were also encouraged. Some of the loans were quite large, like those made during the 1830s to Esteban de Antuñano, a cloth manufacturer friend of the minister's in Puebla. After Alamán was forced out of the government over his putative role in the killing of Vicente Guerrero, he himself received several large loans for the enormous textile factory he and some partners established near Orizaba in the late 1830s. The Banco lasted for a dozen years, then was shut down by Santa Anna during one of his presidencies. But the idea that the national government might take a hand in encouraging industrialization survived in the form of a bureau for that purpose under Alamán's directorship during much of the 1840s, charged with gathering statistics, organizing industrial trade fairs, establishing a school for the training of industrial technologists, and promoting other activities in favor of industrial manufacturing. This entity was woefully underfunded and had no money to make loans or grants, its recommendations were rarely followed, and the school was a bust, but it did represent a notional effort in the direction of shifting the center of the national economy away from mining to factory-scale industry.

There is little question that the Banco de Avío had a positive effect in encouraging the large-scale mechanization of the cotton textile industry during the late 1830s and 1840s even though during its life its investment in loans to entrepreneurs totaled less than a million pesos. Between 1835 and 1844 forty-seven factories in spinning and weaving were in operation, the number reaching fifty-five by 1851, and just short of one hundred by 1879, well beyond the end of our period. Not all of these enterprises were funded by the Banco, and of those that were the capital supplied by the bank tended to be a minority share of the total. The number of mechanized spindles, the metric by which textile productive capacity was typically measured at the time, grew vertiginously, in 1843 processing about 12,000 tons of raw cotton into yarn and cloth at the hands of about 10,000 workers. The woolen textile industry also recovered from the destructive effects of the 1810–1821 insurgency. Principal areas of production included those cities with already established industries, including Mexico City, Puebla, Querétaro, and Guadalajara, but also several places in the states of Yucatán, Coahuila, Nuevo León, Durango, Colima, and Guerrero. But the cotton textile industry faced numerous problems, already alluded to in a general way, so that by the 1840s levels of profitability had apparently begun to falter. A major problem was the scarcity and unpredictability of the raw material, cotton, mostly produced in the state of Veracruz. Also plaguing the industry was the relatively high cost of specialized labor, the expense of costly imported machinery, the primitive transportation system of the country, and the central government's practice of diverting funds intended for the Banco to other purposes, making the funding stream unpredictable. Furthermore, the domestic demand for mass-produced, inexpensive cottons did not grow as robustly as its proponents had predicted due to stubbornly low per capita incomes among most of the population, so that oversupply quickly became a problem even in the face of the erratic availability of raw cotton. As in other economic activities those men who benefited most from Banco loans and other advantages conceded by the government were part of personal social networks with privileged access to high officialdom, including Santa Anna at those times he headed the state; in other words, the institution ran on cronyism. While most economic historians assert that the mechanized textile industry faltered badly after the 1840s, there is some evidence to indicate that in fact it only slowed its rate of expansion but continued to grow until the more definitive takeoff of the Porfirian period, a small nuance, perhaps, but a significant one. In the words of the Banco de Avío's best historian, Robert Potash:

> After all is said against it, the fact remains that as of 1846, a mechanized textile industry had been created; the level of employment in manufacturing, agriculture, transportation, and other fields had been raised, and concomitantly the income of a goodly number of working people. The creation of the industry, moreover, was not a transitory achievement. It was to survive the shock of foreign invasions and civil wars; it was to witness the growth of plant capacity and of the value and variety of output; and it was to constitute, in the hands of its predominantly Mexican entrepreneurs, a viable and profitable sector of the economy well before the economic transformation of the Porfirian era.[9]

Even if this remarkably sanguine evaluation of the Banco de Avío specifically, and of the state of the textile industry in the middle decades of the nineteenth century more generally, is darkened a tone or two in keeping with the consensus of a number of other scholars, the picture by mid-century was at least mixed. There were some successes and some failures.

As in the country's attempt to revive the mining economy, Lucas Alamán's experience was both central to and illustrative of the problems that plagued the textile startups. Relying heavily on technical advice from his friend Antuñano in Puebla, in 1836 Alamán established with two French partners, the brothers Legrand, an enormous, water-powered textile factory at Cocolapan, near the town of Orizaba in the state of Veracruz, for a time the largest factory in Mexico. He had little in the way of financial capital of his own to invest, which would turn out later to be a major complaint as the enterprise went bankrupt, the major investors tried to salvage what they could of their funds, and the concern's failure spurred complicated litigation in the 1840s. The affair damaged Alamán's reputation seriously, leaving him under a debt overhang lasting until his death in 1853. But at the end of the 1830s prospects for a very successful business seemed strong, the former government minister supplying the human capital in the form of management skills, social connections, and the considerable gloss of his name. What eventually brought the business down was the scarcity of raw cotton, the falling price of yarn and cloth due to overproduction, the saturation of the market by contraband, disagreements among the investors, and the political situation of the country. After Alamán left the enterprise under a cloud Cocolapan was purchased for a fraction of its assessed value in 1848 by one of the relatively few entrepreneurs of the time who achieved large-scale success, Manuel Escandón y Garmendía (1804–1862), in whose family it remained into the twentieth century. Escandón was also involved in the construction of the first railroad line in the country, a successful diligence (stagecoach) service, speculation in the public debt, mining, land ownership, and several other lines of investment. He and some partners also acquired a majority ownership stake in an important textile factory in the Guadalajara area that not only manufactured cotton goods but also served as a cover for the introduction into Mexico of contraband British cotton cloth marketed as a domestic product.

MEXICAN SOCIETY AT MID-CENTURY

What is striking about Mexican society toward the end of the early republican period is the stability of its social structure and practices, especially in rural Mexico, so that much of the description offered in chapter 2 still held true three decades after independence was won. The national population grew from about 6,000,000 in 1810 to some 8,000,000 fifty years later, a rate of increase of less than 1 percent annually, while the population of the capital fluctuated between 120,000 and 200,000 from 1820 to 1890. The failure of Lucas Alamán's giant textile enterprise at Cocolapan points indirectly to some clues about the state of Mexican society by mid-century. Although still water powered as the age of steam came to dominate the Atlantic world, the concern's excess installed capacity was relative, of course, to the purchasing power of ordinary Mexican consumers over and above their most basic needs, what economists would call the elasticity of demand. Outside the country's cities and even within them this was low, limited to the small middle social sector and the urban elites. Even had there been abundant capital, the limited incentives for investment would tend to discourage technological innovation in Mexico originating either domestically or as imported from abroad, thus stalling perhaps the single most important motor of social change affecting the lives of most people in the modern world. The age of steam had taken hold in Britain and was well established in the United States in the form of steamboats (from just after 1800), steam-powered manufacturing equipment, and of course the railroad (somewhat later in the United States than in Britain). The major Mexican industrial activities, textile manufacture and sugar and silver refining, would remain in the presteam era for several decades for the apparently trivial reason that in many areas of the country wood was too scarce to feed steam boilers. The meaning of this is that the technological changes that significantly altered people's lives, most of them involving steam and/or electricity, for the most part did not show up in Mexico until the last quarter of the century. There was change in the early republican decades, of course, but it occurred almost entirely in the political sphere and to a lesser degree in the area of social relations. To say this is not to reduce all social change to economic and technological development, but it does mean that the pace of change in most people's lives was slow and would not have been very noticeable until 1875 or so. Innovation in the economy consisted chiefly of the new or wider application of technological elements already on the scene. Manuel Escandón, for example, established the first regular diligence service in the country in the early 1830s, running between Mexico City and Veracruz. There were already horses and carriages, of course, so put them together with a half-way decent road and a bit of capital and—voilà!—stagecoach service. Those better-off Mexicans who could afford the fare and dared to expose themselves as targets to the constant bandit attacks on the highways might avail themselves of this faster and more convenient mode of transportation, saving a good deal of time in traveling between the two cities, but this entrepreneurial innovation clearly affected the lives of only a tiny part of the population.

One area of change, as I have already noted, appears to have been the somewhat more fluid notions and practices regarding the racial hierarchy ushered in by the republican period, although racial and class borders were still patrolled informally, as in the appropriateness of marriage partners, especially as one ascended the social ladder. Blacks were already blending into the general population except in certain coastal enclaves such as Veracruz and Acapulco. A number of men of color made their way to the heights of political and military life and to other sorts of positions foreclosed to them in former times. Lower-class women of color enjoyed as much, or perhaps more, freedom of action. They were less subject to the control of fathers, husbands, elder brothers, or even adult sons than they had been in the late colonial era. Because they might well be widowed early, women of color were necessarily self-supporting and needed to work, conferring on them an independence in the everyday world (within limits) largely unknown to their wealthier white sisters. Peasant women, whether Indigenous or of mixed race, devoted themselves to domestic duties while their men performed agricultural labor as they always had, whether on their own account or as waged employees. The saying from German imperial times describing a woman's place in the social scheme of things, "Kinder, Küche, Kirche"—children, kitchen, church—might well be applied to Mexican rural women, or middle-and upper-class urban women, for that matter. As historian Mark Wasserman has noted:

> Rural women arose at four [a.m.] to grind maize. They drew the water, brought the wood for the fire, cared for the children, prepared three meals, did the wash, and spun and weaved. They made pottery and then hauled it to the Sunday market. It was very common that, if the men hired on at the hacienda, the women's

work was included either as a field hand or as a domestic in the hacienda house. Women received no pay.[10]

When one arrived in cities, however, the situation for women was somewhat different. The research of historian Silvia Arrom has done much to illuminate the condition of women in Mexico City from the end of the colonial era to the mid-nineteenth century.[11] Middle-and upper-class women in the capital and larger cities, often widowed in middle age, might be thrust into the position of head of household because under the inheritance practices prevailing into the nineteenth century they could come into property of their own, not to mention the dowries they might bring to marriage. One has the impression that this became somewhat more common in early republican times. Their educational opportunities were very limited, however, and their activities basically restricted to the domestic sphere. The working class of Mexico City and other cities embraced many women; about 25 percent of the female inhabitants of the capital worked, mostly Indigenous women and other women of color. Many of these people were domestics, the number of domestic servants in a given household increasing as one ascended the social hierarchy. Working women of color also dominated the urban markets where household shopping was done on a daily basis, they had a significant role in small retail establishments, and they worked in food preparation mostly from their own modest homes. But gaining a living as an independent worker was difficult, making vital the family incomes combining the earnings of domestic partners and even children. In analyzing the composition of Mexican armies at the time of the war with the United States, historian Peter Guardino makes the point that whether men were drafted into the regular army or joined militia units, the pay was so miserably low and irregular that women and their children might be thrust into destitution in the absence of the adult males in the family.[12] This is one reason, aside from the sexual, subsistence, and personal (for example, laundry) services they provided, why such prodigious numbers of women were to be found as *soldaderas* with the Mexican armies of the time and of the Revolution of 1910.

RURAL LIFE

Where the countryside was concerned, little seems to have changed in rural Mexico during the three decades after 1821. The abolition of noble titles in the republic and of African slavery, both in the 1820s, affected ordinary people very little if at all. By 1850 many areas continued to be dominated by haciendas, which could recover relatively quickly from the destructive effects of the 1810 insurgency, as I have suggested, mostly because their technology was so simple. By the eve of the 1910 Revolution one inventory of the country's mines and haciendas (of which the definition at the time was admittedly rather vague and the count itself incomplete) put the number at around 5,000. This may well have been the high water mark of the great estate in Mexico before the land redistribution initiated after the Revolution, particularly during the 1930s when the regime of President Lázaro Cárdenas (1895–1970) broke many of them up and left many others reduced to unviability, shorn of their land. Haciendas were probably considerably fewer in our period, before the Porfirian era's nonfarming population growth, the advent of the railroad, and the surveying and giveaway of state-owned lands to private owners increased their number and economic vitality.[13] The countryside, however, was not a moonlike landscape in which large estates were the only agrosocial units on which rural people lived and worked. There were the smaller, family-worked properties called by various names according to size, area of the country, and local conventions, but which for purposes of convenience we can think of as ranchos even though their primary productive activity might not have revolved around the livestock we often associate with such entities. And because rural Mexico remained substantially Indian in ethnic terms (there were approximately 4,000,000 Indigenous people by the 1840s), there were still hundreds and hundreds of Indigenous towns, villages, and hamlets, most numerous where the population was densest, as in the state of Oaxaca. There was a complex rural social ecology established in colonial times, surviving intact through the nineteenth century, and in evidence even in our own era. Of these entwined relationships the most important was that between the village, primarily Indigenous in the mid-nineteenth century, and the hacienda. This was a mutual if asymmetrical dependency favoring the large estate until the imbalance was reversed by state action following the Revolution of 1910, so that the extended, family-owned rural estate, modern forms of agribusiness aside, was virtually extinguished through postrevolutionary land reform. During the 1750–1850 period, however, the hacienda needed labor and the villagers needed sources of income beyond what they might earn as individual farmers or community members. The asymmetry consisted in the fact that the hacienda had pushed peasant villagers off their lands to then hire them back as laborers to farm some of the same lands of which they had been dispossessed.

The hacienda was a highly protean entity: despite its apparent solidity really a nexus of variables whose mix of characteristics varied greatly with the geography, so it is difficult to pin down its social shape definitively. The "typical" personnel structure included an absentee or only intermittently on-site owner at the top, an administrator and perhaps another employee or two (an accountant, a storekeeper, and some foremen), and a work force that might or might not live on site and tended to fluctuate in numbers. Life on the early republican hacienda revolved around the seasonal demands of agricultural pursuits, as it had during the late colonial decades. On larger estates temporary wage workers were hired and discharged as necessary to supplement the labor of the resident peons. Sharecroppers and renters might live on the estate in a somewhat more dispersed pattern, whereas a permanent wage labor force might occupy an area of simple, single-family housing, sometimes known as the *cuadrilla*, near the central hacienda buildings. There might even be a chapel attached to the main house where an itinerant priest administered the sacraments and held mass for the residents of the property. In such a case the workers' living arrangements might mimic to some degree a village community, although it lacked the political structure of an autonomous pueblo. These arrangements varied widely in scale, composition of the workforce, relationship of *hacendado* to workers, and other characteristics according to the region of the country, roughly along the lines set forth in table 3.1. Some owners lived on their properties, others in nearby cities from which they might visit periodically. Lucas Alamán, for example, had a resident manager and a few other employees between him and the labor force on his hacienda near Celaya, in the Guanajuato area, but visited from Mexico City as frequently as his other occupations there permitted. In the 1840s Fanny Calderón described a typical sugar-producing hacienda in the Cuernavaca area to the south of Mexico City. Such an enterprise would naturally be more highly capitalized because of the intensive agricultural practices associated with the growing of sugar cane and the industrial process of sugar refining. But the elements of her description, including the isolation of such estates, their occasionally run-down, melancholy condition, the elemental nature of furnishings in the main house, etc., can also be read in many of her observations of rural estates elsewhere in the country:

> As for the interior of these haciendas, they are all pretty much alike . . . a great stone building, which is neither farm nor country house . . . but has a character to itself—solid enough to stand a siege, with floors of painted brick, large deal tables [a simple, multipurpose table made of pine or other soft wood], wooden benches, painted chairs, and whitewashed walls; one or two painted or iron bedsteads, only put up when wanted; numberless empty rooms; kitchen and outhouses; the courtyard a great square around which stand the house for boiling the sugar, whose furnaces burn day and night; the house with machinery for extracting the juice from the cane.[14]

THE GREAT CAPITAL

Mexico City, as I have noted, had by 1850 already long displayed what has been called the "primate city" pattern, a disparity that would continue to grow so markedly into the twentieth century. Although the capital was (and remains) sui generis among Mexican cities in many ways, a look at it as it stood in 1850 gives some general sense of urban life at the close of our period. For one thing, it was not a very healthy place to live because inadequate or nonexistent sewage disposal and the vulnerability to contamination of the water supply were problems not addressed until the Porfirian era. The age-old tendency of parts of the city to flood at various times of the year, a problem admittedly peculiar to a capital sitting in a geologically unstable basin surrounded by lakes, produced dangerous conditions including a prime environment for water-borne disease. Repeated outbreaks of smallpox (1825–1826, 1828–1830, 1839–1840), scarlet fever (1822, 1825, 1838, 1842, 1844, 1846), and measles (1822, 1826, 1836, 1843, 1848) exacted a high death toll, not to mention the virulent killers typhoid, cholera, and gastrointestinal diseases that attacked other cities as well. Infant mortality was high even under ordinary conditions. Natural replacement of the urban population was impossible in these circumstances, so that replenishment depended upon constant cityward immigration from smaller towns and the countryside. Given the nature of work available in the city most immigrants were female, young, dark-skinned, and single and mostly went into domestic service. Of those inhabitants of the city gainfully employed in 1850 or so, about one-third were artisans of various sorts, about a quarter service providers (porters, water sellers, coachmen, domestics, and so on), and a fifth the perennially turbulent soldiers. The rest, historian Mark Wasserman estimates, was made up of what might be construed as the middle-and upper-income groups. As many as 20,000 in the population were extremely poor, including the famous *capitalino* criminal class of pickpockets, cutpurses, prostitutes, and the homeless *léperos* (the socially marginal, but not actually leprous). But the city was also the capital of an extensive nation, even after 1848, so it thronged with men of all sorts who had some direct stake in matters of government, including politicians secular and ecclesiastic, bureaucrats, clerks, and military officers, as well as professionals such as doctors and lawyers. Popular entertainment for people of modest means included gambling, cockfights (Santa Anna was a notable patron of this pastime), bullfights, and street dances, while the better heeled might attend one of several theaters whose presentations and ticket prices corresponded to economic means and tastes. Not untypically of even the most sympathetic of foreigners traveling or living in Mexico, Brantz Mayer, for a number of years secretary of the American legation in Mexico

City, remarked in his 1844 account of the country that the chief diversions of the Mexicans were revolutions, earthquakes, and bullfights, in that order, although this statement may say more about Mayer than his surroundings.

The French traveler Louis de Bellamare (the pseudonym of Gabriel Ferry the elder [1809–1852]) remarked that the city was by far the most beautiful the Spaniards had established in the Americas but that the conditions of the streets contrasted shockingly with the elegance of the buildings. The physical layout of the city centered on the public square, what came to be known as the Zócalo after Santa Anna's attempt in 1843 to build a monument to independence there to replace an enormous equestrian statue of King Charles IV removed in 1822. This project got only as far as the construction of the base, or *zócalo* (plinth), from which the impressive space thence derived its popular name. The Cathedral stands on its north side, the National Palace on the east, the municipal buildings to the south, and portals with cafés, booksellers, and shops to the west. As in virtually all Mexican cities, the moneyed class lived toward the center on streets radiating out at right angles from the Zócalo, where a number of their impressive mansions can still be seen today, converted to other purposes. These substantial houses were two and three stories high, constructed entirely or at least surfaced with the reddish volcanic rock called *tezontle*. Arched gateways with massive wooden doors sized to accommodate carriages led to interior courtyards surrounded by colonnades, various outbuildings, stables, and so forth. Well-off families usually occupied the upper floors while street-level premises were leased to commercial concerns. As one went further out from the center into the *barrios populares* (popular neighborhoods) housing became progressively humbler, with the working poor living in *casas de vecindad* (essentially tenements). By 1840 the city had many religious establishments and was home to upward of 2,000 regular and secular clergy. There were about sixty churches, twenty-three male monastic complexes, and fifteen female convents, many shortly to be destroyed or repurposed in a spasm of anticlerical legislation under the ascendant liberals in the mid-1850s. The scores and scores of popular eating and drinking establishments, boardinghouses, and restaurants had dreadful reputations for the most part concerning their cleanliness, their amenities, and the quality of the fare served in them. And this was to say nothing of the 400 or so *pulquerías*— basically bars, some exceedingly primitive, for the consumption of pulque, the generation of brawls, and the diffusion of subversion. An 1837 analysis of the temporarily suppressed Federal District and its suburbs noted that crime was rampant despite a substantial police presence. A few years later the largest element in the income of the municipal budget was derived from licensing fees for these watering holes and the largest single expenditure for the jails. While the municipal and federal authorities spent a fair amount on attempting to control street crime, attention paid to public hygiene and individual health was left almost entirely in the hands of the Church as a religious obligation. Hospitals were scarce in the capital, as in provincial cities. In Mexico City most foreign travelers, among them the American military officials whose forces occupied the city in 1848, were impressed by the medical services offered at the Hospital de Jesús, a pious foundation established by Fernando Cortés in the early sixteenth century (which still exists today as a modern hospital) for the medical care of Indigenous people and managed for many years by Lucas Alamán.

All this would have been recognizable to a Mexican of 1800 or even earlier. One aspect of urban life that did change in the early republican era, however, was the increase in the number of foreigners even in provincial capitals and larger towns and the proliferation of foreign luxury goods and items of European manufacture available to people of means. Newspapers teemed with adds for French dressmakers and hair stylists (whom Fanny Calderón tended to call "scoundrels"); French pastry chefs, carriage makers, and other providers of upmarket goods and services were to be found everywhere. English merchants, engineers, and other technical personnel valued for their commercial and scientific acumen, Italian teachers of voice and instruments, and a scattering of German craftsmen and even American traders were to be found among foreign diplomats, touring artists, and opera and theatrical companies. And of course there were the foreign travelers, scores of who left accounts of Mexican life and customs. Perhaps the most famous of these was Fanny Calderón de la Barca (1804–1882), the Edinburgh-born Scotswoman married to a Spanish diplomat, often quoted in these pages. But there were many others as well, European and American. Many of them projected a strong note of superiority toward Mexicans of all classes and definite traces of the orientalism tinged with eroticism so characteristic of such writers in describing cultures other than their own. One of these was the American poet, literary critic, travel writer, and diplomat Bayard Taylor (1825–1878), whose 1850 travel book on Mexico described social customs quite minutely. In contrasting the custom of the *paseo* in Guadalajara—the evening stroll or promenade, carried out in a park or boulevard, on foot or in a carriage, that one would also have observed in Paris or Berlin—with the way it was practiced in Mexico City, Taylor wrote:

> We sat down on one of the benches, so near the throng of [female] promenaders . . . that their dresses brushed our feet. The ladies were in full dress, with their heads uncovered. . . . The faint clear olive of their complexion . . . the deep, dark, languishing eye . . . the ripe voluptuous lip—the dark hair whose silky waves would have touched the ground . . . and the pliant grace and fullness of the form, formed together a type of beauty which a little queenly ambition would have moulded into a living Cleopatra.[15]

CONCLUSION

Before the substantial loss of life (the numbers are squishy, but let us assume some 600,000 people out of a national population of around six million) and massive destruction of productive capacity wrought by the decade of the independence struggle, signs for the development, or at least the growth, of the economy of New Spain/Mexico were mixed at best. There had been some loosening of commercial restrictions with Spain and Europe under the trade reforms of the 1780s, there was a quickening of trade within New Spain, and urban markets—Mexico City, Guadalajara, the mining centers—had expanded to absorb more commodities that the commercial agricultural/ livestock sector might produce. Because population growth had slackened, however, there were limits to the growth possibilities here. A more modern-ized textile industry had managed to gain a foothold in Puebla, Guadalajara, Querétaro, and a few other cities but bumped up against the limitations of the market for its goods. Silver production was still increasing, but at a shal-lower rate of climb than earlier. Fiscal income from taxes of various kinds was devoted less to infrastructural and other projects within New Spain—to domestic reinvestment, in other words—than to imperial defense against British incursions into the Spanish colonial sphere associated with the Napoleonic wars. So it seems possible that without the push of something like industrialization and the growth it might produce in the real income of ordinary people as consumers, the colonial economy might have reached a natural limit to its expansion.

After New Spain became Mexico in 1821 a debate developed among pub-lic men, generally implicit but sometimes explicit, about the path to modern-ization and prosperity that the new nation might best pursue. Some favored the option of reliance on silver and a handful of other primary products under the model of comparative advantage espoused by Adam Smith's *Wealth of Nations* (1775), which many political decision makers read. Others, the most articulate voice among them Lucas Alamán's, advocated industrialization along the lines seen in the North Atlantic world. If Mexico was to choose the latter path, however, serious difficulties stood in the way. Absent some more efficient transportation system, the difficult Mexican geography and the distances within the country posed a problem of getting inputs to manufac-turing centers and outputs to markets. Perhaps even more fundamental was the difficulty of raising real wages for the mass of the population, most of them Indigenous peasants, so that people could purchase the products of an industrializing sector, beginning with inexpensive textiles. Here a contradic-tion arose among the modernizers favoring the rise of manufactures. Readers will remember that according to an estimate offered earlier real wages for working people had fallen by about 25 percent in the three decades or so following 1775, so the buying power of popular consumers was anything but robust to begin with. Raising the productivity of peasant agriculture to put additional income into the hands of potential consumers would require either some sort of technological breakthroughs in farming or the redistribution of land resources from the commercial hacienda sector to the peasant sector. The sort of social (and arguably political) change that this implied was anathema to conservative modernizers like Alamán and other industrialists unwilling to pay the high price of reducing the social and political predominance they exercised by virtue of their control of land, a case of having their cake and eating it too. So what continued during the early republic was a sort of dual economy with an enormous group of working people and peasants with low purchasing power, a small minority of relatively prosperous urban dwellers with the economic means to buy luxury goods, whether produced domestically or imported from abroad, and a stuttering industrial sector. The general picture of the early republican economy was not completely dark because the strong regionalization of the country produced something of a patchwork when it came to recovering from the shock of independence and moving on. Some regions recovered more quickly than others and even experienced development, while others endured the near stagnation that was the rule rather than the exception.

The political instability of the period—the continual *pronunciamientos*, the coups d'état, the civil wars and near-civil wars, the acrimonious public discourse, political experimentation, and pendulum swings in styles of governance, and the central government's nearly perpetual penury—grew out of the rachitic economic situation while at the same time contributing to the weakness of that economy. Even if potential investors had capital available, the climate for investment was highly insecure because political circumstances were unpredictable, and one never knew from one day to the next what business conditions might be like. Although Tolstoy's aphorism that "all happy families are alike; each unhappy family is unhappy in its own way" can be applied to economic enterprises, Alamán's failure with the Cocolapan textile factory illuminates the situation generally: a weak consumer base, problems with transportation and the supply of raw materials, and overproduction.[16] Moreover, the state's ability to control banditry was very limited, making travel and the transportation of goods risky. The central government's predatory policies of exacting forced loans from the populace to support its (chiefly military) activities in lieu of a steady tax base tended to dictate risk-averse activities to keep visibility low. And the weakness of infrastructure inhibited the movement of goods, services, and people in ways I have mentioned. The country's experience with the Banco de Avío tellingly illustrates the failure of the central government to keep its commitments, whether under Santa Anna's or anyone else's leadership.

NOTES

1. Walter L. Bernecker, *De agiotistas y empresarios: En torno a la temprana industrialización Mexicana (siglo XIX)* (Mexico City: Universidad Iberoamericana, 1992), 120 (translation mine).

2. The important work of Coatsworth is based on statistics that are somewhat doubtful because of imprecise or incomplete recordkeeping by the Mexican government in the early republican period. The figures cited from him are therefore approximations included here to provide orders of magnitude only rather than precise figures.

3. As the previous chapters, this one rests in part upon my own research but also in major respects upon the published work of a number of talented Mexican, European, and American economic historians. Among these (in no particular order, and certainly not a complete list) are Mark Wasserman, John Coatsworth, Stephen Haber, Margaret Chowning, the late Araceli Ibarra Bellón, Walter Bernecker, Guy Thomson, Aurora Gómez-Galvarriato, Sergio Cañedo Gamboa, Gisela Moncada González, Carlos Marichal, and Tom Passananti. Particularly helpful due to its broad scope has been Enrique Cárdenas Sánchez's study *Cuando se originó el atraso económico de México: La economía Mexicana en el largo siglo XIX, 1780–1920* (Madrid: Fundación Ortega y Gasset, 2003). Due to space constraints, and in keeping with my approach of looking into a few important themes more deeply rather than touching on many themes superficially, the emphasis in this chapter is on major sectors of the economy—silver mining, agriculture, and the industrialization of textiles. There were other things going on in the early republican economy—export-import activities, artisanal production, local commerce, and so forth—but I have elected to touch on these only in passing if at all.

4. Margaret Chowning, *Wealth and Power in Provincial Mexico: Michoacán from the Late Colony to the Revolution* (Stanford: Stanford University Press, 1999).

5. Sergio Alejandro Cañedo Gamboa, *Comercio, alcabalas y negocios de familia en San Luis Potosí, México: Crecimiento económico y poder politico, 1820–1846* (Mexico City: El Colegio de San Luis/Instituto Mora, 2015). Full disclosure: Cañedo Gamboa was a doctoral student of mine at the University of California, San Diego.

6. David Sinclair, *The Land that Never Was: Sir Gregor MacGregor and the Most Audacious Fraud in History* (Cambridge, MA: Da Capo Press, 2003).

7. The £3,250,000 of 1825 would be approximately £225 million in today's equivalent currency, an enormous sum; and this was only for one mining company of several large enterprises and a number of smaller ones.

8. Guy P. C. Thomson, "Continuidad y cambio en la industria manufacturera Mexicana, 1800–1870," in Gómez-Galvarriato, *La industria textil*, 53–113, at p. 103 (translation mine).

9. Robert A. Potash, *Mexican Government and Industrial Development in the Early Republic: The Banco de Avío* (Amherst, MA: University of Massachusetts Press, 1983), 165.

10. Mark Wasserman, *Everyday Life and Politics in Nineteenth-Century Mexico: Men, Women, and War* (Albuquerque: University of New Mexico Press, 2000), 150.

11. Silvia Marina Arrom, *The Women of Mexico City, 1790–1857* (Stanford, CA: Stanford University Press, 1985).

12. Guardino, *Dead March.*

13. I owe this observation to Thomas Passananti.

14. Calderón de la Barca, *Life in Mexico*, 376. She was actually describing the sugar hacienda of Atlacomulco, established by Fernando Cortés in the early sixteenth century, inherited in the nineteenth century by his titled Neapolitan noblemen descendant, the Duke of Terranova y Monteleone, and managed by Lucas Alamán for nearly thirty years as a valuable part of the Duke's large holdings.

15. Bayard Taylor, *Eldorado, or, Adventures in the Path of Empire: Comprising a Voyage to California via Panama, Life in San Francisco and Monterrey, Pictures of the Gold Region, and Experiences of Mexican Travel* (New York: G. P. Putnam, 1850), 285–86.

16. Leo Tolstoy, *Anna Karenina: A Novel in Eight Parts*, trans. Richard Pevear and Larissa Volokhonsky (London: Allen Lane, 2000), 1.

Chapter 11

Conclusion

Walking the central, most developed parts of the sprawling Mexican capital, especially toward the west and southwest, one can hardly question that this is a highly modernized city, and if only on a smaller scale much the same conditions will be found in other major cities in the country. The megalopolis embracing the Federal District and much of the Valley of Mexico is the fifth largest urban concentration in the world, whose population of nearly 22,000,000 people sandwiches it in between São Paulo, Brazil, and Cairo, Egypt. Although it annually serves only half the travelers of the Atlanta airport in the United States, Mexico City's airport is the largest and busiest in Latin America. The vehicular traffic in the city is dense, extremely fierce, and one needs to have one's wits about one when crossing major streets as a pedestrian. Tall glass and steel buildings, chiefly in the "international style" but many of more distinguished design, loom over boulevards teeming with well-dressed people hurrying about their business. *Flâneurs* (of which I have occasionally been one) also saunter with apparent aimlessness along the fashionable blocks of high-end stores, showrooms, restaurants, the occasional multiplex movie theater, and of course the ubiquitous Starbucks coffee bars. Penetrate a block or two behind the major thoroughfares, however, and you are likely to find yourself in a lower-rent district where you will encounter modest and informal eating establishments that cater to workers on their lunch hours. For two dollars or so one can still feast on a three-to five-course *comida corrida*, the traditional main meal of the day still widely adhered to in Mexico, eaten at a very sensible 2:00 to 4:00 p.m. While it may emphasize carbohydrates (rice, pasta) and include only small portions of animal protein, this meal in a popular establishment can nonetheless compete in flavor, quantity, and even quality with the pricier fare on offer in the upmarket eateries of the fashionable boulevards. The side streets may also feature shops that open directly onto the street as they did centuries ago. There are also many people of obviously modest means in the tonier parts of town, to say nothing of the Indigenous women, referred to deprecatingly as "Marías," seated in doorways selling yarn dolls, chewing gum, and other small items to tourists (at least in pre-Covid pandemic times) and other passersby. The older city center, in the crowded streets stretching out from the enormous central square, the Zócalo, presents a striking embodiment of the tension between the antique and the modern. This part of town is full of late colonial and nineteenth-century buildings, impressive stone mansions with massive double wooden doors installed to accommodate the passage of carriages and mounted riders. More than one nineteenth-century foreign visitor was prompted to call the capital a "city of palaces" even while sewage ran down open gutters in the middle of the streets. The nearby archaeological sites constantly yield new evidence of the Aztec civilization on whose imperial capital, Tenochtitlán, the invading Spaniards constructed their own city, while one of the world's great subway systems rumbles underneath. All the while, modern Mexico City, built on and around the soft lake beds of the central Valley of Mexico, is slowly sinking, ineluctably swallowed up by the old Tenochtitlán—Moctezuma's truest revenge.

Yet other markers of the modernization overlapping colonial times are to be found on all sides. Primary schools that would look only slightly out of place if at all in a US urban setting are scattered around the enormous city. There are more public and private universities, technological institutes, research centers, and other forms of postsecondary educational and research establishments in the country than one can easily keep track of, a number of them among the foremost in Latin America and world-class institutions in their own right. In a society still heavily characterized by patriarchal values and practices, as of this writing eight out of twenty departmental secretaries in the president's cabinet are women and the mayor of the capital is a woman and potential presidential contender, a Jewish engineer-physicist with a PhD. There is only one female state governor, suggesting that attitudes at the national level, certainly in the president's office, are more liberal than in the states, although the country has implemented a gender quota system for many political and judicial offices. Mexico's overall adult literacy rate is almost 95 percent. At just over seventy-five years, overall life expectancy at birth (not far below that in the United States) has risen nearly thirty years since 1950 and ten just since 1980. Eighty percent of Mexico's population is at least nominally urbanized, about the same percentage as in the United States. Monuments and other forms of symbolic national remembrance in paper, stone, celluloid, and other media abound, signifying that beneath the nearly constant raucous discordances of politics there is a functioning, heroic national mythology on which Mexicans can draw to explain their collective history and identity, their "imagined community." A number of other hallmarks of modernization might be mentioned for Mexico, but most of them tend in the same direction as those I have just cited, many of them counterbalanced by seeming contradictions. Modern societies are not flawless utopias, of course, and the country has many enormous and widely publicized problems: the political and law enforcement systems are by all accounts still riddled with corruption despite the avowed goal of every incoming national administration to sweep it away, and the drug trade is a seemingly insuperable problem nationally and internationally, in large measure responsible for a domestic homicide rate that has quadrupled since 2004. Much of this violence is fed by the enormously profitable market for recreational drugs in the United States, of course, and by American pressure on Mexico to join its war against the industry. Income inequality is extremely high, one data set embracing 132 countries putting Mexico at number 107—that is, higher in terms of inequality than 80 percent of the comparison group. This is hardly unique to Mexico within Latin America, however, because rates of income inequality in the region rank among the highest in the world. Notwithstanding these and other problems it is impossible to deny that Mexico is a society deeply advanced into modernization.

Yet what Mexico might have become—the path to the modern world it took partly by the choice of its elites, partly by ineluctable circumstance and the pace at which that path was followed—was not definitively determined until beyond the end of our period. I have made the point at some length in chapter 8 that independence, the very act that pulled New Spain away from Old Spain, tore down the long-sanctified legitimacy of royal authority and the power that emanated from it, laying the shakiest of foundations for national political life. The failure over many years to replace this with another generally adhered to principle of legitimacy, a consensus among political players and general populace that the locus of loyalty and authority should shift from monarchy to independent Mexican nation, made it difficult to achieve the necessary collective work of decolonization, to put political, economic, and social institutions and practices in sync with independent nationhood. The Mexican-American War prompted a sharpening of the conflict between conservatives and liberals that had already contributed to cost the country more than three decades of political instability often characterized by considerable violence, of which the War of the South (1830) was the most extreme example. With the fall of Santa Anna's last government (1855) there came a clear liberal ascendancy that produced the Constitution of 1857, a charter that would rule national political life at least nominally until it was replaced by another in 1917 that still prevails, although much amended. The liberals pursued a largely successful legislative campaign to reduce the political and economic power of the Catholic Church, restructure much property in land through state intervention, substantially subordinate the army to civil authority, further secularize education, and initiate other steps toward modernization as much of the Euro-Atlantic world was experiencing it. Much of this program was not actualized until the long regime of Porfirio Díaz (1876–1911), an imperfect authoritarianism described by writer Carleton Beals as the "queer frock-coated abortion" of a conjoined liberalism and conservatism.[1]

The elements of a colonial conquest society were not easily expunged, however, and some have become so naturalized that they simply seem part of contemporary Mexico by a sort of implicit, consensual social choice rather than what they are, the legacy of colonial forms of subordination that have been hard to root out or at least correct for. In terms of the spheres of life that in chapter 1 I suggested alter at different velocities in the process of decolonization, political decolonization changed the most quickly. After the episode of Iturbide's empire in 1822–1823, except for a brief return to monarchy forced on Mexico (although with considerable domestic collaboration from Mexican conservatives) by the French in their intervention of 1862–1867, the country became a republic and has remained so, even if far from a perfect democracy. The colonial political arrangements did leave some traces, however, whose lines of descent are difficult to document directly but whose lingering influence may be suggested. One is the deeply embedded practice of corruption—of officials illegitimately using their political powers for private gain and the allied habits of cronyism and nepotism—which certainly had their precedents in colonial administration. The salaries of colonial officials were low, so such corruption was seen as a sort of perquisite of office, an overhead cost of administering a far-flung empire tolerated as long as it was kept within reasonable if not explicitly sanctioned limits. It was a way for such people to make a living, recover what may have been the expenses of obtaining their posts in the first place, and for the Spanish crown to shift the outlay for empire to the imperial subjects, whether impoverished Indigenous peasants or silver mining magnates in silk coats. Another notable political echo from the colonial period is the prevalence in Mexico of very strong presidents cast in a soft authoritarian mold with wide powers that stop just short of true authoritarianism. This pattern certainly marked Santa Anna's presidencies, especially his last (1853–1855); persisted through the latter part of the nineteenth century with presidents Benito Juárez and Porfirio Díaz; and is recurrent in the presidencies of the postrevolutionary century just ending. Political genealogies are hard to establish directly, as I have said, but at least some features of colonial practice do seem to survive in adapted forms and in the political ethos of modern Mexico.

Where its economy is concerned Mexico has experienced the entwined processes of decolonization and modernization in phases that have left it substantially less dependent and more industrialized over time but still exposed to the brisk weather of the global economy in ways that more developed economies (which often make their own weather) are not. The halting measures toward industrialization begun in the early republic, outlined in chapter

10, while they built on some late colonial foundations nonetheless faced the headwinds of regressive taxation systems, inefficient means and very high costs of transportation, low effective consumer demand, foreign competition, scarcity of domestic capital, and so forth. Under the Porfirio Díaz regime many of these problems were partially resolved, or at least attenuated. The advent of the railroads is hard to overestimate in this connection, and the imposition of political stability, even as it imposed high social costs, nonetheless encouraged capital investment and further steps toward the creation of an industrialized economy less dependent upon the export of primary products, principally silver, although these were still important in the overall productive mix, as they remain today. If relatively small in comparative terms, by the beginning of the twentieth century an industrial proletariat had found sufficient voice to make itself heard in political and economic life. The Great Depression of the 1930s initiated a phase of what has been called "import substitution industrialization" in which domestic industrial production within the country to some degree replaced goods, now choked off in the contraction of the international economy, that previously came from more advanced modernized economies, providing yet another jolt to the industrializing process. The 1940–1970 period of economic development, the "Mexican Miracle," especially following World War II, accelerated this trend and saw high rates of growth and a further turn toward manufacturing as it did elsewhere in Latin America. Currently the large majority of the Mexican labor force is found in the service sector, but industrial workers account for twice the number in agriculture. The pattern of dependency in the country's economy is still very strong, with about 75 percent of its exports going to the United States, while the half of its total imports, of which machinery of various sorts is the major item, that come from the United States make up only about 12 percent of US exports. It is often said that when the United States sneezes, Mexico catches a cold. There is a good deal of scholarly and political discussion about what this all means, but from a common sense perspective it looks like Mexico is still locked into a highly asymmetrical relationship, only now with its immediate northern sister republic rather than Spain, as in the colonial period. Whether or not this asymmetry places the country in a "neocolonial" position vis-à-vis the United States has largely to do with how much freedom of action Mexico enjoys in terms of the global economy and the internal allocation of all sorts of resources.

Finally, in modern Mexico the social and cultural strands of society prove difficult to pry apart because formal patterns of hierarchy and barriers of exclusion disappeared with independence or shortly thereafter. Among these were the systems of the "dos repúblicas" and "castas," the titled aristocracy, sumptuary laws mandating social limitations on the consumption of certain prestige goods, exclusions from professions and offices on the basis of racial ascription, Black slavery, and craft guilds. While class distinctions existed in the late colonial era—that is, to put it crudely, differences between those who owned the means of production and those who worked for the owners, with a vast pool of self-employed small-scale producers between the two, themselves often with bonds of dependency to superordinate groups—they reinforced and were reinforced by socioethnic criteria, what was known as *calidad* (quality), and have only emerged clearly over time. This blurring of class distinctions by ethnic ones, by the way, is what has made the 1810–1821 insurgency difficult to cast in the mold of traditional class models of mass political violence and revolution. In the colonial era *calidad* embraced skin color, language (Spanish and/or an Indigenous tongue), place of origin and community membership, and other variables. Most of the *formal* disadvantages adhering to the status of *indio* (Indian), for example, were swept away with independence and the accompanying political changes. I have already mentioned that this paved the way for some upward economic and political, and to some degree social, mobility for men of color, particularly below the top levels of the social and political worlds. Several of the insurgent leaders of color, for instance, survived to carve out regional *cacicazgos* for themselves, and there was a general loosening up of invidious color-based distinctions and barriers in society. Moreover, by mid-century liberal president Benito Juárez, of pure Indigenous origins, led the country through a tempestuous time, and for the last quarter of the nineteenth century and the first decade of the twentieth Porfirio Díaz, of mixed Indigenous and Creole heritage, did the same.[2]

Still, no matter what the semiofficial rhetoric about today's Mexico embodying a "cosmic race," the country is far from being a color- or ethnic-blind society. The stigma of Indianness goes back to the colonial era, when the "Indian" was invented by the invading Spaniards; there were native-born inhabitants of Mesoamerica in 1518, of course, but no Indians as such. The strong traces of colonial attitudes about the inferiority of Indigenous people, and the modern racialist attitudes they engendered, definitely slipped the weave of decolonization and are everywhere visible in Mexican society. If one looks at today's political elite it is difficult to avoid the impression that with few exceptions the upper ranks of the country's leadership look more Mediterranean, or perhaps mestizo, than Indigenous, and the same tendency exists with regard to cultural life, as well as the upper reaches of the economic pyramid. There is upward economic and political mobility in today's Mexico, although how far it extends into the social realms of marriage and other intimate relationships of family, friendship, and elective affinity is difficult to say—probably not far. Recent studies have found that while there is considerable mobility within the middle quartiles (the middle 50 percent) of the population, there is little downward movement from the top quarter of the population and little upward mobility from the bottom quarter. Exemplified by the boy from humble beginnings who achieves wealth and power, often during times of political upheaval and through considerable violence, upward mobility is made much of in literature and film. For example, there are the novels *The Death of Artemio Cruz* (1962, English translation 1991) by Carlos Fuentes (said to have been strongly influenced by the story arc in Orson Welles's film *Citizen Kane* [1940]), the much more recent *El resplandor de la madera* (1999) by Héctor Aguilar Camín, and other works. This is also, of course, a theme in American literature, but the same cultural phenomenon in the two cases has different origins, and for the most part the protagonists face different obstacles in their upward striving. In Mexico it is difficult to say if such mobility is depicted because it is common or celebrated because it is uncommon. But ethnicity and its most readily identifiable markers, color and "Indigenous" features, still play a social role, especially in keeping an ethnically marked underclass from moving up. Much of this stagnation, now ascribed to class position, is fundamentally related to modern forms of *calidad*, although the stereotypes associated with it nowhere appear in visual representations as explicit as the *casta* paintings I described in chapter 2. The handicaps in Mexican society of the dark skin color linked to "Indianness," filtered through the lens of art, are on display in the autobiographical, multiple prize–winning 2018 film *Roma* by Mexican writer-director Alfonso Cuarón. An Indigenous woman from the heavily Indigenous state of Oaxaca is shown as the servant of a middle-class Mexico City family, much loved by the children of the household and up to a point viewed by the parents as a member of the family but in the end still a servant and an Indigenous person with uncertain prospects for advancement in life, at least within the bounds of the film.

Reinventing the country from a colonial society to a modern one was certainly the ambition of many of the men who sought to guide the national fortunes in the early republic, while certain aspects of state-sponsored modernization were put in place by the Spanish Bourbon regime in the late colonial period, if more for the benefit of the metropolitan power than for Mexico itself, which was still seen as an imperial cash cow. The verdict on decolonization and modernization must be a mixed one. In many ways Mexico is a modern society, and in others it still bears the marks of its colonial life after more than two centuries, although to speak of a "colonial heritage" as historians sometimes do seems overly deterministic. Mexico is not alone in these continuities, of course, because all societies carry their past into their present. As historian Tom Passananti has put it eloquently, many modern societies bear the scars or wounds of their colonial past, none more pernicious than the invention and application of categories of race to control colonial subjects.[3] But not all pasts have been colonial, nor all presents as unstable as Mexico's.

Given the country's history, perhaps the remarkable thing is not how much of the present is undecolonized but rather how modern it has become.

NOTES

1. Carleton Beals, *Porfirio Díaz, Dictator of Mexico* (London: J. B. Lippincott, 1932).

2. It is believed that as he grew older Díaz applied face powder to lighten his dark skin to a more acceptable "mestizo" tone.

3. Tom Passananti, personal communication, February 22, 2021.

For Further Reading

Note: I have included here a large number of works in Spanish, almost exclusively by Mexican scholars, on the assumption that many of this book's readers can read Spanish. They may want to consult a broader range of secondary works than the fine studies available in English, and much of the best work on this century has been done by Mexican historians.

CHAPTER 2

Alberro, Solange, et al. *Cultura, ideas y mentalidades.* Mexico City: El Colegio de México, 1992.

Alcubierre Moya, Beatriz. *Niños de nadie: Usos de la infancia menesterosa en el contexto borbónico.* Mexico City: Bonilla Artigas Editores/Universidad Autónoma del Estado de Morelos, 2017.

Arenal, Jaime, and Elisa Speckman Guerra, eds. *El mundo del derecho: Aproximaciones a la cultura jurídica novohispana y mexicana (siglos XIX y XX).* Mexico City: Instituto de Investigaciones Históricas, Universidad Nacional Autónoma de México, 2009.

Ávila, Dolores, Inés Herrera, and Rina Ortiz, eds. *Empresarios y política minera: Primera reunión de la minería latinoamericana.* Mexico City: Instituto Nacional de Antropología e Historia, 1992.

Blázquez Domínguez, Carmen, Carlos Contreras Cruz, and Sonia Pérez Toledo, eds. *Población y estructura urbana en México, siglos XVIII y XIX.* Xalapa: Universidad Veracruzana, 1996.

Brading, David A. *Church and State in Bourbon Mexico: The Diocese of Michoacán, 1749–1810.* Cambridge: Cambridge University Press, 1994.

Brading, David A. *Mexican Phoenix. Our Lady of Guadalupe: Image and Tradition across Five Centuries.* Cambridge: Cambridge University Press, 2001.

Castañeda García, Carmen. *La educación en Guadalajara durante la colonia (1552–1821).* Mexico City: Centro de Investigación y Estudios Superiores en Antropología Social, 2012.

Castañeda García, Carmen. *Violación, estupro y sexualidad: Nueva Galicia, 1790–1821.* Guadalajara: Editorial Hexágono, 1989.

Cooper, Donald B. *Epidemic Disease in Mexico City, 1761–1813.* Austin: University of Texas Press, 1965.

Fisher, Andrew B. "Worlds in Flux, Identities in Motion: A History of the Tierra Caliente of Guerrero, 1521–1821." PhD dissertation, University of California, San Diego, 2002.

Fisher, Andrew B., and Matthew D. O'Hara, eds. *Imperial Subjects: Race and Identity in Colonial Latin America.* Durham: Duke University Press, 2009.

Florescano, Enrique. *Memory, Myth, and Time in Mexico: From the Aztecs to Independence.* Translated by Albert G. Bork with the assistance of Kathryn R. Bork. Austin: University of Texas Press, 1994.

Guardino, Peter. *The Time of Liberty: Popular Political Culture in Oaxaca, 1750–1850.* Durham: Duke University Press, 2005.

Katzew, Ilona. *Casta Painting: Images of Race in Eighteenth-Century Mexico.* New Haven, CT: Yale University Press, 2005.

Katzew, Ilona, and Susan Deans-Smith, eds. *Race Classification: The Case of Mexican America.* Stanford: Stanford University Press, 2009.

Kicza, John A. *Colonial Entrepreneurs: Families and Business in Bourbon Mexico City.* Albuquerque: University of New Mexico Press, 1983.

Knight, Alan. *Mexico: The Colonial Era.* Cambridge: Cambridge University Press, 2002.

Ladd, Doris M. *The Mexican Nobility at Independence, 1780–1826.* Austin: University of Texas Press, 1976.

Lozano Armendares, Teresa. *La criminalidad en la ciudad de México, 1800–1821.* Mexico City: Universidad Nacional Autónoma de México, 1987.

Martin, Cheryl E. *Rural Society in Colonial Morelos.* Albuquerque: University of New Mexico Press, 1985.

Martínez-López, María Elena. *Genealogical Fictions: Limpieza de Sangre, Religion, and Gender in Colonial Mexico.* Stanford: Stanford University Press, 2008.

McCaa, Robert. "The Peopling of Mexico from Origins to Revolution." http://www.hist.umn.edu/~rmccaa/mxpoprev/cambridg3.htm.

Molina del Villar, América, Lourdes Márquez Morfín, and Claudia Patricia Pardo Hernández, eds. *El miedo a morir: Endemias, epidemias y pandemias en México, análisis de larga duración.* Mexico City: Centro de Investigaciones y Estudios Superiores en Antropología Social, 2013.

O'Hara, Matthew D. *A Flock Divided: Race, Religion, and Politics in Mexico, 1749–1857.* Durham: Duke University Press, 2010.

Pérez Rosales, Laura. *Familia, poder, riqueza y subversión: Los Fagoaga novohispanos 1730–1830.* Mexico City: Universidad Iberoamericana, 2003.

Ruiz Guadalajara, Juan Carlos. *Dolores antes de la independencia: Microhistoria del altar de la patria.* 2 vols. San Luis Potosí: El Colegio de San Luis, 2004.

Santiago, Mark. *The Red Captain: The Life of Hugo O'Conor, Commandant Inspector of the Interior Provinces of New Spain.* Tucson: Arizona Historical Society, 1994.

Taylor, William B. *Drinking, Homicide and Rebellion in Colonial Mexican Villages.* Stanford: Stanford University Press, 1979.

Taylor, William B. *Magistrates of the Sacred: Priests and Parishioners in Eighteenth-Century Mexico.* Stanford: Stanford University Press, 1996.

Vinson, Ben, III. *Before Mestizaje: The Frontiers of Race and Caste in Colonial Mexico.* New York: Cambridge University Press, 2018.

Vinson, Ben, III, and Matthew Restall. *Black Mexico: Race and Society from Colonial to Modern Times.* Albuquerque: University of New Mexico Press, 2009.

Viqueira Albán, Juan Pedro. *Propriety and Permissiveness in Bourbon Mexico.* Translated by Sonya Lipsett-Rivera and Sergio Rivera Ayala. Wilmington, DE: Scholarly Resources Books, 1987.

Voekel, Pamela. *Alone Before God: The Religious Origins of Modernity in Mexico.* Durham: Duke University Press, 2002.

CHAPTER 3

Amith, Jonathan D. *The Möbius Strip: A Spatial History of Colonial Society in Guerrero, Mexico.* Stanford: Stanford University Press, 2005.

Barrett, Ward J. *The Sugar Hacienda of the Marqueses del Valle.* Minneapolis: University of Minnesota Press, 1970.

Baskes, Jeremy. *Indians, Merchants, and Markets: A Reinterpretation of the Repartimiento and Spanish-Indian Economic Relations in Colonial Oaxaca, 1750–1821.* Stanford: Stanford University Press, 2000.

Brading, David A. *Haciendas and Ranchos in the Mexican Bajío, León 1700–1860.* Cambridge: Cambridge University Press, 1978.

Brading, David A. *Miners and Merchants in Bourbon Mexico, 1763–1810.* Cambridge: Cambridge University Press, 1971.

Bulmer-Thomas, Victor, John H. Coatsworth, and Roberto Cortés Conde, eds. *The Cambridge Economic History of Latin America. Vol. 1, The Colonial Era and the Short Nineteenth Century.* Cambridge: Cambridge University Press, 2006.

Castleman, Bruce. *Building the King's Highway: Labor, Society, and Family on Mexico's Caminos Reales, 1757–1804.* Tucson: University of Arizona Press, 2005.

Chowning, Margaret. *Wealth and Power in Provincial Mexico: Michoacán from the Late Colony to the Revolution.* Stanford: Stanford University Press, 1999.

Coatsworth, John H. *Los orígenes del atraso: Nueve ensayos de historia económica de México en los siglos XVIII y XIX.* Translated by Juan José Trujilla. Mexico City: Alianza Editorial, 1990.

Couturier, Edith B. *The Silver King: The Remarkable Life of the Count of Regla in Colonial Mexico.* Albuquerque: University of New Mexico Press, 2003.

Del Valle Pavón, Guillermina. *Donativos, préstamos y privilegios: Los mercaderes y mineros de la Ciudad de México durante la guerra anglo-española de 1779–1783.* Mexico City: Instituto de Investigaciones Dr. José María Luis Mora, 2016.

Del Valle Pavón, Guillermina. *Finanzas piadosas y redes de negocios: Los mercaderes de la ciudad de México ante la crisis de Nueva España, 1804–1808.* Mexico City: Instituto de Investigaciones Dr. José María Luis Mora, 2012.

Del Valle Pavón, Guillermina, ed. *Mercaderes, comercio y consulados de Nueva España en el siglo XVIII.* Mexico City: Instituto de Investigaciones Dr. José María Luis Mora, 2003.

Flores Clair, Eduardo. *Minería, educación y sociedad: El Colegio de Minería, 1774– 1821.* Mexico City: Instituto Nacional de Antropología e Historia, 2000.

Florescano, Enrique. *Precios del maíz y crisis agrícolas en México, 1708–1810: Ensayo sobre el movimiento de precios y sus consecuencias económicas y sociales.* Mexico City: El Colegio de México, 1969.

García Martínez, Bernardo. *El Marquesado del Valle: Tres siglos de régimen señorial en Nueva España.* Mexico City: El Colegio de México, 1969.

Garner, Richard L., with Spiro E. Stefanou. *Economic Growth and Change in Bourbon Mexico.* Gainesville: University Press of Florida, 1993.

Greenow, Linda. *Credit and Socioeconomic Change in Colonial Mexico: Loans and Mortgages in Guadalajara, 1720–1820.* Boulder: Westview Press, 1983.

Hamnett, Brian R. *Politics and Trade in Southern Mexico, 1750–1821.* Cambridge: Cambridge University Press, 1971.

Hoberman, Louisa S., and Susan M. Socolow, eds. *The Countryside in Colonial Latin America.* Albuquerque: University of New Mexico Press, 1996.

Humboldt, Alexander von. *Ensayo político sobre el Reino de la Nueva España.* Edited by Juan A. Ortega y Medina. 1803; Mexico City: Editorial Porrúa, 1966.

Ibarra Romero, Antonio. *La organización regional del mercado interno novohispano: La economía colonial de Guadalajara, 1770–1804.* Puebla: Benemérito Universidad Autónoma de Puebla/Universidad Nacional Autónoma de México, 2000.

Ibarra Romero, Antonio, and Guillermina del Valle Pavón, eds. *Redes sociales e instituciones comerciales en el imperio español, siglos XVII a XIX.* Mexico City: Universidad Nacional Autónoma de México/Instituto Mora, 2007.

Konrad, Herman W. *A Jesuit Hacienda in Colonial Mexico: Santa Lucía, 1576–1767.* Stanford: Stanford University Press, 1980.

López Miramontes, Alvaro, and Cristina Urrutia de Stebelski, eds. *Las minas de Nueva España en 1774.* Mexico City: Secretaría de Educación Pública/Instituto Nacional de Antropología e Historia, 1980.

Pérez Herrero, Pedro. *Plata y libranzas: La articulación comercial del México borbónico.* Mexico City: El Colegio de México, 1988.

Salvucci, Richard J. *Textiles and Capitalism in Mexico: An Economic History of the Obrajes, 1539–1840.* Princeton: Princeton University Press, 1987.

Stein, Barbara H., and Stanley J. Stein. *Crisis in an Atlantic Empire: Spain and New Spain, 1808–1810.* Baltimore: Johns Hopkins University Press, 2014.

Suárez Arguello, Clara Elena. *Camino real y carrera larga: La arriería en la Nueva España durante el siglo XVIII.* Mexico City: Centro de Investigación y Estudios Superiores en Antropología Social, 1997.

Taylor, William B. *Landlord and Peasant in Colonial Oaxaca.* Stanford: Stanford University Press, 1972.

Thomson, Guy P. C. *Puebla de los Angeles: Industry and Society in a Mexican City, 1700–1850.* Boulder: Westview Press, 1989.

Tutino, John. *Making a New World: Founding Capitalism in the Bajío and Spanish North America.* Durham: Duke University Press, 2011.

Van Young, Eric. *Economía, política y cultura en la historia de México: Ensayos historiográficos, metodológicos y teóricos de tres décadas.* Translated by Victoria Shussheim. San Luis Potosí: El Colegio de San Luis/El Colegio de Michoacán/El Colegio de la Frontera Norte, 2010.

Van Young, Eric. *Hacienda and Market in Eighteenth-Century Mexico: The Rural Economy of the Guadalajara Region, 1680–1820.* Berkeley: University of California Press, 1981.

Van Young, Eric. *La crisis del orden colonial: Estructura agraria y rebeliones populares de la Nueva España, 1750–1821.* Mexico City: Alianza Editorial, 1992.

Van Young, Eric, ed. *Mexico's Regions: Comparative History and Development.* San Diego: Center for US-Mexican Studies, University of California, San Diego, 1992.

von Wobeser, Gisela. *El crédito eclesiástico en la Nueva España, siglo XVIII.* Mexico City: Universidad Nacional Autónoma de México, 1994.

CHAPTER 4

Alberro, Solange, Alicia Hernández Chávez, and Elías Trabulse, eds. *La revolución francesa en México.* Mexico City: El Colegio de México, 1993.

Benson, Nettie Lee. *The Provincial Deputation in Mexico: Harbinger of Provincial Autonomy, Independence, and Federalism.* Austin: University of Texas Press, 1992.

Brading, David A. *The First America: The Spanish Monarchy, Creole Patriots, and the Liberal State, 1492–1867.* Cambridge: Cambridge University Press, 1991.

Breña, Roberto, ed. *Cádiz a debate: Actualidad, contexto y legado.* Mexico City: El Colegio de México, 2012.

Breña, Roberto. *El Imperio de las circunstancias: Las independencias hispanoamericanas y la revolución liberal española.* Mexico City: El Colegio de México, 2013.

Breña, Roberto, ed. *En el umbral de las revoluciones hispánicas: el bienio 1808–1810.* Mexico City: El Colegio de México, 2010.

Chust, Manuel. *La cuestión nacional americana en las Cortes de Cádiz (1810–1814).* Valencia, Spain: Fundación Instituto Historia Social/Instituto de Investigaciones Históricas de la Universidad Nacional Autónoma de México, 1999.

Chust, Manuel, and Ivana Frasquet, eds. *La Trascendencia del liberalismo doceañista en España y en América.* Valencia, Spain: Generalitat Valenciana, n.d.

Connaughton, Brian F. *Clerical Ideology in a Revolutionary Age: The Guadalajara Church and the Idea of the Mexican Nation (1788–1853).* Translated by Mark Alan Healey. Calgary: University of Calgary Press/University Press of Colorado, 2003.

Díaz Zermeño, Héctor. *La masonería como sociedad de ideas contrapunteadas, en el proceso de la independencia de Hispanoamérica y México, 1782–1833*. Mexico City: Universidad Nacional Autónoma de México-Acatlán, 2009.

Garrido Asperó, María José. *Fiestas cívicas históricas en la ciudad de México, 1765–1823*. Mexico City: Instituto de Investigaciones Dr. José María Luis Mora, 2006.

Ouweneel, Arij. *The Flight of the Shepherd: Microhistory and the Psychology of Cultural Resilience in Bourbon Central Mexico*. Amsterdam: Aksant, 2005.

Rodriguez O., Jaime E., ed. *Mexico in the Age of Democratic Revolutions, 1750–1850*. Boulder: Lynne Rienner Publishers, 1994.

Ruiz Medrano, Carlos. *Las sombrías aventuras del rey tlaxcalteco Juan Vicencio de Córdova y los rebeldes de Colotlán, Jalisco, 1777–1783*. San Luis Potosí: El Colegio de San Luis, 2011.

Serrano Ortega, José Antonio, ed. *El sexenio absolutista: Los últimos años insurgentes, Nueva España (1814–1820)*. Zamora, Michoacán: El Colegio de Michoacán, 2014.

Uribe-Urán, Victor, ed. *State and Society in Spanish America during the Age of Revolution*. Wilmington, DE: Scholarly Resources Books, 2001.

Zepeda Cortés, María Bárbara. "Empire, Reform, and Corruption: José de Gálvez and Political Culture in the Spanish World, 1765–1787." PhD dissertation, University of California, San Diego, 2013.

CHAPTERS 5, 6, AND 7

Alamán, Lucas. *Historia de Méjico desde los primeros movimientos que prepararon su independencia en el año de 1808, hasta la época presente*. Second edition. 5 vols. 1849–1852; Mexico City: Editorial Jus, 1968.

Almada Bay, Ignacio, and José Marcos Medina Bustos, eds. *De los márgenes al centro. Sonora en la Independencia y la Revolución: cambios y continuidades*. Hermosillo: El Colegio de Sonora, 2010.

Anna, Timothy E. *The Fall of the Royal Government in Mexico City*. Lincoln: University of Nebraska Press, 1978.

Annino, Antonio, and Rafael Rojas. *La Independencia*. Mexico City: Centro de Investigación y Docencia Económica/Fondo de Cultura Económica, 2008.

Ávila, Alfredo. *En nombre de la nación: La formación del gobierno representativo en México (1808–1824)*. Mexico City: Taurus/Centro de Investigación y Docencia Económica, 1999.

Brading, David A. *Prophecy and Myth in Mexican History*. Cambridge: Centre of Latin American Studies, Cambridge University, 1984.

Breña, Roberto. *El primer liberalismo español y los procesos de emancipación de América, 1808–1824: Una revisión historiográfica del liberalismo hispánico*. Mexico City: El Colegio de México, 2006.

Bustamante, Carlos María de. *Cuadro histórico de la revolución mexicana, iniciada el 15 de septiembre de 1810 por el C. Miguel Hidalgo y Costilla, cura del pueblo de Dolores en el obispado de Michoacán*. 3 vols. 1823–1832; Mexico City:

Ediciones de la Comisión Nacional para la Celebración del Sesquicentenario de la Proclamación de la Independencia Nacional y del Cincuentenario de la Revolución Mexicana, 1961.

Costeloe, Michael P. *Response to Revolution: Imperial Spain and the Spanish American Revolutions, 1810–1840*. Cambridge: Cambridge University Press, 1986.

De la Torre Villar, Ernesto. *La Independencia mexicana*. 3 vols. Mexico City: Fondo de Cultura Económica, 1982.

Ducey, Michael T. *A Nation of Villages: Riot and Rebellion in the Mexican Huasteca, 1750–1850*. Tucson: University of Arizona Press, 2004.

Esdaile, Charles. *The Peninsular War: A New History*. New York: Palgrave MacMillan, 2003.

Flores Caballero, Romeo. *Counterrevolution: The Role of the Spaniards in the Independence of Mexico, 1804–38*. Translated by Jaime E. Rodríguez O. Lincoln: University of Nebraska Press, 1974.

Florescano, Enrique, and Victoria San Vicente, eds. *Fuentes para la historia de la crisis agrícola (1809–1811)*. Mexico City: Universidad Nacional Autónoma de México, 1985.

González y González, Luis. *Once ensayos de tema insurgente*. Zamora: El Colegio de Michoacán, 1985.

Granados, Luis Fernando. *En el espejo haitiano: Los indios del Bajío y el colapso del orden colonial en América Latina*. Mexico City: Ediciones Era, 2016.

Guedea, Virginia. *En busca de un gobierno alterno: Los Guadalupes de México*. Mexico City: Universidad Nacional Autónoma de México, 1992.

Guerra, François-Xavier. *Modernidad e independencias: Ensayos sobre las revoluciones hispánicas*. Mexico City: Editorial Mapfre/Fondo de Cultura Económica, 1992.

Hamill, Hugh M. *The Hidalgo Revolt: Prelude to Mexican Independence*. Gainesville: University of Florida Press, 1966.

Hamnett, Brian R. *Roots of Insurgency: Mexican Regions, 1750–1824*. Cambridge: Cambridge University Press, 1986.

Jiménez Codinach, Guadalupe. *México en 1821: Dominique de Pradt y el Plan de Iguala*. Mexico City: Ediciones el Caballito/Universidad Iberoamericana, 1982.

León-Portilla, Miguel, and Alicia Meyer, eds. *Los indígenas en la Independencia y en la Revolución Mexicana*. Mexico City: Universidad Nacional Autónoma de México, 2010.

Morelos, José María. *Morelos: Documentos inéditos y poco conocidos*. 3 vols. Mexico City: Secretaría de Educación Pública, 1927.

Ortiz Escamilla, Juan. *Guerra y gobierno: Los pueblos y la independencia de México*. Mexico City: Instituto de Investigaciones Dr. José María Luis Mora, 1997.

Rodríguez O., Jaime E. *The Emergence of Spanish America: Vicente Rocafuerte and Spanish Americanism, 1808–1832*. Berkeley: University of California Press, 1975.

Rodríguez O., Jaime E. *"We Are Now the True Spaniards": Sovereignty, Revolution, Independence, and the Emergence of the Federal Republic of Mexico, 1808–1824*. Stanford: Stanford University Press, 2012.

Simon, Joshua. *The Ideology of Creole Revolution: Imperialism and Independence in American and Latin American Political Thought.* Cambridge: Cambridge University Press, 2017.
Timmons, Wilbert H. *Morelos of Mexico: Priest, Soldier, Statesman.* El Paso: Texas Western Press, 1963.
Tutino, John. *From Insurrection to Revolution in Mexico: Social Bases of Agrarian Violence, 1750–1940.* Princeton: Princeton University Press, 1986.
Van Young, Eric. *The Other Rebellion: Popular Violence, Ideology, and the Mexican Struggle for Independence, 1810–1821.* Stanford: Stanford University Press, 2001.
Villaseñor y Villaseñor, Alejandro. *Biografías de los héroes y caudillos de la independencia.* 2 vols. Mexico City: Editorial Jus, 1962.
Villoro, Luis. *El proceso ideológico de la revolución de Independencia.* Mexico City: Secretaría de Educación Pública, 1986.
Zavala, Lorenzo de. *Ensayo crítico de las revoluciones de México desde 1808 hasta 1830.* 2 vols. Mexico City: Editorial Porrúa, 1969.

CHAPTER 8

Anna, Timothy E. *Forging Mexico: 1821–1835.* Lincoln: University of Nebraska Press, 1998.
Anna, Timothy E. *The Mexican Empire of Iturbide.* Lincoln: University of Nebraska Press, 1990.
Aguilar Rivera, José Antonio. *Ausentes del universo: Reflexiones sobre el pensamiento político hispanoamericano en la era de la construcción nacional, 1821–1850.* Mexico City: Fondo de Cultura Económica, 2012.
Aguilar Rivera, José Antonio, and Rafael Rojas, eds. *El republicanismo en Hispanoamérica: Ensayos de historia intellectual y política.* Mexico City: Centro de Investigación y Docencia Económica/Fondo de Cultura Económica, 2002.
Andrews, Catharine. *Entre la espada y la constitución: El general Anastasio Bustamante, 1780–1853.* Tamaulipas, Mexico: Universidad Autónoma de Tamaulipas/H. Congreso del Estado de Tamaulipas, LX Legislatura, 2008.
Arnold, Linda. *Bureaucracy and Bureaucrats in Mexico City, 1742–1835.* Tucson: University of Arizona Press, 1988.
Avila, Alfredo. *Para la libertad: Los republicanos en tiempos del imperio, 1821–1823.* Mexico City: Universidad Nacional Autónoma de México, 2004.
Bosch García, Carlos. *El mester político de Poinsett (noviembre de 1824–diciembre de 1829).* In *Documentos de la relación de México con los Estados Unidos.* Mexico City: Universidad Nacional Autónoma de México, 1983.
Bosch García, Carlos. *Problemas diplomáticos del México independiente.* Mexico City: El Colegio de México, 1947.
Brading, David A. *The Origins of Mexican Nationalism.* Cambridge: Centre of Latin American Studies, University of Cambridge, 1985.

Bullock, William. *Six Months' Residence and Travels in Mexico, Containing Remarks on the Present State of New Spain* . . . . 1824; Port Washington, NY: Kennikat Press, 1971.

Bustamante, José María de. *Diario histórico de México, 1822–1848.* Edited by Josefina Zoraida Vázquez and Héctor Cuauhtémoc Hernández Silva. 3 vols. on 2 CD-ROMs. Mexico City: El Colegio de México/Centro de Investigaciones y Estudios Superiores en Antropología Social, 2001–2003.

Castellanos, Francisco. *El Trueno, gloria y martirio de Agustín de Iturbide.* Mexico City: Editorial Diana, 1982.

Costeloe, Michael P. *La primera república federal de México (1824–1835): Un estudio de los partidos politicos en el México independiente.* Translation by Manuel Fernández Gasalla. Mexico City: Fondo de Cultura Económica, 1983.

di Tella, Torcuato S. *Política nacional y popular en México, 1820–1847.* Mexico City: Fondo de Cultura Económica, 1994.

Domínguez Michael, Christopher. *Vida de Fray Servando.* Mexico City: Ediciones Era, 2005.

Ferrer Muñoz, Manuel. *La formación de un estado nacional en México: El Imperio y la República federal, 1821–1835.* Mexico City: Universidad Nacional Autónoma de México, 1995.

Fuentes Mares, José. *Poinsett, historia de una gran intriga.* Mexico City: Editorial Jus, 1964.

Gaxiola, Francisco Javier. *Poinsett en México (1822–1828): Notas de un libro inconcluso.* Mexico City: Editorial "Cultura," 1936.

Green, Stanley C. *The Mexican Republic: The First Decade, 1823–1832.* Pittsburgh: University of Pittsburgh Press, 1987.

Hale, Charles A. *Mexican Liberalism in the Age of Mora, 1821–1853.* New Haven, CT: Yale University Press, 1968.

Hernández Franyuti, Regina, ed. *La Ciudad de México en la primera mitad del Siglo XIX.* 2 vols. Mexico City: Instituto de Investigaciones Dr. José María Luis Mora, 1994.

Lafragua, José María. *Vicente Guerrero, mártir de Cuilapam, biografía.* Edited and with notes by Jorge Fernando Iturribarría. Mexico City: Secretaría de Educación Pública, 1946.

Márquez Morfín, Lourdes. *La desigualdad ante la muerte en la ciudad de México: El tifo y el cólera (1813 y 1833).* Mexico City: Siglo Veintiuno Editores, 1994.

Mayer, Brantz. *México, lo que fue y lo que es.* Prologue and notes by Juan A. Ortega y Medina. Mexico City: Fondo de Cultura Ecnómica, 1953.

Memorias de los ministros del interior y del exterior: La Primera República Federal, 1823–1835. Proyecto y estudio preliminar de Tarsicio García. Mexico City: Instituto Nacional de Estudios Históricos de la Revolución Mexicana/Secretaría de Gobernación, 1987.

Méndez Reyes, Salvador. *El hispanoamericanismo de Lucas Alamán (1823–1853).* Toluca: Universidad Autónoma del Estado de México, 1996.

Miño Grijalva, Manuel, ed. *Raices del federalismo mexicano.* Zacatecas: Universidad Autónoma de Zacatecas, 2005.

Nebel, Carl. *Voyage pittoresque e archéologique dans la partie la plus intéressante de Mexique*. Paris: M. Moench, 1836.

Pérez Toledo, Sonia, and Herbert S. Klein. *Población y estructura social de la Ciudad de México, 1790–1842*. Mexico City: Universidad Autónoma Metropolitana-Iztapalapa, 2004.

Poinsett, Joel Roberts. *Notes on Mexico, Made in the Autumn of 1822. Accompanied by an Historical Sketch of the Revolution and Translations of Official Reports on the Present State of that Country*. London: John Miller, 1825.

Reyes Heroles, Jesús. *El liberalismo en México*. 3 vols. Mexico City: Fondo de Cultura Económica, 1974.

Rippy, J. Fred. *Joel R. Poinsett, Versatile American*. Durham: Duke University Press, 1935.

Ruiz de Gordejuela Urquijo, Jesús. *La expulsión de los españoles de México y su destino incierto, 1821–1836*. Madrid: Diputación de Sevilla, Universidad de Sevilla, 2006.

Serrano Ortega, José Antonio. *Hacienda y política: Las finanzas públicas y los grupos de poder en la Primera República federal mexicana*. Zamora: El Colegio de Michoacán, 1998.

Serrano Ortega, José Antonio. *Igualdad, uniformidad, y proporcionalidad: Contribuciones directas y reformas fiscales en México, 1810–1846*. Mexico City: Instituto de Investigaciónes Dr. José María Luis Mora/El Colegio de Michoacán, 2007.

Sims, Harold D. *The Expulsion of Mexico's Spaniards, 1821–1836*. Pittsburgh: University of Pittsburgh Press, 1990.

Staples, Anne, ed. *Educar: Panacea del Mexico independiente*. Mexico City: Secretaría de Educación Pública, 1985.

Stevens, Donald F. *Origins of Instability in Early Republican Mexico*. Durham: Duke University Press, 1991.

Tayloe, Edward Thornton. *Mexico, 1825–1828: The Journal and Correspondence of Edward Thornton Tayloe*. Edited by C. Harvey Gardiner. Chapel Hill: University of North Carolina Press, 1959.

Taylor, Bayard. *El Dorado, or Adventures in the Path of Empire*. Introduction by Robert Glass Cleland. New York: Alfred A. Knopf, 1949.

Tornel y Mendivil, José María. *Breve reseña histórica de los acontecimientos más notables de la nación mexicana desde el año de 1821 hasta nuestros días*. Mexico City: Imprenta de Cumplido, 1852.

Trabulse, Elías. *Ciencia y tecnología en el Nuevo Mundo*. Mexico City: El Colegio de México, 1994.

Valadés, José C. *Alamán: Estadista e historiador*. 1938; Mexico City: Universidad Nacional Autónoma de México, 1977.

Vázquez, Josefina Zoraida. *El establecimiento de federalismo en México, 1821–1827*. Mexico City: El Colegio de México, 2003.

Vázquez, Josefina Zoraida, and José Antonio Serrano Ortega, eds. *Práctica y fracaso del primer federalismo mexicano (1824–1835)*. Mexico City: El Colegio de México, 2012.

Vázquez-Semadeni, María Eugenia. *La formación de una cultura política republicana: El debate sobre la masonería en México, 1821–1830*. Mexico City: Instituto de Investigaciones Históricas, Universidad Nacional Autónoma de México, 2010.

Vincent, Theodore G. *The Legacy of Vicente Guerrero, Mexico's First Black Indian President*. Gainesville: University Press of Florida, 2001.

Waldeck, Frédéric de. *Voyage pittoresque e archéologique dans la province d'Yucatan (Amérique Centrale) pendant les années 1834 et 1835*. Paris: B. Dufour, 1838.

Ward, Henry George. *Mexico in 1827*. London: Colburn, 1828.

Warren, Richard A. *Vagrants and Citizens: Politics and the Masses in Mexico City from Colony to Republic*. Wilmington, DE: Scholarly Resources Books, 2001.

Weber, David J. *The Mexican Frontier, 1821–1846: The American Southwest under Mexico*. Albuquerque: University of New Mexico Press, 1982.

CHAPTER 9

Andrews, Catherine. *Entre la espada y la Constitución: El general Anastasio Bustamante, 1780–1853*. Ciudad Victoria, Tamaulipas: Universidad Autónoma de Tamaulipas, 2008.

Barker, Nancy Nicholls. *The French Experience in Mexico, 1821–1861: A History of Constant Misunderstanding*. Chapel Hill: University of North Carolina Press, 1979.

Beezley, William H., Cheryl English Martin, and William E. French, eds. *Rituals of Rule, Rituals of Resistance: Public Celebrations and Popular Culture in Mexico*. Wilmington, DE: Scholarly Resources, 1994.

Beezley, William H., and David E. Lorey, eds. *¡Viva Mexico! ¡Viva la Independencia! Celebrations of September 16*. Wilmington, DE: Scholarly Resources Books, 2001.

Briseño Senosiáin, Lillian, Laura Solares Robles, and Laura Suárez de la Torre. *Valentín Gómez Farías y su lucha por el federalismo, 1822–1858*. Mexico City: Instituto de Investigaciones Dr. José María Luis Mora, 1991.

Calderón de la Barca, Fanny. *Life in Mexico: The Letters of Fanny Calderón de la Barca, with New Material from the Author's Private Journals*. Edited by Howard T. Fisher and Marion Hall Fisher. New York: Anchor Books, 1970.

Castelán Rueda, Roberto. *La fuerza de la palabra impresa: Carlos María de Bustamante y el discurso de la modernidad*. Mexico City: Fondo de Cultura Económica, 1997.

Chasteen, John C. *Heroes on Horseback: A Life and Times of the Last Gaucho Caudillos*. Albuquerque: University of New Mexico Press, 1995.

Connaughton, Brian F. *Dimensiones de la identidad patriótica: Religión, política y regiones en México, siglo XIX*. Mexico City: Universidad Autónoma de México, Unidad Iztapalapa, 2001.

Connaughton, Brian F., Carlos Illades, and Sonia Pérez Toledo, eds. *Construcción de la legitimidad política en México*. Zamora, Michoacán: El Colegio de Michoacán, 1999.

Chowning, Margaret. *Rebellious Nuns: The Troubled History of a Mexican Convent, 1752–1863*. New York: Oxford University Press, 2006.

Costeloe, Michael P. *The Central Republic in Mexico, 1835–1846: Hombres de bien in the Age of Santa Anna*. Cambridge: Cambridge University Press, 1993.

Fowler, Will. *Independent Mexico: The Pronunciamiento in the Age of Santa Anna, 1821–1858*. Lincoln: University of Nebraska Press, 2016.

Fowler, Will. *Santa Anna of Mexico*. Lincoln: University of Nebraska Press, 2007.

Fuentes Mares, José. *Santa Anna, aurora y ocaso de un comediante*. Mexico City: Editorial Jus, 1967.

García Cantu, Gastón. *El pensamiento de la reacción Mexicana: Historia documental, 1810–1962*. Mexico City: Empresas Editoriales, 1965.

González Pedrero, Enrique. *País de un solo hombre: El México de Santa Anna*. 2 vols. Mexico City: Fondo de Cultura Económica, 2003.

Granados, Luis Fernando. *Sueñan las piedras: Alzamiento ocurrido en la ciudad de México, 14, 15 y 16 de septiembre de 1847*. Mexico City: Ediciones Era, 2003.

Griswold del Castillo, Richard. *The Treaty of Guadalupe Hidalgo: A Legacy of Conflict*. Norman: University of Oklahoma Press, 1990.

Guardino, Peter. *The Dead March: A History of the Mexican-American War*. Cambridge, MA: Harvard University Press, 2017.

Guardino, Peter. *Peasants, Politics, and the Formation of Mexico's National State: Guerrero, 1800–1857*. Stanford: Stanford University Press, 1996.

Hale, Charles A. "The War with the United States and the Crisis in Mexican Political Thought." *The Americas* 14, no. 2 (1957): 153–73.

Henderson, Timothy J. *A Glorious Defeat: Mexico and its War with the United States*. New York: Hill and Wang, 2007.

Henson, Margaret Swett. *Lorenzo de Zavala: The Pragmatic Idealist*. Fort Worth: Texas Christian University Press, 1996.

Hutchinson, C. A. *Valentín Gómez Farías: La vida de un republicano*. Translated by Marco Antonio Silva. Guadalajara: Unidad Editorial, Gobierno de Jalisco, 1983.

Katz, Friedrich, ed. *Riot, Rebellion, and Revolution: Rural Social Conflict in Mexico*. Princeton: Princeton University Press, 1988.

López de Santa Anna, Antonio. *Mi historia militar y política, 1810–1874*. [Mexico City]: Lindero Ediciones, 2001.

Meyer, Jean. *Problemas campesinos y revueltas agrarias (1821–1910)*. Mexico City: Secretaría de Educación Pública, 1973.

Morales Moreno, Humberto, and William Fowler, eds. *El Conservadurismo mexicano en el siglo XIX (1810–1910)*. Puebla, Mexico: Benemérita Universidad Autónoma de Puebla/Saint-Andrews University, 1999.

Morán Leyva, Paula. *Lucas Alamán*. Mexico City: Planeta DeAgostini, 2002.

Ojeda Dávila, Lorena. *El Establecimiento del Centralismo en Michoacán, 1833–1846*. Morelia, Michoacán: Universidad Michoacana de San Nicolás de Hidalgo, 2011.

Oliveira, Ruth R., and Liliane Crété. *Life in Mexico under Santa Anna, 1822–1855*. Norman: University of Oklahoma Press, 1991.

Olveda, Jaime. *Gordiano Guzmán, un cacique del siglo XIX*. Mexico City: Instituto Nactional de Antropología e Historia, 1980.

Palti, Elías José, ed. *La política del disenso: La "polémica en torno al monarquismo" (México, 1848–1850) . . . y las aporías del liberalismo*. Mexico City: Fondo de Cultura Económica, 1998.

Pani, Erika, ed. *Conservadurismo y derechas en la historia de México*. 2 vols. Mexico City: Fondo de Cultura Económica, 2009.

Pérez Toledo, Sonia, René Elizalde Salazar, and Luis Pérez Cruz, eds. *Las ciudades y sus estructuras: Población, espacio y cultura en México, siglos XVIII y XIX*. Mexico City: Universidad Autónoma de Tlaxcala/Universidad Autónoma Metropolitana-Iztapalapa, 1999.

Reid, Stuart. *The Secret War for Texas*. College Station: Texas A&M University Press, 2007.

Reina, Leticia. *Las rebeliones campesinas en México, 1819–1906*. Mexico City: Siglo XXI Editores, 1980.

Reséndez, Andrés. *Changing National Identities at the Frontier: Texas and New Mexico, 1800–1850*. Cambridge: Cambridge University Press, 2005.

Rives, George Lockhart. *The United States and Mexico: A History of the Relations between the Two Countries from the Independence of Mexico to the Close of the War with the United States*. 2 vols. New York: Charles Scribner's Sons, 1913; Krause reprint, 1969.

Rugeley, Terry. *Yucatán's Maya Peasantry and the Origins of the Caste War*. Austin: University of Texas Press, 1996.

Rugeley, Terry. *Rebellion Now and Forever: Mayas, Hispanics, and Caste War Violence in Yucatán, 1800–1880*. Stanford: Stanford University Press, 2009.

Salinas Sandoval, María del Carmen. *Política interna e invasión norteamericana en el Estado de México, 1846–1848*. Zinacantepec, Mexico: El Colegio Mexiquense, 2000.

Salinas Sandoval, María del Carmen, Diana Birrichaga Gardida, and Antonio Escobar Ohmstede, eds. *Poder y gobierno local en México, 1808–1857*. Toluca, Mexico: El Colegio Mexiquense/El Colegio de Michoacán/Universidad Autónoma del Estado de México, 2011.

Sinkin, Richard N. *The Mexican Reform, 1855–1876: A Study in Liberal Nation-Building*. Austin: Institute of Latin American Studies, University of Texas at Austin, 1979.

Smith, Justin H. *The War with Mexico*. 2 vols. New York: Macmillan, 1919.

Solares Robles, Laura. *Una revolución pacífica: biografía política de Manuel Gómez Pedraza, 1789–1851*. Mexico City: Instituto de Investigaciones Dr. José María Luis Mora, 1996.

Sordo Cedeño, Reynaldo. *El congreso en la primera república centralista*. Mexico City: El Colegio de México/Instituto Tecnológico Autónomo de México, 1993.

Soto, Miguel. *La conspiración monárquica en México, 1845–1846*. Mexico City: Editorial Offset, 1988.

Staples, Anne. *Recuento de una batalla inconclusa: La educación mexicana de Iturbide a Juárez*. Mexico City: El Colegio de México, 2005.

Tenenbaum, Barbara. *The Politics of Penury: Debts and Taxes in Mexico, 1821–1854*. Albuquerque: University of New Mexico Press, 1986.

Vázquez, Josefina Zoraida. *Dos décadas de desilusiones: En busca de una formula adecuada de gobierno (1832–1854).* Mexico City: El Colegio de México/Instituto de Investigaciones Dr. José María Luis Mora, 2009.

Vázquez Mantecón, Carmen. *La palabra del poder: Vida pública de José María Tornel (1795–1853).* Mexico City: Fondo de Cultura Económica, 1997.

Zaragoza, José. *Historia de la deuda externa de México, 1823–1861.* Mexico City: Universidad Nacional Autónoma de México, 1996.

CHAPTER 10

Aguirre Anaya, Carlos, Marcela Dávalos, and María Amparo Ros, eds. *Los espacios públicos de la ciudad: Siglos XVIII y XIX.* Mexico City: Instituto de Cultura de la Ciudad de México, 2002.

Arrom, Silvia Marina. *Containing the Poor: The Mexico City Poor House, 1774–1871.* Durham: Duke University Press, 2000.

Arrom, Silvia Marina. *The Women of Mexico City, 1790–1857.* Stanford: Stanford University Press, 1985.

Beatty, Edward. *Technology and the Search for Progress in Modern Mexico.* Oakland: University of California Press, 2015.

Bauer, Arnold J. *Goods, Power, History: Latin America's Material Culture.* Cambridge: Cambridge University Press, 2001.

Bernecker, Walter L. *De agiotistas y empresarios: En torno de la temprana industrialización mexicana (siglo XIX).* Translated by Perla Chinchilla. Mexico City: Universidad Iberoamericana, 1992.

Cañedo Gamboa, Sergio Alejandro. *Comercio, alcabalas y negocios de familia en San Luis Potosí, México: Crecimiento económico y poder político, 1820–1846.* Mexico City: El Colegio de San Luis/Instituto de Investigaciones Dr. José María Luis Mora, 2015.

Cárdenas, Enrique. *Cuando se originó el atraso económico de México: La economía mexicana en el largo siglo XIX, 1780–1920.* Madrid: Fundación Ortega y Gasset, 2003.

Cárdenas, Enrique. *El largo curso de la economía mexicana: De 1780 a nuestros días.* Mexico City: Fondo de Cultura Económica/El Colegio de México, 2015.

Cassidy, T. J. *British Capital and the Mexican Silver Mining Industry, 1820–1850.* Cambridge: Center of Latin-American Studies, Cambridge University, Working Papers, 27, n.d.

Colón Reyes, Linda Ivette. *Los orígenes de la burguesía y el Banco de Avío.* Mexico City: Ediciones el Caballito, 1982.

Gómez-Galvarriato, Aurora. *Industry and Revolution: Social and Economic Change in the Orizaba Valley, Mexico.* Cambridge, MA: Harvard University Press, 2013.

Gutiérrez López, Edgar Omar. *La inversión inglesa en la minería mexicana (Carácter histórico).* Mexico City: Dirección de Estudios Históricos, Instituto Nacional de Antropología e Historia, 1986.

Ibarra Bellón, Araceli. *El comercio y el poder en México: La lucha por las fuentes financieras entre el Estado central y las regiones.* Mexico City: Fondo de Cultura Económica, 1998.

Keremitsis, Dawn. *La industria textil mexicana en el siglo XIX.* Mexico City: Secretaría de Educación Pública, 1973.

Marichal, Carlos. *A Century of Debt Crises in Latin America: From Independence to the Great Depression, 1820–1930.* Princeton: Princeton University Press, 1989.

Moncada González, Gisela. *La libertad comercial: El sistema de abasto de alimentos en la ciudad de México, 1810–1835.* Mexico City: Instituto de Investigaciones Dr. José María Luis Mora, 2013.

Oliver, Lilia V. *Un Verano mortal: Análisis demográfico y social de una epidemia de cólera, Guadalajara, 1833.* Guadalajara: Unidad Editorial, Secretaría General, Gobierno de Jalisco, 1986.

Pérez Toledo, Sonia. *Los hijos del trabajo: Los artesanos de la Ciudad de México, 1780–1853.* Mexico City: Universidad Autónoma de México-Iztapalapa, 1996.

Pérez Toledo, Sonia. *Trabajadores, espacio urbano y sociabilidad en la Ciudad de México, 1790–1867.* Mexico City: Universidad Autónoma de México-Iztapalapa, 2011.

Potash, Robert A. *Mexican Government and Industrial Development in the Early Republic: The Banco de Avío.* Amherst: University of Massachusetts Press, 1983.

Randall, Robert W. *Real del Monte: A British Mining Venture in Mexico.* Austin: University of Texas Press, 1982.

Rippy, J. Fred. *British Investments in Latin America, 1822–1849: A Case Study in the Operations of Private Enterprise in Retarded Regions.* 1959; Hamden, CT: Archon Books, 1966.

Romero Flores, Jesús. *México, historia de una gran ciudad.* Mexico City: B. Costa-Amic Editor, 1978.

Salvatore, Ricardo D., and John H. Coatsworth, eds. *Living Standards in Latin American History: Height, Welfare and Development, 1750–2000.* Cambridge, MA: David Rockefeller Center for Latin American Studies, Harvard University, 2010.

Salvucci, Richard J. *Politics, Markets, and Mexico's "London" Debt, 1823–1887.* Cambridge: Cambridge University Press, 2009.

Trujillo Bolio, Mario. *Empresariado y manufactura textil en la Ciudad de México y su periferia. Siglo XIX.* Mexico City: Centro de Investigaciones y Estudios Superiores en Antropología Social, 2000.

Velasco Ávila, Cuauhtémoc, Eduardo Flores Clair, Alma Laura Parra Campos, and Edgar Omar Gutiérrez López. *Estado y minería en México (1767–1910).* Mexico City: Fondo de Cultura Económica, 1988.

Wasserman, Mark. *Everyday Life and Politics in Nineteenth-Century Mexico: Men, Women, and War.* Albuquerque: University of New Mexico Press, 2000.

Index

Valladolid, city of, *12*, **24**, 87, 120, 121,
132, 133, 138, 275–76, 278
Valladolid conspiracy (1809), 119, 124
Van Buren, Martin, 202, 229,
249, 270n2
Velasco Gómez, José María, *55*
Velázquez, Diego, 162
Venegas, Javier, 134, 136
Veracruz, city, *12*, 25, 30, 212,
256, 287, 298
in Pastry War with France, 240, 241;
Plan de Casa Mata conceived in, 191;
as a port city, 45, 62, 63, 185, 292;
Santa Anna, as hometown of,
189, 221, 227, 228, 237, 243,
261, 262, 266;
Spanish military forces as
bombarding, 171–72, 198;
textile production in, 15, 295, 296;
Treaty of Córdoba signed in, 171
Victoria, Guadalupe, 132, 183, 190,
194, 202, 217
Alamán in regime of, 202, 208, 221;
Guerrero as successor to, 204, 211;
as president, 165, 200, 203, 223, 245,
261–62, 289
Villagrán, José María (El Chito),
144–45, 146–47
Villagrán, Julián, 144–45
Virgin of Guadalupe, 10, 76, 101n3,
112, 124, 125, 160
Voltaire (François-Marie
Arouet), 99, 201

wage decline, 47, 273, 274–75, 305–6
Ward, Henry G., 283, 292
War of the South. *See* Guerra del Sur
War of the Spanish Succession (1701–
1714), 77, 79
Washington, George, 80, 201, 202
Wasserman, Mark, 298–99, 302, 307n3
Wealth of Nations (Smith), 82, 305
Wellington, Arthur Wellesley, 114, 135,
166, 247, 249
William of Orange, 78, 101n4

Yermo, Gabriel de, 118
Yorquinos of York Rite Masonry, 200,
201, 202, 204, 211, 212, 214, 223
Yucatán, state of, *12*, 138, 200, 244, 295
breaking away,
considering, 194, 195;
Caste War of Yucatán (1847–1901),
242, 251, 254, 256–61;
Yucatán Peninsula, 19, 27

Zacatecas, state of, 11, **24**, 147,
195, 247, 275
in cartography, *12*, *256;*
as a rebellious state, 151, 221;
silver mining in, 42, 43, 281
Zapata, Emiliano, 5, 256
Zavala, Lorenzo de, 179, 213, 267
as a Freemason, 200, 202;
as a liberal, 205, 207, 222, 234, 267;
as treasury secretary, 211, 212
Zepeda Cortés, María Bárbara, 96, 99